SCOTT FORESMAN ENGLISH

ON TARGET

TEACHER'S EDITION 1

INTERMEDIATE

Second Edition

James E. Purpura
Teachers College, Columbia University

Diane Pinkley
Teachers College, Columbia University

Teacher's Edition revised by James R. Morgan

Longman

I dedicate this book to the memory of two wonderful parents, Josephine Mercurio Purpura and Michael F. Purpura. JP

I dedicate this book to Georgie, Adrian, José, and Montse, and Jennifer, with appreciation and love. DP

Acknowledgments

We are especially grateful to James R. Herbolich of ESADE Idiomas in Barcelona and to Stephen Gudgel of the Institute of North American Studies in Barcelona for their insightful comments and support throughout this project. A sincere word of thanks to Laura Le Dréan and Joanne Dresner at Pearson Education for believing in us. Thanks to Steve Albanese for being there whenever we needed you.

Reviewers and Piloters

Our thanks to the following reviewers and piloters whose comments and suggestions were of great value in the development of the second edition of *Scott Foresman English.*

Angie Alcocer, Maria Alvarado School, Lima, Peru; **Walter A. Alvarez Barreto,** Santa Teresita School, Lima, Peru; **Chuck Anderson,** Athenée Français, Tokyo, Japan; **Paula Banks Al-Saihati,** Dhahran Ahliyya Schools, Saudi Arabia; **Lourdes Betancourt,** English Resource Center, Caracas, Venezuela; **Elba de Buenafama,** School Hipocampitos, Los Teques-Caracas, Venezuela; **Alexandra Espinoza Cascante,** Instituto Universal de Idiomas, San José, Costa Rica; **Orquídea Flores/Romelia Pérez,** Colegio Nuestra Señora de la Paz, Puerto La Cruz, Venezuela; **Brigite Fonseca,** Colegio Bom Jesus, del Joinville, Santa Catarina, Brazil; **Edmundo Gallardo,** Universidad de Occidente, Culiacán, Sin., Mexico; **Ana María García,** Instituto Tecnológico de Estudios Superiores de Monterrey, Mexico; **Victor A. García,** Universidad de Occidente, Culiacán, Sin., Mexico; **Irma K. Ghosn,** Lebanese American University, Byblos, Lebanon; **Carmina González Molina,** Instituto Cultural, A.C., Mexico City, Mexico; **Lucero González Mendieta,** Universidad de Occidente, Culiacán, Sin., Mexico; **Luz Ma. González,** Universidad de Occidente, Culiacán, Sin., Mexico; **Gloria I. Gutiérrez Vera,** Colegio Regiomontano Country, Monterrey, Mexico; **Tatiana Hernández Gaubil,** Colegio Madre del Divino Pastor, San José, Costa Rica; **Madeleine Hudders,** University of Puerto Rico, San Juan, Puerto Rico; **Denise Khoury,** Notre Dame de Louaize School, Lebanon; **Jerome D. Klena,** Nihon Gaigo Senmon Gakko, Tokyo, Japan; **Jane Lyon Lee,** Chungang University, Seoul, Korea; **Francisco J. Martínez,** Instituto La Salle Preparatoria, León, Mexico; **Javier Murillo,** Universidad de Occidente, Culiacán, Sin., Mexico; **Jorge Obregón Aragón,** Universidad de Occidente, Culiacán, Sin., Mexico; **Paula Sánchez Cortés,** Centro de Idiomas, ENSE de N.L., Monterrey, Mexico; **Nitzie de Stanley/Mireya Miramare,** IFISA, Puerto La Cruz, Venezuela; **Erick Soriano Moreno,** Universidad de Occidente, Culiacán, Sin., Mexico; **Elizabeth Vélez,** Colegio San Agustín, Cabo Rojo, Puerto Rico; **Diana Yupanqui Alvarez,** San Antonio de Mujeres School, Lima, Peru

On Target 1 Teacher's Edition, Second Edition

Copyright © 2000, 1991 by Addison Wesley Longman, Inc.
A Pearson Education Company

Pearson Education, 10 Bank Street, White Plains, NY 10606

Editorial directors: Allen Ascher, Louise Jennewine
Acquisitions editor: Bill Preston
Director of design and production: Rhea Banker
Development editors: Barbara Barysh, Marcia Schonzeit
Production manager: Alana Zdinak
Production supervisor: Liza Pleva
Managing editor: Linda Moser
Senior production editor: Virginia Bernard
Production editor: Lynn Contrucci
Senior manufacturing manager: Patrice Fraccio
Manufacturing supervisor: Edith Pullman
Photo research: Quarasan and Aerin Csigay
Cover design: Charles Yuen
Text design and composition: Quarasan
Photo and illustration credits: See page ii.

ISBN: 0-201-66411-9
1 2 3 4 5 6 7 8 9 10—WC—05 04 03 02 01 00

CONTENTS

Introduction to *Scott Foresman English*, Second Edition

This new edition of *Scott Foresman English* is a theme-based, integrated skills series for secondary and adult students. It is a unique and flexible program with multiple entry levels. The components can be used together as a comprehensive eight-level course or individually as separate mini-courses. The series consists of:

On Your Mark 1 and 2	INTRODUCTORY
In Contact 1 and 2	BEGINNING
On Target 1 and 2	INTERMEDIATE
In Charge 1 and 2	ADVANCED

Key Features of the First Edition

The second edition of *Scott Foresman English* maintains and builds on the key features of the successful and popular first edition.

- **An integrated syllabus** presents the communication skills—listening, speaking, reading, writing—together with functions, notions, and grammar.

- **Thematic units** teach English through a variety of high-interest topics and content.

- **A learner-centered approach** makes students active participants in every lesson by activating their prior knowledge of the topics and encouraging them to share and express their personal experience, ideas, and opinions in English.

- **The development of critical thinking skills** such as classifying, sequencing, making inferences, and drawing conclusions helps students learn more effectively and retain learned material longer.

- **The application of learning strategies** such as applying prior knowledge, scanning for specific information, skimming for main ideas, and getting meaning from context helps students take responsibility for their own learning and become more effective, independent learners.

New Features of the Second Edition

The second edition incorporates many ideas and improvements suggested by teachers from around the world.

- **Revised and updated content** includes new conversations, listening activities, and readings.

- **Summary of skills** charts highlight the new unit organization and identify and summarize key language skills, strategies, and topics in each unit.

- **Grammar presentations and practice** allow students to focus on form, meaning, and use. Many new and revised grammar presentations provide clear explanations and examples. New exercises and activities offer a balance of controlled and communicative practice.

- **Learning strategies** are now highlighted in all levels with the symbol ➡. Many new strategies have been added to promote effective, independent learning and academic success.

- **Review sections** have been added every three units to recycle and reinforce grammar focus and key vocabulary.

- **Teacher's Editions** are easier to use, with unit objectives, listening scripts, and answers to exercises clearly identified and highlighted.

- **Achievement tests** allow teachers and students to assess their progress after each unit.

- **The audio program** is now available in two formats: audiocassettes and audio CDs.

Components of the Program

Each level of *Scott Foresman English*, Second Edition, contains these components.

Student Book

Each Student Book contains twelve thematic units. A new Summary of Skills chart following the Contents highlights and summarizes the important language skills, strategies, and teaching points in each unit. New review material following Units 3, 6, 9, and 12 reinforces key vocabulary and grammar points. Additional material includes a Starting Out section (providing a brief introduction to the course), an irregular verb list, an International Phonetic Alphabet (IPA) chart, a unit-by-unit vocabulary list, and an index.

Workbook

The Workbook provides further practice and reinforcement of vocabulary and grammar, as well as additional interactive speaking activities and listening tasks. A self-test page (Check Your Knowledge) at the end of each unit allows students to assess their own progress.

Teacher's Edition

The Teacher's Edition contains full-size, full-color reproductions of the Student Book pages opposite complete teaching suggestions for the Student Book and references to corresponding Workbook practice exercises. Answers to all Student Book exercises are now highlighted in boxes on the corresponding Teacher's Edition pages. Listening scripts to all Student Book and Workbook exercises, along with the Workbook Answer Key, follow the Student Book pages. Each Teacher's Edition unit ends with suggestions for evaluating language and communication skills. The Teacher's Edition also includes Placement, Mid-Book, and End-of-Book Tests, information on basic teaching techniques, and Scope and Sequence charts. *On Target 1* and *2* also provide Vocabulary Expansion Activities. These reproducible blackline masters provide additional vocabulary enrichment work.

Audio Program

All material appearing on the audio program is indicated in the Student Book and Workbook pages with the symbol ⌒. The audio program is available in two formats, audiocassettes and audio CDs. Both contain conversation models as well as materials for the Warm Up, Listen, and Pronunciation sections in the Student Book and selected listening exercises in the Workbook.

Achievement Tests

The new Achievement Tests provide an additional option for evaluation. The Achievement Test book contains tests for all twelve units and an answer key.

Introduction to *On Target*

About the Authors

James E. Purpura is currently Assistant Professor of Linguistics and Education in the TESOL and Applied Linguistics programs at Teachers College, Columbia University, in New York City. He holds a Ph.D. in TESL/Applied Linguistics from the University of California at Los Angeles.

Dr. Purpura worked at the Institute of North American Studies, Barcelona, Spain, from 1982 to 1990, first as an instructor, then as Director of Courses. In addition, he has taught in France, Iran, Saudi Arabia, and Kuwait. He has also worked as a curriculum specialist in Iran, Saudi Arabia, and San Diego, California, and was involved in curriculum development at Kuwait University. His scholarly publications appear in *Language Learning*, *Language Testing*, and *Issues in Applied Linguistics*.

Diane Pinkley is the Director of the TC TESOL Certificate Program at Teachers College, Columbia University, in New York City. She holds a B.A. from Avila College, Kansas City, Missouri, and an M.A. in English language and literature from the University of Michigan. She is currently pursuing studies leading to an Ed.D. in TESOL at Teachers College, Columbia University.

Ms. Pinkley worked as Curriculum Coordinator at the Michigan Language Center in Ann Arbor, Michigan, as well as instructor and Director of Courses at the Institute of North American Studies in Barcelona, Spain. She has taught American and British literature and American culture, and all levels of EFL/ESL.

A Student Book Unit

In response to teachers' feedback on the first edition, the unit organization of the new edition has been restructured for greater clarity and ease of use. Each unit is divided into four distinct sections, each identified with a different color, which highlight the pedagogic features and language skills.

GETTING STARTED

This unit opening section consists of three parts.

Warm Up

Warm Up activates students' prior knowledge of the unit theme. It introduces the theme by means of a short listening passage. Interactive activities follow to get students talking about how the theme relates to their knowledge, feelings, and life experiences.

Figure It Out

Figure It Out presents the new language in a functional context in the form of a conversation, mini-reading, or questionnaire. Students begin to acquire the language before they analyze it in the Grammar section. Comprehension questions check understanding. A Vocabulary Check exercise helps students discover the meaning of the target vocabulary from context. This exercise is indicated in the Student Book with the symbol ☑.

Talk About It

Talk About It provides students with the opportunity to practice one or more aspects of the target language in a controlled context. This is an intermediary step between cue dependency and real production.

GRAMMAR

This section presents the target grammar of the unit. Grammar presentations and practice focus on structure, meaning, and usage, and are designed to encourage students to analyze the language by means of inductive and deductive reasoning. A variety of exercises gives students the opportunity to practice language structure individually and in pairs or groups. Check Your Understanding exercises allow students to test their understanding of specific situations in which particular tenses and other grammar points are used. These exercises are indicated with the symbol ☑. A culminating Express Yourself activity allows students to use the language communicatively in personalized contexts. This activity is indicated with the symbol ⬚.

LISTENING and SPEAKING

This third section integrates listening and speaking strategies, skills, and activities.

Before You Listen

These activities focus on anticipating meaning and applying prior knowledge to the listening task. These prelistening activities are followed by strategies such as listening for details, making inferences, and organizing information. These strategies are indicated with the symbol ➡.

Speak Out

Speak Out activities develop fluency as the students share information, opinions, and experiences. In addition, each unit focuses on at least one discussion strategy, which is indicated with the symbol ➡.

Pronunciation

This section provides practice in perceiving and producing the phonology of English (sounds, intonation, stress, reduction, etc.).

READING and WRITING

This final section integrates reading and writing strategies, skills, and activities.

Read About It

Read About It contains high-interest readings that reflect and extend the unit themes. Prereading exercises (Before You Read) focus on applying students' prior knowledge. Reading strategies such as scanning, understanding sequence, and getting meaning from context are presented and then checked in comprehension exercises. These strategies are indicated with the symbol ➡.

Think About It

Think About It presents activities that offer students further opportunities to apply strategies and share personal knowledge and experience related to the readings in open-ended, creative ways.

Write

This section focuses on specific writing tasks—such as writing a topic sentence, narrowing a topic, using supporting details—that prepare students to write with confidence in English.

Write About It

Write About It tasks, consistent with the unit themes, are purposeful and communicative because students are writing for a real audience of their peers. A new, culminating Check Your Writing exercise applies the important writing process steps of peer feedback and revision. These exercises are indicated with the symbol ☑.

A Teacher's Edition Unit

Each unit in the Teacher's Edition starts with a list of unit objectives. These objectives are followed by complete teaching information for each section of the Student Book unit.

The teaching information contains suggestions for previewing and presenting material, language and cultural notes, and a rich variety of optional extension activities, including ideas for discussion topics, vocabulary enrichment, spelling, games and competitions, and research projects. These optional activities add flexibility to the course length, depending on how few or how many of the optional activities are used.

- The **Preview** section gives suggestions for introducing content and for developing the target language. During the Preview, you will want to encourage students to say as much as they can about the content or theme. Model correct usage, but remember that the objective here is to get students involved and to give them the language they need to express their ideas.

- The **Presentation** section provides effective, step-by-step suggestions for presenting the lesson, using clear, practical teaching methods.

- A variety of **Options** provides flexibility so that you can adapt the lesson to the needs of your class and offer additional activities for reinforcement and enrichment.

- The **Evaluation** section at the end of each unit contains suggestions for four different ways to evaluate your students' progress. See pages TExi–TExii for more information.

- **Workbook links** suggest points at which the corresponding material in the Workbook may be assigned, indicated with the symbol ▨ .

- **Language Notes** explain colloquial English, foreign words, idiomatic expressions, and provide additional information about usage.

Presenting a Unit

GETTING STARTED

Warm Up

Each unit in *On Target* opens with a Warm Up section that both introduces students to the theme of the unit and involves them in the theme. It typically consists of a listening passage to which students must respond and one or more interactive exercises in which they talk about the unit theme.

Preview suggestions include the introduction of the target language through the use of pictures, realia, mime, and Total Physical Response (TPR) (see page TExiii). Depending on students' abilities, you may wish to skip this section and have the students learn the language directly from the recording and the Student Book pages.

In general, all the target language appears in the Warm Up and Figure It Out sections. These sections have been carefully designed so that students can discover the meaning of the new language through the pictures and context. Because of this, you should begin the presentation of each unit by reading the unit title and the Warm Up section with the class. Encourage students to say as much as they can about the pictures and text. Model any language they need. Use the Preview suggestions to clarify or for reinforcement or review.

Play the recording and have students complete the corresponding exercises. Use the procedures outlined in Listen on page TEix.

Figure It Out

This section demonstrates the use of the new language in functional situations.

There are several ways to present this section to students. You will want to choose the method that best suits your classroom and your method of teaching.

Whatever method you use, first have students comment on the pictures and predict what the section is about. Using prior knowledge and anticipating meaning are valuable comprehension tools.

Most of the units contain conversations. In presenting them, you can emphasize listening and aural comprehension by reading the conversations aloud or playing the recording two or more times as students listen with their books closed. For each listening, you will want to set up a comprehension task. For some classes, ask a simple factual question and tell students to listen for the answer. For more advanced students, you should set more difficult tasks, such as inferring where the speakers are, what their relationship is, etc. You may find it valuable to have students read the comprehension questions before they listen.

Next, read the conversations or play the recording one or more times as students follow along in their books. If necessary, a few yes/no questions will help students focus on meaning.

Then have students work in pairs or groups to read the conversations aloud. They might also answer the comprehension questions and do the meaning-from-context exercise at this time.

Finally, ask for volunteers to perform the conversations for the class. Encourage students to adapt or add to the conversations by introducing new topics or adding additional speakers as their level of proficiency permits. Simple props will make performing the conversations fun and meaningful.

For units that contain mini-readings or questionnaires, see Read About It on page TEx for ideas and suggestions.

Presenting Vocabulary

Active and Receptive Vocabulary

On Target includes both active and receptive vocabulary. The active vocabulary has been selected for its usefulness and frequency of occurrence in real communication. A list of the active vocabulary for each unit is included in Unit Vocabulary at the back of the Student Book (see page 132). In addition, receptive vocabulary appears throughout the unit. Students are not expected to learn these non-target words. Instead, they should learn to develop a tolerance for ambiguity with respect to unknown vocabulary. As long as they can complete the activities, understanding every word is not necessary. Students should be encouraged not to use dictionaries but to try to make intelligent guesses about meaning based on the use of context, cognates, word families, and other strategies.

Introducing Vocabulary

Every opportunity should be taken to involve students in the learning process. Introduce vocabulary through pictures, realia, or TPR (see page TExiii). Encourage students to provide synonyms, antonyms, examples, or simple definitions. Many English words are similar in form and meaning to words in other languages. Students should be trained to recognize these cognates (and cautioned on the dangers of false cognates).

Help students understand and use the techniques of paraphrasing and circumlocution to elicit and communicate new, unfamiliar vocabulary—for example, to say "the thing you cut bread with" for *knife*, or "go behind (someone)" for *follow*. As often as possible, help them understand meaning through the use of word associations. For example, the meaning of many verbs can be demonstrated through the use of different complements—e.g., *run out of gas* on the highway, *run out of money* at the store, *run out of eggs* while making a cake.

Finally, encourage students to use only monolingual dictionaries. Bilingual dictionaries force students to see English in terms of their own language instead of as a distinct tool for communication. Translation should be used only as a last resort.

Vocabulary Notebooks

Encourage students to keep notebooks of new vocabulary, to include both the words they learn in the Student Book and words they want to know in order to express their own ideas. Have students make up sentences to illustrate the meaning of the new words. This can be done individually or in pairs or groups. Write the best examples on the board for students to copy into their notebooks. If students group the words by meaning and function, at the end of the year they will have their own personal dictionaries. (You may want to collect and check the notebooks periodically to make sure that students' example sentences are correct.)

Talk About It

This mini-dialogue presents a series of connected conversational cues (a discourse chain) that trains students to relate roles, functions, and language possibilities. Have students work in pairs to read the situation and identify the roles; for example, in Unit 1 the situation is an interview, and the roles are a TV marketing manager and a person being interviewed about his or her viewing habits. Assign or let students choose roles. Have them read the functions (printed in small type) and the mini-dialogue aloud. Answer any questions about vocabulary or grammar. Then focus attention on the exercise cues; in Unit 1, these cues are the categories on the TV Questionnaire (see Student Book, page 3). Do one example with a student or ask a pair to do one example as a model. Then have the pairs work together to complete the exercise. Encourage students to add examples as their proficiency permits.

GRAMMAR

In this section, students are given a brief grammatical description of the target language and are asked to apply those rules (deductive reasoning), or they are given a number of examples and are asked to use the examples to formulate rules (inductive reasoning).

This presentation is followed by exercises designed to accomplish one of two purposes: to train students to use the language accurately and to encourage them to use it fluently. The exercises designed for accuracy can be done by the students independently, in class or as homework; however, you will probably find it preferable to have students complete them in pairs or small groups. In this way, students can help each other form the correct answers. Check Your Understanding exercises follow to allow students to test their understanding of the specific situations in which the particular points are used. These exercises are done individually and then students are encouraged to check their answers with a partner. The Express Yourself exercises should be done in pairs to promote fluency and proper use of new vocabulary. Cooperative learning and peer correction are invaluable in developing both accuracy and fluency.

LISTENING and SPEAKING

Listen

The listening selections on the audio program provide practice in understanding ordinary English discourse. Each listening section begins with Before You Listen prelistening questions, which establish the context and help students activate and share prior knowledge. The prelistening questions are followed by the presentation of a specific listening strategy, highlighted with ➡. You will want students to answer the prelistening questions, to comment on any pictures, charts, etc., and to discuss the strategy before you play the recording or read the selection aloud. Always remind students that they don't have to understand every word of the selection in order to do the exercise.

The first time you play the recording or read the selection aloud, have students listen with their books closed. Set a purpose for listening by asking a simple, factual question and having students listen for the answer. When they answer the question, have them tell you anything else they can remember about what they heard.

Have students open their books and reread the directions. Play the recording or read the selection again and tell them to listen for the specific information the exercise asks for. According to students' ability, you can have them mark the exercise at this time or during a third listening.

After students have written their answers, play the recording or read the selection again for students to check their work.

Pronunciation

To communicate understandably, a speaker must pronounce individual sounds correctly and use the patterns of word stress, intonation contours, and rhythms that are characteristic of a language. The listener, too, must participate actively, using his or her knowledge of those elements to derive meaning. Good pronunciation evolves only gradually. However, students should be encouraged from the start to listen carefully to the way English sounds are produced and to attempt the pronunciation of all of them.

A book alone cannot teach pronunciation; it can only serve as a guide. It is your voice and the voices on the recordings that must provide the models for the class. Speakers on radio and TV, recordings, and class visitors who are native speakers can provide additional models. Good models, consistent patterns, and ample opportunity to listen and speak are essential for developing good pronunciation.

On Target focuses on perceiving and producing such aspects of English phonology as plural and past tense endings, word and sentence stress, intonation, reduction, and elision. Most students will not be able to produce such things as intonation and stress with perfect accuracy. Concentrate instead on their hearing and understanding these aspects of English.

Have students read the explanation and make any predictions about the target sound. Play the recording or read the examples several times while students listen. Remember that they must be able to perceive a sound before they can produce it. Next, play the recording or repeat each word or sentence first for the class, then for groups, and finally individuals to repeat. Then have students complete the exercises and formulate the rule if required.

You will find it valuable to have students work in pairs or groups to read the examples to each other. This gives additional, needed practice in forming the sounds correctly.

Speak Out

Begin by setting up a situation in which the target discussion strategy highlighted with ➡ would be used. For example, if the strategy focuses on persuading, you might ask students how late they are allowed to stay out on weekday evenings and how they would try to get permission from their parents to stay out later. Elicit examples from the class and/or refer them to the strategy presentation box in the Student Book. Have one or more pairs of students use the expressions in a conversation based on your example.

Divide students into pairs or groups according to the activity and have them read the directions. Answer any questions they have. For some units, you may wish to model a conversation for the class or have students do so. Then have students complete the activity. Monitor the groups, but do not interrupt for correction. Instead, take note of repeated errors for later reteaching or review.

Encourage students to use the language in the strategy boxes as much as possible, inside and out of class. The purpose of this activity is to help students gain confidence in their oral performance. The constant reinforcement of this language will result in greater fluency.

Read About It

The reading selection in Read About It extends the theme of the unit and provides the opportunity for improving reading strategies and critical thinking skills. The section opens with Before You Read prereading questions, which introduce the content and help students recall prior knowledge of the subject. Commenting on any illustrations along with using such reading strategies as skimming and scanning further preview the selection. In most units, the prereading questions are followed by specific reading strategies (highlighted with ➡) aimed at helping students focus their attention on reading for specific information, examples, or main ideas. In other units, reading strategies immediately follow the reading selections and focus on guessing meaning from context and making inferences.

Most reading done for information or pleasure is silent reading, so students should read the selections silently. Encourage them to read without dictionaries. Stopping to look up unknown words interrupts the flow of reading and makes it more likely that students read word for word rather than for general meaning. In addition, the selections have all been carefully written to enable students to use cognates and to understand meaning from context.

The reading may be assigned as homework, but you will probably find it more beneficial to have students read in class. Set a time limit to encourage them to keep reading without stopping at each unknown word. Watch to make sure they are not relying on their dictionaries.

Think About It

A final Think About It section presents challenging, creative activities related to the reading. Some exercises check comprehension, the ability to get meaning from context, and other reading skills. These exercises can be completed in pairs or small groups. Other open-ended activities offer students further opportunities to develop critical thinking skills and share personal knowledge and experience in imaginative ways.

Write

In the Write sections, specific elements of paragraph writing are presented—such as identifying what makes a good paragraph, narrowing a topic, writing a topic sentence, adding supporting details, and writing a concluding sentence—along with other important academic writing skills and forms such as summarizing and writing instructions. The presentations are immediately followed by one or more exercises that allow students to apply and practice the target elements or skills.

Write About It

Write About It tasks are purposeful and communicative. Students write for a real purpose related to the unit theme and for a real audience of their peers

On Target also incorporates key elements of the writing process to help students brainstorm and organize ideas, write their first drafts, and then edit and revise their paragraphs. The new Check Your Writing exercises at the end of each unit focus students' attention on key points from the unit and help them edit and revise their drafts, applying the important writing process steps of peer feedback and revision. The following steps highlight and summarize key aspects of the writing process. Depending on your teaching objectives and classroom situation, you may follow these steps as guidelines for using the writing process more extensively and comprehensively.

1. Prewriting

Prewriting includes the important strategies of brainstorming, focusing, and organizing information. These strategies help students to generate, select, and organize ideas so that they can write a first draft of a paragraph about a specific topic.

In **brainstorming**, students make a list of as many ideas about a particular topic as they can. The purpose of brainstorming is to generate and explore lots of possible ideas. Students should not worry at this point whether or not their ideas are good or bad but should just write them down.

Once students have a list of possible ideas, they can then focus on choosing the best, most useful ideas for inclusion in a paragraph. In **focusing**, students should keep the ideas that relate to the topic they will write about and eliminate ideas that do not.

After students choose the ideas they want to write about, they are ready to organize them in a paragraph. Each Write section focuses on a specific element—such as writing topic sentences, narrowing a topic, or writing supporting sentences—for **organizing** ideas in a paragraph. These sections have been expanded and improved in the new edition to include more examples and models of the target elements.

Most students find it beneficial to do some or all prewriting with a partner because this enables them to invent and generate more new ideas from each other's ideas.

2. First Draft

Many students do not realize that good writing is usually the result of many revisions or drafts. Knowing that they will write more than one draft allows students to focus on different aspects of their writing in each draft. As students write their first drafts, they should concentrate on composition, not mechanics (such as grammar, spelling, and punctuation). Have them work with partners to write good topic sentences. Remind them that every supporting sentence should amplify the topic sentence and that the sentences should be in a logical order. Assure them that good writers revise several times.

3. Revision

Revising includes making such changes as adding new information, deleting nonessential information, and arranging the information in the best order. Editing for mechanics—to check grammar and proofread for correct spelling and punctuation—is a final step of revision. Students should understand that you expect correct grammar, spelling, and punctuation in the final copy, but that revision of these comes last in the writing process.

Peer editing is an effective tool for second-language writers. Have students exchange papers with a partner and read the partner's paper for interest and accuracy of content. Do they understand what the other person is trying to say? Do they have any questions they would like answered to make the passage clearer? Do they see anything that is out of place or irrelevant? The new, culminating Check Your Writing exercises can help students focus their attention on these and other questions. After peer editing, have students work independently to improve their drafts. Partners can then get back together to discuss the improvements and to work on mechanics. You may wish to have partners sign each other's final drafts. This gives each person a stake in the other's success.

4. Correction

When correcting students' writing, concentrate on paragraph structure and ideas over grammar, punctuation, and spelling. You might use one color pencil to comment on content and another to mark errors in mechanics.

Student compositions will probably contain many mechanical errors. For this reason, you may wish to concentrate only on one aspect in a particular composition. For example, if a student is having difficulty with English punctuation, you might mark only the punctuation errors. Or you may wish to mark only the errors in the target language of the unit.

However you do it, be sure to let students know that you and the rest of the class are interested in what they have to say by providing some means of presenting their work.

5. Presenting

All writing should be done with an audience in mind. Public acceptance of the writer's product validates both the writer and the writing process. Therefore, you should arrange to have students present their writing to the class—*if they so wish*.

Following are some suggestions for presenting:

- Have students read their articles or paragraphs aloud to a group or to the class.
- Display the papers on a bulletin board.
- Place a number of samples from an assignment in a notebook to be shared by interested members of the class.

Using these elements of paragraph writing for the writing process makes students confident writers, providing them with both a blueprint and the tools for constructing paragraphs.

Remember that good readers often become good writers. By providing a variety of English language materials for students to read (magazines and newspapers as well as books, fiction as well as nonfiction), you will be increasing their understanding of writing in English.

Evaluation

The second edition of *On Target* offers a new supplementary test booklet for each level, containing an individual achievement test for each unit. These new achievement tests complement and expand on the three other ways of evaluating students' progress provided in the first edition: a self-test of vocabulary and grammar, a dictation for aural comprehension and writing, and a check of oral proficiency.

Achievement Tests

The new Achievement Test booklet for each level contains tests for all twelve units. Each unit test measures students' progress in grammar, vocabulary, pronunciation, reading, and writing. There are separate scales for different parts of the test, so you can test all or selective skills, depending on your teaching objectives.

Self-Test

Each unit in the Workbook ends with a self-test called Check Your Knowledge, allowing students to assess their own progress. Encourage students to complete these tests without looking back at their student books. Although you may want to have students complete the tests in class so that you can record their scores, the tests are best treated as a learning experience. Students are interested in their own progress and will take responsibility for review if they know that their mistakes here will not be held against them in their final grades.

Dictation

Dictation can be a valuable diagnostic tool. By careful correction, you can discover which areas need reteaching or review. For example, if students consistently drop the third person singular simple present tense ending, you will want to do additional practice on hearing, saying, and spelling that ending. Information on giving and correcting dictations can be found on page TExv.

Evaluating Oral Communication Skills

Oral communication has one primary goal—to get the message across as clearly as possible. The ability to communicate orally in a second or foreign language involves a complex set of competencies or abilities, each of which may develop at its own pace. We define oral communication skills in terms of five competencies. See the Oral Communication Skills Assessment Scale.

Oral assessment can make students anxious, so use strategies that help students feel safe. Engaging in small talk before the beginning of an oral exam—for example, asking students how they are or talking about the weather and other simple topics—can help students feel more relaxed and at ease. You can also make students feel more comfortable by using clear directions and procedures so that they know what to expect.

You may choose to assess students individually or to have them work in pairs or small groups, depending on your objectives. (For example, if you want to assess students' ability to manage a discussion, you need to have students interacting in small groups.) Audio- or videotaping students during oral exams is an effective tool for learning and assessment. This allows you to listen several times and score what you observe. Audio- or videotaping also gives you the option of involving students in self- or peer assessment—that is, students can listen/observe and evaluate themselves or each other.

However you conduct oral assessment, introduce students gradually to the criteria of correctness so that they understand the objectives and know how to improve. In the beginning, assess only one or two of the following abilities. Gradually add more. Use the number scale in the box to rate the abilities. You can modify the scale to meet your specific needs.

Oral Communication Skills Assessment Scale

3 = excellent	1 = fair
2 = good	0 = poor

1. **COMMUNICATIVE EFFECTIVENESS**
   Using language to convey ideas
   3 2 1 0

2. **GRAMMATICAL ACCURACY**
   Using grammar forms and vocabulary correctly
   3 2 1 0

3. **GRAMMATICAL APPROPRIATENESS**
   Using appropriate forms in context (with appropriate formality, politeness)
   3 2 1 0

4. **INTELLIGIBILITY**
   Using accurate pronunciation and intonation
   3 2 1 0

5. **INTERACTIVE EFFECTIVENESS**
   Using strategies to keep communication going
   3 2 1 0

Vocabulary Expansion Activities

The twelve reproducible, supplementary activities (one for each unit in the student book) provide students with additional tools for becoming independent learners by increasing their active and receptive vocabularies. They present vocabulary-building skills such as recognizing prefixes and suffixes, understanding noun compounds, and inferring extended meanings. Topics of other activities include idioms, empty verbs (*take, have, break*, etc.), phrasal verbs, and other specific difficulties of English vocabulary.

The language presented in each activity has always been introduced in the corresponding Student Book unit. A good time to present the activity is after students have completed the unit. Students should be familiar with the language and can apply strategies for getting meaning from context to help them understand the target skill or topic in each activity. As students complete each activity, encourage them to think of as many additional examples of the specific topic as possible. Answers to the vocabulary expansion activities appear at the end of the teaching notes for each unit.

Teaching Techniques

Using Realia

The use of realia in the classroom will motivate students and make them realize the relevance of their language study. Realia includes anything from the real world: native speakers, radio and TV programs, films, records and tapes, printed materials such as brochures, tickets, schedules, ads, maps, menus, and objects such as food, clothing, toy vehicles and furniture, photos and other pictures. *On Target* incorporates the use of realia in the introduction of vocabulary and in many of the Options.

Total Physical Response

Total Physical Response (TPR), developed by James J. Asher, plays an important role in developing language skills. This technique relieves the pressure on students to speak before they are ready to do so, allowing students to respond without fear or hesitation. TPR is especially helpful at the early stages of learning, when students might not be capable of producing a verbal response. In fact, research shows that many students go through a "silent period" before they begin to speak. During this time they require intense listening practice to help them acquire the language. TPR is ideal for learners at this stage.

To begin, give a command or series of commands while performing the actions with the students. For example, *Stand up. Sit down. Open your book. Close your book. Stand up. Sit down.* Repeat, modeling the actions with the whole class or individual rows or groups. Then give the commands again, this time waiting a second or two to see if students respond correctly. If students cannot follow the directions, model the actions again until they are able to respond.

Next, give the commands without modeling the actions. Be sure to vary the order to make sure everyone understands and is not just doing a memorized series of actions. As vocabulary builds, one of the best ways to check understanding is to give a humorous or unexpected command: *Stand on your chair. Sit under the table.*

When students are able to follow your commands without confusion or delay, have individual students give commands to the class, to a small group, or to a partner. Encourage them not to use their hands or give other visual clues. At this point, do not stop students to correct pronunciation as long as they are being understood.

Once students understand basic commands, you can use TPR to build vocabulary. Provide pictures or props for each student. Give such commands as *Point to the bus. Point to the car. Show me the taxi.* Gradually add the target vocabulary: *Point to the plane. Point to the pilot. Show me the airport.*

TPR techniques can also be used to clarify verb tenses and question/answer patterns. For example, give a student a command: *Peter, go to the window.* As the student is doing so, model *Peter is going to the window. What's he doing? He's going to the window.* For past tense, simply wait until the student arrives and say, *Peter went to the window. What did he do? He went to the window.*

Once you and your students are used to using these techniques, you will find them well suited not only for introducing and practicing new language but also as a quick change of pace after sedentary practice. Give a series of quick commands to vary the routine and to let students move around. Everyone will feel better after a break.

Working in Pairs and Groups

Most of the language practice and skill development activities in *On Target* can be done in pairs or in groups of three or four. There are many advantages to having students work in pairs or groups.

Student involvement and participation are maximized. Each student gets the opportunity to speak many times during each class. In addition, each student practices all the examples in an exercise instead of eight or ten students each practicing one example.

Students are able to collaborate on answers and rehearse them before speaking in front of the whole class. The pair or group is responsible for each member's participation. Students can confirm their knowledge or learn from their partners or groups. Anxiety is reduced, which increases success.

Face-to-face interaction simulates real-life social contact, encouraging the use of eye contact, proper intonation, emotional tone, rejoinders, exclamations, etc., which are difficult when reciting in front of the class.

Forming the Groups

You will want to give each student in the class the opportunity to work with as many different partners or groups as possible during the term or year. You might assign partners and/or groups at the beginning of each week or even at the beginning of each class. You can do this in a variety of ways. The simplest is just to have students sitting next to or in front of and behind each other work together. You can put two to four slips of paper numbered 1, two to four slips numbered 2, etc., in a bag for the students to draw from. (The 1s work together, the 2s work together, etc.) Or you can put the names of half the students in the bag for the other half to draw from. Sometimes you may want to have students choose their own partners or groups.

No matter how you assign the groups, you will want one member of each group to act as leader. It is the group leader's task to keep the group working smoothly and talking in English. The reader should take any necessary notes and report any conclusions to the class. At first you may want to choose those students who have greater English fluency for this position, but it is important that every student be given the opportunity to act as a group leader.

Procedures

Always make sure everyone understands what to do. Have students read the instructions and any examples or models. They can do this silently or by reading aloud to each other. To encourage effective reading of the directions, set a time limit. Then have students close their books and tell each other what they are supposed to do. Answer any questions the pairs or groups have.

Always read the example, or model one of the items with a student. If you like, you can then ask for volunteers to do the next item as an additional model for the class.

Establish a time limit. This will help keep students on task. Most activities in *On Target* can be completed in no more than five minutes. Longer activities can have a longer time limit, but don't let students continue beyond their ability to speak English.

As students are talking, walk around the class and monitor as many groups as possible. Encourage students to speak only in English. Answer questions and provide any language they need. Students will make mistakes, but don't interrupt for error correction. Students should feel free to express themselves however they can. Repeated errors should be noted for later reteaching and review.

Remind students that error correction is the learner's responsibility as well as the teacher's. Encourage them to recognize their own mistakes. Peer- and self-correction are valuable tools in learning because students feel less pressure than they do from teacher correction. Train students to help each other give the correct answers before you step in to help. You might give them copies of the evaluation scale on page TExii to help them evaluate themselves and each other. Keeping a record of their performance in each unit will help them assess their progress.

Conclude the activity by having a few pairs do parts of the activity for the class or by having the group leader report the group's conclusions.

Remember that this kind of practice gives all students the chance to use their new language often. This extended listening and speaking time will greatly improve their confidence and ability.

Pair or group work can result in a noisy classroom, but remember—it's the sound of students communicating in English!

Games and Activities

Chain Drills

For some classes, a chain drill is an excellent intermediary step for practicing language after modeling by the teacher and before working in pairs. It can be done in small groups or as a class. In a typical chain drill, each student holds an object or picture or focuses on a picture in the Student Book. You begin the chain by showing an object or picture to the first student and asking a question. After answering, that student turns to the next student and asks the question. Continue until everyone has had a chance both to ask and to answer.

Teacher: (*Shows eraser*) What's this?
Student A: It's an eraser. (*Shows pen to Student B*) What's this?
Student B: It's a pen. (*Shows book to Student C*) What's this?

Spelling Bees

Spelling bee techniques can be adapted for many kinds of language practice. You will find suggestions for various kinds of "bees" throughout *On Target*. To begin a typical spelling bee, ask students to stand. Give the first student a word to spell. If that person spells the word incorrectly, he or she must sit down and the second student gets a chance to spell the same word. If that student spells it correctly, the next student is given a different word to spell. The game continues until only one student is left standing.

The game can be played in teams or in small groups with the group leader giving the words.

Surveys

Having students survey each other provides real language practice. Students enjoy surveys because they find out new information about their classmates and because they can compare their own lives and attitudes with those of their peers.

Begin a survey by having students tell you the questions they want answered about a topic. Write the questions on the board. You need one question for each student to ask. Have each student ask every other student his or her question and record the answers. (If your class is large, have students do the survey in groups with one member of each group asking the same question.)

Next, have each student summarize his or her results and write them on the board. You may wish to have students make a graph of the class's responses.

Finally, talk about the answers. Were any of them surprising? Which questions was the class evenly divided about? Were there any that everyone answered the same?

Dictations

Dictations are an excellent means for students to gain proficiency in aural comprehension and writing. Dictations can also be valuable diagnostic tools. By careful correction, you can discover which language skills need reteaching or review. For example, if a student consistently drops past tense endings, you will want to give that student extra practice in hearing and saying those sounds.

There are many kinds of dictations—single words, sentences, short dialogues, or paragraphs. Here are a few simple rules and ideas.

- At first, dictate passages that are familiar to the students. For example, after students have listened to a dialogue, read it silently, and answered comprehension questions, you can use it as a dictation. You may wish to have students prepare by reading the passage again as homework.

- Mark the passage for pauses before you read it to the students. The pauses should be after logical phrase groups and at the ends of sentences. (You may want to practice reading the passage aloud.)

- For the first few dictations, you might name the punctuation marks as you read. First, write the marks on the board and present the English names. Then, as you read the passage, name the marks as they occur. As students become more familiar with English, you can begin to omit the names of the punctuation marks in your reading.

- Write proper names, unknown vocabulary, and words with unusual spellings on the board. If you are dictating a dialogue, write the speakers' names so that the passage is easier to follow.

- Read the selection three times. First, read it at a normal pace while students listen. Next, read it with pauses so that they can write. Allow a few minutes for them to check their work. Then read it again, this time at a pace slightly slower than normal but without long pauses. (In some classes, you may want to vary the speed of the last reading and/or read the passage a fourth time.) In all readings, try to use normal stress and intonation.

There are many ways to correct dictations. You might simply mark all the errors. However, for beginning students especially, this may result in a lot of red marks! Another method is to mark only those mistakes in vocabulary and structure that are covered in the unit you are working on. Or you might correct those errors in red and other errors in a different color. However you decide to do it, be sure to praise students for what they do get right.

Tests

Placement Test

On Target was designed for learners who have had approximately 140 to 360 hours of instruction in English. However, you may have students whose level you are unsure of. These guidelines and the Placement Test on page TExviii will help you place those students in the appropriate level of *Scott Foresman English*.

Guidelines for Testing

Try to make the testing conditions as relaxed as possible. Remember that a test is almost certainly viewed by the student as a threatening experience. You will want to do everything possible to lessen the tension. Smile. Aim for a conversational approach.

First, ask basic questions. Find out the student's name, address, occupation, and favorite subject in school. Ask about the student's hobbies, what the student did yesterday, what the student will do after school, how long the student has lived in your city, etc. If the student cannot answer these questions, he or she should begin with *In Contact*, Level 1. If the student answers appropriately, go on to the Placement Test on page TExviii.

A student who answers fewer than six of the questions in the test on page TExviii correctly should take the Placement Test in *In Contact*, Level 2. A student who answers fewer than ten questions correctly should begin with *On Target*, Level 1. A student who answers between ten and twenty questions correctly should begin with *On Target*, Level 2. If a student answers more than twenty questions with no difficulty, you will want to continue with the Placement Test in *In Charge*.

Procedures for Testing

Make a copy of the test for every student. Go over the test with the students. For the Listening section, play the recording or read the audioscript aloud two or more times. Then allow sufficient time for students to complete the test. *Note:* The Listening section for the Placement test appears before Unit 1 on the Student Book audiocassette and CD.

Listening Audioscript

Jack: Hi, Jane. What've you got there?

Jane: Hi, Jack. It's a letter from my cousin Bonnie.

Jack: Oh, really? What's she been doing?

Jane: Really amazing things! She sent me this letter from Africa. She's been there for over a month.

Jack: Wow! What's she been doing there?

Jane: She's been taking photographs of wild animals for *Discoveries Magazine*. She says that after she finishes her job there, she's going to go to Alaska to take more pictures.

Jack: Wow! What a change! I must say, though, that I like cold weather better than hot weather. I'd love to go to Alaska.

Jane: Well, Jack, if you'd saved your money instead of buying a new car, you'd be able to go there.

Jack: Well, I could have saved it, but I wanted that car!

Jane: Do you still have it? I don't see you driving it these days.

Jack: Of course I still have it. Right now it's at the garage. It's being fixed.

Answers
A. 1. She's in Africa. **2.** She's a photographer. **3.** Next she's going to Alaska. **4.** Jack does. **5.** No, he didn't. **6.** He bought a new car. **7.** Yes, he does. **8.** He's having his car fixed.
B. 1. playing **2.** had escaped **3.** missed **4.** had studied **5.** haven't finished **6.** to let **7.** has been having **8.** didn't build **9.** will be able to **10.** have collected *or* have been collecting
C. 1. must have been **2.** might go or may go **3.** must be **4.** must have missed
D. 1. Apples are grown all over the world. **2.** My computer is being fixed. **3.** Eric wasn't invited to the party. **4.** My car was stolen.

Mid-Book Test

Procedures for Testing

Make a copy of the Mid-Book Test on pages TExix–TExx for every student; then follow the procedures for the Placement Test. *Note:* The Listening section for the Mid-Book Test appears after Unit 6 on the Student Book audiocassette and CD.

Listening Audioscript

A: So, Ron, how was your vacation?

B: Nice. I went to the Forest Hotel.

A: Really? How was it?

B: Well, I saw an ad in the newspaper for it. It didn't seem to be very expensive, so I decided to stay there. When I got there, the clerk told me that my room was being cleaned and that I would have to wait in the lobby. After about twenty minutes, he showed me to a room above the kitchen. It was really clean, but it was so small that there was room only for a bed and a chair. And every morning, noise from the kitchen woke me up.

A: That's too bad!

B: Yes, but at least the food was good. Every meal I had was delicious.

A: Well, did you go swimming or do anything else fun?

B: Well, the ad said that the hotel had a pool, but when I got there the pool was empty. But the hotel had a fun club. I went dancing there every night. But when I wanted to go shopping, I had to drive for miles. What about you? How was your vacation?

A: I went to the Palace Hotel.

B: How was it?

A: Well, my room was very expensive, but it was nice. It had a living room, a private kitchen, and two balconies. The hotel was huge. It had two pools and four restaurants, but the food wasn't very good. So every day I went shopping in the hotel mall and cooked in my room.

B: Did you have fun?

A: Well, every morning I went to the health club to exercise. Then I went to the pool to relax and have a drink. In the afternoons, I went to the beach or shopped in the mall. But there wasn't much to do at night. There was no place to dance or listen to music, so usually I went to my room and read a good book.

B: Gosh, I'm glad that I went to the Forest Hotel. It was small, but it was a lot of fun.

Answers

A. 1. Forest Hotel **2.** Palace Hotel **3.** Forest Hotel **4.** Palace Hotel **5.** Palace Hotel **6.** Forest Hotel **7.** Palace Hotel **8.** Palace Hotel **9.** *Answers will vary. Follow the correction instructions on page TExi.*

B. 1. huge **2.** appointment **3.** damage **4.** accident **5.** perform **6.** towel

C. 1. was riding **2.** played **3.** am talking **4.** decided **5.** do (you) know **6.** bought **7.** was washing **8.** have **9.** is eating **10.** thinks

D. 1. larger than **2.** the best **3.** the most powerful **4.** the worst **5.** more expensive than.

Score three points for each correct answer in A items 1–8, one point for each correct answer in B, five points for each correct answer in C, and four points for each correct answer in D, for a total of 100 points.

End-of-Book Test

Procedures for Testing

Make a copy of the End-of-Book Test on page TExxi for every student; then follow the procedures for the Placement Test. *Note:* The Listening section for the End-of-Book test appears after Unit 12 on the Student Book audiocassette and CD.

Listening Audioscript

A: Well, I see that you have had a lot of experience working in restaurants.

B: Yes, that's right. I started out when I was in college. I worked as a waitress in a small restaurant in order to pay for my education. It was hard work, and I didn't make much money, but I liked my job a lot.

A: What did you do after that?

B: Well, after I graduated, I wanted a better job. I liked working in restaurants, so I went to work as the head waitress of the Harbor Restaurant here in the city. I was in charge of all of the waiters and waitresses.

A: How did you like your job?

B: It was great! I really liked making sure that the customers enjoyed their meals. While I was head waitress, the Harbor became one of the most popular restaurants in the city.

A: But you don't work there now. Why?

B: Well, I wanted a much more important job. A couple of years ago the owners of a new restaurant offered me the job of manager. It was a much larger restaurant, and the salary was much higher. Also, it gave me the chance to be in charge of the kitchen.

A: And why do you want to work with us?

B: Well, the Hollywood Hotel has four restaurants. Up to now, I've been manager of only one restaurant. I'd like to try running four restaurants at the same time.

A: Very interesting, Ms. Keating.

Answers

A. 1. waitress **2.** wanted more money **3.** head waitress **4.** wanted a better job **5.** manager **6.** wants to be manager of four restaurants **7.** manager of four restaurants **8.** *Answers will vary. Follow the correction instructions on page TExi.*

B. 1. stressed out **2.** driver's license **3.** complain **4.** bills **5.** advice **6.** amazing

C. 1. has worked *or* has been working **2.** used to play *or* played **3.** will understand **4.** ought to take *or* should take *or* had better take **5.** used to live **6.** has been traveling **7.** ought to go swimming *or* should go swimming **8.** haven't seen **9.** wins, buy

D. 1. (that) **2.** who **3.** (that) **4.** that **5.** who

Follow the scoring instructions for the Mid-Book Test.

Placement Test

🎧 **A.** Listen to the conversation. Answer the questions.

1. Where is Jane's cousin Bonnie?_____

2. What is her job? _____

3. Where is she going next? _____

4. Who likes cold weather? _____

5. Did Jack save his money for a vacation? _____

6. What did Jack buy? _____

7. Does he still have it? _____

8. What is Jack having done? _____

B. Write the correct form of the verb on the line.

1. Steve really enjoys **(play)** _____ basketball.

2. By the time the police arrived, the thief **(escape)** _____.

3. Paul isn't at work yet. I guess that he **(miss)** _____ his train to the city.

4. I wish that I **(study)** _____ for my driving test more. Now I have to take it again next week.

5. You still **(finish, neg.)** _____ your homework! Get busy right now!

6. Ms. Jackson refused **(let)** _____ her children attend the concert.

7. Carmen said that her new boss **(have)** _____ a lot of problems with the employees lately.

8. They have to tear down that new building because they **(build, neg.)** _____ it correctly.

9. I'm not sure that Judy **(be able to)** _____ come with us to the concert next week. I think that she has other plans.

10. I **(collect)** _____ coins for over twenty years. I really enjoy working on my collection!

C. Write **may**, **might**, **must**, **may have**, **might have**, or **must have** and the correct form of the verb on the line.

1. Did you hear that loud noise? There **(be)** _____ an accident at the corner.

2. Gerardo **(go)** _____ to California on vacation, but he's not sure.

3. Tim isn't here today. He **(be)** _____ on vacation.

4. The boss is late today. He **(miss)** _____ his train.

D. Write the following sentences again. Use the new subjects.

1. People grow apples all over the world.

Apples _____.

2. Someone is fixing my computer.

My computer _____.

3. No one invited Eric to the party.

Eric _____.

4. Someone stole my car.

My car _____.

Mid-Book Test (Units 1–6)

A. Listen to the conversation and circle the name of the correct hotel.

1. Cheap	Forest Hotel	Palace Hotel
2. Large room	Forest Hotel	Palace Hotel
3. Delicious food	Forest Hotel	Palace Hotel
4. Quiet	Forest Hotel	Palace Hotel
5. Swimming	Forest Hotel	Palace Hotel
6. Dancing	Forest Hotel	Palace Hotel
7. Shopping mall	Forest Hotel	Palace Hotel
8. Health club	Forest Hotel	Palace Hotel

9. Which hotel do you want to stay in? Explain in a sentence or two.

_____

_____

B. Write the correct word on the line.

accident	appointment
damage	embarrassing
huge	jealous
perform	talent
towel	turn on

  1. The Joneses bought a new house. It's really
  _____. It has twenty rooms!

  2. I have an _____ with Dr. Dominique
  tomorrow at 4 o'clock.

  3. The hurricane did a lot of _____.
  Over 300 houses were destroyed.

  4. I saw a terrible _____ this morning.
  A truck hit a train.

  5. The newspaper says that the Broken Bones band is going to _____ this
  Saturday night at the City Theater. Let's see if we can get tickets!

  6. Take a _____ with you to the pool!

C. Write the correct form of the verb on the line. Use the simple present tense, the present
progressive tense, the simple past tense, or the past progressive tense.

  1. Jennifer **(ride)** _____ her bike when she
  found the money.

  2. Kevin **(play)** _____ basketball after school yesterday.

  3. I can't come right now, Mom. I **(talk)** _____ on the phone. I'll be there
  in a minute.

  4. Juana **(decide)** _____ to study biology at the City University. I think
  that she did the right thing.

  5. Sunja, **(know)** _____ you _____ Hiroko? Come on, I'll
  introduce you.

  6. Liz and Frank **(buy)** _____ a new computer last week.

  7. Tomiko **(wash)** _____ the car when it
  began to rain.

8. I can't meet Thursday for lunch. I **(have)** _____ a meeting every Thursday at that time.

9. Look at that man over there! He **(eat)** _____ his fourth hamburger!

10. My doctor **(think)** _____ that I need to get more exercise. I am going to start running every day after work.

D. Write the correct form of the adjective on the line.
Use a comparative or superlative adjective or **as ... as ...** .
Use **the** or **than**, if necessary.

1. The Waxmans' house is **(large)** _____ the Johnsons' house.

2. The Waxmans' garden is **(good)** _____ .

3. The Long's car is **(powerful)** _____ .

4. The Waxmans' car is **(bad)** _____ .

5. The Waxman's house is **(expensive)** _____ the Johnson's house·

End-of-Book Test (Units 7–12)

A. Listen to the interview and fill in the information.

	Job	Reason for leaving
first job	1.	2.
second job	3.	4.
third job	5.	6.
job she wants now	7.	8.

9. Do you think that she should get the job? Why or why not? Explain in a sentence or two.

_____

_____

B. Write the correct word or phrase on the line.

advice	amazing
Better luck next time!	bills
Congratulations!	complain
driver's license	disappoint
jealous	stressed out

  1. I have two tests tomorrow. I'm really
  _____!

  2. Tim got his _____ last month, and now
  he takes his car everywhere.

  3. You fixed this TV three times, but it still doesn't work correctly.
  I'm going to _____ about it to the manager.

  4. Alice can't pay all of her _____ this month. She asked me to lend her
  some money until she gets paid.

  5. Kelly is having a problem with her children. She needs some _____.

  6. What an incredible story! It's really _____!

C. Write the correct form of the verb on the line.

  1. Ann **(work)** _____ for the Smythe Company for over twenty years.
  She really likes her job.

  2. When I was a child, I **(play)** _____ football every day after school.

  3. If you explain your problem to the boss, I'm sure that she **(understand)** _____.

  4. I think that you **(take)** _____ your umbrella with you. I think that it's
  going to rain.

  5. I **(live)** _____ in Barcelona, but now I live in Chicago.

  6. Joan **(travel)** _____ around the world for over two months. She's
  going to come back next month.

  7. Mary, I don't think that you **(go swimming)** _____. It's very cold out.

  8. Where's Mary Jane these days? I **(see, *neg.*)** _____ her for several days.

  9. If Bill **(win)** _____ the lottery, he **(buy)** _____ a new car.

D. Write **who** or **that** on the line. If the relative pronoun is not necessary, write it in parentheses.

  1. The car _____ I bought was not very expensive.

  2. The doctor _____ wrote a book about weight loss is giving a speech at
  our club tonight.

  3. The tickets _____ Tim and Gloria bought for the opera were very expensive.

  4. Give me the book _____ is on the top shelf. I want to return it to the library.

  5. The woman _____ won the prize is from New York.

On Target 1 **TExxi**

SCOTT FORESMAN ENGLISH

ON TARGET 1

INTERMEDIATE

Second Edition

James E. Purpura
Teachers College, Columbia University

Diane Pinkley
Teachers College, Columbia University

Photos: p. vii, PhotoDisc, Inc.; p. 1, The Kobal Collection; p. 3, PhotoDisc, Inc.; p. 4, Handout/Reuters/Archive Photos; p. 7, PhotoDisc, Inc.; p. 11, PhotoDisc, Inc.; p. 18, Image provided by MetaTools; p. 20, PhotoDisc, Inc.; p. 25, PhotoDisc, Inc.; p. 26, PhotoDisc, Inc.; p. 27, Corbis/Digital Stock; p. 28, © R. Hutchings/PhotoEdit; p. 29, Courtesy BMW of North America; p. 33, Shooting Star (Elvis Presley); Corbis/Reuters (Placido Domingo); Paul Fenton/Shooting Star (Madonna); p. 33, (tl) Manny Hernandez/Archive Photos; (bc) Scott Harrison/Archive Photos; (br) Fotos International/Archive Photos; p. 35, Archive Photos; p. 36, (t) AP/Wide World Photos (The Beatles); p. 36, (b) AP/Wide World Photos (John Lennon and Yoko Ono); Corbis/Bettmann-UPI (Rosemary Brown); p. 40, (t) Photo by Michael Terranova/Courtesy New Orleans Convention and Visitors Bureau; (c, b) Archive Photos; p. 42, Lyric Opera of Chicago's production of Verdi's *Aida* (1994). Photo by John Reilly; p. 43, (tl, tr, cl, cr, bl, bc) Corbis/Digital Stock; (tc, c, br, b) PhotoDisc, Inc.; p. 50, Archive Photos; p. 51, Corbis/Digital Stock; p. 53, (t) © Cosmo Condina/Tony Stone Images; (cl, cr) PhotoDisc, Inc.; (bl) Image provided by MetaTools; (br) The Corel Corporation; p. 54, from *The Guinness Book of World Records* published by Sterling Publishing Co., Inc. New York, N.Y. © 1990 by Guinness Superlatives Ltd., Bobbi Lane/Tony Stone Images; p. 55, Courtesy BMW of North America; p. 59, PhotoDisc, Inc.; p. 60, PhotoDisc, Inc.; p. 64, PhotoDisc, Inc.; p. 65, Michael Newman/PhotoEdit; p. 66, PhotoDisc, Inc.; p. 67, PhotoDisc, Inc.; p. 68, PhotoDisc, Inc.; p. 70, PhotoDisc, Inc.; p. 71, Courtesy NASA; p. 72, Culver Pictures; p. 73, Culver Pictures; p. 75, PhotoDisc, Inc.; p. 82, PhotoDisc, Inc.; p. 83, PhotoDisc, Inc.; p. 86, PhotoDisc, Inc.; p. 88, PhotoDisc, Inc.; p. 89, PhotoDisc, Inc.; p. 91, PhotoDisc, Inc.; p. 92, (t) Owen Franken/Stock Boston; p. 92, (b) Liane Enkelis/Stock Boston; p. 93, (t) Uniphoto, Inc.; p. 93, (m) Rick Brady/Uniphoto, Inc.; p. 93, (b) AP/Wide World Photos; p. 93, PhotoDisc, Inc.; p. 94, PhotoDisc, Inc.; p. 97, Reuters/Mike Blake/Archive Photos; p. 101, PhotoDisc, Inc.; p. 102, The Kobal Collection; p. 104, AP/Wide World; p. 105 (t), UPI/Bettman Newsphotos; (b), *The Guinness Book of World Records 1998* by Mark C. Young © Used be permission of Bantam Books, a division of Random House, Inc.; p. 107, (bkgrnd) PhotoDisc, Inc.; p. 112, (t) Corbis/Bettmann-UPI; p. 112, (b) Corbis/Reuters; p. 115, (t) Owen Franken/Stock Boston; p. 115, (b) Corbis/Bettmann; p. 116, PhotoDisc, Inc.; p. 120, PhotoDisc, Inc.

Illustrations: Andrea Baruffi pp. 11 (t), 80; Chris Celusniak pp. 23, 48; T. R. Garcia pp. 22, 118; Patrick Girouard pp. 98, 110; Brian Karas pp. 47, 52, 99; Judy Love p. 6; Robert Porazinski pp. 43, 77; Philip Scheuer pp. 14, 21; Steve Schindler pp. 56, 121; Terry Sirrell pp. 2, 17, 107, 124; George Thompson pp. 108, 117; George Ulrich pp. 24, 85; Randy Verougstraete pp. 12, 13, 44, 45.

Cover photos: Gotham Studio/Jan Cobb (dartboard); Jim Barber/The Stock Rep (keyboard); © 1999 Jim Westphalen (type).

CONTENTS

SUMMARY OF SKILLS

Theme	Grammar	Listening and Speaking	Reading and Writing
Unit 1 **What's on TV?** Page 1	Simple Present Tense; Future Events Frequency Adverbs and Expressions	**Listening:** Coming Soon! ➡ Listening for Specific Details **Pronunciation:** -s/-es ending **Speaking:** What's Your Opinion? ➡ Expressing Opinions	**Reading:** TV Programs ➡ Scanning **Writing:** The Paragraph
Unit 2 **People Watching** Page 11	Present Progressive Tense: Present Time; Future Time Stative Verbs	**Listening:** Where Are They? ➡ Making Inferences **Pronunciation:** Syllables **Speaking:** The Meeting ➡ Making Appointments	**Reading:** The Right to Privacy ➡ Guessing Meaning from Context **Writing:** Narrowing a Topic
Unit 3 **Keeping Up with the Joneses** Page 21	Comparative Adjectives; *Not as ... as;* Talking about Similarities	**Listening:** Choosing a Restaurant ➡ Listening for Criteria **Pronunciation:** Stressed Syllables **Speaking:** Alternatives ➡ Agreeing and Disagreeing	**Reading:** Mall Crawlers: A Teenage Stereotype ➡ Identifying Main Ideas **Writing:** The Topic Sentence

Review (Units 1–3)

Theme	Grammar	Listening and Speaking	Reading and Writing
Unit 4 **And the Beat Goes On!** Page 33	Simple Past Tense; Adverbs of Sequence	**Listening:** Music Around the World ➡ Listening to Complete a Chart **Pronunciation:** -ed ending **Speaking:** First-Time Experiences ➡ Keeping a Conversation Going	**Reading:** The Story of Jazz ➡ Noticing Chronological Order **Writing:** Supporting Sentences
Unit 5 **Close Calls** Page 43	Simple Past and Past Progressive Tenses; Time Clauses with *When, While, As*	**Listening:** A News Story ➡ Listening for Sequence **Pronunciation:** Content vs. Function Words **Speaking:** A Close Call ➡ Telling a Story	**Reading:** The San Francisco Earthquake of 1906 ➡ Making Predictions **Writing:** The Concluding Sentence
Unit 6 **The Best in Life** Page 53	Superlative; Making Comparisons with Adverbs and Nouns	**Listening:** Advertisements ➡ Listening to Draw Conclusions **Pronunciation:** Numbers **Speaking:** Five Thousand Dollars ➡ Arguing, Counterarguing, Conceding	**Reading:** The World of Advertising ➡ Noticing Examples **Writing:** Ordering Supporting Sentences

Review (Units 4–6)

STARTING OUT

Note: This unit provides a brief introduction to the course. Keep the activities moving quickly. Spend no more than one or two class sessions on this unit.

You may wish to read Introducing Vocabulary, page TEvii, and Working in Pairs and Groups, page TExiii, before proceeding with the lesson.

Getting Acquainted

Preview

- Write **language** and **communication** on the board. Emphasize that students must actively participate (communicate) in class to do well.

- Check understanding of **culture.** Have students define the word (ideas, customs, and beliefs shared by a society) and tell you important aspects of their home culture: music, special foods, etc. Put a list on the board.

- Explain the difference between **acquaintance** and **friend.** Ask, *What activities would you enjoy with a friend? Would you do the same activities with an acquaintance?* Introduce students to the expression **getting acquainted.**

- Check understanding of **hobby** by saying, *In my free time, I like to (do something).* Ask selected students to share their hobbies with the class.

Presentation

❶ Review the vocabulary in the chart. Put students into pairs to write a question or questions for each category. Tell students to use the question words in the box for help. Circulate to offer assistance. Once

Tvii

students have finished working, go over their answers as a class. Correct any problem sentences on the board as a class.

Possible Questions

a. What's your name? **b.** Where are you from? What's your hometown? **c.** What do you do? Where do you go to school? **d.** Where do you go to school? What grade are you in? What is/was your major? When did/will you graduate? **e.** Why are you studying English? Why are you taking this class? **f.** How many people are in your family? **g.** What are your hobbies? **h.** What's your favorite food? **i.** Who's your favorite actor or actress? **j.** What's your favorite restaurant? **k.** What do you like to do on the weekend? What's your favorite weekend activity? **l.** *Questions will vary.*

---

❷ Students should switch partners and ask their new partner all the questions in the chart, taking notes as they listen.

❸ Each student should introduce his/her partner to the class, using the notes from Exercise 2. [Students should start out by saying, *This is (name) and he's/she's …*] In this way, everyone in the class will get acquainted.

Language Note: Students may have trouble explaining their answer to question **d** about education since educational systems differ widely from country to country.

Option: Bring a small ball to class. Form a circle with the class. Say your name and throw the ball to a student. That student catches the ball, repeats your name, says his/her name, and throws the ball to another student. Continue until each student has had a turn (saying the name of the other student, and then saying his/her name before throwing the ball to another student). In the same circle you can also call out a name and throw the ball to that students, who has to catch the ball, say the name of another student, and throw the ball to that student. Students can also say their nationalities and/or occupations.

Language is communication. In this class, you will communicate in English. You will talk about your ideas, feelings, experiences, and culture. Begin the class by getting to know the other students and the teacher.

Getting Acquainted

1 When you get acquainted with people, you find out information about them. What questions do you ask when you are getting acquainted with someone? Look at the categories. Write an information question for each category. Use the question words from the box for help.

Question Words	
who	where
what	what kind of
how	how often
why	which
when	how long
how many	how much

Categories	Questions
a. name	*What's your name?*
b. hometown or country	
c. job/school	
d. education	
e. reason for studying English	
f. family	
g. hobbies	
h. favorite food	
i. favorite actor/actress	
j. favorite restaurant	
k. favorite weekend activity	
l. other information	

2 Find a partner and get acquainted. Ask each other your questions. Write your partner's answers on a sheet of paper.

3 Introduce your partner to the class.

Getting Down to Business

4 When you are ready to begin work, you "get down to business." In a new class, you ask questions about the course. Look at the class information chart. Use question words to ask your teacher about your course. Write your teacher's answers in the chart.

Class Information	
a. number of units to finish	
b. number of exams	
c. date of final exam	
d. homework	
e. number of compositions	
f. grading	
g. attendance	
h. other information	

What Do You Say?

5 What would you say in each situation? Write the letter of the appropriate expression next to the situation. You can use a letter more than once.

Situation

_____ **1.** You don't know the meaning of a word.

_____ **2.** You don't know a word in English. You know it in your language.

_____ **3.** You didn't hear something.

_____ **4.** You don't understand something in English. You want your teacher to explain it to you.

_____ **5.** You are trying to say something in English, but you are not sure if it's correct.

_____ **6.** People in your culture do something differently than in another culture.

_____ **7.** You want to write a word. You can't write it correctly.

_____ **8.** A classmate says something. You have the same opinion.

_____ **9.** A classmate says something. You have a different opinion.

_____ **10.** You know that two things aren't the same. You want to know why they aren't the same.

Language Expressions

a. Well, in my country, _____.

b. Is it possible to say _____ in English?

c. How do you spell _____?

d. Oh, I don't know. In my opinion, _____.

e. What does _____ mean?

f. Excuse me, I need some help.

g. How do you say _____ in English?

h. What's the difference between _____ and _____?

i. Could you repeat that, please?

j. I agree with you.

Getting Down to Business

Preview

Explain that **getting down to business** means deciding to do something seriously.

Presentation

❹ Have students go over the vocabulary in the class information chart and ask any questions. If necessary, allow students time to work with a partner to write out some questions. When they are ready, have volunteers ask you one question each. Tell the entire class the answers.

Possible Questions

a. How many units are there? How many units will we finish (this term/semester)? **b.** How many exams will we have? How many exams will there be? **c.** What is the date of the final exam? When will we have our final exam? **d.** How much homework will there be? What will we have to do for homework? **e.** How many compositions will we have to write? **f.** How will we be graded? How do you figure out the final grade? **g.** What is the policy on attendance? How often can we miss class? **h.** *Questions will vary.*

✪ Option: If any categories do not apply to your class, substitute others, such as policies on late papers, use of the language laboratory, etc.

What Do You Say?

Preview

Explain to students that they will first work alone to do this activity and then check answers with a partner.

Presentation

❺ Have students read the instructions. Circulate and provide help with vocabulary as students raise their hands.

Answers

1. e **2.** b or g **3.** i **4.** f **5.** b **6.** a **7.** c **8.** j
9. d **10.** h

✪ Option: Have students cover up the right-hand column and write down what they would say in each situation. Then have them check their answers against the list of language expressions.

✪ Option: Put students into groups. Have the members of each group find five things that they have in common. Set a time limit. Have each group report its findings to the class, for example, "We all have cars."

✪ Option: Have each student write one false and two true statements about himself/herself on a sheet of paper. Have individuals read their sentences to the class. The class has to discover which statement is false by asking questions.

✪ Option: Draw a tic-tac-toe square on the board. Number the squares and write the answer to an information question in each one. Divide the class into two teams, the X team and the O team. Tell the teams that the goal is to get three of their marks in a row horizontally, vertically, or diagonally by forming information questions. Have team members work together to form nine information questions, then take turns reading them aloud. When a team member reads a correct question, the team can put its mark in the square.

1. I'm thirty years old.
2. I'm a lawyer.
3. She collects stamps and coins.
4. I have two brothers and three sisters.
5. We're from Barcelona, Spain.
6. Her name is Rosa.
7. I go to International University.
8. Brad Pitt is our favorite actor.
9. He's in fifth grade.

✪ Option: Make a list of sentences, such as the following. Write it on the board or make a copy for every student. Tell the class that they have to find a student for whom each statement is true. They can use any student's name only one time unless the class is small. Set a time limit. The winner is the student who completes the list the fastest.

1. _____ has been to Washington D.C.
2. _____ was born under the zodiac sign of Cancer.
3. _____ is sixteen years old.
4. _____ likes the color red best.
5. _____ likes Tom Cruise a lot.

WHAT'S ON TV?

OBJECTIVES

- To talk about TV viewing habits
- To express opinions
- To agree and disagree
- To use the simple present tense
- To use frequency adverbs and expressions
- To listen for specific details
- To practice –s and –es endings
- To use the technique of scanning
- To identify elements of a paragraph
- To use two-word verbs

GETTING STARTED

Warm Up

Preview

- Students name some TV programs. Make a list on the board. Identify the channel of a program: *(X Files) is on Channel 2.* Have students make similar sentences about other programs.

- Ask, *How can you find out the channel of a program if you don't know it?* Show a real TV program guide (or use the guide on page 9). Ask, *What information can you find in a TV guide?*

- Look at the photo. Ask students to name the movie *(Godzilla)* and to say what Godzilla is (a monster, a dinosaur). Ask, *What other movie monsters do you know? (Possible answers*: Frankenstein, Dracula, etc.)

- Identify one type of TV program—for example, *Godzilla is a movie. It's a science fiction movie.* Ask, *What other types of TV programs do you know?* Have students identify the type of each program you listed on the board. Write the type of

program next to its name. Introduce other types by giving examples, such as, *Money Talk is a talk show.* (*Possible types:* comedy, talk show, game show, cartoon, soap opera, movie, sports program, detective show, news, documentary, science fiction.)

Presentation

❶ Ask students to describe each type of program and add other types to the list.

❷ Read the instructions. Play the recording one or more times. Tell students that they do not have to understand every word to do the activity.

Audioscript: The audioscript for Exercises 2 and 3 appears on page T152.

> **Answers**
> Channel 5: *Science Fiction Theater;* Channel 2: *The World of Nature;* Channel 4: *Women Today;* Channel 3: *The $10,000 Test;* Channel 1: *Nikki Danger–Police Officer*

Option: Before doing Exercise 3, have students list words they expect to hear in each program. (*Example:* For *Science Fiction Theater,* they might list **monsters, aliens, robots.**) After students listen, ask which words helped them figure out the correct answers.

❸ Students may need to listen again to do the activity.

> **Answers**
> *Science Fiction Theater:* movie; *The World of Nature:* documentary; *Women Today:* talk show; *The $10,000 Test:* game show; *Nikki Danger–Police Officer:* detective show

 Workbook: Practice 1

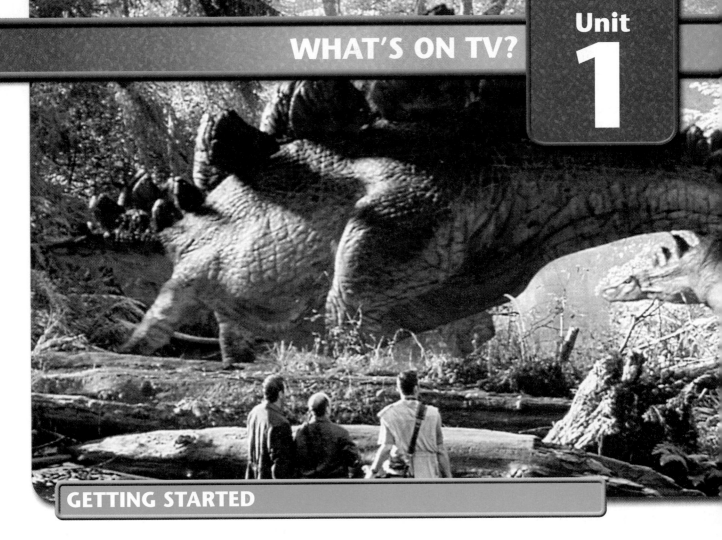

GETTING STARTED

Warm Up

1 TV is a popular form of entertainment. Here are some types of TV programs. Describe each one. Can you add two other types of programs?

| talk show | docu-mentary | game show | detective show | soap opera | movie | | |

2 You are going to hear parts of five different TV programs. What channel is each program on? Write the channel number in the box.

☐ *Science Fiction Theater* _____

☐ *The World of Nature* _____

☐ *Women Today* _____

☐ *The $10,000 Test* _____

☐ *Nikki Danger—Police Officer* _____

3 Match the program names above with the correct type of program. Write the answers on the lines.

Figure It Out

4 Some people only want to sit on the couch and watch TV. We call these people "couch potatoes." Are you a couch potato? Check the appropriate boxes in the questionnaire below to find out.

		100% Always	Usually	Often	Sometimes	Seldom	0% Never
a	How long is your TV on every day?	☐	☐	☐	☐	☐	☐
b	How often do you eat while you are watching TV?	☐	☐	☐	☐	☐	☐
c	How often do you watch TV when you have guests?	☐	☐	☐	☐	☐	☐
d	How often do you fall asleep with the TV on?	☐	☐	☐	☐	☐	☐
e	How often do you think about your favorite programs before you plan other activities?	☐	☐	☐	☐	☐	☐
f	How often do you turn on the TV right after you get home from work or school?	☐	☐	☐	☐	☐	☐
g	How often do you watch TV instead of reading, going out with friends, or playing sports?	☐	☐	☐	☐	☐	☐

5 Figure out your total points; then look at the information below.

Always = 5 points *Often = 3 points* *Seldom = 1 point*
Usually = 4 points *Sometimes = 2 points* *Never = 0 points*

0–11 Points	**12–19 Points**	**20–27 Points**	**28–35 Points**
You're not a couch potato! In fact, you're not even a potato chip. You seldom watch TV. You probably have a love for real life and enjoy many activities. However, remember that there are some good programs on TV. Do you ever watch the news, a good documentary, or a good movie?	You're not a couch potato, but you watch TV sometimes. You probably use your time to participate in sports, hobbies, and other fun activities. Make sure that the TV programs you watch are good ones!	You probably watch TV a little too much. You're going to be a couch potato soon if you're not careful! Think of other ways to spend your time. Visit a friend, go to the movies, or read a book. Learn something new, start playing a sport, or begin a new hobby.	You're a real couch potato! Watch out or you'll become a french fry! You probably almost always watch TV in your free time. You don't have many other interests or activities. You need to find new things to do. Start a hobby! Make new friends! Try turning off the TV once in a while!

Figure It Out

Preview

- Ask students how much TV they watch every day. Ask them if they think some people watch TV too much. Ask how many hours is too much.
- Ask students what a **questionnaire** is and what it is used for. Ask if anyone in the class has ever filled one out. If so, have students describe their experiences.

Presentation

❹ Look at the picture. Ask students to describe the man and what he is doing. Students read the directions silently. Ask if they know any "couch potatoes." Ask if they are couch potatoes. If so, ask why. Students can complete the questionnaire individually in class or as homework.

Language Note: The term **couch potato** is an example of informal English. It describes a person who would rather sit at home on the couch watching TV than participate in more active or social pastimes, such as playing sports or visiting friends.

Option: Have students work in pairs and complete the questionnaire by interviewing each other. Student A asks Student B the questions and checks the boxes; then B interviews A.

❺ Students follow the instructions to figure out their total points. Ask, *How many people scored between 0 and 11 points? Between 12 and 19 points? 20 and 27 points? 28 and 35 points?* Write the number of students in each category on the board. Discuss the results of the questionnaire. Ask if the descriptions in the categories are accurate. Why or why not? Ask what the good and bad points about watching TV are. (*Possible good points:* Some TV programs—like news and documentaries—are very educational. Watching TV in English is a good way to practice and improve listening skills. *Possible bad points:* Watching too much TV makes you passive and lazy. People need to get information from many sources— for example, from reading and talking with people—not just from TV.)

Option: You may want to have students keep vocabulary notebooks. (See page TEviii.)

- Students may write down new vocabulary and expressions from the Student Book and from class discussions. They can also make up sentences to illustrate the meaning of new words and expressions.
- Another way to use vocabulary notebooks to build and review vocabulary is to make word maps. This strategy helps students organize and show relationships among terms and new information. Here are examples of possible word maps for two types of TV programs.

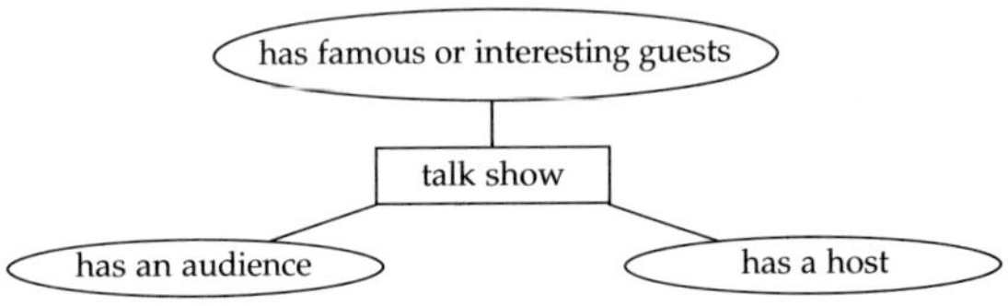

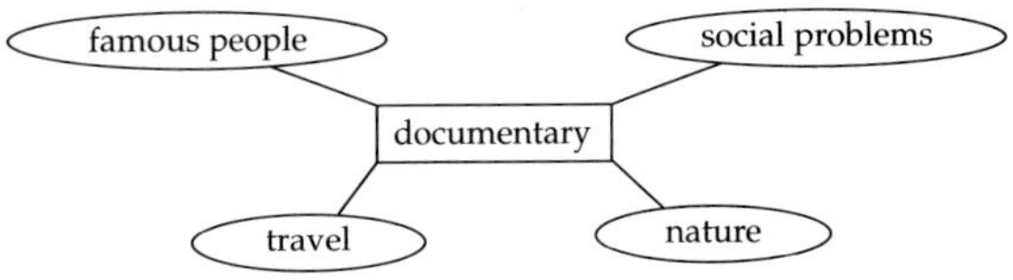

☑ ❻ **Vocabulary Check** Students read the instructions and complete the matching exercise.

Answers
1. e 2. f 3. d 4. b 5. a 6. c

 Workbook: Practice 2

Talk About It

 Option: If you feel your students need extra help with the simple present tense, you may postpone doing Exercises 7, 8, and 9 until after the grammar presentation on page 4. You may also ask students to first do Workbook Practice 4.

Presentation

❼ Ask a volunteer to make up a question for questionnaire item **a.** Then ask students to write questions for the other items; they may work alone, in pairs, or in small groups (see page TExiii).

Answers
a. What's your favorite TV program?
b. How many hours of TV do you watch per week? **c.** When do you usually watch TV? **d.** How often do you watch the news?

Option: Write additional cues on the board for students to write questions about, for example, their favorite TV actor and actress or how often they watch the news (sports, etc.).

❽ Ask students to work in pairs. One student in each pair is the interviewer. When pairs finish the interview, ask them to switch roles and repeat the activity.

❾ Ask volunteers to report on the most interesting facts they learned about their partners.

Option: Ask for volunteers to perform their interviews for the class. Encourage students to expand their conversations by using greetings, asking for permission to do the interview, thanking the interviewee, etc.

 Workbook: Practice 3

6 **Vocabulary Check** The frequency adverbs in column A are from the questionnaire. Match the other frequency adverbs and expressions in column B with the correct adverbs in column A.

Column A
___ **1.** always
___ **2.** usually
___ **3.** often
___ **4.** sometimes
___ **5.** seldom
___ **6.** never

Column B
a. rarely
b. once in a while
c. not at all
d. frequently
e. all the time
f. generally

Talk About It

TV marketing managers often interview people about their TV viewing habits. Look at the dialogue.

Ask about favorite program.
A: What's your favorite TV program?

State favorite program.
B: My favorite program is *Nikki Danger—Police Officer*.

Ask about frequency.
A: How often do you watch it?

Tell frequency.
B: I watch it every week.

7 Look at the categories in the questionnaire. On a sheet of paper, write an interview question for each category.

8 Work with a partner. Interview your partner and write his or her answers in the questionnaire.

9 Discuss your interviews with the class.
a. What is your class's favorite TV program?
b. What is the average number of hours that people watch TV per week?

TV Questionnaire

Categories	Responses
a. Favorite TV program	
b. Hours watching TV per week	
c. Usual time to watch TV	
d. Frequency of watching news	

The Simple Present Tense

We use the simple present tense to talk about actions and states in the present that do not usually change. Look at the different uses.

Present Habits	Marco Jobim **watches** sports on TV every night. He almost always **falls asleep** in front of the TV.
Ideas, Opinions, and Feelings	Marco **doesn't enjoy** soap operas. His wife **thinks** he watches too much TV. She **knows** he is becoming a couch potato.
General Truths and Facts	Teenagers in the United States **watch** about twenty-one hours of TV a week. Cable TV and satellite dishes **give** people many more channels.

 1 **Check Your Understanding** Why do we use the simple present tense? Read the sentences below. Write **H** for habits, **G** for general truths and facts, or **I** for ideas, opinions, and feelings.

_____ **a.** Marco Jobim likes TV very much.

_____ **b.** He turns on the TV as soon as he gets home.

_____ **c.** He always watches music videos.

_____ **d.** His TV gets twelve channels.

_____ **e.** At night he often falls asleep in front of his TV.

_____ **f.** His mother thinks he watches too much TV.

_____ **g.** She believes that a lot of TV is bad for people.

Work with a partner. Compare your answers.

2 Write three sentences of your own. Write one sentence for each use.

3 Look at a partner's sentences. Can you name the use for each sentence?

Hanson, a popular musical group

The Simple Present Tense: Future Events

You can also use the simple present tense to talk about future events with timetables and calendars. Look at the examples.

Future Events	A new talk show **starts** next Monday at 9:00 p.m. The World Cup match **is** on TV tomorrow afternoon at 3:00 p.m. My exams **finish** on Friday.

GRAMMAR

The Simple Present Tense

Preview

- Introduce or review the word **habit** by giving examples: Smoking is a bad habit. Ask students for other examples of good and bad habits.

- Contrast **fact** with **opinion.** Explain that the difference between fact and opinion is not always clear. Facts can be proved by scientific evidence. Opinions are what people think or believe to be true. Give an example of each: It is a *fact* that water becomes ice at 32 degrees Fahrenheit/0 degrees Celsius. *John thinks Godzilla is a very scary movie.* Ask students for some additional facts and opinions.

Presentation

Students read the grammar explanation and the examples in the box. You may assign this for homework or have students read it in class.

☑ ❶ **Check Your Understanding** This exercise asks students to identify specific situations (categories) for using the simple present tense.

Answers
a. I b. H c. H d. G e. H f. I g. I

❷ Ask for volunteers to share their sentences with the class. Ask the class to identify the correct category.

❸ Partners read each other's sentences and identify the uses of the simple present tense.

 Workbook: Practices 4, 5

✪ **Option:** Bring in magazine or newspaper articles for students to look at. Have them find examples of the simple present tense and classify them by category (use the same categories as in Exercise 1).

✪ **Option:** Ask students to write as many sentences as they can about activities they do every day. Who can write the most sentences in three minutes?

The Simple Present Tense: Future Events

Preview

- Ask students to name places where they can find schedules. (*Possible answers:* bus and train stations, schools, newspapers and magazines—for TV program and movie schedules)

- Ask what information schedules contain. (*Possible answers:* arrival and departure times of buses and trains, times and room numbers when/where classes meet, names, channels, and times of TV programs, names and times of movies)

Presentation

Students read the explanation and the examples in the box.

❹ Students use the cues to make sentences in the simple present tense. (*Answers will vary.*)

Language Note: We can use the verbs **open** and **close** to refer to the start and finish of a movie, play, or other special event (such as an art show or the Olympic Games).
Examples:
The new *Star Wars* movie **opens** on Friday.
The Van Gogh exhibit **closes** on June 5.

✲ **Option:** Bring in real schedules for buses, trains, school, TV, or movies, etc. Students talk about the schedules using the simple present tense, for example, "The bus to Miami leaves at one o'clock."

❺ In describing their TV habits, students may talk about their favorite programs, what types of programs they like and don't like to watch, how often they watch these programs, their favorite actors and actresses.

Frequency Adverbs and Expressions

Preview

Introduce or review **once** and **twice**. Perform a simple action, such as dropping a pencil, two times. Say, *I dropped my pencil twice.*

Then drop your pen only once. Say, *I dropped my pen once.* Ask students questions with **how often**. Encourage them to answer with **once** or **twice**.
Example:
A: How often do you go to the movies?
B: Twice a month.

Presentation

❻ Students study the grammar chart and answer the questions.

> **Answers**
> a. Frequency adverbs come before the verb.
> b. Frequency expressions come after the verb.

☑ ❼ **Check Your Understanding** The words and expressions that can be used with the simple present tense are **seldom, every Saturday, once a year, next Friday.** (*Students' sentences using these words will vary.*)

✲ **Option:** Students work in small groups to list all the frequency adverbs and expressions they can. Set a time limit, such as one minute. Then find out how many frequency adverbs and expressions each group wrote. Write them on the board. The group with the largest number wins.

Talk about future events using the words and phrases below.

Example: The Olympic Games start next week.

Events	Verbs	Future Time Words
a new science fiction movie	start	next week (month, year)
final exams	finish	tomorrow (morning, afternoon, night)
summer classes	is (on)	tonight
the Olympic Games	open	on Friday (Saturday, …)
a documentary on UFOs	close	at 7 p.m.

5 Work in groups of three. Take turns describing your TV viewing habits.

Example:
A: I watch the news on TV every night.
B: Not me. I only watch sports and game shows.
C: Me too. My favorite show is *Jackpot Shop.*

Frequency Adverbs and Expressions

We use frequency adverbs and expressions to talk about how often an action happens. We ask questions with *How often* or *ever*.

	Subject	Frequency adverb	Verb phrase
How often do you watch the news?	I	**seldom**	watch the news on TV.
	I	**usually**	read the newspaper.
Do you **ever** get news from the Internet?	I	**sometimes**	do.

	Subject	Verb phrase		Frequency expression
Do you **ever** go to the ballet?	We	go		**twice a year.**
How often do you get that magazine?	I	get	it	**weekly.**
How often does your son watch TV?	He	watches	TV	**every day.**

6 Look at the chart above.

    a. Where do frequency adverbs come in a sentence?
    b. Where do frequency expressions come in a sentence?

 7 **Check Your Understanding** Circle the words and expressions you can use with the simple present tense. Then write a sentence about yourself in the simple present tense for each word you circled.

seldom	once a year
yesterday	next Friday
every Saturday	last night

8 The Yang family always shares the housework. Mr. Yang, Mrs. Yang, Ann, and Mike do different chores.

a. Look at the word box. Match the verbs on the left with the words on the right to make phrases. Write the phrases on the lines under pictures 1 to 8. The first one is done for you.

b. Work with a partner. Describe the Yang family. Who does the chores? How often? Make sentences in the simple present tense.

Example:

Mrs. Yang often irons the clothes on the weekend.

washes	the food
mows	the car
irons	the plants
fixes	the floor
mops	the dog
cooks	the clothes
feeds	the lawn
waters	the dishes

1.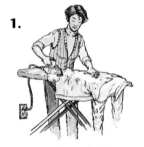

irons the clothes
often/on the weekend

2.

_____
sometimes/on Saturday

3.

_____
always/on weekdays

4.

_____
usually/Saturday morning

5.

_____
normally/every day

6.

_____
generally/twice a week

7.

_____
often/after dinner

8.

_____
usually/Friday evening

 9 **Express Yourself** Work with a partner. Who does the chores at your house? How often? Take turns asking and answering questions.

Example:

A: Who usually washes the dishes at your house?

B: I usually do.

A: How often do you wash them?

B: Twice a day.

Unit 1

❽ Students look at the picture of the Yang family and read the paragraph.

    a. Students do the matching exercise.

Answers

1. irons the clothes **2.** fixes the car **3.** cooks the food **4.** mops the floor **5.** feeds the dog **6.** waters the plants **7.** washes the dishes **8.** mows the lawn

    b. Students take turns making sentences in pairs.

Answers

1. Mrs. Yang often irons the clothes on weekends. **2.** Mr. Yang sometimes fixes the car on Saturday. **3.** Mrs. Yang and Mike always cook the food on weekdays. **4.** Mike usually mops the floor Saturday morning. **5.** Ann normally feeds the dog every day. **6.** Mrs. Yang generally waters the plants twice a week. **7.** Ann and Mike often wash the dishes after dinner. **8.** Ann usually mows the lawn Friday evening.

 ❾ **Express Yourself** These activities are communicative and interactive. They connect the grammar point—in this case, frequency adverbs and expressions—to the students' personal lives. (*Answers will vary.*)

Link   *Workbook: Practices 6, 7, 8*

LISTENING and SPEAKING

Listen: Coming Soon!

Presentation

❶ Before You Listen As a class or in pairs, students answer the prelistening questions.

➡ **Listening for Specific Details** This is the first of several learning strategies that appear in every unit. The purpose of these strategies is to help students learn more effectively and independently.

Have students read the strategy. Ask students to think of examples from their own experience where they might listen for details. (*Possible examples:* listening for a gate number in an announcement at a train station or airport; listening for a telephone number on someone's answering machine)

You might point out that listening for details is a useful strategy in any language, but it is especially useful when learning a second or foreign language.

🎧 **❷** Before students listen, they study the chart. Ask, *What kinds of information do you see on the chart?* Explain that looking at the chart before listening can help them predict the information they will hear. Then play the recording or read the audioscript aloud one or more times.

Audioscript: The audioscript for Exercise 2 appears on page T152.

❸ Having students check answers in pairs allows for more independent language practice. If students need help getting started, you might help them ask questions such as *What day is The Big Question on? What kind of program is Nikki Danger—Police Officer?*

Answers
1. Monday **2.** detective show, 8:00
3. *Amazing Animals*, documentary **4.** science fiction movie, Wednesday **5.** Thursday, 7:00

 Workbook: Practice 9

Speak Out

➡ **Agreeing and Disagreeing** Introduce or review the language for agreeing and disagreeing. As a way of modeling the strategy, you can ask a student, *What do you think is the best program on TV?* Use one of the expressions in the box to agree with him/her. Ask another student, *Who do you think is the best pop singer?* This time, use one of the expressions to disagree and give your own opinion.

Presentation

❹ Students read and complete the questionnaire individually. (*Answers will vary.*)

Option: Write some additional statements on the board for students to add to their questionnaires, for example, *There are too many commercials on TV.*

Listen: Coming Soon!

 Before You Listen

    a. What TV programs can you watch tonight?
    b. What type of program is each one?
    c. What time is each program on?

 Listening for Specific Details We often listen for details such as a name, a date, or a time. We may not understand every word, but we listen for the specific information we need.

Name of Program	Kind of Program	Day	Time
1 The Big Question	game show		7:30
2 Nikki Danger— Police Officer		Monday	
3		Tuesday	4:00
4 Spaceship Theater			8:30
5 Music City	music		

 The program *Coming Soon!* is on TV every Sunday. It tells people about next week's programs. Read the chart carefully. Then listen and fill it in.

 Work with a partner. Compare charts and check your answers.

Speak Out

 Agreeing and Disagreeing When someone expresses an opinion in a discussion, it is important to know how to agree and disagree politely. Look at the language below.

Agreeing	Disagreeing
Right, I think so too because …	I'm sorry, but I disagree …
I don't think so either …	Well, I'm not sure. I think …
Yeah, I agree with you because …	

 What are your opinions about TV? Read the statements in the chart. Check the boxes.

TV Opinions	I agree	Maybe	I disagree
1. Violent programs make people violent.			
2. Parents need to check the programs their children watch.			
3. Watching TV makes people passive.			
4. You can learn a lot watching TV.			
5. Governments need to control the programs on TV.			

Work in groups of three. Share your TV opinions. Use language for
agreeing and disagreeing.

Example:

A: I think violent programs make children violent.

B: Well, I'm not sure about that. I watch thrillers all the time and I'm not violent.

C: I don't think so, either.

Pronunciation

The –s/–es ending

In English, we pronounce the –s/–es ending of simple present tense verbs in three ways.
The pronunciation depends on the final sound of the verb.

/s/ as in li<u>k</u>es   /z/ as in fa<u>ll</u>s   /ɪz/ as in wa<u>tch</u>es

  Listen to the verbs. Do you hear /s/, /z/, or /ɪz/? Write the verbs in
the correct boxes below.

/s/ as in *likes*	/z/ as in *falls*	/ɪz/ as in *watches*

 Work with a partner. Look at the pictures on page 6 again. Ask and
answer questions about the Yang family, using the example. Pay
special attention to your pronunciation of –s and –es.

Example:

A: Who mop<u>s</u> the floor?

B: Mike Yang usually mop<u>s</u> it.

READING and WRITING

Read About It

 Before You Read Predict the kinds of information you could find
in a television guide. Circle the letters:

a. program names   **d.** main actors   **g.** program costs

b. program writers   **e.** program types   **h.** program descriptions

c. program times   **f.** number of commercials   **i.** channel numbers

STRATEGY **Scanning** When you read, you often want to find a fact—a name, a date,
a price—quickly. You look for the fact and do not read every word. This
kind of reading is called scanning.

5 The purpose of this discussion activity is to encourage fluency. Students need to be free to speak without fear of interruption for error correction. If you notice errors as you walk around the class listening to different groups, take notes. When the activity is finished, write the errors on the board and ask students to help you correct them.

Pronunciation

Preview

Write **gets** and **knows** on the board and ask students to pronounce them. Ask students if the letter *s* sounds the same in each word. (No.) Have students hold their fingers to their throats as they pronounce the words. They will feel their vocal chords vibrate as they pronounce the –*s* ending in **knows**, which sounds like /z/.

Presentation

Students read the explanation in the box in class or as homework.

6 Play the recording or read the audioscript aloud two or more times and have students fill in the words. Pause between words to allow students time to write.

Audioscript: The audioscript for Exercise 6 appears on page T152.

Answers

/s/: sleeps, makes, asks, laughs, wants, hikes

/z/: goes, learns, calls, comes, believes, describes

/ɪz/: teaches, changes, uses, fixes, washes, misses

---

7 Walk around the class as students ask and answer questions. Make sure they are paying attention to the –*s* and –*es* endings.

 Workbook: Practices 10, 11

Option: To give students more practice in spelling and pronunciation of third person singular verbs, have a spelling bee. Read aloud a list of verbs for students to pronounce and spell. Have students work in teams. The team that spells and pronounces the most verbs correctly wins.

READING and WRITING

Read About It

Presentation

1 **Before You Read** Individually or in pairs, students do the prereading exercise. Predicting is another useful learning strategy.

➡ **Scanning** Students read the strategy. Ask students, *What kinds of reading materials do you usually scan?* Make a list on the board and ask them to explain their answers. (*Possible answers:* a telephone book, a television guide, a menu, a train or bus schedule, a newspaper or magazine article, a table of contents or index) We scan these types of reading to look for specific information only, not to read every word.

❷ Students scan the TV program guide and check their predictions from Exercise 1.

Answers
a, c, d, e, h, i

❸ Students complete the exercise individually or in pairs. You might want to set a time limit (for example, one minute) to encourage students to learn to scan quickly.

Answers
a. three b. *The Rich and the Famous*
c. documentary d. *$20 Million Prize* e. 37
f. science fiction g. three h. Gloria Esteban

☯ **Option:** Ask additional scanning questions:
- What is the Chinese chef going to cook? (Szechwan chicken and fried bananas)
- When was *The Return of King Kong* made? (1989)
- What does Mike Walters explain on *Ninety Minutes?* (how to stop watching TV)
- Who stars in the movie *The New Doctors?* (George Mendel and Judy Grant)

☯ **Option:** Have students write five scanning questions independently, in pairs, or in groups. Then have students ask each other their questions.

Think About It

Presentation

❹ Students do the activity in pairs, in small groups, or as a class.

❺ After students work in pairs, you might have them share their programs with the class. Then the class might vote on which three programs they like best.

☯ **Option:** Ask students the following additional discussion questions:
- Which programs do people watch for fun?
- Which programs are educational?
- You are watching TV. Which shows will you watch at 6:00, 6:30, and 7:00. Why?

☯ **Option:** In groups, pairs, or individually, have students look at a real television guide and find three entertaining programs and three educational programs. Students decide whether or not they want to watch each one. Students discuss their answers. Ask individuals to explain why they want or don't want to watch each program.

☯ **Option:** Students write their own television guides, using the guide shown as a model. They might include the descriptions of the three programs they discussed in Exercise 5. Encourage students to use the simple present tense.

☯ **Option:** In pairs, students use the television guide shown or a real television guide to write a listening activity like Exercise 2 on page 7. They should make a chart with missing information, then write a script that describes what programs are on TV that night. When they finish, students join another pair and exchange charts. They take turns reading their scripts and filling in the missing information.

2 Scan the program guide. How many of your predictions from Exercise 1 were correct?

3 Scan the program guide again to find the answers to these questions:

  a. How many channels show the news at 6:00 p.m.?

  b. What's on channel 10 at 7:00 p.m.?

  c. What kind of program is *The First Cartoons*?

  d. On which program can you win $20 million?

  e. On which channel can you see a tennis match?

  f. What kind of show is *Z Files*?

  g. How many documentaries are in the program guide?

  h. Who does Ken Cleveland interview?

Think About It

4 Look at the program guide. Which programs would these people like?

- a businessman
- an eleven-year-old girl
- a mother of a small child
- a teenage boy

5 Imagine you own a TV station. With a partner, describe three programs you would like to show on your channel. When you finish, join another pair of students. Describe your programs. Which program do you like best?

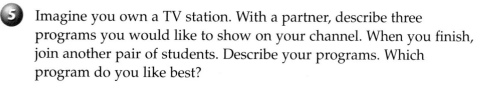

TV Programs

6:00

6 21 NEWS

7 OK FOR KIDS *Talk Show.* Children discuss latest kids' movies.

19 $20 MILLION PRIZE *Game Show*

53 The New Doctors *(1984) Movie* George Mendel and Judy Grant are doctors in love in a big-city hospital.

55 24 HOURS *Talk Show* Opera Winfield interviews the first woman in space, Valentina Tereshkova. She describes her work on Space Station Venus.

6:30

2 7 10 NEWS

6 A DAY IN MY LIFE *Comedy* Lance asks Betty to marry him. He gives her a week to decide.

19 MONEY TALK *Talk Show* David Montoya, President of City Bank, discusses the high cost of living. He describes ways to save money.

37 SPORTS WORLD *Tennis* Live from Wimbledon, England

39 THE FIRST CARTOONS *Documentary* Paul Dismay tells stories of early cartoons.

55 CHINESE CHEF *Cooking* The chef explains how to cook Szechwan chicken and fried bananas.

7:00

2 NINETY MINUTES *Documentary* Mike Walters reports on teen-age couch potatoes. He explains how to stop watching TV.

6 LIVING TODAY *Documentary* A Mexican teenager describes his first parachute jump.

7 The Return of King Kong *(1989) Movie* King Kong returns to New York. He climbs the World Trade Center this time.

10 THE RICH AND THE FAMOUS *Talk Show* Ken Cleveland interviews singer Gloria Esteban. He visits her one hundred-room mansion.

19 Z FILES *Science Fiction* A doctor thinks his new neighbors are aliens. He asks Mouldy and Smelly to find out.

31 FIX IT YOURSELF *Home Repair* Jack and Julie explain how to fix a broken window.

Write: What Is a Paragraph?

A paragraph is a group of sentences that develops one main idea. In a well-written paragraph, all the sentences are about this one main idea. The first sentence in a paragraph is generally indented from the left-hand margin.

 Here are two paragraphs. Read them and answer the questions below.

Paragraph A

My favorite TV program is 60 Minutes. It usually has three different stories about people or events in the news. Frequently, there is an interview with a musician, singer, or other famous person in politics, sports, business, or the arts. Sometimes the stories are about ordinary people who do something special or unusual. 60 Minutes has excellent reporters and a variety of interesting stories on many topics. I always learn something new from 60 Minutes, so I try to watch it every week.

Paragraph B

My favorite TV program is Cinema 13. Cinema 13 is on every Saturday night at 9:00 on channel 13. Every week, they show a different movie. I like old movies, especially movies from different countries. You can learn many things about different countries by watching movies. I really like Japanese and French movies. My favorite Japanese film is Rashomon, directed by Akira Kurosawa. Channel 13 is a public TV station, so I don't have to pay for it.

1. Which paragraph has one main idea ?   A B
2. In which paragraph are all the sentences about one idea?   A B
3. Which paragraph is indented?   A B
4. Which is an example of a well-written paragraph?   A B

Write About It

 Write a paragraph about your favorite TV program. In the first sentence, give the name of the program. Then discuss what type of program it is, when it is on, and other information about it.

  Check Your Writing You can improve your writing by having other people read and comment on it. This is called getting feedback. Work with a partner. Read and discuss your paragraphs. Revise your paragraphs if necessary. Use the checklist below to help you.

- Is there one main idea? What is it?
- Do all sentences in the paragraph develop the main idea?
- Is the paragraph indented?

Write: What Is a Paragraph?

Students read the presentation in class or for homework.

Presentation

❻ Students may read the paragraphs and answer the questions individually, in pairs, or as a class.

> **Answers**
> 1. ∧ 2. A 3. A 4. A

Write About It

Presentation

❼ Students complete the writing task in class or for homework. Students can use Paragraph A as a model for their paragraphs.

☑ **❽ Check Your Writing** Reading each other's paragraphs provides students with feedback to help them revise their writing if necessary. The editing checklist helps students focus attention on a few key points as they edit their writing.

 Workbook: Practice 12

Vocabulary Expansion: Two-word verbs See page T140.

Note that the last unit objective refers to the Vocabulary Expansion Activities.

> **Answers**
> 1. c 2. a 3. d 4. e 5. b 6. f

EVALUATION

See page TExi.

Unit 1 Achievement Test

Self-Check See **Check Your Knowledge** on page 8 of the Workbook.

Dictation Have students review the sentences in Exercise 1 on page 4. Then present the sentences as a dictation. (See instructions on page TExv.)

Communication Skills

1. Ask students to talk about their TV viewing habits. As they speak, pay attention to their use of the simple present tense and adverbs of frequency.

2. Ask students to discuss their opinions about TV. You might use one or more of the questions from the survey in Exercise 4 on page 7. As they speak, listen for their of use of language for stating opinions and for agreeing and disagreeing.

PEOPLE WATCHING

OBJECTIVES

- To describe people and what they are doing
- To use the present progressive tense to talk about actions happening now
- To use the present progressive tense to talk about plans in the future
- To identify stative verbs
- To make inferences
- To make appointments
- To count syllables
- To guess meaning from context
- To narrow a writing topic
- To use expressions with **have**

GETTING STARTED

Warm Up

Preview

- Ask students if they ever engage in people watching. If so, when and where do they do it? Why do they do it?

- Check understanding of **bald, band,** and **ring** by having students identify them in the picture. Ask them to make sentences: "He's a bald man." "He's holding a ring." Check understanding of **wig.** Ask, *Who do you think is wearing a wig?* Explain that some bald people wear wigs.

- Check understanding of **public.** Identify some public places such as the public library. Explain that public places and services are provided for everyone to use. They are often owned or run by the government. See if students can come up with the opposite word for **public** (private).

- Check understanding of **politician.**

- Ⓐ **Option:** Before students listen to the recording for Exercise 1, have them list key words that they think they might hear. After students listen, ask them which words helped them get the correct answers.

Ⓐ **Option: Vocabulary Notebooks** See page TEviii.

Presentation

🎧 ❶ Read the instructions for Exercise 1. Play the recording one or more times. Tell students they do not need to understand every word to do the activity.

Audioscript: The audioscript for Exercise 1 apperars on page T152.

Answers
1. C 2. D 3. A 4. B

Ⓐ **Option:** Have students listen to the recording again and answer these questions:

Conversation A: Are the members of the band professional musicians? (no) Who are they? (students from the university)

Conversation B: What is the man going to give the woman? (a ring)

Conversation C: Does the woman's boss have blond hair? (no) What is she wearing? (a wig)

Conversation D: How would you describe the man with the camera? (He is bald.)

❷ Have students read Exercise 2. Ask, *What are some well-known newspapers and magazines that feature articles about the private lives of famous people? What do you call these magazines/newspapers?* (tabloids) Lead a class discussion about tabloid newspapers/magazines. If there is time, compile a list on the board of the good and bad points of tabloids.

Ⓐ **Option:** As a follow-up activity, ask students to bring in photos of famous people from magazines or newspapers. Have them work in small groups. They should write dialogues, imagining what people watchers might say about the famous people in the photos. Have selected groups perform their dialogues for the class.

Ⓐ **Option:** Alternatively, if there is less time, bring in copies of fan magazines. Have students identify the famous people and say what they are doing.

GETTING STARTED

Warm Up

1 Two people watchers are at a sidewalk cafe. Who are they talking about? Listen to their conversations. Write the letter of the conversation in the corresponding box in the picture.

2 Newspapers and magazines often have articles about the private lives of movie stars, TV actors and actresses, musicians, politicians, and other famous people. Do you ever read any of them? Why or why not?

Figure It Out

Paparazzi are professional people watchers. They are photographers who take embarrassing pictures of events in the private lives of famous people. Paparazzi sell their photos to magazines and newspapers, sometimes for a lot of money.

Rock N. Roller, the famous singer and guitarist of the rock band The Broken Bones, is taking a vacation with his wife, Raquel Roller. They are staying at the Royal Hideaway Hotel so they can relax in private, away from the public eye.

Gino and Hank are paparazzi. They work for the magazine *The Rich and the Famous*. Gino and Hank want to take pictures of Rock and Raquel for their magazine.

A. **GINO:** Look, there they are!

HANK: Where?

GINO: Sitting over there by the pool. Give me the telephoto lens and some more film. Hurry! I don't want to miss anything.

HANK: What are they doing?

GINO: They're laughing and talking. They look like they're having a good time. [*click*] Wait. Rock's giving something to Raquel.

HANK: What is it?

GINO: I don't know. Wait. Raquel is opening it. Look! It's a ring. [*click*] Wow! It's huge! I'm sure it cost a fortune! [*click*] This is fantastic. Wait! Now they're getting up. I think they're going to the beach.

HANK: Let's follow them. Hurry!

Figure It Out

Preview

- Ask, *What is your favorite band?* Explain that the reading is about a famous singer in a rock band.

- Lead a discussion about fan magazines. Ask, *How do you think these magazines get photos of famous people? How do you think famous people feel about being featured in these magazines?*

- Have students read the definition of **paparazzi** at the top of the page. Ask, *Do you know any famous people who have had trouble with paparazzi?* Encourage students to name international celebrities as well as famous people in their own country.

Language Note: **Paparazzi** comes from Italian. The singular is **paparazzo.**

Have students read the introduction to the conversations. Check understanding of **embarrassing.** Give students an example of something embarrassing that happened to you. (*Possible answer:* I was walking up the stairs when I tripped and fell. Everyone saw me. It was embarrassing.) Ask students if they can remember any embarrassing moments.

Language Note: Something that happens to you is **embarrassing.** You feel **embarrassed** about it.

Check understanding of (conversation A) **miss, have a good time, follow;** (conversation B) **come off;** and (conversation C) **security guard** (pictures on page 13). Say, for example, *Raul was late to school this morning. He missed the first part of the lesson.* Ask students what they do to **have a good time** with their friends. You can use pantomime to **follow** a student around the classroom and then show your hat **coming off.**

Ⓧ **Option: Vocabulary Notebooks** See page TEviii.

Explain that **click** in the dialogue refers to the sound a camera makes when you're taking a picture.

Presentation

Read the conversations aloud or have students read them silently themselves. After they've read the conversations once, have them practice in pairs. Ask students to go back and find two idiomatic expressions that refer to money. [cost a fortune (conversation A), make millions (conversation C)]

Language Note: In informal English, a **nut** is someone who is crazy. In the expression **health nut**, the "nut" refers to someone who is "crazy" (very eager) about leading a healthy lifestyle.

❸ Have students work in pairs to answer the questions.

Answers

a. They are staying there so that they can relax in private, away from the public eye. **b.** They are taking pictures of Rock and Raquel for their magazine. **c.** They found out that he wears a wig. (They also found out that he gave Raquel a ring and that he's a good swimmer.) **d.–e.** *Answers will vary.*

 Option: Ask additional comprehension questions:

- Where are Rock and Raquel staying? (at the Royal Hideaway Hotel)

- How often does Rock exercise? (He exercises twice a day at home. He plays tennis every morning and swims every afternoon.)

- How do Hank and Gino feel when Rock's wig comes off? (They can't believe it. They are very excited.)

 Option: Have students close their books and retell the story in their own words. You may want to give them some key vocabulary to get them started.

Option: Send students out to a public place to people-watch. (This activity can be done as homework.) Ask them to take notes on their observations and report their findings to the class. The class can then vote on the student who observed the most interesting scenario.

Option: Ask, *Is people watching polite? Why do we watch people?* Lead a discussion on the positive and negative aspects of people watching.

Link *Workbook: Practice 1*

☑ ❹ **Vocabulary Check** Have students work alone and then check answers with a partner.

Answers

a. bald **b.** fortune **c.** holding **d.** relax **e.** band **f.** security guards **g.** get out of **h.** missed **i.** nut **j.** towel

---

Link *Workbook: Practice 2*

B. HANK: What's happening now?

GINO: Rock's still lying on the towel, but Raquel isn't reading anymore. Wait! Rock's getting up. He's going into the water.

HANK: Is he swimming?

GINO: Yes, and he looks like a good swimmer. [*click*]

HANK: They say he's a health nut. He exercises twice a day at home. Plus, he plays tennis every morning and swims every afternoon after the band practices.

HANK: Wait. He's standing up now. Hey, look at Rock's hair! What's happening?

HANK: It's coming off! It's a wig! Quick! Take a picture!

C. GINO: I can't believe it! What a story! [*click click click*] Wait until Rock's public finds out he's bald! The magazine will pay millions for this!

HANK: Look out! The hotel security guards see us! They're running this way.

GINO: Let's get out of here!

3 Answer the questions.

a. Why are Rock and Raquel staying at the hotel?

b. What are Hank and Gino doing?

c. What did Hank and Gino find out about Rock?

d. Would you like to be famous? Why or why not?

e. Do photographers and reporters have the right to follow famous people everywhere? Why or why not?

4 **Vocabulary Check** Complete the sentences with words or phrases from the box.

band	fortune
bald	relax
get out of	security guards
holding	towel
missed	voice
wig	nut

a. Look! Rock has no hair! He's _____.

b. Rock and Raquel earned millions of dollars last year. They made a _____.

c. Gino is _____ the telephoto lens in his left hand.

d. Rock was very tired after the band's tour. He wanted to _____ for a few days at the Royal Hideaway Hotel.

e. There are five musicians in Rock's _____.

f. The hotel has several _____ to keep guests safe.

g. The police are coming. Let's _____ here before they catch us.

h. Joe arrived late. He _____ the first part of the show.

i. Hank loves to take pictures. He's a photography _____.

j. Jim is over there lying on the _____.

Talk About It

An executive of the Royal Hideaway Hotel is talking to a security guard about what's happening in various parts of the hotel.

 With a partner, take turns being the executive and the guard. Look at the pictures. Ask and answer questions about the different places in the hotel.

Ask about present actions.

A: What's going on in the restaurant? Is anything happening there?

State present actions.

B: Well, people are eating. The waiters are serving people. Everything's fine.

GRAMMAR

The Present Progressive Tense: Present Time

To talk about habitual actions in the present, we use the simple present tense. To talk about actions that change or are happening at the present time, we use the present progressive tense.

Simple Present	Present Progressive
Rock **practices** every day.	The band **is practicing** now.

We use *still* with the present progressive to describe an action that continues in the present without changing. We use *anymore* to describe an action that stopped.

> The paparazzi **are still waiting** to get a good shot of Rock.
>
> Rock **isn't lying** on the beach **anymore**. He's swimming.

1 You meet an old friend and you want to know what's new in his or her life. With a partner, ask and answer questions using the topics and the verbs in parentheses.

Example: Apartment (live)

A: So, are you still living in the same old apartment?

B: Yeah, I'm still living on Third Avenue.

A: And is your brother still living with you?

B: No, actually he's not living with me anymore. He moved out.

Unit 2

14

Talk About It

⊛ Option: If students need extra practice with the present progressive tense, postpone this activity until after you've completed the grammar exercises for this unit or Workbook Practice 4.

Preview

- Lead a discussion on vacations and hotels. Ask, *Do you stay with relatives or in hotels when you go on vacation?* Have students comment on one they've stayed in.

- Look at the illustration. Check understanding of **gym, restaurant, snack bar, shops, lobby,** and **kitchen.** Ask students if they know the meaning of the word **executive** (a high-ranking employee in a company, often the president).

⊛ Option: Vocabulary Notebooks See page TEviii.

Presentation

Note: The purpose of this activity is to develop fluency. The students should be free to speak without fear of interruption for error correction. If you note persistent errors, write them down for later reteaching or review.

❺ Have students read the instructions, and ask volunteers to model the dialogue. Then have students work in pairs asking and answering questions about each part of the hotel. Circulate and offer assistance. Make notes of student errors, but don't interrupt to correct them; you want to encourage fluency. Have volunteers perform their dialogues for the class. Refer to your notes and write errors on the board without identifying who made them. Then correct the errors as a class.

⊛ Option: Give students additional locations in the hotel to discuss: the parking lot, the conference room, etc. Bring in hotel brochures for students to refer to in their conversations.

⊛ Option: For homework, have students choose two locations and write out their dialogues.

⊛ Option: Have students bring in photographs that show people doing something: hiking, swimming, talking on the telephone, etc. Ask them to describe what's happening using the present progressive tense.

⊛ Option: For a major project, have students take photographs of their classmates and write articles about them. Help students assemble the articles into a magazine and make a copy for each student.

GRAMMAR

The Present Progressive Tense: Present Time

Preview

- Review the simple present tense from Unit 1 by asking students to tell you when it is used. Then contrast it with the use of the present progressive tense. Ask students to say additional sentences in the simple present and the present progressive.

- Explain that **still** can be used with the present progressive to imply surprise that the action is not finished. It often is placed before the verb: "I can't believe it! It's **still** raining!" On the other hand, **anymore** is usually placed at the end of the sentence. In American English, when it refers to time, it is written as one word. The use of **anymore** with the present progressive indicates that an action that continued for a time has now stopped: "Gino isn't taking pictures anymore. He's talking to Hank." Give additional examples using **still** and **anymore.**

Presentation

Students read the grammar explanation and the examples in the box. You may assign this activity for homework or have students read it in class.

❶ Students discuss various topics using the present progressive tense. (*Answers will vary.*)

 Workbook: Practices 3, 4, 5, 7

The Present Progressive Tense: Future Time

Preview

Emphasize that the present progressive tense is also used to talk about arrangements or plans in the future, especially when they are fixed.

Presentation

❷ Students complete sentences with the correct form (simple present or present progressive) of the verbs in parentheses.

> **Answers**
> **1.** is playing **2.** are staying **3.** are performing **4.** practices **5.** plays **6.** is lying **7.** is recording **8.** is leaving

☑ ❸ **Check Your Understanding** In this exercise, students must explain their answers in Exercise 2 by writing H (for **h**abit or routine), N (for action happening **n**ow), or F (for **f**uture action).

> **Answers**
> **1.** F **2.** N **3.** F **4.** H **5.** H **6.** N **7.** F **8.** F

 Workbook: Practices 6, 8

❹ Have students read through the conversation silently and aloud. Then put them in pairs and ask them to take turns playing the caller and the hotel operator. The operator should think of believable reasons why the hotel employee cannot come to the telephone. Other hotel employees to whom students can refer: **bellhop, concierge, business center receptionist.**

✦ **Option:** Have students make a schedule (fictitious or real) for the future and then tell a partner what they plan to do: "Next Thursday, I'm going on a trip." "Tomorrow I'm visiting my grandmother."

✦ **Option:** Have students research what's happening where you live and tell you about it, using the present progressive: "A new action movie is showing at the movie theater downtown." Students can discuss sports events, plays, concerts, movies, etc.

a. Job or school (work/study/teach)

b. Vacation plans (take/go)

c. Problems (have trouble/worry)

d. Free-time activities (read/paint/play)

e. Ideas of your own

The Present Progressive Tense: Future Time

We can use the present progressive to talk about planned actions in the future. We often use future time words like *next, tomorrow, later, on Monday*.

> The Royal Hideaway Hotel **is having** a party **tonight**.
>
> Raquel and I **aren't leaving** until **next week** some time.

2 Write the correct form of the simple present or present progressive tense on the line.

Reason

_____ **1.** The Broken Bones Band **(play)** _____ in Brazil later this week.

_____ **2.** They **(stay)** _____ at the Royal Paulista Hotel.

_____ **3.** Next week they **(perform)** _____ in Salvador de Bahia.

_____ **4.** Rock **(practice)** _____ alone for an hour every day.

_____ **5.** The band only **(play)** _____ rock music.

_____ **6.** Sticks, the drummer, **(lie)** _____ on the beach now.

_____ **7.** The band **(record)** _____ a new album next month.

_____ **8.** The band **(leave)** _____ for Salvador de Bahia after the concert on Monday.

 3 **Check Your Understanding** Now give your reason for using the simple present or the present progressive in Exercise 2. Write **H** (habit or routine), **N** (action happening now), or **F** (future action). Then compare your answers with a partner's.

4 People are calling the hotel to speak to some of the hotel employees. With a partner, take turns being the operator and the caller.

Example:

OPERATOR: Hello, Starlight Hotel.

CALLER: Hi, I'd like to speak to Ms. Aziz, the hotel manager, please.

OPERATOR: I'm sorry. She can't come to the phone right now. She's talking to the chef. Would you like to leave a message?

CALLER: No, thanks. I'll call back later.

a. Billie Jean, the tennis instructor

b. Julia, a waitress in the restaurant

c. Paolo from the flower shop

d. Sherlock from security

e. Tomoko from the front desk

f. Marta from housekeeping

g. Angelo from the kitchen

h. Idea of your own

Stative Verbs

Generally, we do not use the present progressive with stative or non-action verbs—verbs that refer to states rather than actions. To express a continuing action with stative verbs, we usually use the simple present tense.

Common Stative Verbs	Examples
Verbs that describe mental processes: *know, remember, think, believe*	Rock **remembers** the words to all the songs.
Verbs that express feelings: *want, like, love, hate, prefer, need*	Raquel **doesn't like** the paparazzi.
Verbs that describe appearance: *be, seem, look like, appear*	Rock and Raquel **seem** happy.
Verbs that show possession: *have, own, belong*	Rock **has** seven cars.
Verbs of perception: *see, hear, taste, smell, feel, notice*	Rock and Raquel **feel** relaxed.

5 Complete the conversation with the simple present or present progressive tense. Some answers may be negative.

A: What **(1. read)** _____ you _____?

B: An article about Liz Tyler's latest marriage. It says that Liz really **(2. love)** _____ her new husband, Rudolph Valenti. They **(3. seem)** _____ so happy. Right now, in fact, they **(4. travel)** _____ around the world.

A: Everyone says her new husband **(5. be)** _____ super rich.

B: That's right. He **(6. own)** _____ homes in Paris, Rio, Zurich, and Madrid, and he **(7. build)** _____ a new house in Miami.

A: **(8. think)** _____ you _____ they will stay married?

B: I **(9. know)** _____. He's her eighth husband!

6 **Check Your Understanding** In which situations are you likely to use the present progressive tense?

- [ ] Talking about your vacation plans
- [ ] Describing a normal day at the office
- [ ] Giving your opinion about television
- [ ] Reporting the activities at a football game
- [ ] Talking about new changes in your life

Compare your answers with a partner's. Do you agree?

7 **Express Yourself** With your partner, choose one of the situations you checked above. Imagine yourselves in the situation and write a dialogue.

Stative Verbs

Preview

Explain to students that some verbs do not use the present progressive tense because they refer to states (mental processes, feelings, appearances, etc.) rather than actions. See if the students can name any of these verbs before opening their books to the grammar page.

Presentation

❺ Students complete the conversation using either the simple present or the present progressive of the verb in parentheses. Have pairs of students read parts of the conversation aloud so that the class can check their answers.

> **Answers**
> 1. are (you) reading 2. loves 3. seem
> 4. are traveling 5. is 6. owns 7. is building
> 8. Do (you) think 9. don't know

Option: Give students more stative verbs, such as **agree, imagine, owe, promise, realize, cost, become, suppose,** and **wish.** Tell them to add to the list as they learn more verbs that fit into this category.

Option: Toss a ball to a student and call out a stative verb. The student who catches the ball has to immediately make a sentence using the verb and then pass the ball on to another student as he/she calls out another stative verb. Students are out of the game when they (1) can't come up with a sentence quickly enough; (2) can't think of another stative verb when they pass the ball along; or (3) make a grammatically incorrect sentence. Don't be too choosy about accuracy, but students should be penalized if they make sentences with stative verbs in the present progressive.

Option: To help students remember stative verbs, play a memory game. First, a student says a stative verb. The next student repeats the first student's verb and then adds his/her own. A third student has to repeat the first two verbs in order before adding another stative verb. To make the game more interesting, students can also say their name before each verb: "Marta, know," "Jose, seem," etc. Students who can't remember what was said before them are out of the game.

☑ ❻ Check Your Understanding In this exercise, students decide when they would use the present progressive tense.

> **Answers**
> Talking about your vacation plans,
> Reporting the activities at a football game,
> Talking about new changes in your life

❼ Express Yourself In this activity, pairs of students choose one of the appropriate situations in Exercise 6 and write dialogues using the present progressive. After they've practiced, ask selected students to perform their dialogues for the class.

Option: Explain that some stative verbs may be used in the present progressive, but their meaning changes. Have students discuss these sentences and explain the difference:

- What do you *think* of this class?
- What are you *thinking* about?

- I *see* a mountain in the distance.
- I am *seeing* my friend tomorrow.

- I *have* a new car.
- I'm *having* a good time.

- Peanuts *taste* salty.
- I'm *tasting* the peanuts.

LISTENING and SPEAKING

Listen: Where Are They?

Presentation

❶ Before You Listen As a class or in pairs, students answer the prelistening questions.

➡ **Making Inferences** Go over the listening strategy.

🎧 **❷** Check understanding of the vocabulary. Students should then listen to the recording and circle the location of each speaker. Remind students that they don't have to understand every word of the selection to do the activity. Stress that students will have to infer from what they hear exactly where the people are located. Pause after each conversation to give students time to make their choices.

Audioscript: The audioscript for Exercises 2 and 3 appears on page T153.

> **Answers**
> **a.** on the tennis court **b.** in the TV room
> **c.** in the restaurant **d.** at the beach
> **e.** in the hotel security room

🎧 **❸** Play the recording again and have students write down the key words that helped them figure out their answers.

☯ **Option:** Have students listen again and answer these comprehension questions:

Conversation A: How is Bob playing today? (Not well. He's missing a lot of balls.) Why? (He's tired.)

Conversation B: Is Bill enjoying the show? (No, he's not.) What does he want to watch? (the detective show)

Conversation C: What is Liz Tyler eating and drinking? (She's eating a hot dog and drinking pineapple juice.) What is Mary going to do? Why? (She's going to order the same thing because it looks great.)

Conversation D: What's the weather like? (It's really hot.) What are they going to do? (go swimming)

Conversation E: What's happening at the pool? (Rock N. Roller is trying to swim, but hundreds of people are watching and screaming at him.)

Speak Out

➡ **Making Appointments** Circulate around the class and make appointments with different students. Say, *I need to talk to you about something. Are you busy after class?* or *I'd like to talk to you about your homework assignment. Can we meet tomorrow afternoon?* Try to schedule an appointment when you know a student has another class or is otherwise engaged. Don't correct students at this point. Next, go over the patterns in the box and have students practice them.

Presentation

❹ Have pairs of students take turns role-playing the detective and the TV executive. Then have them switch roles. After a while, have students switch partners and work with someone new. Circulate and offer assistance. Make notes of student errors, but don't interrupt to correct them; you want to encourage fluency. Later, refer to your notes and write errors on the board without identifying who made them. Then correct the errors as a class.

☯ **Option:** Hand out a schedule from a daily planner (with blanks for each hour from 9 a.m. to 6 p.m.) and have students fill in their schedules for tomorrow. Tell them to complete their schedules but to leave three blanks open. Then have students circulate around the class and make appointments with fellow classmates. Students are finished when their three blanks are filled in.

Listen: Where Are They?

1 **Before You Listen**

    a. What are some different places in a hotel?

    b. What do people usually do in each place? Make a list.

 Making Inferences Sometimes you can guess certain information that is not directly stated because of the other words you hear. Listen for words that help you make inferences or guesses about the situation.

2 Listen to the conversations. Where are the people? Circle the place.

a. in the clothing boutique	in the hotel lobby	on the tennis court
b. in the bookstore	in the TV room	in the hotel lobby
c. at the swimming pool	in the restaurant	in the gym
d. in the snack bar	on the tennis court	at the beach
e. in the hotel security room	in the restaurant	at the pool

3 Which words helped you figure out where the conversations were taking place? Listen to the conversations again and write the words on a sheet of paper. Compare your answers with a partner's.

Speak Out

 Making Appointments When you want to meet with another person, you use certain expressions to suggest and arrange a meeting time.

Suggesting a meeting time	Can we meet at (nine o'clock)? Are you busy at (ten o'clock)?
Accepting a suggestion	That sounds good. I'll meet you in the lobby.
Suggesting another time	Sorry. I'm busy at (nine). How about (ten)? I'm busy at (ten). Are you free at (eleven)?

4 A TV executive hired a private detective to get information about another TV channel. Work with a partner. One of you is the detective and the other is the TV executive. Use the expressions above and the information in the appointment books to find a time for the meeting.

Pronunciation

> **Syllables**
>
> Every word has one or more beats, or syllables. For example, **needs** (needs) has one syllable, **begin** (be•gin) has two syllables, and **remembers** (re•mem•bers) has three.

5 Say the words to yourself. Predict the number of syllables for each. Then listen to the words. Write the number of syllables you hear.

a.	believe _____	**g.**	fantastic _____
b.	guitarist _____	**h.**	beaches _____
c.	camera _____	**i.**	embarrassing _____
d.	relaxes _____	**j.**	guards _____
e.	photographer _____	**k.**	actress _____
f.	exercises _____	**l.**	actresses _____

6 With your partner, take turns saying the words. Be careful to say the correct number of syllables.

READING and WRITING

Read About It

1 **Before You Read** The following article is about privacy. What do people watching and privacy have to do with each other?

The Right to Privacy

Many people enjoy learning about the rich and the famous. They spend millions of dollars yearly on newspapers and magazines that tell
5 about the private lives of rich and famous people. However, the people who enjoy reading about the private lives of others do not always like it when people watch them!

10 In the past, performers, politicians, and other people in the public eye were the only ones who worried about the right to a private life. Now, however, even ordinary people are complaining about losing their privacy. They say that they have the right to be left
15 alone and that now, because of technology, it is getting too easy to violate this right.

Today, new technology makes it possible to investigate the most private parts of people's lives. For example, some employers watch everything their employees do. They listen to personal phone calls, and they check how long their workers are at their computers. Some employers even check their employees' e-mail.

Pronunciation

Preview

Explain that every word has at least one syllable. To determine how many syllables a word has, lightly tap a table (or your knee) once for each syllable as you say the word aloud slowly. Practice saying the following words from the box with the students as you tap out the syllables: **needs, begin, remembers.**

Presentation

Students read the explanation in the box in class or as homework.

5 Play the recording or read the audioscript aloud two or more times and have students write the number of syllables. Pause between words to allow students time to write.

> **Answers**
> a. 2 b. 3 c. 3 d. 3 e. 4 f. 4 g. 3 h. 2 i. 4 j. 1 k. 2 l. 3
>
> **Note: Camera** can also be pronounced as two syllables /kam-rə/.

6 Have students work with a partner and go over their answers. They should say each word aloud, being careful to say the correct number of syllables. Then go over the answers as a class.

 Workbook: Practices 9, 10

Option: Have students review the vocabulary they've learned in Units 1 and 2 and determine how many syllables each word has. Encourage students to write down the number of syllables when they enter new words in their vocabulary notebooks.

READING and WRITING

Read About It

Presentation

1 **Before You Read** Have students work in pairs to do the prereading exercise. In addition to discussing the question in their books (*What do people watching and privacy have to do with each other?*), ask students to look at the title of the article. What do they think the article is going to be about? Have selected pairs share their answers with the class.

➡ **Guessing Meaning from Context**

Students read the strategy. Write the word **anonymous** on the board and ask students what it means. Then write, *Famous people don't like to be watched all the time. Sometimes they would prefer to be* **anonymous.** Ask students for the definition again (unknown, unidentified). Explain that this procedure is an example of guessing the meaning of a word from context.

❷ Students should work alone and then compare answers with a partner. Have selected students read aloud each item and their answer.

> **Answers**
> **a.** normal, usual **b.** a kind of detective
> **c.** something that others don't know
> **d.** writing you keep **e.** equality between
> two things

❸ Students should stay with their partner and work together to match the words with their definitions.

> **Answers**
> 1. c 2. e 3. a 4. d 5. b

�় **Option:** After Exercise 4 on page 20, you may wish to ask additional comprehension questions about the article:

- Who used to worry about the right to a private life? (performers, politicians, other well-known people) Who worries now? (even ordinary people)

- How can employers watch their employees? (They can listen to personal phone calls, check how long workers are at their computers, check workers' e-mail.)

- What can investigators do? (They can put secret microphones in houses or cars and then listen from far away. They can use tiny radios to follow drivers. They can use video cameras at home.)

- What kind of personal information is kept on computers? (records on military service, health, school grades, work performance) What are people saying about these records? (They are asking why organizations need all this information.)

- What kind of balance needs to be respected? (the balance between the public's right to know and the individual's right to privacy)

20   Many employees know that their companies watch them at work, but they do not realize that they might be watched at home. Investigators can put secret microphones in houses or cars when no one is looking and then listen from far away. They can use tiny radios to follow drivers in their cars. And they can use video cameras to record people's actions at home—even at night when the lights are off.

25   Computers now have records on military service, health, school grades, and work performance. People are beginning to ask why these organizations need all this information. They are also concerned because investigators can get this information without telling them. It is not surprising, then, that more and more people are worried about invasion of privacy. As a result, they are asking organizations to respect the

30   balance between the public's right to know and the individual's right to privacy.

STRATEGY **Guessing Meaning from Context** When you don't understand a word, you can often use other information in the text—the context—to figure out the meaning. Look at surrounding sentences and words to guess the meaning from context.

2 Below are five words from the reading. Use the context to figure out the meaning of each word. Choose the correct definition from the box.

> writing you keep
> equality between two things
> normal, usual
> a kind of detective
> something that others don't know
> strange, not normal

   a. **ordinary** (line 13) The sentence before this one was about famous people. This sentence refers to other people who are worried about privacy, so ordinary means _____.

   b. **investigators** (line 21) Investigators get information about people, so investigator means _____.

   c. **secret** (line 21) This sentence refers to microphones that investigators put in people's homes or cars when no one is looking, so secret means _____.

   d. **records** (line 25) This sentence is about information on health, school grades, and work performance. People keep records on computers, so records means _____.

   e. **balance** (line 30) This sentence refers to two things that have the same importance, the public's right to know and the individual's right to privacy, so balance means _____.

3 Find each of the following words in the reading. Using the context, guess the meaning of each. Write the letter on the line.

   _____ **1.** to complain (line 14)   **a.** worker
   _____ **2.** to violate (line 15)   **b.** to pay attention to
   _____ **3.** employee (line 17)   **c.** to say something is wrong
   _____ **4.** concerned (line 27)   **d.** worried about
   _____ **5.** to respect (line 29)   **e.** to break

Think About It

 Do famous people have the right to complain about an invasion of their privacy? Why or why not?

 Is it a good idea to control employees at the workplace? (For example, phone calls, e-mail, drug and alcohol tests.) Why or why not?

Write: Narrowing a Topic

When you start with a general topic, you need to narrow it down so that you can discuss it in one paragraph. Look at the example:

General Topic:		Vacations	
Narrowed Topics:	A special vacation I took	The location for my next vacation	A fun but inexpensive vacation

 Here are some general writing topics. Narrow each one so that it is more suitable for one paragraph. Use your own paper.

Example:

privacy

- *the privacy teenagers need*
- *ways to protect your privacy*

a. television

b. hotels

c. music

d. sports

Write About It

 Write a paragraph about one of your narrowed topics from the previous exercise. Remember that all the sentences in the paragraph should be about your main idea.

 Check Your Writing Read your paragraph again. Does it say what you want it to say? Use the questions in the checklist to help you. Then revise your paragraph as needed.

- Is the topic narrow enough for one paragraph?
- Is there one main idea? What is it?
- Are the verb tenses correct?

Think About It

Presentation

4 After reading the article on page 18, ask, *Do famous people have the right to complain about an invasion of their privacy?* Have students make a list of reasons supporting both sides.

5 Have students work in pairs or small groups or as a class to think of reasons to support both sides.

Option: Ask additional discussion questions:

- What kind of privacy do children need? teenagers? adults?

- Is it a good idea to keep records on computers? Why or why not?

- Some countries **take a census** every few years: the government counts the population and interviews a lot of people who are asked personal questions about where they live, who they live with, where they work, etc. Do you think this is an invasion of privacy? Why or why not?

Option: Students can have a class debate in teams, using one or both of the questions in Exercises 4 and 5. Encourage them to come up with evidence and examples to support each of their points.

Write: Narrowing a Topic

Students read the presentation in class or for homework.

Presentation

6 Students should work alone to narrow each of the general writing topics. Then they can compare ideas with a partner. Remind students that their topic should be narrow enough for one paragraph.

 Workbook: Practice 11

Write About It

Presentation

7 Students complete the writing task in class or for homework.

☑ 8 Check Your Writing Have students refer to the checklist to revise their paragraph before they turn it in.

Option: Students work in pairs and give each other peer feedback. Have students answer these questions about their partner's writing:

- What is one thing that you learned after reading your partner's paragraph that you didn't know before?

- What is something you read that you would like to hear more about?

Option: For an end-of-unit vocabulary expansion exercise, bring in a camera and introduce new vocabulary as you demonstrate how to use it: **load the film, focus the lens, press the button, take the picture, develop the film.** Have selected students practice using the vocabulary and demonstrate how to use the camera.

Vocabulary Expansion: Expressions with *have*
See page T141.

Answers
Part A: **1.** f **2.** d **3.** e **4.** a **5.** g **6.** c
7. h **8.** b Part B: A. 6 B. 5 C. 3 D. 1
E. 2 F. 7 G. 4 H. 8

EVALUATION

See page TExi.

Unit 2 Achievement Test

Self-Check See **Check Your Knowledge** on page 16 of the Workbook.

Dictation Have students review the sentences in Exercise 4 on page 13. Then present them as a dictation. (See instructions on page TExv.)

Communication Skills

1. Show pictures of people doing various activities and ask students to describe what they're doing. As students speak, pay attention to their use of the present progressive tense to describe present time.

2. Ask students to describe their schedule for the next week. As they speak, pay attention to their use of the present progressive tense to describe future time.

KEEPING UP WITH THE JONESES

OBJECTIVES

- To use the comparative form of the adjective to compare people, places, and things
- To use **(not) as … as** to talk about similarities and differences
- To listen for criteria
- To identify stressed syllables
- To agree and disagree
- To identify main ideas
- To write a topic sentence
- To use nouns, adjectives, and their opposites

GETTING STARTED

Warm Up

Preview

- Lead a discussion about competition. Why do students think that people try to compete with each other? What are the good and bad effects of competition?

- Have students read the introduction to the listening. Check understanding of **compare, possessions, jealous, neighbors, long, wide, deep.** Show students some of your possessions (watch, pen, etc.) and ask them what possessions they have. Point out the two houses and the people. Say, *They are neighbors.* Ask students if they ever feel jealous of anyone who has more possessions than they do.

- Show students pictures of two houses (interiors or exteriors). Try to elicit comparative expressions such as **older, more expensive,** etc.

- Teach the noun forms of **long (length), wide (width),** and **deep (depth).** Have students practice pronouncing them. Demonstrate measuring a box: *This box is 10 inches deep,* etc.

Language Notes: Jones is a common family name in English. In the expression **keep up**

with the Joneses, "Joneses" refers to other people or people in general. Ask students for common family names in their language(s). **Home** refers to any place that is the center of one's family life; **house** refers only to a building.

🌐 **Option: Vocabulary Notebooks** See page TEviii.

Presentation

🎧 ❶ Make sure that everyone understands the exercise and the expression **keep up with the Joneses.** Play the recording. Tell students that they do not have to understand every word to do the activity.

Audioscript: The audioscript for Exercises 1 and 2 appears on page T153.

Answers
a. yes **b.** yes **c.** no

🌐 **Option:** Before students listen, have them list key words that they think they might hear. After students listen, ask them which words helped them figure out the correct answers.

🌐 **Option:** Have students listen again and answer these questions:

Conversation A: What do the people speaking think of their own car? (It's getting old and it's very small.)

Conversation B: Why is the pool owner happy with the new swimming pool? (It's longer, wider, and deeper than the neighbor's pool.)

Conversation C: What does Maria tell Paula? (Maria tells Paula that she can watch her favorite programs at Maria's house.)

❷ Ask students to make a list of the possessions being discussed. Play the recording again as necessary. Put students in pairs to compare answers.

 Workbook: Practice 1

Figure It Out

See page T22.

KEEPING UP WITH THE JONESES

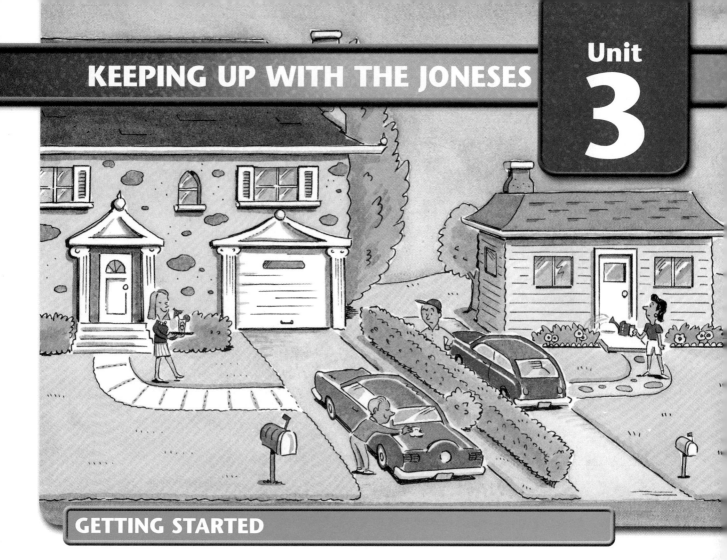

GETTING STARTED

Warm Up

People often compare their cars, their homes, and their other possessions to what other people have. Sometimes they feel jealous. They want their things to be as good as or better than everyone else's. We say that they want to "keep up with the Joneses."

1. Listen to each conversation. Are the people trying to "keep up with the Joneses"? Circle the answer.

   a. yes/no   **b.** yes/no   **c.** yes/no

2. What possessions are the people comparing in the conversations? What else do people compare?

Figure It Out

A.   **VAL:**   Hey, look Roxy. There's a moving truck next door. I hope the new neighbors are friendly.

   ROXY: Well, I'm sure they'll be friendlier than the old ones!

   VAL: Roxy, be nice. Our old neighbors weren't as bad as you thought.

B.

VAL: I wonder if the new neighbors have any children.

ROXY: There's room for a lot of children in that house. It's much bigger than yours or mine. And the yard is huge.

VAL: Oh, Roxy, why do you always think other people's possessions are better than yours? Your yard is smaller, but a little yard is easier to take care of.

ROXY: You're right, and I still think my garden is more beautiful than theirs.

VAL: Yeah, well, it's still not as pretty as mine.

ROXY: That's only because your gardener is better than mine.

C.

ROXY: Wow! Look at the size of that TV! It's enormous! And look! They have another TV. It's even bigger than the first one!

VAL: Oh, look. Here come the new neighbors. And they have two children. The older daughter looks about the same age as your son. Isn't she pretty? Gee, she's a lot prettier than the other girls in the neighborhood.

ROXY: She's gorgeous! She's a lot richer than the other girls in the neighborhood, too! Val, don't you think she and my son will make a perfect couple?

VAL: Sure, Roxy, now I understand. If you can't keep up with the Joneses, you'll have your son marry one of them!

ROXY: That's right! If you can't beat them, marry them!

3 Answer the questions.

   a. Whose house is larger, Roxy's or the new neighbors'?

   b. Whose garden is prettier, Val's or Roxy's?

   c. What does Roxy want her son to do? Why?

   d. Why do people want to "keep up with the Joneses"?

   e. Do you know anyone who tries to "keep up with the Joneses"?

   f. Moving to a new house or neighborhood has advantages and disadvantages. What are they?

Figure It Out

Preview

Ask students to talk about their neighbors. Do they know them? What kind of people are they? Do they compete with them? How?

Presentation

Read the dialogues aloud or have students read them silently. Then have them practice in pairs.

Check understanding of (dialogue A) **truck;** (dialogue B) **yard, huge, garden, gardener;** (dialogue C) **size, gorgeous, couple.** Show a picture of a **truck,** a **yard,** and a **garden.** Explain that a **gardener** works in a garden. Refer to the illustration on page 21 to show a **couple.** Explain that **gorgeous** means very attractive or beautiful. (It is used to refer to people or things and is somewhat dramatic.) Compare two objects of different sizes. Point to pictures of two dogs or trucks and say, *One is large and one is small. They're different sizes.* Explain that people often compare things by price and size. **Price** refers to the cost of something. **Size** tells if an object is big or little. Explain that something that is very big is **huge** or **enormous** (dialogue C).

Language Note: Yard refers to the land surrounding a house. The land is part of the owner's property and usually the owner takes care of it. People often refer to the front, back, and/or side yards. Usually, a yard has a lawn, which is an area covered with grass. Many people put gardens in their yards. A garden is a specific area in which people plant flowers or vegetables.

❸ Place students in pairs to answer the questions.

> **Answers**
> **a.** the new neighbors' **b.** Val's **c.** Roxy wants her son to date the new neighbors' daughter because she's prettier and richer than the other girls in the neighborhood. **d.–f.** *Answers will vary.*

🜨 **Option:** Ask additional comprehension questions:

- Did Roxy like her old neighbors? (No.)
- Why does Val think a small yard is better? (It's easier to take care of.)
- How old is the new neighbors' daughter? (She's the same age as Roxy's son.)
- What is Roxy's idea about keeping up with the Joneses? (If you can't beat them, marry them.)

🜨 **Option:** Ask additional discussion questions:

- Do you think Roxy and Val should encourage Roxy's son to go out with the neighbors' daughter?
- What kind of people do you think worry most about keeping up with the Joneses: younger people, older people, richer people, etc?
- How do you feel about Roxy and Val: too materialistic, too competitive, etc.?

Cultural Note: Ask, *How do people in your culture welcome new neighbors?* (*Example:* Bring them gifts, meals, etc.)

🜨 **Option:** You may want to review possessive adjectives (**my, your, his, her, its, our,** and **their**) as well as emphatic possessive pronouns (**mine, ours, his, hers, ours,** and **theirs**).

☑ ❹ **Vocabulary Check** Have students work alone on the exercise and then check answers with a partner.

> **Answers**
> **a.** neighborhood **b.** yard **c.** wonder **d.** gorgeous **e.** size **f.** huge **g.** possessions

🌀 **Option:** Before you do Vocabulary Check, you many wish to review possessive nouns. Write examples on the board and elicit rules from students.

1. cousin → cousin's
2. cousins → cousins'
3. children → children's
4. James → James's

Review rules.

1. Add 's to form the possessive of singular nouns.
2. Add only an apostrophe to form the possessive of plural nouns.
3. Add 's to form the possessive of plural nouns that do not end in s.
4. Add 's to form the possessive of names that end in s.

🌀 **Option: Vocabulary Notebooks** See page TEviii.

Talk About It

🌀 **Option:** If students need extra practice with the comparative, postpone this activity until after you've completed the grammar exercises for this unit or Workbook Practice 3.

Preview

- Lead a discussion about houses. Ask, *Where do you live now, in a house or an apartment? What kind of houses do you like? If you could buy your dream house, what would it look like? How much would it cost?*

- Review the names of the different rooms in a house: **bedroom, living room, dining room, bathroom, kitchen**, etc. Check understanding of words such as **attic** and **basement**.

Presentation

❺ Have students read the instructions, and ask selected students to model the dialogue for the class. Then have students work in pairs asking and answering questions about the houses on Lake Street and Pine Street. Circulate and offer assistance, encouraging students to use the adjectives in the chart. Make notes of student errors, but don't interrupt to correct them; you want to encourage fluency. Have selected pairs perform their dialogues for the class. Refer to your notes and write errors on the board without identifying who made them. Then correct the errors as a class.

🌀 **Option:** To make the activity more challenging, introduce additional words that students can use in their discussion of the two houses: **den, family room, garage, pantry, porch, study,** etc.

 Workbook: Practice 2

④ Vocabulary Check Complete the sentences with words from the box.

couple	neighborhood
deep	wonder
gorgeous	possessions
huge	price
jealous	size
yard	

   a. I don't like living in this part of the city. I want to move to another _____.

   b. The Joneses have a pool and a garden in their _____.

   c. Val and Roxy _____ if the new neighbors have children.

   d. Mrs Jones's daughter is really _____. I think she's the most beautiful girl in school.

   e. Look at the _____ of that TV! It's enormous.

   f. The Joneses' TV is larger than ours. It's _____.

   g. Some people with many _____ are unhappy, but others with just a few are happy anyway.

Talk About It

⑤ A real estate agent is trying to sell a house to a buyer. With a partner, take turns being the agent and the buyer. Use the information in the chart below to ask and answer questions.

Pine Street

A: I have two great houses for sale.
    Ask for a comparison.

B: Tell me about the size of the houses. Which one is larger, Lake Street or Pine Street?
    Make a comparison.

A: Lake Street is larger than Pine. It has four bedrooms.
    Ask for a comparison.

B: Which house is newer?
    Make a comparison. Ask about preference.

A: Pine Street is newer. It's only ten years old. Which do you like better?
    State preference.

B: I like Lake Street better because I prefer older houses.

Lake Street

	Lake Street	**Pine Street**	**Useful Adjectives**
size	4 bedrooms, 2 baths	3 bedrooms, 1 1/2 baths	big, little, large, small
age	15 years old	10 years old	new, old
price	$275,000	$300,000	expensive, inexpensive
style	traditional	modern	modern, traditional
location	near the center	far from the center	near, far

GRAMMAR

The Comparative: Talking About Differences

To talk about differences between two people, places, or things, we use the comparative form of the adjective.

One-syllable adjectives usually: add **–er**	Janet's pool is **longer than** Val's.
Two-syllable adjectives ending in **–y**: change **y** to **i** and add **–er**	Janet's garden is **prettier than** Val's.
Adjectives with two or more syllables: use **more** or **less** … **than**	Janet's house is **more modern than** Val's. Janet's couch is **less expensive than** Val's.
Exceptions: good → better than bad → worse than far → farther than	Janet's garden is **better than** Val's.

 1 Look at the pictures of Nola and Atina and compare them.

Example:

A: What do you think about Nola's skirt?

B: It's shorter than Atina's and more fashionable.

a. height (tall/short)

b. appearance (pretty/attractive)

c. weight (heavy/light)

d. personality (interesting/boring/funny)

e. age (old/young)

f. clothes (expensive/cheap/fashionable)

g. hair (long/short/curly/straight)

Atina   **Nola**

 2 Compare the following items. Use an adjective that fits the category.

Example:

(size) Luxemburg/Lithuania

Luxemburg is a smaller country than Lithuania.

a.	(size)	Mexico City/Cairo
b.	(price)	apartment in New York/apartment in Tokyo
c.	(age)	Buenos Aires/Madrid
d.	(appearance)	modern furniture/antique furniture
e.	(distance)	Mars/Jupiter
f.	(height)	Mt. Fuji/Mt. Everest
g.	(quality)	German cars/American cars
h.	(length)	The Amazon River/The Nile River

GRAMMAR

The Comparative: Talking About Differences

Preview

Before looking at the grammar presentation box, see whether students can tell you the rule for forming the comparative. After they've offered an explanation, go over the information in the box.

Option: Write **thin** on the board. Ask students if they know how to form the comparative adjective. After they've offered explanations, introduce the rule for one-syllable adjectives ending in one (a single) consonant: *generally double the consonant and add* **–er** (thin → thinner; big → bigger).

Option: You may wish to have students go back to Figure It Out on pages 21 and 22 and circle all of the comparative adjectives. Have students work in pairs or as a class to compare their findings. Make a list on the board. Students can make additional sentences with these words.

Presentation

❶ Students compare Nola and Atina and write sentences using the comparative. Have students write two sentences per item.

Answers
a. Nola is taller than Atina. Atina is shorter than Nola. **b.** Nola is prettier than Atina. Atina is less attractive than Nola. **c.** Atina is heavier than Nola. Nola is lighter than Atina. **d.** Nola is more interesting than Atina. Atina is more boring than Nola. Atina is funnier than Nola. **e.** Atina is older than Nola. Nola is younger than Atina. **f.** Nola's clothes are more expensive than Atina's. Atina's clothes are cheaper than Nola's. Nola's clothes are more fashionable than Atina's. Atina's clothes are less fashionable than Nola's. **g.** Nola's hair is longer than Atina's. Atina's hair is shorter than Nola's. Atina's hair is curlier than Nola's. Nola's hair is straighter than Atina's.

❷ Students write sentences using the comparative.

Answers
a. Mexico City is larger than Cairo. Cairo is smaller than Mexico City. **b.** An apartment in Tokyo is more expensive than an apartment in New York. An apartment in New York is cheaper than an apartment in Tokyo. **c.** Madrid is older than Buenos Aires. Buenos Aires is younger than Madrid. **d.** *Answers will vary.* **e.** Mars is closer to the Earth than Jupiter. Jupiter is farther from the Earth than Mars. **f.** Mt. Everest is taller than Mt. Fuji. Mt. Fuji is shorter than Mt. Everest. **g.** *Answers will vary.* **h.** The Nile River is longer than the Amazon River. The Amazon River is shorter than the Nile River.

Language Note: The rules for forming the comparative have many exceptions. You may wish to point out that the comparative of **fun** is formed with **more**, not **–er,** and that the comparatives of **stupid** and **quiet** can be formed with either **–er** or **more.**

Option: Give students a list of other adjectives that form the comparative with **–er** (**big, large, rich, warm, safe, dry,** etc.) as well as ones that form it with **more/less** (**friendly, comfortable, helpful, popular, modern,** etc.).

Option: Have students bring in pictures of family members and friends and introduce and describe them to the class: "This is my brother. He's older than I am."

Option: Show students pictures of celebrities and have them make comparative sentences about them: "Madonna's music is better than Cher's."

 Workbook: Practices 3, 4, 5, 7

Talking About Differences: *not as ... as*

Preview

Before reading the grammar box, give students this sentence: *My watch is cheaper than yours.* Then write, *My watch isn't ... yours* and ask students to complete the sentence. Explain that the second sentence is a less direct way of presenting the same information. Then go over the information in the grammar box.

Presentation

❸ Students rewrite the sentences to use the less direct way of talking about differences.

> **Answers**
> **a.** Val's garden isn't as beautiful as Roxy's.
> **b.** Janet's couch isn't as comfortable as Roxy's. **c.** Janet's car isn't as fast as Roxy's.
> **d.** Val's daughter isn't as attractive as Roxy's. **e.** Roxy isn't as polite as Janet.

🌀 **Option:** Have students rewrite their sentences from Exercise 1 on page 24 to make them less direct.

 Workbook: Practices 6, 8

Talking About Similarities

Preview

Check understanding of **age, height, weight, rich,** and **poor.** Go over the information in the grammar box.

Presentation

❹ Students make sentences using the two grammar patterns presented. If necessary, answer any questions regarding vocabulary before students begin.

> **Answers**
> Franny is the same age as Pia. / Franny is as old as Pia.
> Franny is the same height as Pia. / Franny is as tall as Pia.
> Franny is the same weight as Pia. / Franny is as heavy as Pia.
> Franny's eyes and hair are the same color as Pia's.
> Franny's grades are as good as Pia's.
> Franny is as active and popular as Pia.
> Franny is as wealthy and generous as Pia.

☑ ❺ **Check Your Understanding** This exercise asks students to identify specific situations (categories) for using comparatives.

> **Answers**
> Deciding which computer to buy, Choosing between two people for a job, Deciding on a vacation spot.

Talking About Differences: *not as ... as*

We also use *not as ... as* to talk about the difference between two items. This form is common because it is less critical.

Less critical		More critical
Roxy's kitchen is**n't as clean as** Val's.	=	Val's kitchen is **dirtier than** Roxy's.
It is**n't as modern as** Val's either.	=	Val's kitchen is **less modern than** Roxy's.

 3 Rewrite the sentences to be less critical.

Example: Roxy's house is smaller than Val's.
Val's house isn't as large as Roxy's.

a. Val's garden is less beautiful than Roxy's.
b. Janet's couch is less comfortable than Roxy's.
c. Janet's car is slower than Roxy's.
d. Val's daughter is less attractive than Roxy's.
e. Roxy is less polite than Janet.

Talking About Similarities

We use *as* + adjective + *as* and *the same* (+ noun +) *as* to show that two items are the same. To show that two items are almost the same, we use *like* and *similar to*.

Roxy's car is **as old as** Val's.	=	Roxy's car is **the same age as** Val's.
Roxy's furniture is **like** Val's.	=	Roxy's furniture is **similar to** Val's.

4 Read about Franny and Pia and make a list of their similarities.

     Franny and Pia are good friends. They were both born in 1985. Both are 5 feet 7 inches tall. They each weigh 120 pounds. Both girls have brown eyes and dark hair. Each gets excellent grades at school. Both girls are active in school events and very popular. They are both wealthy and generous. Too bad they don't exist!

Example:

Franny is the same age as Pia.

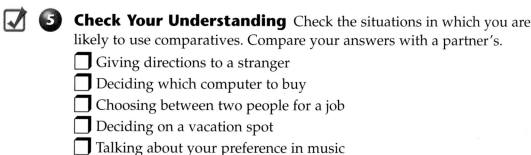 **5** **Check Your Understanding** Check the situations in which you are likely to use comparatives. Compare your answers with a partner's.

☐ Giving directions to a stranger
☐ Deciding which computer to buy
☐ Choosing between two people for a job
☐ Deciding on a vacation spot
☐ Talking about your preference in music

6 **Express Yourself** Work with a partner. Choose one of the situations from Exercise 5, and write a dialogue using comparative forms.

Example:

A: So, who do you think is the better candidate for the job?

B: Well, Tony's more experienced, but he doesn't seem as bright as Sandra.

A: I think Sandra's a lot friendlier, and she'll get along better with her colleagues.

B: So, do we agree on Sandra?

Now practice the dialogue with your partner.

LISTENING and SPEAKING

Listen: Choosing a Restaurant

1 **Before You Listen** What do you consider when you buy or rent a house or apartment? Number your answers from 1 (most important) to 8 (least important). Compare your choices with those of a partner.

_____ price   _____ number of rooms   _____ yard   _____ age

_____ size   _____ location   _____ garden   _____ view

 Listening for Criteria When comparing items, it is normal to use criteria or standards. Listening for the criteria will help you understand the comparison.

2 Listen to the conversation. A woman is trying to pick out a restaurant. Look at the criteria in the box. Circle the ones she uses.

age	price
size	food
cleanliness	noise
popularity	service

3 Listen to the conversation again. Check the correct column.

Criteria	Andy's Restaurant	Starlight Diner
cheaper	❑	❑
newer	❑	❑
noisier	❑	❑
cleaner	❑	❑
smaller	❑	❑
better food	❑	❑
more crowded	❑	❑

⑥ Express Yourself In this exercise, pairs of students choose one of the appropriate situations from Exercise 5 and write a dialogue about it. Circulate as students work and offer help as necessary.

Option: Have selected students perform their dialogues for the class. After they've finished, the other students should identify which situation the dialogue was describing.

LISTENING and SPEAKING

Listen: Choosing a Restaurant

Presentation

❶ Before You Listen Have students complete this exercise individually and then compare answers with a partner. Have selected students report to the class. Ask, *How were your priorities different? Were you surprised? Why did you put _____ as your first priority? Why was _____ your last? Are there any items you would add to this list?*

Option: Take a class survey of the most popular **criteria** and tally the results on the board.

➡ **Listening for Criteria** Explain what **criteria** means and then have students look at the vocabulary in the box. Check that they understand the words. Ask students to name the adjectival forms for some of these nouns (**cleanliness–clean; popularity–popular; noise–noisy**). Explain that once you know the criteria you are listening for, it's easier to anticipate what you're going to hear.

Language Note: You may want to point out that **criteria** is an irregular plural that does not end in –s. The singular is **criterion:** *Cleanliness is an important* **criterion** *in choosing a restaurant.*

❷ Play the recording or read the audio-script aloud one or more times. Students should circle the criteria they hear mentioned. Have the students check answers with a partner.

Audioscript: The audioscript for Exercises 2 and 3 appears on page T153.

> **Answers**
> price, cleanliness, noise, food

❸ Play the recording or read the audio-script aloud one or more times. Have students check the correct box for each criterion listed and compare answers with a partner.

> **Answers**
> Andy's Restaurant: cheaper, newer, cleaner, better food; Starlight Diner: noisier, smaller, more crowded

Option: To better personalize the listening, have students rank the criteria in the box that they would use to select a restaurant. Then skip Exercise 2 and have students complete Exercise 3. Ask, *Which restaurant would you choose? Which one better satisfies your criteria?*

Option: Have students make a list of their friends, family members, and teachers. Have them decide which restaurant they think each person would choose and give reasons why. Ask, *Do certain groups of people (older people, teenagers, parents of young children, etc.) follow different criteria when choosing a restaurant?* Have students discuss their findings in pairs or small groups.

 Workbook: Practice 9

Pronunciation

Preview

Review with students what syllables are and how to count them.

Presentation

Students read the explanation in the box in class or as homework.

 ❹ Play the recording or read the audioscript aloud two or more times and have students underline the syllables that are stressed. Pause between words to allow students time to write.

> **Answers**
> a. enter<u>tain</u> b. ga<u>rage</u> c. <u>cus</u>tomer d. under<u>stand</u> e. <u>nois</u>ier f. at<u>trac</u>tive g. disa<u>gree</u> h. ex<u>pen</u>sive i. e<u>nor</u>mous

❺ Have students work with a partner to go over their answers. They should say each word aloud, being careful to stress the correct syllable. Then go over the answers as a class.

🔗 *Workbook: Practice 10*

☸ **Option:** Prepare a list of words ahead of time and divide the class into teams. One member from each team should come to the front. As you read a word aloud, the chosen students have to call out whether the first, second, third (or other) syllable is the stressed one. The student who says the correct answer first wins a point for his/her team. Students should rotate so that every team member gets a chance to play.

☸ **Option:** Have students review the words they've written in their vocabulary notebooks and underline the stressed syllable in each word.

Speak Out

➡ **Agreeing and Disagreeing** Introduce or review the language for agreeing or disagreeing. As a way of modeling the strategy, make a statement such as *I like winter vacations best. Do you feel the same way?* Call on selected students to agree or disagree and explain how they feel. Students should then read the sentences in the chart and practice them with a partner.

Presentation

❻ Have students read the instructions, and ask selected students to model the conversation for the class. Then have students work in pairs discussing which alternatives they prefer. Circulate and offer help. Make notes of student errors, but don't interrupt to correct them—you want to encourage fluency. Have selected pairs perform their dialogues for the class. Refer to your notes and write errors on the board without identifying who made them. Then correct the errors as a class.

 Option: Give students some additional alternatives to discuss in class or to write about for homework:

- having a cat/having a dog
- sightseeing with a tour group/sightseeing with a friend
- traveling by train/traveling by airplane
- big cars/small cars
- large families/small families

🔗 *Workbook: Practice 11*

Pronunciation

 Listen to the words. Underline the stressed syllable in each word.

a. entertain	**d.** understand	**g.** disagree
b. garage	**e.** noisier	**h.** expensive
c. customer	**f.** attractive	**i.** enormous

5 Work with a partner. Take turns saying the words aloud, focusing on correct syllable stress.

Speak Out

 Agreeing and Disagreeing In conversation, it's customary to ask if others agree with you. It's also common to explain why you agree or disagree with someone.

Asking for Agreement	Agreeing	Disagreeing
Do you agree?	I think so too, because …	I'm sorry, but I don't agree with you because …
Do you feel the same way?	Yes, I know how you feel.	No, I don't feel that way because …
What do you think?	I don't think so either.	I'm sorry, but I think …

 In small groups, discuss which of the two alternatives you like better. Give reasons.

Example:

Tom: I think city life is better than country life.

Ann: So do I. There is so much more to do. What do you think?

Bob: I agree with Tom.

Sue: Well, I don't agree. I like the country better because you don't have to face crowds.

Ed: I disagree. Farm life is hard work.

a. country life/city life

b. car/motorcycle

c. private/public school

d. living with your family/living alone

e. vacation in summer/vacation in winter

Read About It

1 **Before You Read**

a. We all have certain ideas about different groups of people such as movie stars, people from other countries, or politicians. We call these ideas stereotypes. What other groups of people do we stereotype? Make a list.

b. Work in a small group. Give examples of stereotypes. Do you think that most stereotypes are true? Explain your answer. Why do people form stereotypes? How can we break them?

> **STRATEGY** **Identifying Main Ideas** As you read, you should always try to identify the main ideas. Each paragraph has its own main idea, often stated in the first sentence in the paragraph. The other sentences give more information about the main idea.

MALL crawlers
A Teenage Stereotype

Many people believe that American teenagers think only about buying goods. They say teens today want all the fashionable clothes, shoes, music, and sports equipment that their
5 friends have, all the things that they see advertised on TV and in magazines. When American teens get money, the critics say, they walk around the shopping mall for hours at a time. Teens who pass the time this way are called "mall crawlers." Is this
10 stereotype of American teenagers true?

It is true that more American teens have money to spend and that they are spending it at the mall. Research companies tell us, for example, that 12- to 19-year-olds spent over $109 billion in
15 1995, a 38% increase over 1990. Those numbers are even bigger today because almost 50% of teens 16 and older have part-time jobs after school or on weekends. In addition, experts predict that the teenage population will be larger
20 than ever before, reaching almost 35 million by the year 2010. This means that teenage consumers will play an even more important economic role in the future of the United States.

American teens are wealthier and work harder than before, but not all of their interests center on clothes, music, and movies at the mall. Around 30% of working teens save money in order to go to college. Others help in the purchase of a family computer or contribute to the family grocery budget. In addition, many American teens give their time to volunteer work and community service. And of course at school, competition for good grades to get into college is as tough as ever. With so many important responsibilities, it is unlikely that American teens spend all their time and money crawling the mall. It is easy but unfair to stereotype them in such a way. ■

READING and WRITING

Read About It

Presentation

❶ Before You Read Have students work in pairs to discuss the question in part **a.** For part **b,** have students work in small groups. They should be able to come up with at least three examples of stereotypes, three reasons for forming them, and three ways of breaking them. Have selected students report to the class about what their group discussed.

Option: Ask students to discuss this question: *Are stereotypes dangerous?* Alternatively, the question can be assigned as written homework.

➡ **Identifying Main Ideas** Ask students to explain what a main idea is. (Refer them to page 10, if necessary, to refresh their memories.) Explain that each paragraph in "Mall Crawlers" has one main idea. Main ideas are usually presented in the first sentence. The remaining sentences in the paragraph support the main idea.

❷ Have students read the article and find the main idea for each paragraph. They should identify the sentences and then check their answers with a partner.

Answers

Main idea for paragraph 1: Many people believe that American teenagers think only about buying goods. (sentence 1, line 1)

Main idea for paragraph 2: It is true that more American teens have money to spend and that they are spending it at the mall. (sentence 1, line 11)

Main idea for paragraph 3: American teens are wealthier and work harder than before, but not all of their interests center on clothes, music, and movies at the mall. (sentence 1, line 24)

❸ Have students work alone to match the expressions from the reading with their definitions. You might want to set a time limit for this exercise to encourage students to scan and think quickly. After they've finished, have students compare answers with a partner.

Answers

1. e **2.** f **3.** a **4.** h **5.** c **6.** d **7.** b **8.** g

☸ **Option:** Ask additional comprehension questions:

- What do critics say that American teens do when they get money? (walk around a shopping mall for hours at a time)

- Why do experts think teenagers will play an important economic role in the future? (The teenage population will be larger than ever before and many will be working.)

- What kind of responsibilities do American teens have? (They are saving money for college, contributing to the family budget, volunteering for community service, and competing for good grades.)

☸ **Option:** Ask students to discuss which of the following they do or would like to do and explain their reasons:

- Save money for college
- Contribute to the family budget
- Volunteer for community service

Think About It

Presentation

❹ Have students work in pairs or small groups. They should brainstorm and come up with a list of other stereotypes about teenagers and decide whether they are true or false.

☸ **Option:** Divide the class into debate teams. One side should represent people who believe negative stereotypes about teenagers. They should develop several arguments and support them with evidence. The other team should represent teenagers and develop arguments that show the positive side to teen life. Ask some students to judge the debate and vote on the team with the best arguments.

❺ Students should discuss this question and explain the reasons for their opinions.

Write: The Topic Sentence

Preview

With students' books closed, check their knowledge of writing good topic sentences. Ask them to imagine that they are going to write a paragraph about a hobby they have. Have students write a topic sentence, and then ask selected students to read theirs aloud. Do not correct at this stage. Next, have students open their books and read the explanation and the example sentences. Explain the importance of writing a topic sentence that is neither too general nor too narrow.

2 What is the main idea of each paragraph of the reading? In which sentence does the main idea occur? Check your answers with a partner.

3 Use the context to match the words from the reading with their meanings.

_____ **1.** fashionable (line 3)   **a.** rise in number

_____ **2.** mall crawlers (line 9)   **b.** to give money or help

_____ **3.** increase (line 15)   **c.** people who buy goods

_____ **4.** population (line 19)   **d.** buying

_____ **5.** consumers (line 21)   **e.** popular at the moment

_____ **6.** purchase (line 29)   **f.** people who walk around a mall

_____ **7.** to contribute (line 30)   **g.** money set aside

_____ **8.** budget (line 30)   **h.** number of people

Think About It

4 What are some other stereotypes about teenagers? Are they true or false? Explain your answers.

5 Do teenagers have the right to spend all the money they earn on themselves? Why or why not?

Write: The Topic Sentence

The main idea of a paragraph is usually introduced in the first sentence. This is called the topic sentence. The topic sentence is the most important sentence in the paragraph. It focuses the topic by giving the writer's main idea, opinion, or feeling about the subject.

A good topic sentence is not too general or too narrow. Imagine you want to write about your neighbor's new car. Look at three possible topic sentences and the comments about each:

a. My neighbor has many possessions.
Too general. This sentence is not focused on the new car.

b. My neighbor's new car is metallic blue.
Too narrow. This sentence is about only one aspect of the car.

c. My neighbor's new car is fantastic.
Just right. This paragraph can explain why the car is fantastic.

6 Decide if the topic sentences below are too general, too narrow, or just right. Discuss your answers with the class.

   a. Houses are expensive.

   b. My TV cost $450.00.

   c. My new TV has several amazing features.

   d. My roommate sometimes annoys me.

   e. There are four important criteria in choosing a house.

   f. The topic of this paper is television.

Write About it

7 Write a paragraph about one of your favorite possessions. Explain why the possession is important to you. Look at the model.

> Over the years I have collected many items, but my most valuable possession is a ring my husband gave me. He gave it to me a few months before we were married. He spent a long time looking for the right ring, and he was very proud of his choice. The ring is a sapphire set on a simple gold band. The sapphire is deep blue and is surrounded by two small diamonds. The ring is beautiful and was probably expensive, but I treasure it because it reminds me of my husband. Every time I wear it, I am closer to him.

8 Exchange papers with a partner. Give feedback to your partner to help him or her make the paragraph as clear as possible.

9 **Check Your Writing** Use your partner's comments and the questions below to revise your paragraph.

- Is the paragraph indented?
- Does the paragraph have a topic sentence? Where is it? Does it state the main idea of the paragraph?
- Is the topic sentence neither too general nor too narrow?

Presentation

❻ Have students work alone and then compare answers with a partner.

> ### Answers
> **a.** too general **b.** too narrow **c.** just right
> **d.** just right **e.** just right **f.** too general

 Workbook: Practice 12

Write About It

Presentation

❼ Go over the model paragraph together. Explain that the topic sentence introduces the topic (the woman's favorite possession, her ring) and the other sentences give specific details about it. Have students read the paragraph silently and then close their books. Ask selected students to give one detail about the ring. Students should next write their own paragraphs about a favorite possession. They can do the writing in class or as homework. Before students write at home, have them brainstorm in class. Students should work alone on their paragraphs.

❽ Students exchange papers and do peer-editing. Make sure each student makes at least one positive comment about his/her partner's paragraph.

Option: Students can finish the paragraphs for the topic sentences they wrote (about their hobbies) in the Preview section on page T29. Then have them exchange with a partner for feedback.

☑ **❾ Check Your Writing** Students should use their partner's feedback and the questions to revise their paragraphs. In addition, you can have students answer these questions:

- Are all the details clearly written?
- Are there any additional details you would like to include?

Vocabulary Expansion: Nouns, adjectives, and their opposites See page T142.

> ### Answers
> **A. 1.** short **2.** width **3.** high, short **4.** small
>   **5.** fat, light
> **B. 1.** long **2.** wide **3.** height **4.** weight
>   **5.** light or small **6.** size **7.** high **8.** narrow

---

EVALUATION

See page TExi.

Unit 3 Achievement Test

Self-Check See **Check Your Knowledge** on page 24 of the Workbook.

Dictation Have students review the sentences in Exercise 4 on page 23. Then present them as a dictation. (See instructions on page TExv.)

Communication Skills

1. Show students objects or pictures of places and objects. Have students describe them. Pay attention to students' use of adjectives.

2. Have students compare objects of different sizes, shapes, etc. Pay attention to students' use of comparatives and superlatives.

Review Units 1–3

Review unit exercises can be assigned as homework or done in class. You can use them in different ways.

- Give the review exercises as a quiz. Students work alone and turn in their answers to you.

- Use these review exercises as you would other exercises in the book. Students work alone and then compare answers with a partner.

- Have students work alone and then review answers as a class. Have selected students write their answers on the board and correct any errors together.

❶ Have students read the instructions and complete the exercise. For general notes on the simple present, have them refer to Unit 1, page 4. For general notes on the present progressive tense, have them refer to Unit 2, pages 14–15. For a comparison of the simple present and the present progressive tense, have students refer to Unit 2, page 14.

Answers
1. spend 2. are watching/are enjoying
3. watch/enjoy 4. knows 5. is learning
6. think/know 7. learn 8. watch

❷ Have students read the instructions and complete the exercise. For general notes on the simple present, have them refer to Unit 1, page 4. For general notes on the present progressive tense, have them refer to Unit 2, pages 14–15. For a comparison of the simple present and the present progressive tense, have students refer to Unit 2, page 14.

Answers
1. are (you) doing 2. 'm/am listening
3. hear 4. like 5. don't know 6. are (you) doing 7. Do (you) want 8. sounds 9. have
10. 'm/am meeting

❸ Have students read the instructions and complete the exercise. For a review of frequency expressions, have students refer to Unit 1, page 5.

Answers
a. every year b. rarely c. tonight
d. right now e. once in a while f. always

1 Complete the passage with the correct form of the verbs in the box. Use the simple present or present progressive tense.

learn	watch
think	love
enjoy	know
spend	

Many parents think that their children (1.) _____ too much time in front of the TV, but TV can be educational. For example, Sylvia and Eddie (2.) _____ an interesting TV program on animals now. Another program they (3.) _____ is about the latest developments in computer technology. Sylvia now (4.) _____ how to send e-mail and how to use the Internet. Eddie (5.) _____ about all the new computer games. Sylvia and Eddie's parents don't worry about TV; they (6.) _____ their children (7.) _____ a lot from the programs they (8.) _____.

2 Complete the conversation with the correct form of the verbs in parentheses. Use the simple present or present progressive tense.

BOB: Hey, Pat. What (1. do) _____ you _____?

PAT: Hi, Bob. I (2. listen) _____ to the latest CD by The Broken Bones Band.

BOB: Oh yeah? I (3. hear) _____ they have some great songs on there.

PAT: They do. I really (4. like) _____ "Crash" and "Forget About It."

BOB: I (5. know, *neg.*) _____ those songs, but I love their old ones.

PAT: What (6. do) _____ you _____ after class? (7. want) _____ you _____ to come over to my place and listen to their new CD?

BOB: That (8. sound) _____ great, but I can't. I (9. have) _____ an appointment. I (10. meet) _____ an old friend this evening.

PAT: Too bad. Another time, maybe.

3 Complete the sentences with the appropriate time expression from the box.

right now	every year
this year	tonight
once a day	once in a while
always	rarely

a. The Broken Bones Band works hard and records a new album _____.

b. David _____ watches TV on weekends; he likes to be outdoors.

c. We are going to the movies _____ after dinner.

d. My favorite news program is coming on _____.

e. If you are a couch potato, you should try turning off the TV _____.

f. The boss is not happy because Mary is _____ late for work.

4 Complete the paragraph with the comparative form of the adjectives in parentheses.

Mark's computer is **(1. new)** _____ than Zack's. It also has a **(2. powerful)** _____ processor and a much **(3. large)** _____ memory. Mark's computer is **(4. fast)** _____ than Zack's, too. However, Zack's computer is **(5. easy)** _____ to use. Zack's is also **(6. small)** _____ and **(7. attractive)** _____ in design. I think Zack's computer is **(8. good)** _____ than Mark's, but I wonder which one was **(9. expensive)** _____.

5 Rewrite the comparative sentences so that the meaning is the same.

a. Marty's house is dirtier than Teddy's.   _Marty's house isn't as clean as Teddy's._

b. Lou's new bike is cheaper than Jan's.   _____

c. _____   Mark's garden isn't as pretty as Tim's.

d. Pauline is less intelligent than Eve.   _____

e. _____   Susan's writing isn't as good as Mia's.

f. Bob is poorer than Sam.   _____

Vocabulary Review

Use the words in the box to complete the sentences.

commercial	enormous
crowded	relax
bored	follow
embarrassing	miss
jealous	security
possession	wonder

1. Look! There's Rock! Let's _____ him and try to take his picture!

2. I'm _____. Can't you find a more interesting program to watch?

3. Rock and Raquel Roller went to a luxury hotel to get away from fans and _____.

4. That is the biggest swimming pool in this neighborhood. It's _____!

5. I think Roxy is _____ of Val's prize-winning garden.

6. Let's go somewhere else to eat. It's too _____ here.

7. Rock! Call _____! Someone is taking photos of us through the window!

8. Our program will continue right after this _____. Stay tuned!

9. I _____ if Rock N. Roller wears a wig. I'd love to find out.

10. I never _____ my favorite TV shows.

❹ Have students read the instructions and complete the exercise. For a review of the comparative, have students refer to Unit 3, pages 24–25.

Answers
1. newer 2. more powerful 3. larger
4. faster 5. easier 6. smaller 7. more attractive 8. better 9. more expensive

❺ Have students read the instructions and complete the exercise. For a review of the comparative, have students refer to Unit 3, pages 24–25.

Answers
a. Marty's house isn't as clean as Teddy's.
b. Lou's new bike isn't as expensive as Jan's.
c. Mark's garden is less attractive than Tim's.
d. Pauline isn't as intelligent as Eve.
e. Susan's writing is worse than Mia's.
f. Bob isn't as rich as Sam.

Vocabulary Review

Have students read the instructions and complete the exercise.

Answers
1. follow 2. bored 3. relax 4. enormous
5. jealous 6. crowded 7. security
8. commercial 9. wonder 10. miss

AND THE BEAT GOES ON!

OBJECTIVES

- To talk about music
- To use the simple past tense to talk about events in the past
- To use adverbs of sequence with the simple past tense
- To listen to complete a chart
- To pronounce the **–ed** endings of regular past tense verbs
- To keep a conversation going
- To notice chronological order
- To write supporting sentences
- To use nouns ending in **–ance** and **–ment**

GETTING STARTED

Warm Up

Preview

Have students work in small groups to name as many different kinds of music as they can. Ask selected groups to share their lists with the class and write them on the board. If necessary, clarify **classical, country and western, folk, jazz, opera, rock,** and **soul.**

Presentation

❶ Have students work in pairs or small groups to discuss the questions. They can refer to the lists you wrote on the board in their discussions.

✪ **Option:** Have students explain in detail why they like certain kinds of music. You may want to introduce some music-related vocabulary: **beat, lyrics, singers, performers,** etc.

🎧 ❷ Play the recording one or more times. The recording contains short excerpts of rock, soul, opera, jazz, and country and western music. If you do not have the recording, bring in examples or ask students to bring in recordings of as many different kinds of music as possible.

Answers
1. rock and roll 2. soul 3. opera 4. jazz
5. country and western

✪ **Option:** Ask students to explain how they figured out their answers.

✪ **Option:** Ask students to make a list of adjectives to describe each genre of music. Alternatively, they could choose a feeling, color, or any other descriptive word that they associate with each type of music. Students should explain their lists in small groups.

✪ **Option:** Introduce or review additional music-related vocabulary. First, draw a staff with a treble clef and notes on the board. Identify the **staff, notes,** and **clef.** If any of your students are knowledgeable about music, ask them to explain musical notation in greater detail. Next, display pictures of musical instruments and have students identify them. Name any musical instruments students cannot identify. Then name the major types of instruments, such as **strings, brass, woodwinds,** and **percussion.** Ask students to sort the musical instruments by type. Say, *What kind of musical instrument is a (violin)?*

 Workbook: Practice 1

Figure It Out

Preview

Introduce **singer, dancer, award,** and **contest.** Ask students to name their favorite singers and dancers and award shows. Use realia to introduce **album** and **conductor.** For **appearance** talk about a concert or show that students are familiar with. Check understanding of **millionaire.** Explain that a **millionaire** has made a **million** dollars.

Presentation

❸ Ask students what they know about each performer. Ask them to name recordings, songs, roles, films, or performances for

(Exercise 3 continues on page T34.)

AND THE BEAT GOES ON!

Ricky Martin

Madonna

Placido Domingo

Elvis Presley

Celine Dion

Will Smith

GETTING STARTED

Warm Up

1 People in all cultures enjoy music. What kinds of music are popular in your country? What kinds do you like?

2 You are going to listen to different selections of music. What kind of music is each one? Write the number of the selection on the line.

_____ classical   _____ jazz

_____ opera   _____ rap

_____ folk   _____ soul

_____ country and western _____ rock and roll

Figure It Out

3 Look at the singers above. What do you know about them? Think about:

- biographical information
- albums and songs
- personal life

4 Which singer is each article about?

A. _____

He was born in the United States in the city of Philadelphia. When he was only twelve, he showed great talent as a rapper.
5   With Jazzy Jeff, his childhood friend and partner, he made two albums which sold thousands of copies and won important music awards. In fact, because of his rap music hits, he
10 was already a millionaire at eighteen! In 1990, he surprised his fans and became the star of a popular TV comedy series, which lasted until 1996. Then he decided
15 to perform in movies. He acted in a film almost every year from 1993 to 1998. He became even more popular after he made an adventure movie in which he wore a black suit
20 and black sunglasses and saved the world.

B. _____

One of fourteen brothers and sisters, she spent her childhood in Charlemagne, a town in Quebec, Canada. At age five, she already showed talent as a songwriter and
25 singer in French. She recorded a "demo" (demonstration album) when she was only twelve, and two years later became a performing star in Quebec. Well known in Canada and France, she participated in the Eurovision Song Contest in 1988, and won. As a result, people in
30 Europe, Russia, Australia, and the Middle East bought her albums. She longed to be popular in the United States and England too, and so she worked very hard to learn English. Her songs in English became instant hits, and she won many awards for her albums and for songs on movie
35 soundtracks such as *Titanic*.

C. _____

He was born in Spain in 1941, but moved to Mexico with his family when he was eight years old. As a child, he did not know
40 whether he wanted to be a soccer player or an orchestra conductor when he grew up. Both his parents were well-known singers. He made his first appearance in a musical comedy, but later became an opera singer. He performed in operas all over the world. His dream of becoming a conductor came true, too—he made his first appearance as a conductor in London. He also recorded albums of popular songs, which made him even more famous.

 5 **Vocabulary Check** Use the context to match the words with the correct meaning.

_____ **1.** talent (line 4)   **a.** to change from child to adult
_____ **2.** awards (line 8)   **b.** ability to do something well
_____ **3.** hits (line 9)   **c.** famous
_____ **4.** to perform (line 15)   **d.** to want very much
_____ **5.** to participate in (line 28) **e.** prizes
_____ **6.** to long (line 31)   **f.** songs or shows that are successful
_____ **7.** instant (line 33)   **g.** immediate
_____ **8.** conductor (line 41)   **h.** to enter
_____ **9.** to grow up (line 42)   **i.** to act, sing, or dance for the public
_____ **10.** well-known (line 43)   **j.** person who directs an orchestra

Talk About It

 6 A reporter from a music magazine is interviewing Rock N. Roller. Look at the start of their interview. With a partner, take turns being the reporter and Rock. Use the cues to continue the interview.

which each one is famous. Ask, *Have you ever seen any of these performers in person? Which ones are your favorites? Why?*

Language Note: Two common suffixes used to denote people who do things are **–er** and **–or.** Ask students to name as many nouns as they can: **dancer, conductor, actor, teacher, performer, sailor, singer,** etc.

ⓧ **Option: Vocabulary Notebooks** See page TEviii.

❹ Have students work alone, reading the articles and deciding which singer is being described. Students should then compare answers with a partner.

Answers
a. Will Smith **b.** Celine Dion **c.** Placido Domingo

ⓧ **Option:** Alternatively, have students work in groups of three. Have each student skim and then summarize the article for other students in the group. The group should try to guess the singer based on the summary.

ⓧ **Option:** Ask additional comprehension questions:

Article A: Where was Will Smith born? (in Philadelphia, Pennsylvania, in the United States) What are some of his well-known achievements? (As a young musician he made two albums that sold thousands of copies and won important music awards. He was already a millionaire at eighteen. He was the star of a popular TV comedy series.) What did he wear in a popular adventure movie? (a black suit and black sunglasses) What was the name of that film? (*Men in Black*)

Article B: What is Celine Dion's first language? (French) What happened in 1988? (She won the Eurovision Song Contest and became popular in Europe, Russia, Australia, and the Middle East.) Why did she study English? (She wanted to be popular in the United States and England, too.)

Article C: As a child, what did Placido Domingo want to be when he grew up? (a soccer player or an orchestra conductor) What are some of his well-known achievements? (He became an opera star and performed all over the world. He also became a conductor. He recorded albums of popular

songs.) What was his dream and where did it come true? (He dreamed of becoming a conductor; in London.)

ⓧ **Option:** Have each student write a profile of a singer or other well-known performer similar to the articles in Exercise 4 and present it to the class. The other students should try to guess the person.

ⓧ **Option:** Have students imagine that a visitor to their country wants to learn about the local music scene. What singer/group would they introduce to the visitor as being representative of music in their country? Why? In order not to overwhelm the visitor, they should present only one or two people/groups.

☑ ❺ **Vocabulary Check** Have students work alone and then check answers with a partner. Assign this exercise as homework if there isn't time to finish it in class.

Answers
1. b **2.** e **3.** f **4.** i **5.** h **6.** d **7.** g **8.** j
9. a **10.** c

 Workbook: Practice 2

ⓧ **Option: Vocabulary Notebooks** See page TEviii.

Talk About It

ⓧ **Option:** If students need extra practice with the simple past tense, postpone this activity until after you've completed the grammar exercises for this unit or Workbook Practices 3 and 4.

Presentation

❻ Have students read the instructions. Ask selected students to model the interview for the class. Then have students work in pairs taking turns being the reporter and Rock as they ask and answer all the questions. Circulate and offer assistance. Make notes of student errors, but don't interrupt to correct them; you want to encourage fluency. Have selected pairs present their interviews for the class. Refer to your notes and write errors on the board without identifying who made them. Then correct the errors as a class.

GRAMMAR

The Simple Past Tense: Past Events

Preview

- With students' books closed, review spelling rules for past tense forms of regular verbs.

  1. Most regular forms add –ed: **worked, started, visited**

  2. Verbs ending in **e** add –d: **hoped**

  3. Verbs ending in one stressed vowel + one consonant (except **w** or **y**) double the consonant and add **–ed: shopped, regretted**

  4. Verbs ending in a consonant + **y** change **y** to **i** and add **–ed: hurried, cried, studied**

- Explain that the past tense is used to talk about many kinds of past events and is often used in storytelling. Ask students to describe when they think it would be appropriate to use the past tense.

- Go over the dialogue in the grammar box. Have students read the past tense verbs.

Presentation

❶ Students work individually on the exercise and then compare answers with a partner.

Answers

was, grew up, sang, noticed, gave, included, didn't go, became, was, had, performed, listened, recorded, made

---

A: So, Rock, when did you decide to become a rock singer?

Tell about past action.

B: When I was twelve or thirteen. At first I wanted to be a doctor. Then I changed my mind.

Question	**Answer**
a. reason for becoming a rock singer	love of rock music
b. date of first performance	July 15, 1996
c. place of first performance	the Rock Land Club, New York City
d. date of first CD	January 21, 1998
e. people important to your music	my first guitar teacher, Mr. Segovia
f. training and musical education	four years at Jillian School of Music

GRAMMAR

The Simple Past Tense: Past Events

We use the simple past tense to talk about actions completed in the past. For regular verbs, add *–ed* or *–d* to the base verb. For irregular verbs, see pages 129–130.

A: The band U2 **performed** at Tower Theater last night. Everyone **loved** the concert. It **turned out** great.

B: **Did** they **sing** their latest hit?

A: Of course. But they **didn't play** my favorite song, "Indigo."

B: Maybe they only **wanted** to do their new songs.

A: Yeah probably. Anyway, we **had** a fantastic time.

1 Read the passage and underline the past tense verbs.

Oum Kalsoum

Oum Kalsoum was one of the most famous Arab singers of the twentieth century. She grew up in a village in Egypt. Her father sang religious songs at weddings and other events. When he noticed his daughter's voice, he gave her lessons and included her in his performances. She didn't go to the university, but she soon became very successful.

Oum Kalsoum was popular because she had a powerful voice. When she performed, people really listened. She recorded 300 songs and made six movies. Even today you can hear her music all over the Middle East.

2 Now put the verbs that you underlined in Exercise 1 in the correct category.

Regular Verbs   **Irregular Verbs**

_____   _____

_____   _____

3 Work with a partner. Use the cues to make questions about Oum Kalsoum. Then use the information from Exercise 1 to answer them.

Example: Who/Oum Kalsoum

A: Who was Oum Kalsoum?

B: She was one of the most famous Arab singers of the twentieth century.

a. Where/grow up   d. Why/popular
b. What/father/do   e. How many songs/record
c. go/university

4 Complete the passage with the correct form of the verb. Some answers may be negative.

John Lennon **(1. be)** _____ born in 1940 in Liverpool, England, where he **(2. grow up)** _____. As a teenager, he **(3. meet)** _____ Paul McCartney, and they **(4. begin)** _____ to write songs together. After several years, they **(5. form)** _____ a new group called The Beatles with George Harrison and Pete Best. However, Best **(6. stay)** _____ in the group. Ringo Starr **(7. join)** _____ the group in place of Best. In 1964, the group **(8. perform)** _____ its first hit song, "Love Me Do." Between the years 1962 and 1968, The Beatles **(9. be)** _____ the most famous group in the world.

In 1970, The Beatles **(10. break up)** _____, and Lennon **(11. decide)** _____ to perform alone. Between 1969 and 1972, he and his wife, Yoko Ono, **(12. do)** _____ a series of charity concerts together. In 1975, John and Yoko **(13. have)** _____ a son. John **(14. leave)** _____ his music career to raise their child. Five years later, he **(15. go)** _____ back to his music. Tragically, in 1983, Lennon was shot in New York. Lennon's life **(16. end)** _____, but his music lives on today.

❷ Have students work alone and then compare answers with a partner.

> **Answers**
> **regular verbs:** noticed, included, performed, listened, recorded; **irregular verbs:** was, grew up, sang, gave, didn't go, became, was, had, made

 Workbook: Practices 3, 4

❸ Have students work with a partner to form questions. Ask selected students to share their answers and put them on the board. Check them as a class.

> **Answers**
> **a.** Where did she grow up? She grew up in a village in Egypt. **b.** What did her father do? Her father sang religious songs at weddings and other events. **c.** Where did she go to the university? She didn't go to the university. **d.** Why was she popular? She was popular because she had a powerful voice. **e.** How many songs did she record? She recorded 300 songs.

Option: Have students research a famous singer who is no longer alive. Ask them to write a short article about the singer using the past tense to describe his/her life. Have them write questions about that person using the past tense. Then have students work in pairs to read each other's articles and answer the questions. Circulate and encourage students to answer the questions in complete sentences using the simple past tense.

❹ Have students work alone and then compare answers with a partner. Go over the answers as a class.

> **Answers**
> 1. was 2. grew up 3. met 4. began
> 5. formed 6. didn't stay 7. joined
> 8. performed 9. were 10. broke up
> 11. decided 12. did 13. had 14. left
> 15. went 16. ended

Option: Write the following exercise on the board or make a copy for every student. Have students complete the paragraph with verbs in the simple past tense.

On January 28, 1985, forty-five rock stars **(1. get)** _____ together in a Los Angeles record studio to sing a simple song. They **(2. call)** _____ it "We Are the World." Michael Jackson and Lionel Richie **(3. write)** _____ the song. Some of the performers who **(4. give)** _____ their time to record the song **(5. be)** _____ Harry Belafonte, Ray Charles, Bruce Springsteen, Cyndi Lauper, Billy Joel, Tina Turner, Paul Simon, Kim Carnes, Bob Dylan, and Diana Ross. Millions of people **(6. hear)** _____ the song and **(7. buy)** _____ the record. The money from the sales of this record **(8. help)** _____ hungry people in Africa.

> **Answers**
> 1. got 2. called 3. wrote 4. gave 5. were
> 6. heard 7. bought 8. helped

 Workbook: Practices 5, 6, 7, 8

❺ Have students work with a partner to ask and answer questions about these famous people. Circulate to provide help, as students may not be familiar with all the names on the list.

Answers

a. Who composed the opera *Carmen*? Georges Bizet did. b. Who composed the opera *Aida*? Giuseppe Verdi did. c. Who painted the painting *Guernica*? Pablo Picasso did. d. Who built the Taj Mahal? Shah Jahan did. e. Who composed/wrote the song "Yesterday"? Paul McCartney did. f. Who wrote the novel *Don Quixote*? Miguel de Cervantes did. g. Who discovered electricity? Benjamin Franklin did. h. Who invented the piano? Bartolomeo Cristofori did. i. Who wrote the play *Hamlet*? Shakespeare did.

☾ **Option:** Have students work in pairs to draw up a list of people who are famous in the contemporary world. They can be famous in the students' country or internationally well known. Each pair should then exchange their list with another pair. Using the model in Exercise 5, they should all make sentences using the past tense. If a name is unfamiliar, students should ask the pair who wrote it to explain who the person is and why he/she is famous.

☑ ❻ **Check Your Understanding** In this exercise, students determine in which situations the past tense is used. They should work alone and then compare answers with a partner.

Answers

Telling a story, Describing your first concert, Talking about the life of Mozart

---

Adverbs of Sequence with the Simple Past Tense

Preview

With students' books closed, write some adverbs of sequence on the board. Explain that they are used to give the order of events when you are telling a story. Ask students to add any expressions they can to your list.

Presentation

❼ Have students read through the paragraph alone, underlining the adverbs of sequence. Then they should compare answers with a partner.

Answers

first, (Many years) later, (Some time) later, Soon afterward, Finally

---

☾ **Option:** Ask comprehension questions:

- How old was Rosemary Brown when she first saw the spirit of Franz Liszt? (seven)

- What happened in 1964? (Liszt returned and gave Rosemary compositions he wrote after his death.)

- What other spirits did Rosemary meet? (the spirits of Bach, Beethoven, Chopin, Mozart, and other composers)

- What did Rosemary do that was surprising? (With only two years of musical training, she wrote down more than 500 pieces of music.)

- What did Rosemary do in 1971? (She recorded the album of spirit compositions.)

☾ **Option:** After students have underlined the adverbs of sequence, have them close their books and retell Rosemary's story in their own words. If necessary, they can use the comprehension questions to remind them of the main points.

5 Work with a partner. Use the information in the chart to take turns asking and answering questions.

Example:

A: Who composed the opera *Carmen*?

B: Georges Bizet did.

Who	Did	What?
a. Georges Bizet		the opera *Aida*
b. Giuseppe Verdi	paint	the piano
c. Pablo Picasso	write	electricity
d. Shah Jahan	build	the play *Hamlet*
e. Paul McCartney	compose	the painting *Guernica*
f. Miguel de Cervantes	invent	the Taj Mahal
g. Benjamin Franklin	discover	the novel *Don Quixote*
h. Bartolomeo Cristofori		the opera *Carmen*
i. William Shakespeare		the song "Yesterday"

 6 **Check Your Understanding** In which situations are you likely to use the past tense? Check your answers with a partner's.

☐ Talking about your next vacation

☐ Telling a story

☐ Describing your first concert

☐ Explaining how to make coffee

☐ Talking about the life of Mozart

Adverbs of Sequence with the Simple Past Tense

> To tell the order of events, we can use adverbs of sequence, such as *first, later, next, then, after that, soon,* and *finally.*

7 Read the paragraph and underline all the adverbs of sequence.

Although Franz Liszt, the famous composer, died in 1886, a woman in England, Rosemary Brown, says she first saw his spirit when she was seven. Many years later, in 1964, she says Liszt returned and gave her compositions he wrote after his death. Some time later, he introduced her to the spirits of Bach, Beethoven, Chopin, Mozart, and other composers. Soon afterward, they too asked her to write down the music they composed after their deaths. With only two years of musical training, Rosemary wrote down more than 500 pieces of music. Many experts believed the dead composers had actually written the compositions. Finally, Rosemary recorded the album of spirit compositions in 1971.

Rosemary Brown

8 Can you replace the adverbs of sequence in the paragraph from Exercise 7 with any of these? If so, where?

a. then
d. after that
b. in the end
e. next
c. before then

 9 **Express Yourself** Pick one of your favorite musicians or artists. Prepare a short biographical sketch of the artist. Use the passages in this unit as models. Take notes to organize your ideas.

Then, in a small group, present your artist. Be sure to use the past tense and adverbs of sequence to show the order of events. Be prepared to answer questions from members of your group.

LISTENING and SPEAKING

Listen: Music Around the World

1 **Before You Listen**

a. People use music in many different ways. For example, people use music to put babies to sleep. List as many uses of music as you can.

b. Why do you listen to music?

 Listening to Complete a Chart When you listen and take notes, you sometimes have to complete a chart. Charts help organize information. Before listening, look at the chart carefully to see what to listen for.

Wooden drums

Steel drums

Camels in the desert

❽ Have students work in pairs and then go over the answers as a class.

> **Answers**
> **a.** *then* could replace *many years later* or *some time later* or *soon afterward* **b.** *in the end* could replace *finally* **c.** *before then* cannot be used **d.** *after that* could replace *many years later* or *some time later* or *soon afterward* **e.** *next* could replace *some time later* or *soon afterward*

Ⓧ Option: Introduce other adverbs of sequence to add to students' lists: **afterward, before long, eventually, later on, within minutes/hours/days/years, beforehand, in advance, first, second, third.**

❾ Express Yourself These activities are communicative and interactive. They connect the grammar points—in this case, the simple past tense and adverbs of sequence— to the students' personal likes. When students write their biographical sketches, have them pay close attention to these points. If they've done this exercise already as an optional activity, they can expand on their previous sketch or write about a different person.

Ⓧ Option: Have students pretend to be the person they've written the biographical sketch about. The other students then ask yes/no questions and try to guess who the person is.

 Workbook: Practice 10

LISTENING and SPEAKING

Listen: Music Around the World

Presentation

❶ Before You Listen Have students read items **a** and **b**. Students should work in small groups to brainstorm different uses of music and reasons they listen to music. Then call on selected students and write their ideas on the board. Take a class survey to see how many people listen to music to relax, to cheer up, to exercise to, etc.

➡ **Listening to Complete a Chart** Have students read the strategy. If necessary, introduce or review **origin** (beginning).

❷ Play the recording or read the audio-script aloud one or more times. Have students complete the chart.

Audioscript: The audioscript for Exercise 2 appears on page T154.

> **Answers**
> 1. Western Africa 2. to accompany singing and dancing at village festivals 3. Japan 4. to tell stories and poetry 5. Arabian countries

Option: Ask additional comprehension questions:

- What are drums in the West Indies made from? (metal oil containers)
- Where can the rules for Vedic song be found? (in very old writings)
- What does the rhythm of Huda song imitate? (the rhythm of a camel's walk)

Pronunciation

Preview

Students read the explanation in the box in class or as homework and practice saying the past tense ending of regular verbs in the three different ways.

Presentation

 ❸ Play the recording or read the dialogue aloud. Students should write their answers and then compare them with a partner's.

> **Answers**
> /t/: There are no words that end in the /t/ sound.
> /d/: loved, learned, discovered, used
> /ɪd/: visited, recommended, rented, suggested, started, visited

Option: Have students identify past tense endings of regular verbs throughout the unit. Students should practice pronouncing these verb forms aloud.

Link *Workbook: Practices 11, 12*

Speak Out

➡ **Keeping a Conversation Going** Discuss why it is important to learn expressions that are used to show interest in what someone is telling you.

Presentation

❹ Discuss the exercise. Then read the questions and expressions in the box aloud. Have students work in groups to talk about one of their first-time experiences. Students who are listening should use the expressions to keep the conversation going.

Option: Have selected students retell a first-time experience they heard. Ask the class to vote on which experience sounded most interesting.

Link *Workbook: Practice 9*

T39

2 You are going to listen to part of a talk about different kinds of music. Look at the chart to see what information you will have to fill in. Then, listen carefully and fill in the chart.

Type of Music	Place of Origin	Use
1. wooden drums		to communicate
2. steel drums	Barbados, West Indies	
3. koto music		to accompany plays
4. Vedic song	India	
5. Huda song		to stop spirits

Pronunciation

The _–ed_ Ending

We pronounce the past tense ending of regular verbs in three ways, depending on the final sound of the verb.

/t/ after voiceless sounds: tal**ked**, hel**ped**, wi**shed**

/d/ after voiced sounds: perfor**med**, li**ved**, liste**ned**

/ɪd/ after **–d** and **–t** endings: wan**ted**, recor**ded**, visi**ted**

  3 Listen to the dialogue, focusing on the underlined past tense endings. For each ending, decide if you hear **/t/**, **/d/**, or **/ɪd/**. Then practice saying the dialogue.

A: So you visit<u>ed</u> the exhibit on African-American music I recommend<u>ed</u>?

B: Yes, and you were right. I lov<u>ed</u> it. I rent<u>ed</u> the Tour on Tape just as you suggest<u>ed</u>.

A: So, tell me what you learn<u>ed</u>.

B: I discover<u>ed</u> that rap start<u>ed</u> out in the streets of New York City in the 1970s. Performers us<u>ed</u> bits of funk and hard rock and other sounds as background to their lyrics.

A: Yeah, I know. I visit<u>ed</u> the exhibit three times.

Speak Out

 Keeping a Conversation Going You can keep a conversation going by asking questions and by showing interest.

 4 Work with a partner. Think of one of your first-time experiences, such as your first concert or your first airplane flight. What happened? How did you feel? Take turns talking about your experiences. Use the expressions in the box to keep your conversation going.

> What happened after that?
>
> How interesting!
>
> Then what?
>
> Oh, no!
>
> Oh, really?
>
> That's amazing.

Read About It

1 **Before You Read** In a small group, brainstorm the topic of jazz. Make a list of everything that comes to your mind when you hear the word "jazz." Share your ideas with the class.

STRATEGY **Noticing Chronological Order** When you read, it is important to understand the order in which events happen in time. Pay attention to signals such as dates, and adverbs of time, such as *then, next, after that,* and *later.*

The Story of Jazz

The word "jazz" has just four letters, but it covers a multitude of sounds. No definition completely describes it. In the approximately 100 years of its history, jazz has gone through many changes in style—from the earliest blues, to
5   Dixieland, to the Charleston, to swing, to boogie-woogie, to mambo. Jazz musicians of all these different styles do two things in common: they all make sudden, surprising changes in rhythm, and they all improvise (freely compose and invent music as they play, spontaneously). In other words, jazz
10 singers and musicians follow their own inspiration, but they come together to speak the same musical language.

The musical language of jazz began in New Orleans, Louisiana, and came from the mixture of cultures there at that time—old French, new American, Black, and Indian. People
15 used music to accompany daily life, and gradually this music took on all the feelings and emotions of daily life, such as happiness, sadness, anger, and resignation. The more emotion players put into jazz, the more popular it became.

Soon, jazz spread from New Orleans to Memphis and,
20 after that, to Chicago. In Chicago, the music changed to reflect the 1920s, a time of illegal alcohol and gangsters like Al Capone. At this time, jazz was not considered very respectable. Jazz became more respectable in the 1930s as "big bands" filled dance halls and ballrooms with thousands
25 of people, and fans supported their favorite bands just as they did their favorite baseball teams. In the 1940s and 1950s, individual musicians such as Charlie Parker and Duke Ellington received more attention than the bands, and the popularity of jazz continued to grow.
30 Today jazz lives on. We hear it in musical comedies, movies, TV programs, and TV commercials. Jazz musicians of today still experiment with new forms, and performers such as Gato Barbieri, Wynton Marsalis, and Geri Allen continue to delight their fans with creative and exciting music.

Preservation Hall, New Orleans

Preservation Hall Jazz Band

Louis Armstrong

READING and WRITING

Read About It

Presentation

❶ Before You Read Have students work in small groups brainstorming the topic of jazz. Write all the words they suggest on the board and then lead a class discussion. Explain that jazz was popular in the United States in the 1920s and ask students what they know about that time in American history.

Cultural Note: You may want to explain to students that in the 1920s, the United States prohibited the consumption of all alcoholic beverages. This period was called Prohibition. Some people continued to want to consume these drinks, so they either made them at home or bought them from illegal sources. Gangsters such as Al Capone became rich supplying illegal alcohol. Prohibition ended in 1934.

➡ **Noticing Chronological Order** Explain to students that events in a reading are not always presented in a strict chronological order. To figure out the order in which events happened, it is important to pay attention to dates and adverbs of time.

❷ Have students read the text and answer the questions.

Answers
a. It is difficult to define because it covers a multitude of sounds. b. Because it was associated with illegal alcohol and gangsters. c. Big bands began to be popular in the 1930s.

🅐 Option: Ask additional comprehension questions:

- What are some of the styles of jazz that are mentioned? (blues, Dixieland, Charleston, swing, boogie-woogie, mambo)
- What are two things all jazz musicians do in common? (They make sudden, surprising changes in rhythm, and they improvise—freely compose and invent music as they play.)
- Where did jazz begin? (New Orleans, Louisiana) What cultures created it? (Old French, new American, Black, and Indian)
- Who was popular in the 1940s and 1950s? (individual musicians such as Charlie Parker and Duke Ellington)
- Where can we hear jazz today? (in musical comedies, movies, TV programs, and TV commercials)

🅐 Option: Ask additional discussion questions:

- Do you like jazz? Why or why not?
- What other kinds of music or dance do you like? Why?

❸ Have students work alone putting the events in order. Then they should compare answers with a partner.

Answers
5, 2, 4, 1, 3, 6

❹ Have students work alone guessing the meanings of the words from context. Go over the answers as a class.

Answers
1. b 2. a 3. a 4. c 5. b 6. a

🅐 Option: Have pairs of students pick out other difficult words from "The Story of Jazz" on page 40, then exchange words with another pair and practice guessing the meaning of the words from context. Finally, have the class share answers so that everyone can benefit from the exercise.

🅐 Option: Vocabulary Notebooks See page TEviii.

Think About It

Presentation
❺ Have students discuss the question in small groups and present their ideas to the class.

❻ Have students describe a style of music that is famous in their region or country. Encourage them to bring a sample to class. Before playing the music, students should prepare a brief history of the music, instruments used, well-known performers, etc.

Write: Supporting Sentences

Preview
Students read the presentation in class or for homework. Explain that supporting sentences are important because they provide the "evidence" that supports or adds information to the topic sentence. They must always relate to the idea presented in the topic sentence.

Presentation
❼ Have students read the paragraph silently, underlining the topic sentence. Then have them count the supporting sentences. They should compare answers with a partner before you review the answers as a class.

Answers
a. In our city, there are several places where you can listen to music in the summer. b. 3 (They begin At least; In Tranquility; Finally, on Saturday) c. They give three specific places where you can listen to music in the summer: the Miller Outdoor Theater in Herman Park, Tranqulity Park, and the downtown Pavilion.

2 Answer the questions.

    a. Why is it difficult to define jazz?

    b. Why wasn't jazz very respectable in the 1920s?

    c. When were big bands popular?

3 Put the events in the correct order. Write 1 (first) to 6 (last).

    _____ Individual musicians got more attention than big bands.

    _____ Jazz spread from New Orleans to Memphis to Chicago.

    _____ Jazz became more respectable as the big bands filled dance halls.

    _____ Jazz started in New Orleans almost 100 years ago.

    _____ In the 1920s, jazz reflected the times of illegal alcohol and Al Capone.

    _____ Jazz performers continue to delight audiences.

4 Use the context to guess the meanings of the words. Circle the letter.

1. a multitude of (lines 1–2)
    a. few
    b. many
    c. composition

2. history (line 3)
    a. past
    b. present
    c. future

3. blues (line 4)
    a. a jazz style
    b. a color
    c. a jazz singer

4. spontaneously (line 9)
    a. very quickly
    b. with singing
    c. without planning

5. to accompany (line 15)
    a. to change
    b. to go together with
    c. to improve

6. spread (line 19)
    a. traveled
    b. went away
    c. changed

Think About It

5 Why do you think music exists in every culture of the world?

6 Is your country well known for a certain type of music? Explain.

Write: Supporting Sentences

The topic sentence of a paragraph is followed by a number of other sentences called supporting sentences. These sentences make up the body of a paragraph. In a well-written paragraph, all of the supporting sentences give more information about the topic sentence.

7 Read the paragraph and answer the questions below.

    a. What is the topic sentence?

    b. How many supporting sentences are there?

    c. What information do the supporting sentences give about the topic sentence?

> In our city, there are several places where you can listen to music in the summer. At least twice a month, the City Orchestra performs in the Miller Outdoor Theater in Hermann Park. These concerts are especially popular because they are free. In Tranquility Park, rock groups sometimes come and give open-air concerts. Finally, on Saturday and Sunday evenings, jazz musicians perform in the downtown Pavilion. The summer is a great time for music lovers in our city.

8 Read the following paragraphs. In each paragraph, find the one sentence that does not support the topic sentence. Cross it out.

A.

GIUSEPPE VERDI, a well-loved composer of opera, had a very simple musical beginning. His first musical lessons came from a priest in his church. He also liked to read. When he was ten years old, he moved to the small city of Busseto to play music for the church there. Two years later, he became the main church organist. In four years, Verdi became the best organist of the area.

Verdi's opera *Aida*

B.

Verdi's music is full of emotion. The stories of his operas are full of love, death, romance, and excitement. He used his music to show these feelings. He didn't like the music of Richard Wagner, another opera composer. He worked hard on melody, the main part of a song, because he thought that melody was a very important way to show emotion.

Write About It

9 Write a paragraph about your favorite composer, singer, or musical group. First, brainstorm everything you know about the artist. Focus on one central idea. Write a topic sentence and develop it with supporting sentences.

10 Exchange papers with a partner. Ask questions about parts where you want more information.

11 **Check Your Writing** Make revisions based on your partner's comments and the questions below.

- Does the paragraph have a topic sentence? Is there one main idea?
- Do all the supporting sentences give information about the topic sentence?
- Is the sequence of events clearly marked with adverbs of sequence or dates?

❽ Have students read both paragraphs and cross out the sentence in each that doesn't belong. Ask students to explain how they made their choices.

> **Answers**
> **a.** He also liked to read. **b.** He didn't like the music of Richard Wagner, another opera composer.

Option: Bring in newspapers and magazines and ask students to read specific paragraphs. Have students underline the topic sentence and study the supporting sentences. They should say whether the supporting sentences successfully support the topic sentence or not.

Write About It

Preview

Have students underline the topic sentences in the two paragraphs in Exercise 8. What additional information do the supporting sentences provide?

Presentation

❾ Have students write their own paragraph about their favorite composer, singer, or musical group. Remind them to focus on one central idea (which differentiates this paragraph from Express Yourself on page 38 and other optional exercises that have them writing paragraphs). They can write in class or as homework. If students do their writing at home, first have them brainstorm in class so you that can check this step.

❿ Students exchange papers and do peer-editing. Make sure each student makes at least one positive comment about his/her partner's paragraph.

Option: Students can also answer these questions while they're editing:

- What is one thing that you learned that you didn't know before?

- What is one thing that was mentioned that you'd like to hear more about?
- Was there anything left out that you think should have been mentioned?

☑ **⓫ Check Your Writing** Students revise their assignments based on the suggestions given.

Vocabulary Expansion: Nouns ending in –ance and –ment See page T143.

> **Answers**
> A. 1. performance 2. disappearance
> 3. appearance 4. attendance 5. accompaniment 6. entertainment 7. agreement
> 8. disagreement 9. excitement 10. retirement
> B. 1. perform 2. disappear 3. appearance
> 4. attend 5. accompany 6. entertainment
> 7. retirement 8. disagreement 9. excitement 10. retire

EVALUATION

See page TExi.

Unit 4 Achievement Test

Self-Check See Check Your Knowledge on page 32 of the Workbook.

Dictation Have students review the sentences in Exercise 3 on page 41. Then present them as dictation. (See instructions on page TExv.)

Communication Skills

1. Ask students to talk about their favorite kind of music or the different musical styles popular in their country. Pay attention to students' use of vocabulary to talk about music.

2. Ask students to tell a story about their first day at school or some other significant past event in their lives. Pay attention to students' use of the simple past tense and adverbs of sequence.

3. Tell a story of your own and have students use appropiate expressions to keep the conversation going.

CLOSE CALLS

OBJECTIVES

- To talk about close calls and disasters
- To use the simple past and past progressive tenses to tell stories
- To use time clauses with **when, while, as**
- To listen for sequence
- To identify stressed and unstressed words
- To tell a story
- To make predictions
- To write concluding sentences
- To use expressions with **get**

GETTING STARTED

Warm Up

Preview

- With students' books closed, ask for a definition of **close call.** Then have students work in pairs to think of situations that could result in having a close call. Ask selected students to report to the class and compile a list on the board.

- Check understanding of the words used to describe the pictures on this page: **thunderstorm, accident, flood, tornado, blizzard, snowstorm,** and **fire.**

Language Notes: You may want to tell students that **damage** means "to harm or injure in such as way as to lessen the value of something."

A **tornado** is a very strong and destructive storm that takes the form of a funnel cloud and moves very quickly, often without warning, along a narrow path. Tornadoes are very common in the spring and fall in the midwestern United States. Synonyms for tornado include **cyclone** and the colloquial **twister.**

Typhoons, tropical storms with strong winds and heavy rains, occur over the Pacific Ocean. Similar storms are called **hurricanes** in the United States and the West Indies.

Introduce or review **earthquake** (a shaking

or sliding of a portion of the earth, caused by movement of the earth's surface).

Check understanding of **alarm.** Ask students if they use an alarm to wake up in the morning. Ask, *At what other times do you hear alarms?*

Option: Vocabulary Notebooks See page TEviii.

Presentation

❶ Make sure everyone understands the exercise. Play the recording one or more times. Tell students they do not have to understand every word to do the activity.

Audioscript: The audioscript for Exercise 1 is on page T154.

> **Answers**
> **Top row:** C, A, extra picture
> **Bottom row:** D, E, B

 Workbook: Practice 1

❷ Have students discuss this question in pairs. Circulate and encourage students to ask their partners questions to keep the stories going.

Option: Focus the discussion for Exercise 2 on storms. Ask students if they've had any experience with **snowstorms, thunderstorms, hurricanes, tornadoes, typhoons, earthquakes.**

Option: Ask students if they know what to do in different kinds of emergencies. Have groups of students do research and present their findings to the class so that everyone can learn the dos and don'ts of facing a dangerous situation.

Option: Have students bring in an article from a newspaper or magazine about someone who had a close call. Ask students to tell the class what happened, using their own words.

GETTING STARTED

Warm Up

1. If you escape a dangerous situation, we say you had a "close call."
   Listen to the conversations and look at the pictures. Write the letter of
   the conversation in the box. There is one extra picture.

2. What do people do in these emergencies?

Figure It Out

Read the following news report to
find out people's reactions to a
close call with a tornado.

And now …
today's weather. A tornado
struck Park City Airport at 11:15 this
morning. It damaged the airport
building and destroyed a plane.
Several people were hurt. Let's go
to Al Stevens at the airport …

A.

AL STEVENS: For the people at Park City Airport, this morning's tornado was a real close call. Let's get these people's reactions. [*to airport official*] Excuse me, Ma'am. What was happening here at the airport when the storm struck?

AIRPORT OFFICIAL: Well, everything was going fine. Planes were taking off and landing on time. Passengers were waiting at the gate to get on Flight 62. Then, suddenly, we saw a black cloud coming closer and closer!

AL STEVENS: What happened then?

AIRPORT OFFICIAL: The tornado hit the plane and destroyed it. There was baggage and broken glass all over. I thought it was the end! I was really afraid.

AL STEVENS: Well, that's not surprising. Thank you, Ma'am.

B.

AL STEVENS: Excuse me, Sir. Could you tell me about this morning's tornado?

TICKET AGENT: Well, I was having a problem with an awful person. While passengers were checking in, this man tried to get ahead of a woman and her children. She got angry and told him to wait his turn, and he started to shout at her. They were having a terrible argument.

AL STEVENS: Then what happened?

TICKET AGENT: Well, all of a sudden, the storm hit and the windows shattered. Glass was all over the floor. People were screaming and running away from the windows. Babies were crying and alarms were ringing. Naturally, I hid behind the counter.

Figure It Out

Preview

- Tell students that they will read three dialogues about a close call in an airport. Elicit vocabulary used in an airport, such as the following: **airplane**, **boarding pass**, **check-in counter**, **flight, gate**, **landing**, **runway**, **take off**. Have students anticipate the words they think they'll encounter in the dialogues. Then give them time to skim the dialogues and see which words were actually used.

- Check understanding of **argument** (a loud verbal disagreement), **shatter** (break into many pieces that fly in all directions), and **salad bar** (a long table of greens, vegetables, and other salad ingredients that restaurant customers use to make their own salads). Ask students if they've ever been to a restaurant with a salad bar. Have them name ingredients they would expect to find there.

Language Note: When we talk about storms occurring, we use the verbs **strike** and **hit**. Introduce or review **destroy** in reference to the pictures on page 43. You may wish to tell students that **destroy** means "to make useless by breaking into pieces, taking apart, burning, or ruining in another way."

- **Option: Vocabulary Notebooks:** See page TEviii.

  - Have students skim the dialogues and then close their books. With a partner, they should try to reconstruct what the airport official, ticket agent, and teenager saw or did. Don't correct their answers at this point.

Presentation

❸ Have students answer the questions.

> ### Answers
> **a.** this morning **b.** Everything was going fine. Planes were taking off and landing on time. Passengers were waiting at the gate to get on Flight 62. **c.** As he was taking his food back to the table, the lights went out, and he fell into the salad bar. **d.** *Answers will vary.*

 Option: Ask additional comprehension questions:

- What did the airport official see? (a black cloud coming closer and closer) How did she feel? (really afraid)

- What problem was the ticket agent having? (A man tried to get ahead of a woman and her children. They were having an argument.)

- Where were the teenager and his friend Jeff when the tornado struck? (getting some lunch at the snack bar)

Option: You might want to teach additional words that students are likely to hear at airports: **baggage claim area**, **customs**, **direct flight**, **duty free shop**, **flight attendant**, **layover**, **pilot**, **skycap**. Have students write these words in their vocabulary notebooks and use them in sentences.

Option: Have students play the roles of Al Stevens, the airport official, the ticket agent, and the teenager. They should write their own dialogue and perform it for the class. Encourage students to add other characters to their skit and to make it dramatic or humorous.

❹ **Vocabulary Check** Have students work alone and then check answers with a partner. Assign this exercise as homework if there isn't time to finish it in class.

> ### Answers
> **a.** checking in **b.** close call **c.** taking off
> **d.** landing **e.** passengers **f.** get ahead of
> **g.** struck **h.** caused **i.** argument **j.** shouting
> **k.** hid

Link *Workbook: Practice 2*

Option: **Vocabulary Notebooks** See page TEviii.

C. **AL STEVENS:** What about you? What were you doing when the storm struck?

TEENAGER: Well, my friend Jeff and I were getting some lunch at the snack bar. As he was taking his food back to the table, the lights went out, and he fell into the salad bar. At first I was afraid, but later I thought it was funny when I saw he had lettuce in his hair!

AL STEVENS: Thank you. [*to camera*] And those are some of the reactions to this morning's tornado. This is Al Stevens at the Park City Airport.

3 Answer the questions.
  a. When did the tornado strike?
  b. What was happening when the tornado struck?
  c. What happened to Jeff?
  d. Are there dangerous weather conditions in your country? What are they? How often do they occur?

4 **Vocabulary Check** Read the sentences. From the words in the box, find a synonym for the underlined word or words below and write it on the line.

argument	hid
get ahead of	passengers
shouting	landing
caused	taking off
damaged	struck
close call	checking in

  _____ **a.** People were giving their tickets and suitcases to the agent.
  _____ **b.** We had a dangerous experience, but we didn't get hurt.
  _____ **c.** Planes were leaving on time.
  _____ **d.** Planes were arriving on time.
  _____ **e.** The people who are traveling on the plane are waiting in line.
  _____ **f.** A man tried to move in front of a woman.
  _____ **g.** The tornado hit at 11:15.
  _____ **h.** The tornado created a lot of damage.
  _____ **i.** Two customers were having an angry conversation.
  _____ **j.** A man and a woman were speaking loudly at each other.
  _____ **k.** A ticket agent got behind the counter so that no one could see him.

Talk About It

A reporter is interviewing more people at the airport.

Ask about continuing actions in the past.

A: What were you doing when the storm hit?

Tell about continuing actions in the past.

B: I was waiting to check in.

5 With a partner, take turns being the reporter and one of the interviewees.

a. a cook in the snack bar
b. a clerk at the magazine stand
c. a pilot in a plane
d. a passenger at the gate
e. a passenger at the baggage claim
f. a taxi driver at the taxi stand

GRAMMAR

The Simple Past and the Past Progressive Tenses

To talk about a finished action in the past, we use the simple past tense. We use the past progressive tense (*was/were* + verb–*ing*) to show a continuing action or an incomplete action in the past interrupted by another action.

Simple Past	Yesterday, a tornado **struck** the airport. (*finished*)
Past Progressive	A baby **was crying** at the airport. (*continuing*)
	Passengers **were checking in** when the storm hit. (*interrupted*)

1 Read the sentences and circle the appropriate verb form.

When the storm hit, ...

_____	**a.** an agent	was checking in/checked in	passengers.
_____	**b.** passengers	were standing/stood	in line.
_____	**c.** the airport official	was seeing/saw	the black cloud.
_____	**d.** the lights	were going/went	out.
_____	**e.** the windows	were shattering/shattered.	
_____	**f.** people	were screaming/screamed.	
_____	**g.** alarms	were ringing/rang.	

2 In Exercise 1, which of the actions finished quickly and which were continuing? Write **F** for finished and **C** for continuing on the lines.

Time Clauses with *When, While, As*

When, while, and *as* introduce time clauses that show that two actions happened at the same time. *While* and *as* usually introduce a continuing action; *when* introduces a finished or completed action.

Talk About It

 Option: If students need extra practice with the simple past and past progressive tenses, postpone this activity until after you've completed the grammar exercises for this unit or Workbook Practice 4.

Presentation

❺ Ask selected students to model the dialogue for the class. Then have students work in pairs taking turns being the reporter and one of the interviewees as they work through all the items. Circulate and offer assistance. Make notes of student errors, but don't interrupt to correct them; you want to encourage fluency. Have selected pairs perform their dialogues for the class. Refer to your notes and write errors on the board without identifying who made them. Then correct the errors as a class.

Link *Workbook: Practice 3*

GRAMMAR

The Simple Past and the Past Progressive Tenses

Preview

With students' books closed, explain that the simple past tense is used to describe finished actions in the past. The past progressive tense is used to describe continuing, incomplete, or interrupted actions in the past. Give an example sentence: *Jeff was getting some lunch when the storm hit.* Draw a line on the

board to illustrate the continuing action in the past progressive (*Jeff was having some lunch*). Then draw an "X" on the line to show that the action in the simple past (when the storm hit) interrupted it. Give selected students key words (for example, *watch TV, phone ring*) and have them make a sentence: "I was watching TV when the phone rang."

Presentation

❶ Have students work alone and then compare answers with a partner.

Answers
a. was checking in **b.** were standing **c.** saw
d. went **e.** shattered **f.** were screaming
g. were ringing

❷ Students work alone and then compare answers with a partner.

Answers
a. C **b.** C **c.** F **d.** F **e.** F **f.** C **g.** C

Link *Workbook: Practices 4, 5*

 Option: Students tell a real or imaginary story about a close call using the simple past and past progressive tenses.

Time Clauses with *When, While, As*

Preview

Introduce **when**, **while**, and **as** and their uses. Explain that they can join sentences in the simple past and past progressive tenses.

❸ Have students work alone and then compare answers with a partner. Check answers as a class.

> **Answers**
> 1. was working 2. hit 3. jumped
> 4. exploded 5. was swimming 6. was trying
> 7. saw 8. saved 9. was waiting 10. ate
> 11. drank 12. started 13. found
> 14. was recovering 15. invited

Option: Write the following exercise on the board or make a copy for every student. Have students complete the sentences with the simple past or the past progressive of the verbs. When students have finished, go over the answers as a class. Ask students how they decided which tense to use.

1. We (**see**) _____ an accident while we (**wait**) _____ for the taxi.

2. When the *Titanic* started to sink, some passengers (**wear,** *neg.*) _____ life jackets.

3. As the children (**play**) _____ outside, it started to rain.

4. Pete (**take**) _____ my picture while I (**look,** *neg.*) _____.

> **Answers**
> 1. saw, were waiting 2. weren't wearing
> 3. were playing 4. took, wasn't looking

❹ Have students work alone and then ask and answer questions with a partner. Have selected students read items to the class.

> **Answers**
> **a.** What was Gloria doing when she heard the noise? Gloria was waiting at a traffic light when she heard the noise. **b.** What was Bonnie doing when she smelled smoke? Bonnie was buying a newspaper when she smelled smoke. **c.** What was Tim doing when he felt the explosion? Tim was working at his desk when he felt the explosion. **d.** What was Neal doing when he saw the accident? Neal was crossing the street when he saw the accident. **e.** What was Liz doing when she heard the explosion? Liz was getting (the) coffee when she heard the explosion. **f.** What was Mike doing when he felt the explosion? Mike was talking to his boss when he felt the explosion. **g.** What was Marco doing when he saw the fire? Marco was eating lunch when he saw the fire. **h.** What was Sue doing when she heard the crash? Sue was waiting for the bus when she heard the crash.

Option: Have students work in pairs to create sentences similar to the ones about famous events in history. Then have each pair pass their sentences to another pair to complete.

 Workbook: Practices 6, 7, 8

> **While** we were checking in, the tornado struck.
>
> **As** the plane was landing, a tornado hit.
>
> **When** the storm came in, I was driving to the airport.

Time clauses can come before or after the main clause, but the punctuation changes.

> **When the storm hit**, I was driving to the airport.
>
> I was driving to the airport **when the storm hit**.

3 Complete the passage with the correct form of the verb.

Poon Lim, a Chinese sailor, had a close call in 1943. He **(1. work)** _____ on a British ship when a torpedo **(2. hit)** _____ it. Poon Lim **(3. jump)** _____ into the water. The ship **(4. explode)** _____ while he **(5. swim)** _____ away from it.

Poon Lim was afraid. Then as he **(6. try)** _____ to keep his head above water, he **(7. see)** _____ a raft. The raft **(8. save)** _____ his life!

Poon Lim got into the raft. There was food inside. While he **(9. wait)** _____ for help, he **(10. eat)** _____ the food and **(11. drink)** _____ rainwater. When the food was gone, he **(12. start)** _____ to fish.

Poon Lim was on the raft for 133 days. Then, some Brazilian fishermen **(13. find)** _____ him on August 3, 1943. While he **(14. recover)** _____ from his close call, the United States **(15. invite)** _____ him to live in the U.S.A.

4 Yesterday afternoon at 12:30, a helicopter hit the side of a tall building. Describe what people were doing when the accident happened. With a partner, ask and answer questions using the cues below.

Example: (Mary/hear/sirens) (shop at mall)

A: What was Mary doing when she heard the sirens?

B: She was shopping at the mall when she heard the sirens.

a. (Gloria/hear/noise)   (wait/traffic light)
b. (Bonnie/smell/smoke)   (buy/newspaper)
c. (Tim/feel/explosion)   (work/desk)
d. (Neal/see/accident)   (cross/street)
e. (Liz/hear/explosion)   (get/coffee)
f. (Mike/feel/explosion)   (talk/his boss)
g. (Marco/see/fire)   (eat/lunch)
h. (Sue/hear/crash)   (wait/bus)

5 **Check Your Understanding** In which situations are you likely to use the simple past and the past progressive tense? Check your answers with the class.

- ☐ Talking about a close call
- ☐ Describing an earthquake experience
- ☐ Explaining why you were late
- ☐ Talking about a strange event on the bus
- ☐ Describing your recent trip to Bangkok
- ☐ Comparing a hurricane to a tornado

6 **Express Yourself** Work with a partner. Choose one of the situations you checked above. Imagine yourselves in the situation and write a dialogue.

LISTENING and SPEAKING

Listen: A News Story

1 **Before You Listen** How often do you listen to the news? What is your favorite part of the news—the local news, the international news, human interest stories, the sports, or the weather?

STRATEGY **Listening for Sequence** To understand the sequence of events in a story, listen for time words such as *first*, *then*, *after*, *finally*, *when*, *while*, and *as*.

2 Listen to the news story. Put the events in the correct order by numbering them from 1 to 7.

_____ **a.** Ms. Martin pushed the man while he was trying to run away.

_____ **b.** Ms. Martin hit the man with a bottle of milk.

_1_ **c.** Ms. Martin went shopping with her children.

_____ **d.** The police took the man away.

_____ **e.** A man walked toward her while she was putting the groceries in the trunk.

_____ **f.** The man fell over a bag of groceries.

_____ **g.** The man grabbed her purse.

☑ ❺ **Check Your Understanding** In this exercise, students determine in which situations the simple past and past progressive tenses would be used together. Students should work alone and then compare answers with a partner.

Answers
Both simple past and past progressive: Talking about a close call, Describing an earthquake experience, Explaining why you were late, Talking about a strange event on the bus
Simple past only: Describing your recent trip to Bangkok

❻ **Express Yourself** This activity is communicative and interactive. It connects the grammar points—in this case, the simple past and past progressive tenses—with students' personal lives. Have students write their dialogues and perform them for the class.

LISTENING and SPEAKING

Listen: A News Story

Presentation

❶ **Before You Listen** Have students work in small groups to read the questions and discuss what kind of news they like to watch and why. What are some of the news stories they remember listening to recently? Have selected students report to the class.

➡ **Listening for Sequence** With students' books closed, elicit which words students listen for when they are trying to determine the sequence of events. Then have students open their books, and introduce the time words listed there.

🎧 ❷ Play the recording or read the audioscript aloud one or more times. Then have students put the events in order.

Audioscript: The audioscript for Exercises 2 appears on page T154.

Answers
a. 4 b. 6 c. 1 d. 7 e. 2 f. 5 g. 3

✆ **Option:** Ask additional comprehension questions:
- What day does Mrs. Martin usually go grocery shopping? (Saturday)
- Where was Mrs. Martin when she first noticed the man? (in the parking lot)
- What did the thief fall over? (a bag of groceries)
- What happened when the thief woke up? (The police were waiting to take him away.)

✆ **Option:** Have students listen and write down verbs they hear in the simple past and past progressive tenses. Then have them retell what happened to Mrs. Martin in their own words.

 Workbook: Practices 9, 10

Pronunciation

Preview

- With students' books closed, read several sentences or a short dialogue aloud and have students take note of the words that are stressed and unstressed.

  Example:

  A: *Do **Kate** and **Beth** **like** their **jobs**?*
  B: *No, they **hate** their **jobs**.*
  A: *Why haven't they **left** their **jobs**?*
  B: *They **make** a lot of **money**.*

  Ask, *What do you notice about the stressed words? The unstressed words? Can you come up with any rules about which words are stressed and unstressed?* Next, have students open their books and go over the information in the chart. Were their predictions correct?

- Students read the explanation in the box in class or as homework.

Presentation

🎧 ❸ Play the recording or read the dialogue aloud. Students should listen the first time, practice saying the words along with the recording the second time, and read it with a partner (without the recording) the third time.

✳ **Option:** For further practice, have students identify the parts of speech of all the stressed and unstressed words in the dialogue.

🎧 ❹ Have students underline the stressed words and compare answers with a partner. Then play the recording or read the dialogue aloud one or more times so students can check their predictions.

Answers

A: can people predict earthquakes
B: Not really, 1975, Chinese predicted, 7.3 quake, two days before, struck, city, Haicheng
A: Wow, 7.3, Was, lot, damage
B: Yes, destroyed, 90 percent, buildings
A: How, know, coming
B: They noticed, series, minor quakes, beforehand, also, changes, water levels, wells, animals, acting strangely
A: that's amazing

---

❺ After checking correct word stress, have selected students read the dialogue for the class.

 Workbook: Practice 11

Speak Out

➡ **Telling a Story** Introduce the expressions in the box used to sequence events in a story.

✳ **Option:** You might want to teach some additional sequencing expressions: **as soon as, at that moment, before that, just then, later, suddenly, when.** Go over these expressions with students and give examples of their use. Have students practice using them in sentences.

Presentation

❻ Have students work alone to come up with a story of a close call. (If they've never had such an experience, have them tell an imaginary story.) To help them focus their thoughts, put these questions on the board:

- Where were you when it happened? What time was it? Who were you with?
- What exactly happened?
- How did you react?
- How did you feel before the event? After the event?

Students should practice telling their stories to a partner. The partner should ask questions to clarify the content of the story, for example, "And then what happened?" "What did you do next?" "What happened after that?" "How did it end?" Then ask selected students to tell their stories to the class.

✳ **Option:** Have the partners of selected students retell the stories they heard to the class.

Pronunciation

Content and Function Words

In speaking, the content words of a sentence are stressed and the function words are usually unstressed.

Content Words			Function Words		
Nouns	flood	fire	Pronouns	he	him
Verbs	strike	hit	Auxiliary Verbs	is	do
Adjectives	awful	afraid	Other Adjectives	my	this
Adverbs	quickly	suddenly	Articles	the	a/an
Question Words	who	what	Prepositions	on	in
Negatives	no	didn't			

  Listen to the dialogue. The stressed words are in bold type. Practice saying the dialogue with a partner.

A: **What** was **Andy doing when** the **volcano erupted**?

B: He was **reading** a **novel**.

A: **What** did he **do when** the **fire started**?

B: He **jumped** into the **pool**.

  Read the dialogue. Predict which words are stressed by underlining the words. Then listen to the dialogue to check your predictions.

A: Can people predict earthquakes?

B: Not really, but in 1975 the Chinese predicted a 7.3 quake two days before it struck in the city of Haicheng.

A: Wow! 7.3! Was there a lot of damage?

B: Yes, it destroyed 90 percent of the buildings.

A: How did they know it was coming?

B: They noticed a series of minor quakes beforehand. They also saw changes in the water levels of the wells. And the animals were acting strangely.

A: That's amazing!

5 With a partner, practice reading the dialogue, focusing on word stress.

Speak Out

 Telling a Story When you tell a story, you can use certain expressions to show the sequence of events.

 Have you ever had a close call? Was it an accident, a flood, a fire, a hurricane, or something else? Try to remember everything about it (e.g., time, place, people, your reactions and feelings). Work with a partner. Take turns telling your stories.

> It all began with …
> First of all …
> Then/After that …
> Finally …

Read About It

 Before You Read

  a. What causes earthquakes?

  b. What happens during an earthquake?

 Making Predictions Before you read a text, you should try to predict what it is about. To do this, preview the reading by looking at the title, headings, and any pictures and captions that come with the text.

 Look at the title of the article and the picture. Predict the kinds of information you will find in the text. Make a list and share it with the class.

The San Francisco Earthquake of 1906

The west coast of California is part of the Great Pacific Basin. More than 80 percent of the world's earthquakes occur in this area. In fact, California has about 1,000 earthquakes a year. Many of these
5 earthquakes are minor. They are so small that only animals and seismographs (machines that measure earthquakes) feel them. But about every 100 years, a major earthquake causes terrible losses of life and property. The famous San Francisco earthquake of
10 April 18, 1906, is an example.

At 5:15 on that spring morning, a few people were waking up, getting dressed, having breakfast, waiting for streetcars, or walking to work, but most San Franciscans were sleeping when the ground began to shake. One of the first buildings to fall was the city hall. Damages to this building alone totaled $7 million. Thousands of other
15 buildings followed. Broken electric wires and gas lines started many fires. Broken streets and water lines made it impossible for firefighters to put out the fires. Within twenty-four hours, the city was destroyed. Over 28,000 buildings burned. About 2,500 people died and 250,000 lost their homes.

One of the survivors was Enrico Caruso, the famous opera singer. When the
20 earthquake struck, he was staying at the Palace Hotel. The hotel's decorative glass dome shattered. Caruso escaped. He put a towel around his throat to protect his voice, grabbed his autographed picture of President Theodore Roosevelt, and ran out of the building.

Architects and engineers rebuilt San Francisco. In three years, over 20,000
25 buildings were built. All of them were bigger, stronger, and safer than the ones that were destroyed. Many scientists believe that San Francisco will experience a much stronger earthquake before 2006, the year this hundred-year cycle ends. Will San Francisco be able to survive another huge earthquake?

READING and WRITING

Read About It

Presentation

❶ Before You Read Have students work in small groups to discuss the questions. Don't correct at this point. Students should try to explain their ideas in their own words.

➡ **Making Predictions** Explain to students that they can often predict some of the content of an article by looking at its title, pictures, and captions.

❷ Have students work in groups to come up with questions they think will be answered in the article. Then put their ideas on the board. As students read the article, they can check to see if their questions were answered. Some of the questions the class might come up with:

- When (day and time) did the earthquake occur?
- Was there a lot of damage?
- How many people were hurt?
- What exactly happened?
- Was there a fire? A **tidal wave** (huge wave caused by strong winds)?
- Why do earthquakes happen in California?
- What did people learn from the earthquake of 1906?

Cultural Note: You may wish to share the following information about San Francisco with the class.

California, originally settled by Spain, was ceded to the United States in 1848. The population of San Francisco jumped from about 500 in 1846 to 25,000 in 1849 because of the discovery of gold in the surrounding area. In the rush to the gold fields, people did not take time to build safe buildings. In fact, most of the city was made of tents and wooden buildings. As a result, the city was built, burnt, and rebuilt six times between 1849 and 1851.

The earth's surface is divided into great moving plates. The San Andreas Fault is the boundary between two of these plates. The many earthquakes in the San Francisco area are the result of the San Andreas Fault. Hundreds of minor earthquakes occur each year as southwestern California slips to the northwest. Major earthquakes, such as those of 1906 and 1989, happen as a result of the pressure of the grinding plates.

❸ Have students read the text and answer the questions.

> **Answers**
> **a.** in the Great Pacific Basin **b.** No, most of these earthquakes are minor. They're noticed only by animals and seismographs. **c.** They were sleeping. **d.** before 2006

✦ **Option:** Ask additional comprehension questions:

- About how often does a major earthquake occur in the Great Pacific Basin? (about every 100 years)

- What was one of the first buildings to fall? (the city hall)

- What else happened during the earthquake? (Thousands of buildings fell. Broken electric wires and gas lines started many fires. The city was destroyed.)

- How many buildings burned? How many people died? How many people lost their homes? (Over 28,000 buildings burned. About 2,500 people died. About 250,000 people lost their homes.)

- What did Enrico Caruso do in the earthquake? (He put a towel around his throat, grabbed his autographed picture of President Theodore Roosevelt, and ran out of the Palace Hotel.)

- How long did it take architects and engineers to rebuild San Francisco? (about three years)

❹ Have students work alone to guess the meanings of the words from context. Go over the answers as a class.

> **Answers**
> **1.** i **2.** j **3.** a **4.** c **5.** d **6.** g **7.** b **8.** f **9.** h
> **10.** e

✦ **Option:** Have pairs of students pick out three or four other difficult words from the article. Each pair should hand their words to a neighboring pair and partners should try to guess the meaning of the words from context. Have students share their answers so everyone can benefit from the exercise.

✦ **Option: Vocabulary Notebooks** See page TEviii.

Think About It

Presentation

❺ Have students discuss the question in small groups and present their ideas to the class. Ask, *Would you ever move to an area if you knew it was in a dangerous location? If you already lived in such an area, would you stay?*

❻ Have students discuss the questions in pairs. Ask, *What would be some of the advantages to controlling nature? Are there any disadvantages?* Lead a class discussion.

✦ **Option:** Have students do research on a major disaster that happened in history. They should present their findings to the class and use illustrations, photos, and graphs to show what happened.

Write: The Concluding Sentence

Students read the presentation in class or for homework. Explain that a concluding sentence ties everything together to finish a paragraph or essay. A good concluding sentence gives a general idea about the paragraph topic.

3 Answer the questions.

    a. Where do about 80 percent of the world's earthquakes occur?

    b. Do people notice many of these earthquakes?

    c. What were most San Franciscans doing when the earthquake struck?

    d. When do scientists think there will be another major earthquake in San Francisco?

4 Use the context to guess the meanings of the words in the left column.

    ____ **1.** to occur (line 3)   **a.** important

    ____ **2.** minor (line 5)   **b.** to break into pieces

    ____ **3.** major (line 8)   **c.** destruction

    ____ **4.** losses (line 8)   **d.** to extinguish

    ____ **5.** to put out (line 16)   **e.** a repeating period of time

    ____ **6.** survivors (line 19)   **f.** to keep from danger

    ____ **7.** to shatter (line 21)   **g.** people who had a close call

    ____ **8.** to protect (line 21)   **h.** to take suddenly

    ____ **9.** to grab (line 22)   **i.** to happen

    ____ **10.** cycle (line 27)   **j.** not important

Think About It

5 Many people live in areas where dangerous events such as earthquakes and floods happen frequently. Why do people stay in these areas when they know about the danger?

6 Scientists have many instruments to help them get information about natural disasters such as earthquakes and volcanic eruptions. Do you think we will ever know enough to really control nature? Why or why not?

Write: The Concluding Sentence

A paragraph generally ends with a concluding sentence. This sentence pulls the paragraph together and tells the reader the paragraph is finished. The concluding sentence often restates the main idea in different words or summarizes the major points. It should follow naturally from the body of the paragraph.

7 Read the two paragraphs. For each, write a topic sentence on the line. Then check the best concluding sentence.

a.

_____.

First of all, I got to the train station late and I felt tired. Then, while I was waiting in line, a woman got ahead of me with her two screaming children. When I told her that I was first, she got angry and began shouting at me. Then, when I got on the train, I discovered that I had lost my ticket. When I got home, I was tired and angry.

☐ It was the last train ride I'll ever take.

☐ I take the train a lot.

b.

_____.

We were driving home when it started to rain. Suddenly, it began to rain harder and harder. In fact, it was raining so hard that we couldn't see anything. We were driving very slowly when we realized that the water was halfway up the side of the car.

☐ It was definitely a frightening experience.

☐ Tornadoes are dangerous too.

Write About It

8 Write a paragraph about a bad experience or a close call. Use time words in your story. Be sure you have a focused topic sentence, supporting sentences, and a concluding sentence.

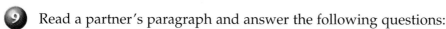

9 Read a partner's paragraph and answer the following questions:

a. Do all the supporting sentences relate to the main idea?

b. Are there any places where you would like additional information?

c. Does the conclusion follow naturally from the body of the paragraph?

 10 **Check Your Writing** After getting feedback from your partner, revise your paragraph as necessary. Use the questions below.

- Does the paragraph say what you want it to say?
- Are time words used to signal the order of events?
- Are verb tenses used correctly?

Presentation

❼ Tell students to first read each paragraph, choose the best concluding sentence, and then write a topic sentence on the line. They should read the paragraphs silently and ask any vocabulary questions.

> **Answers**
> a. **Possible topic sentence:** The last time I took the train, I had a bad experience.
> **Best concluding sentence:** It was the last train ride I'll ever take.
> b. **Possible topic sentence:** Traveling by car is not always safe.
> **Best concluding sentence:** It was definitely a frightening experience.

☻ Option: Have students write their topic sentences (anonymously) on a slip of paper and hand them in. Write some of the sentences on the board, and have students discuss why some make better topic sentences than others.

 Workbook: Practice 12

Write About It

Presentation

❽ Review words used to indicate the sequence of events. Have students write their own paragraph about a bad experience or a close call. They can do it in class or as homework. If students will do their writing at home, have them first brainstorm in class so that you can check that step. (Students may wish to write their paragraph about the close call stories they told to their partner in Exercise 6 in the Speak Out section on page 49.)

☻ Option: Since students have already dealt with this topic in the unit, you might want to have them write about a recent close call in the news or a famous close call in history. Before writing, students may need to do some research. Make sure they retell the story in their own words.

❾ Students exchange papers and do peer-editing. Make sure each student makes at least one positive comment about his/her partner's paragraph.

☻ Option: Students can also answer these questions when they're editing:

- Was the sequence of events clear?
- Was the story exciting? How can you make it more interesting for the reader?
- What would you like to learn about in greater detail?

☑ ❿ Check Your Writing Students should revise their paragraphs based on the suggestions given. Have them review the use of the simple past and past progressive tenses if necessary.

Vocabulary Expansion: Expressions with *get* See page T144.

> **Answers**
> A. 1. up 2. X 3. in 4. out of 5. on 6. off 7. to 8. X 9. X
> B. 1. c 2. h 3. e 4. a 5. b 6. g 7. d 8. f

EVALUATION

See page TExi.

Unit 5 Achievement Test

Self-Check See **Check Your Knowledge** on page 40 of the Workbook.

Dictation Have students review five or six of the sentences in Exercise 4 on page 45. Then present them as dictation. (See instructions on page TExv.)

Communication Skills

1. Ask students to tell you about a real or imaginary trip by plane. Pay attention to their use of airport vocabulary and sequencing words.

2. Ask students to tell you a story about a close call. Pay attention to their use of the simple past and past progressive tenses and time words.

THE BEST IN LIFE

OBJECTIVES

- To talk about advertising
- To use the superlative to compare three or more objects
- To make comparisons with adverbs and nouns
- To listen to draw conclusions
- To identify stressed syllables of numbers
- To argue, counterargue, and concede
- To notice examples
- To order supporting sentences
- To use adjectives ending in –able/–ible and –ful

GETTING STARTED

Warm Up

Preview

- With students' books closed, read the title of the unit. What do students think the unit is going to be about? What things/qualities/experiences do they think are the best in their lives? Lead a class discussion.

- Tell students about the English saying, "The best things in life are free." Do they agree? Can they give some examples? Is there a similar saying in their language?

- Check understanding of **product**, **ad(vertisement)**, and **persuade**. Show pictures of products from various magazine ads to explain those words. Ask what kinds of information are usually in an ad (color, size, price, etc.). You may wish to list these items on the board. Explain to students that the ads are trying to persuade the readers to buy the products shown.

🌀 Option: **Vocabulary Notebooks** See page TEviii.

Presentation

❶ Ask students if they usually read the ads in newspapers and magazines or if they generally ignore them. Have students work in pairs and then small groups to discuss the questions. First have students make a list of five or six things they have bought in the last two months. How did they find out about the products—by word of mouth or from a TV commercial? What persuaded them to buy the products? (You may wish to refer back to the information on the board.) Where did they buy them? Students should choose two items from their list to tell the other students about.

🌀 **Option:** Have students draw a picture of a product they have recently purchased. They should explain to the class why and where they bought it.

🌀 **Option:** Bring in several magazine ads in English and discuss them. Which ads are most convincing? Why? Take a survey and have students vote on the most effective ad.

🌀 **Option:** Before doing Exercise 2, have students anticipate the key words they might hear in the listening. Students should make a list and then check the key words they actually hear.

🎧 ❷ Make sure that everyone understands the exercise. Play the recording one or more times. Tell students they do not have to understand every word to do the activity.

Audioscript: The audioscript for Exercise 2 appears on page T155.

Answers
1. C **2.** A **3.** extra picture **4.** B

Language Note: You may want to tell students that **commercials** are ads on TV or radio. **Ad** is a more general term that includes advertisements printed in magazines and newspapers as well as commercials. You may want to have students discuss whether print ads or commercials are more effective.

 Workbook: Practice 1

GETTING STARTED

Warm Up

1 We often find out about new products from advertisements or "ads." Think of one or two products you bought because of ads. Where did you see the ads? How did the ads persuade you to buy the products?

2 You are going to hear three radio ads. What product is each trying to sell? Write the letter of the ad on the line. There is one extra picture.

1. _____

2. _____

3. _____

4. _____

Figure It Out

3 Describe your dream car. Is it a sports car or a luxury car? What special features does it have? Make a list. Compare your list with a partner's.

4 Look at the car in the ad below. What unusual features do you think the car has? Check the boxes.

- ☐ powerful engine
- ☐ bed
- ☐ stereo
- ☐ refrigerator
- ☐ TV
- ☐ telephone
- ☐ radio
- ☐ swimming pool
- ☐ microwave oven
- ☐ sauna

How much do you think this car costs? _____

How many drivers do you think it needs? _____

New From Luxury Motors!
The American Dream Car

Here is your chance to own the American Dream Car! You work hard to get the best things in life. Don't you deserve to have the very best car?

5 Now you can enjoy the most exciting car of your life—the American Dream! The American Dream is the longest, biggest, and most modern luxury car in the world.

10 The American Dream is the most comfortable car on the road! It is 60 feet (18.3 meters) long, and fifty of your closest friends can ride in it at the same time. Some of its special features 15 include a pool, a water bed, a refrigerator, a radio, ten telephones, three color TVs, a microwave oven, a stereo system, and more. It even has a landing pad for your helicopter!

The American Dream is the most 20 advanced, up-to-date car in the world. This amazing car has six wheels in front and ten wheels in back. The American Dream can go faster than any other car on the road. Its two 25 large, high-powered engines make it the most powerful car in the world. This car is so advanced that it needs two drivers, just like a jet plane!

The American Dream is the finest 30 car that you will ever own! Buy it for yourself or for your husband or wife. Luxury Motors will build an American Dream car for you for only $2 million.

Call your Luxury Motors salesperson 35 *right away and make an appointment today!*

Figure It Out

Preview

- Check understanding of **modern, feature**, and **amazing**. Show a picture of a computer or other complex machine and say, *The computer is a modern invention. It has a lot of amazing features*. Then list some of the features. (You may wish to refer to the list in the Warm Up Preview section.)

- Check understanding of **deserve**. Explain to students that if they work hard in class, they **deserve** to get a good grade.

Language Note: You might want to explain the phrase **the American Dream**. First ask students if they can guess what it refers to. Then explain that it has been used to describe what many Americans have traditionally felt was the ideal life: to own a house and a car, to have a good job at which they are successful because of their hard work, to be happily married and have children, and so on.

Option: Have students describe what a "dream life" would be like in their country. How is it similar to/different from the American dream?

Presentation

❸ Have students work in groups to make a list of special features in their dream car. Students should first decide on the type of car and proceed from there. You may want to introduce such types of cars as **convertible, hatchback, van, sedan, station wagon.**

Option: Have students come up with an ad for their dream car. What features are most important to highlight? Alternatively, have students think of an ad campaign for a car that is different from their dream car.

❹ Have students work alone to predict the unusual features they think the American Dream Car has and to answer the questions. Then have students compare predictions with a partner. Have students skim the article to check their predictions.

❺ Have students read the article on page 54 and find the answers. Review the answers as a class.

> **Answers**
> **a.** a pool, a water bed, a refrigerator, a radio, ten telephones, three color TVs, a microwave oven, a stereo system, a landing pad for a helicopter **b.** It has two large, high-powered engines. **c.–d.** *Answers will vary.*

◉ **Option:** Ask additional comprehension questions:

- How long is the American Dream Car? [60 feet (18.3 meters)] How many people can ride in it? (50 friends and 2 drivers)

- How many wheels does it have? (16—6 in front and 10 in back) How many drivers does it need? (2)

- How much does the car cost? ($2 million)

◉ **Option:** Ask additional discussion questions:

- Is the current trend (fashion direction) to build larger or smaller cars? What do you think is the reason for this trend?

- What would be some disadvantages to owning the American Dream Car?

◉ **Option:** After students have read the article, have them close their books. Ask students to recall the luxury features of the car.

☑ ❻ **Vocabulary Check** Have students work alone and then check answers with a partner. Assign this exercise as homework if there isn't time to finish it in class.

> **Answers**
> **1.** f **2.** d **3.** h **4.** j **5.** g **6.** a **7.** b **8.** c **9.** e **10.** i

 Workbook: Practice 2

◉ **Option: Vocabulary Notebooks** See page TEviii.

◉ **Option:** Have students play a memory game. The first student finishes the statement "The American Dream … " with a fact about the car; for example, "The American Dream is the biggest luxury car in the world." The next student has to repeat what the first student said and add an additional fact; for example, "The American Dream is the biggest luxury car in the world and it has a refrigerator." Each student adds a fact until someone makes a mistake. That person is out and the game resumes again.

Talk About It

◉ **Option:** If students need extra practice with the superlative or the comparative, postpone this activity until after you've completed the grammar exercises for this unit or Workbook Practice 4.

Presentation

❼ Ask selected students to model the dialogue for the class. Then have students work in pairs taking turns being the customer and the salesperson as they work through all the items. Circulate and offer assistance. Make notes of student errors, but don't interrupt to correct them; you want to encourage fluency. Have selected pairs perform their dialogues for the class. Refer to your notes and write errors on the board without identifying who made them. Then correct the errors as a class.

 Workbook: Practice 3

5 Answer the questions.

    a. What are the main luxury features of the American Dream?

    b. What makes the American Dream the most powerful car in the world?

    c. Would you like to own a car like this? Why or why not?

    d. Is having an expensive car important for a person's "image"? Why or why not?

6 **Vocabulary Check** Match the words with the correct meaning.

_____ **1.** chance (line 1)	**a.**	ahead of others
_____ **2.** to own (line 1)	**b.**	machine that converts energy into motion
_____ **3.** to deserve (line 4)	**c.**	strong
_____ **4.** luxury (line 9)	**d.**	to have, possess
_____ **5.** features (line 14)	**e.**	now
_____ **6.** advanced (line 21)	**f.**	opportunity
_____ **7.** engine (line 26)	**g.**	characteristics, qualities
_____ **8.** powerful (line 27)	**h.**	to have the right to
_____ **9.** right away (line 36)	**i.**	a time to meet
_____ **10.** appointment (line 36)	**j.**	very comfortable and expensive

Talk About It

A Luxury Motors salesperson is trying to persuade a customer to buy an American Dream car. Look at their conversation.

State a feature.

A: I'm looking for a really big car.

Persuade by describing the feature.

B: Then you'll like the American Dream. It's the biggest car in the world!

Ask for proof.

A: Is it really the largest car in the world?

Give proof.

B: Oh, yes. It's so big that you can land a helicopter on it.

7 With a partner, continue the conversation. The customer asks about:

a. length	**f.** power
b. comfort	**g.** speed
c. price	**h.** number of features
d. luxury	**i.** quality of engines
e. safety	**j.** reliability

The Superlative: Comparing Three or More Items

When we compare three or more items, we use the superlative form
of the adjective.

One-syllable adjectives: add **the –est**	The XE20 is **the fastest** computer in this store.
Two-syllable adjectives ending in **–y**: *change* **y** *to* **i** *and add* **the –est**	It is **the easiest** of all to use.
Adjectives with two or more syllables: use **the most** or **the least**	Naturally, the XE20 is **the most expensive**.
Exceptions: good → the best bad → the worst far → the farthest	But it's also **the best** computer on the market.

1 Complete the ad for Skyways with the superlative form of the
adjectives in parentheses.

Fly the best airline in the sky!

1. Fly _____ **(Good)** Airline in the Sky!

SKYWAYS is ...

2. _____ (safe) of all airlines.
3. _____ (friendly) in the skies.
4. _____ (reliable) in the air.
5. _____ (comfortable) in the world.
6. It serves _____ (good) food!
7. And it's _____ (expensive) anywhere!

Fly **SKYWAYS!** The Way to Get There Fast!

GRAMMAR

The Superlative: Comparing Three or More Items

Preview

- With students' books closed, introduce the superlative. Put three pens on your desk and say, *Which pen is the largest? Which pen is the most expensive?* etc. Can students come up with rules for forming the superlative?

- With students' books open, go over the information about forming the superlative in the chart. Review the comparative and superlatives for **good, bad, far**. You might also want to teach the irregular forms of the determiners **little** and **much/many**.

Adjective	Comparative	Superlative
good	better	the best
bad	worse	the worst
far	farther	the farthest
little	less	the least
much/many	more	the most

- You may wish to point out that one-syllable adjectives ending in a consonant add **–est** (fast → fastest), but one-syllable adjectives ending in a vowel add **–st** (large → largest). And some one-syllable words ending in a consonant (a consonant, a vowel, and a consonant: CVC) double the final consonant before adding **–est** (big → biggest). Review the information on irregular forms.

- Explain to students that there are many exceptions to the rules presented in the chart in their book. Advise them to consult a dictionary when in doubt. You may want to present some other exceptions.

Adjectives with two syllables that don't use *more/most*	Comparative	Superlative
narrow	narrower	the narrowest
simple	simpler	the simplest
clever	cleverer	the cleverest
quiet	quieter	the quietest

Adjectives with two syllables that can take either form	Comparative	Superlative
polite	politer more polite	the politest the most polite

Presentation

❶ Have students work alone and then compare answers with a partner.

Answers
1. the best **2.** the safest **3.** the friendliest **4.** the most reliable **5.** the most comfortable **6.** the best **7.** the least expensive

🌀 **Option:** Have students work in groups to prepare a skit about Skyway Airlines that they can perform for the class. Assign the following roles: narrator/announcer, passenger, flight attendant, and pilot. Students should talk about how wonderful the airline company is. Encourage students to exaggerate their skits to make them outrageous and funny.

❷ Have students work alone and then compare answers with a partner.

Answers
a. The most enormous b. the most famous
c. The most noticeable d. the greatest
e. The highest

 Option: Have students do some research and come to class with records from their city or country: the tallest building, the coldest recorded temperature, etc. They should present their findings to the class.

❸ Have students work alone making sentences using the superlative and supporting their opinions. (*Answers will vary.*)

Link *Workbook: Practices 4, 5, 6*

Note: You may wish to review the comparative form of the adjective (Unit 3, page 24, grammar chart) before students do Workbook Practice 4.

❹ Students should discuss their opinions with a partner. Alternatively, have students form small groups and discuss their opinions.

 Option: After students have completed Exercise 3, have them take a survey. They should interview five students and record their responses to the topics. Are there any matches? Students should report their findings to the class; for example, "I think Rome is the most beautiful city in the world. Maria likes Rome, too, but she thinks the most beautiful city is San Francisco."

 Option: Have students design an original form of transportation or an original house. Students should present their designs to the class and explain their drawings. The class should vote on which design is the most original, the funniest, the most comfortable, the most expensive, the most advanced, the prettiest, etc.

Making Comparisons with Adverbs and Nouns

Preview

• Review the information in the chart about the comparative and superlative of adverbs.

• Review the information in the chart about the comparative and superlative of nouns on page 58. If necessary, review the information on the irregular forms of **little** and **much/many** on page T56.

2 Complete the passage with the correct form of the adjectives in parentheses.

Advertising Signs

(a. enormous) _____ advertising sign in the world is in Kowloon, Hong Kong. It is 210 feet (64 meters) long and 55 feet (16.7 meters) high.

Every city in the world has signs telling people that they are entering the city, but the one in Hollywood, California is **(b. famous)** _____ in the world. It is in the hills above the city. Its letters are 30 feet (9 meters) wide and 45 feet (13.7 meters) tall.

(c. noticeable) _____ sign in the world was probably the Citroën sign on the Eiffel Tower. People could see it from as far as 24 miles (38.6 kilometers) away. It also had **(d. great)** _____ number of lightbulbs of any sign ever built, over 250,000. It was put up in 1925 and taken down in 1936.

(e. high) _____ sign in the world is on the top of a seventy-two-floor building in Toronto, Canada. It advertises a bank.

3 Give your opinion about the topics and then support your opinion.

Example: good/singer

In my opinion, Maria Bethania from Brazil is the best singer in the world because her voice is so beautiful.

a. beautiful/city	**d.** bad/habit	**g.** dangerous/sport
b. exciting/car	**e.** interesting/book	**h.** good/movie
c. nice/restaurant	**f.** enjoyable/music	**i.** idea of your own

4 Discuss your opinions with a partner. If you don't agree, give a reason. Use the model.

A: In my opinion, Garth Brooks is the best singer in the world.

B: I don't agree. I think Celine Dion is the best.

A: Really? Why do you think that?

B: She sings great songs in French and English.

Making Comparisons with Adverbs and Nouns

To form the comparative and superlative of adverbs, we use the same rules as for adjectives (see page 24).

Comparative

You know, the new XTR runs **faster** and **more efficiently than** the old XTR.

Superlative

Yes, in fact, it runs **the fastest** and **the most efficiently** of all computers on the market.

We can also use nouns in the comparative and superlative.

> **Comparative**
>
> The new XTR costs **less money** and has **more features than** the old one.
>
> **Superlative**
>
> And it uses **the least energy**, but has **the most power of** any computer on the market.

5 Complete the passage about Sam DuGood. Use the comparative or superlative form of the adjective, adverb, or noun in parentheses.

Only one month ago, Sam DuGood was tired and overworked. He was **(a. productive)** _the least productive_ of all the secretaries in the office. But now, thanks to vitamins and healthy living, he's **(b. good)** _____ secretary in the office. He arrives at work **(c. early)** _____, stays **(d. late)** _____, and he has **(e. energy)** _____ of everyone. He does **(f. work)** _____ and has **(g. talent)** _____ any of the other secretaries. In fact, he's **(h. efficient)** _____ secretary in the company. Don't let Sam DuGood do **(i. good)** _____ you!

6 Check Your Understanding In which situations are you likely to use the superlative? Compare you answers with a partner's.

- ☐ Choosing one of several possible gifts to buy someone
- ☐ Describing a frightening experience in your life
- ☐ Refusing an invitation to a party
- ☐ Persuading your colleagues to give an award to a fellow colleague
- ☐ Deciding to go to college in your country or abroad

7 Express Yourself With a partner, choose one of the situations you checked above. Imagine yourselves in the situation and write a dialogue.

LISTENING and SPEAKING

Listen: Advertisements

1 Before You Listen Describe two or three ads that you like a lot. Why do you remember them? What were the ads trying to sell? Who were the advertisers trying to sell their product to?

STRATEGY **Listening to Draw Conclusions** When you listen, you can draw conclusions from information that is directly stated and from information that is not.

2 Listen to four different ads. What products are the ads trying to sell?

a. _____ b. _____ c. _____ d. _____

Presentation

⑤ Have students work alone and then compare answers with a partner. Check answers as a class.

Answers

a. the least productive **b.** the best **c.** the earliest **d.** the latest **e.** the most energy **f.** more work **g.** more talent than **h.** the most efficient **i.** better than

Option: Have students write a brief paragraph or give a short oral presentation about one of the following topics:

- The best teacher I've ever had
- The most fun I've ever had
- The most challenging experience of my life

Option: Have a spelling contest for the superlative forms. Divide the class into two teams. Say an adjective. The first player from each team must go to the board and write the superlative form. Award a point for each correct spelling. The team with the most points wins.

Option: Have students work in small groups to play a description game. One student thinks of a classmate and the others must figure out who it is by asking questions with comparatives and superlatives. You may wish to write this example on the board:

A: Is he the tallest person in the class?
B: No, he isn't.
A: Well, is he taller than I am?
B: No, he's not as tall as you.
A: Is he one of the friendliest students in the class?
B: Yes, he is.
A: Is it Marco?
B: No. Try again.

 Workbook: Practice 7

☑ ⑥ Check Your Understanding In this exercise, students determine in which situations the superlative would be used. They should work alone and then compare answers with a partner.

Answers

Choosing one of several possible gifts to buy someone, Describing a frightening experience in your life, Persuading your colleagues to give an award to a fellow colleague, Deciding to go to college in your country or abroad

⑦ Express Yourself Have students work in pairs to write their dialogues and perform them for the class.

LISTENING and SPEAKING

Listen: Advertisements

Presentation

❶ Before You Listen Have students work in small groups to read the questions. Then have them bring in ads from newspapers and magazines to talk about. Ask, *Who is the target audience for each ad? How can you tell? Is the ad successful at appealing to that audience?*

➡ **Listening to Draw Conclusions** Explain to students that when we make conclusions from information that isn't stated, we are making inferences. Making inferences is an important skill when reading and listening in English.

❷ Play the recording or read the audioscript aloud one or more times. Have students write down what products are being sold.

Audioscript: The audioscript for Exercises 2 and 3 appears on page T155.

Answers

a. (Click) pens **b.** (Wheeler's Country Style) soups **c.** (Marie de Nouvelle Swiss) watches **d.** (Mary Jane's Flower Shop) flowers

🎧 ❸ Play the recording or read the audio-script aloud again. Have students take notes and guess who they think the ads are targeted at. Then have them compare answers with a partner.

Answers
Other answers are possible.
a. teenagers **b.** mothers, working women
c. adults **d.** children

 Workbook: Practices 8, 9

⊛ **Option:** Ask additional comprehension questions:

Ad 2: What does the woman do? (She's president of Skyways Airlines.) Why does she like Wheeler's Country Style Soup? (They taste better than homemade soup, and her family loves them.)

Ad 3: How are the Swiss watches described? (the most beautiful, most elegant, most expensive, and most accurate watches ever made)

Ad 4: Why are Jimmy and Dee Dee going to Mary Jane's Flower Shop? (It's their mother's birthday tomorrow.) When is the shop open? (from 9 a.m. to 9 p.m. Monday through Saturday and from 9 a.m. to 5 p.m. Sunday)

⊛ **Option:** Lead a class discussion. Ask, *Which ad did you find most interesting? Most annoying? Why?*

❹ Have students work in groups to discuss the questions. Ask selected students to report to the class.

⊛ **Option:** Explain to students that advertisers often target various groups: people of certain social groups, ages, incomes, or people with certain hobbies, etc. Give each pair or group of students a piece of paper with a different target audience (for example, women in their twenties) and have them design an ad for a product that would appeal to that audience.

Pronunciation

Preview

With students' books closed, say several numbers aloud. Have students raise their right hand if they hear the ending **–teen** and their left hand if they hear the ending **–ty**.

Presentation

🎧 ❺ Play the recording or read the phrases aloud. Students listen the first time, practice saying the phrases along with the recording the second time, and underline the correct syllables the third time.

Answers
a. teen, thir **b.** teen, for **c.** teen, fif
d. teen, six **e.** teen, seven **f.** teen, eigh

❻ Have students answer the questions.

Answers
The numbers ending in **–ty** (thirty, forty, etc.) have the stress on the first syllable. The numbers ending in **–teen** (thirteen, fourteen, etc.) have the stress on the second syllable.

⊛ **Option:** Divide the class into two teams. Turn away from the students so that they can't watch your mouth. Say a number. The first two representatives from each team have to rush to the board and write the number down. The first to write it correctly wins a point for his or her team. To make the game more challenging, read entire sentences so students have to listen to use of the number in context.

Speak Out

➡ **Arguing, Counterarguing, Conceding**
Introduce the different expressions used in giving opinions. Point out that expressions used for counterarguing include words like **yes**, **but**, and **maybe** to soften the tone.

Presentation

❼ Have students read the three paragraphs and work in groups to decide which person they think deserves the money. Circulate to make sure they use expressions for arguing, counterarguing, and conceding. Each group should then report to the class and explain their decisions. Tally the results on the board.

 Workbook: Practice 10

3 Advertisers try to sell their products to certain groups of people, such as adults, teenagers, children, or women. Listen to the ads again. Which group does each ad target?

a. _____ b. _____ c. _____ d. _____

4 Which of these products would you buy? Why? What information helped you draw your conclusions?

Pronunciation

> **Numbers: –teen vs. –ty**
>
> The **–teen** numbers (e.g. fifteen) and the **–ty** numbers (e.g. fifty) have different stressed syllables.

5 Pronounce each phrase after you hear it, and draw a line under the stressed syllable in each number.

a.	thir teen,	not	thir	ty	pesos
b.	four teen,	not	for	ty	dollars
c.	fif teen,	not	fif	ty	escudos
d.	six teen,	not	six	ty	francs
e.	seven teen,	not	seven	ty	pesetas
f.	eigh teen,	not	eigh	ty	drachmas

6 Which numbers have the stress on the first syllable? _____
Which numbers have the stress on the second syllable? _____

Speak Out

Arguing, Counterarguing, Conceding In giving opinions, you use expressions to argue your point, to counterargue (argue back), and to concede (give in).

Arguing	Counterarguing	Conceding
I'm sure you agree that …	Yes, but …	Well, maybe you're right.
Don't forget that …	Well, I think that …	I agree.
Don't you think that …	Well, maybe but …	You have a point there.

7 Every year the Drexel Company gives $5,000 to the worker who works the hardest and is the most needy. Work in groups. Decide which of these workers deserves the money. Use comparatives, superlatives, and the expressions above.

> **Peter Rosen** is a secretary. He works ten to twelve hours a day and is never absent from work. He has three children and his wife is in the hospital. Her hospital care is very expensive, and they don't know how they are going to pay for it.

Rodolfo Sanchez is an electrician. Last month, he put out a fire that was going to burn down the company office building. He has two children, a son and a daughter. He doesn't make much money and says that he only has enough money to send one of the children to college.

Alice Kim is a computer scientist. She just wrote a new computer program that will earn the company millions of dollars. She earns a lot of money. However, she has to pay back the money she used to pay for her college education.

READING and WRITING

Read About It

1 Before You Read

a. What kind of information would you expect to find in an article about advertising? Make a list.

b. How much money do you think U.S. companies spend on ads in a year? Write your prediction on the line. _____

 STRATEGY **Noticing Examples** When you read, you will understand more if you pay attention to examples that writers use to illustrate their ideas. Watch for expressions such as *for example, namely, that is,* and *for instance.* These signal that the writer is about to give an example.

The World of Advertising

Advertising is probably as old as the products it persuades us to buy. The first advertisements were oral. People with something to sell shouted the name of
5   the product and its cost in the street for everyone to hear. For example, people sold animals and food in this way. Written ads developed early, too. For instance, an ad from Greece over 3,000
10 years old mentioned a shop with the best cloth, and in ancient Rome, ads announced circuses. In the Middle Ages, advertisers used drawings as most people did not know how to read. In the 1600s, after the invention of printing, ads began to appear in newspapers. Since the 1700s, advertising has become increasingly important.

15   In today's world, it is difficult to imagine what it would be like without the hundreds of ads we see and hear every day. Advertising has so much importance now that companies spend billions of dollars every year to call attention to their products. In 1997, for example, U.S. companies spent over $180 billion on advertising.

give power to your eyes

mistica K2350

M

The new K2350. Taking pictures. Higher.™   **mistica cameras**

Option: Have different groups explain why their candidate should get the money. Give each group time to develop their arguments before presenting them to the class. Alternatively, this presentation could be done as a debate.

READING and WRITING

Read About It

Presentation

❶ Before You Read Have students work in small groups to discuss the questions. Students should try to explain their ideas in their own words. Don't correct at this point. Students should be prepared to explain how they reached their prediction for **b.** They should practice using expressions for arguing, counterarguing, and conceding.

➡ **Noticing Examples** Go over expressions used to introduce an example: **for example, namely, that is,** and **for instance.** Ask students if they can add any more expressions to the list.

Option: You may want to teach additional expressions used to introduce examples: **such as; Take _____, for example; An example of this is _____; To illustrate the point; To give you an example.**

❷ Have students read through the article and look for the answers to their predictions. Then have students read the article again and answer the questions.

Answers
a. over 3,000 years ago **b.** because they know ads are the most effective means of persuasion **c.** techniques include using a famous person in the ad to recommend the product, focusing on the customers' emotions, and using scientific test results

✪ **Option:** Draw a chart with these headings on the board. Ask the class to write in the examples:
- Three examples of early advertising
- One example of huge spending for ads
- Three examples of advertising techniques

✪ **Option:** Ask additional comprehension questions:
- What were the first advertisements like? (They were oral. People shouted the name and cost of their product in the street so everyone could hear.)
- What happened to advertising in the 1600s? (After the invention of printing, ads began to appear in newspapers.) What has happened to advertising since the 1700s? (Advertising has become increasingly important.)
- How much money did U.S. companies spend on advertising in 1997? (over $180 billion)
- How do advertisers focus on customers' emotions? (They try to make people feel bad or guilty because they don't use a certain product.)

✪ **Option:** Ask additional discussion questions:
- Why do you think some advertising techniques are better than others for certain products? Give examples.
- Should advertisers be controlled by the government?

- Should products such as alcohol or cigarettes be advertised on TV? Give reasons.

❸ Have students work alone to guess the meanings of the words from context and then compare answers with a partner. Go over the answers as a class.

Answers
1. f **2.** h **3.** g **4.** c **5.** b **6.** a **7.** e **8.** d

✪ **Option: Vocabulary Notebooks** See page TEviii.

❹ Have students work alone and then compare answers with a partner.

Answers
For example, people sold animals and food in this way.
For instance, an ad from Greece over 3,000 years ago ...
In 1997, for example, U.S. companies spent over $180 billion on advertising.
In some ads, for example, actors, sports stars, or singers recommend products.

Think About It

Presentation

❺ Have students bring in or describe their favorite ads. Alternatively, they can describe their favorite commercials. Encourage students to explain why they like the ads/commercials. Discuss the techniques and effectiveness of the various ads/commercials.

❻ After students have discussed their opinions with a partner, lead a class discussion.

❼ Have students discuss the question with partners. Can they think of any problems that could arise from dishonest advertising? Have pairs make a list of possible problems and share it with the class.

20 Advertisers spend these huge sums of money because they know that ads are the most effective means of persuasion. The writers of the best ads use many different techniques to persuade the public. In some ads, for example, actors, sports stars, or singers recommend products. The advertiser hopes that the public will believe the person because he or she is famous. Another method focuses on the customers' emotions. These ads try to make people feel bad or guilty because they don't use

25 a certain product like a brand of cereal or a kind of detergent. Another method, the scientific approach, uses scientific test results to show that products work well.

Advertisers use all of these methods and many more in the hope that people will buy the newest, best, and most exciting product—theirs.

2 Answer the questions.

   a. When did printed ads first appear?

   b. Why do advertisers spend so much money on ads?

   c. What are two techniques that advertisers use to persuade buyers?

3 Use the context to match each word with its meaning.

   _____ **1.** oral (line 3)   **a.** quantities

   _____ **2.** to announce (line 12)   **b.** to get people to notice

   _____ **3.** drawings (line 12)   **c.** to be seen in

   _____ **4.** to appear (line 14)   **d.** way

   _____ **5.** to call attention to (line 17)   **e.** to say something is good

   _____ **6.** sums (line 19)   **f.** said or spoken

   _____ **7.** to recommend (line 22)   **g.** pictures

   _____ **8.** method (line 25)   **h.** to inform the public about

4 Scan the article for phrases that introduce examples and underline them. Then identify the example that each phrase introduces. Compare your answers with a partner's.

Think About It

5 Describe some of your favorite ads. Why do you like them? What techniques do they use?

6 Do you think it is right for advertisers to spend so much money on ads? Why or why not?

7 Is advertising honest? Explain your opinion.

Write: Ordering Supporting Sentences

One way to organize a paragraph is using chronological order. Another way to order supporting sentences is according to importance (from the most important to the least or from the least important to the most). This is called rank order. We use words and expressions such as *first of all, second, main,* and *most importantly* to show rank order.

8 In your opinion, what are the most important criteria? Rank the criteria from 1 (most important) to 5 (least important).

   a. Advantages of buying a new car:

      ____ low price   ____ comfortable seats   ____ nice color

      ____ large size   ____ powerful engine

   b. Advantages of buying a house:

      ____ many rooms   ____ large pool   ____ close to work, school

      ____ big yard   ____ friendly neighborhood

9 Read the sentences below. Write **T** in front of the topic sentence. Number the supporting sentences in order from 1 to 4. Write **C** in front of the concluding sentence.

   ____ **a.** When you get to California, rent your car from Honest Joe's Car Rental Service and visit California the right way!

   ____ **b.** There are many advantages to visiting California by car.

   ____ **c.** Also, most roads are toll free and in good condition.

   ____ **d.** However, the best reason of all is that public transportation is slow, inconvenient, expensive, or often unavailable.

   ____ **e.** Another advantage is that gasoline is cheap and available everywhere.

   ____ **f.** First of all, there is an extensive system of roads, which connects every point on the map.

10 How did you decide on the order of the sentences? Underline all the words and phrases that helped you order the sentences.

Write About It

11 Write a paragraph persuading your audience to buy a particular product or service. First, choose a product or service that you know well. Brainstorm and focus your ideas. Then write your paragraph. Include a topic sentence, at least five supporting sentences, and a concluding sentence. Use words that show order of importance.

 12 **Check Your Writing** Exchange paragraphs with a partner. Use the questions below to suggest areas that need revision. Discuss your papers and revise as needed.

- Is the paragraph persuasive?
- Are the supporting sentences ranked by importance?
- Are words used to signal the order of importance?

Write: Ordering Supporting Sentences

Students read the presentation in class or for homework.

Presentation

8 Have students work alone ranking the criteria for buying a new car and buying a house. Explain that there is no single correct answer. Students should rank the items according to how *they* feel about them. Take a class survey. Did most of the class rank the criteria in a similar way? (*Answers will vary.*)

9 Have students read the sentences, choose the topic sentence and concluding sentence, and then rank the supporting sentences. Review the answers as a class.

> **Answers**
> a. C b. T c. 2 or 3 d. 4 e. 2 or 3 f. 1

10 Ask selected students to explain how they ordered the sentences. Point out the words and expressions **also** (c), **another** (e), and **first of all** (f).

Write About It

Presentation

11 Have students choose a product or service and write a paragraph persuading their audience to buy it. They can do this exercise in class or as homework. If students will do their writing at home, have them first brainstorm in class so that you can check that step.

 Workbook: Practice 11

Option: If students are having trouble getting started on the given topic, write this exercise on the board or duplicate and hand out copies. Have students rank the supporting sentences for each topic and then write a paragraph including topic and concluding sentences.

Advantages of living in a foreign country:

_____ Learn a new language

_____ Get acquainted with a new culture

_____ Understand your own culture better

_____ Buy lots of souvenirs

☑ 12 Check Your Writing Students revise their paragraphs based on the suggestions given. Have them review making comparisons if necessary.

Option: Students can also answer these questions when they're editing:

- What could have made the paragraph more persuasive?

- What was the most/least convincing argument?

Vocabulary Expansion: Adjectives ending in *–able/–ible* **and** *–ful* See page T145.

> **Answers**
> A. 1. helpful 2. beautiful 3. careful
>   4. comfortable 5. collectible 6. believable
> B. 1. helpful 2. beauty 3. careful
>   4. comfortable 5. collect 6. believe

EVALUATION

See page TExi.

Unit 6 Achievement Test

Self-Check See **Check Your Knowledge** on page 48 of the Workbook.

Dictation Have students review five or six of the sentences in Exercise 2 on page 57. Then present the sentences as a dictation. (See instructions on page TExv.)

Communication Skills

1. Bring in several objects and have students describe and compare them using the superlative.

2. Ask students to bring in a picture of a product and persuade you to buy it. Pay attention to their language of persuasion and sequencing of ideas.

Review Units 4–6

The review exercises can be assigned as homework or done in class. You can use them in different ways.

- Give the review exercises as a quiz. Students work alone and turn in their answers to you.

- Use the review exercises as you would other exercises in the book. Students work alone and then compare answers with a partner.

- Have students work alone and then go over answers as a class. Have selected students write their answers on the board and correct any errors together.

❶ Have students read the instructions and complete the exercise. For a comparison of the simple past and past progressive tenses, have students refer to Unit 5, pages 46–48.

Answers
1. bought 2. took 3. was playing 4. went out 5. called 6. was dialing 7. remembered 8. didn't pay

❷ Have students read the instructions and complete the exercise. For a comparison of the simple past and past progressive tenses, have students refer to Unit 5, pages 46–48.

Answers
1. tried 2. was 3. Were (you) talking 4. was using 5. was 6. Were (you) working 7. was listening 8. got

❸ Have students read the instructions and complete the exercise. For a review of adverbs of sequence (time expressions), have students refer to Unit 4, pages 37–38. For a review of **when** and **while**, have students refer to Unit 5, pages 46–47.

Answers
1. After 2. when 3. then 4. While 5. soon 6. finally

1 Complete the passage with the correct form of one of the verbs in the box. Use the simple past or past progressive tense.

buy	play
call	remember
dial	take
go out	pay

Yesterday I **(1.)** _____ a new CD by Rock N. Roller and the Broken Bones Band. I **(2.)** _____ it home to listen to right away. While I **(3.)** _____ it, the electricity **(4.)** _____ . I **(5.)** _____ the electric company to complain, but as I **(6.)** _____ their number, I **(7.)** _____ I **(8. neg.)** _____ the bill last month!

2 Complete the conversation with the correct form of the verbs in parentheses. Use the simple past or past progressive tense.

KIM: Hey, Pam. I **(1. try)** _____ to call you last night, but your line **(2. be)** _____ busy.

PAM: Hi, Kim. I know. I'm sorry.

KIM: **(3. talk)** _____ you _____ to your boyfriend?

PAM: No. I **(4. use)** _____ my computer. I **(5. be)** _____ on the Internet.

KIM: Oh. **(6. work)** _____ you _____ on your project for history class?

PAM: No. I **(7. listen)** _____ to a live interview with the Broken Bones Band.

KIM: Really? I just **(8. get)** _____ their new CD. I really like it.

3 Complete the paragraph with an appropriate time expression from the box.

after	then
finally	when
soon	while

Last night was Rock N. Roller's big concert. **(1.)** _____ Rock N. Roller finished singing, he smashed his guitar on stage. Karen was watching Rock on stage **(2.)** _____ a piece of his guitar hit her on the head. Karen didn't think she was hurt, but **(3.)** _____ she noticed she had a lump on her head, so she went to the first aid station. **(4.)** _____ she was waiting at the first aid station, a reporter took her picture. An article about Karen **(5.)** _____ appeared in the local paper. Karen saved that piece of Rock's guitar for a while, but she **(6.)** _____ sold it to a rock and roll collector for several hundred dollars!

4 Complete the paragraph with the correct form of the adjectives in parentheses.

And now, here's the weather. As you listeners know, a tornado struck Park City Airport yesterday morning. Since then, two more tornadoes have done damage in the area. The last of the three was **(1. serious)** _____. It lasted **(2. long)** _____ and caused **(3. great)** _____ damage. Local business owners say that this tornado was **(4. bad)** _____ in the area's history. The mayor, however, has good news. Park City will receive **(5. large)** _____ share of money from the state's emergency relief fund. And now, back to our music. Here's **(6. popular)** _____ song from Will Smith's new CD.

5 Write sentences comparing the three vases of flowers. Use comparative and superlative forms of adjectives in the box.

elegant	large
expensive	simple
good	pretty

a. _____

b. _____

c. _____

d. _____

e. _____

Vocabulary Review

Use the words in the box to complete the sentences.

advertising	luxury
damage	performance
deserve	power
feature	survivors
height	talent

1. The American Dream car is the biggest _____ car in the world.

2. Celine Dion's _____ of her hit song was wonderful!

3. The flood caused eight million dollars' worth of _____ to the area.

4. Many international companies spend millions of dollars on _____.

5. The _____ I like the best about the American Dream car is the swimming pool!

6. The _____ of the plane crash waited two days before help came.

7. Ben and Betty _____ the award because they worked the hardest.

8. My cousin has real _____ as a country singer; you should hear her.

❹ Have students read the instructions and complete the exercise. For a review of the superlative, have students refer to Unit 6, pages 56–58.

Answers
1. the most serious 2. the longest
3. the greatest 4. the worst 5. the largest
6. the most popular

❺ Have students read the instructions and complete the exercise. For a review of the comparative, have students refer to Unit 3, page 24. For a review of the superlative, have students refer to Unit 6, pages 56–58.

Answers
Other answers are possible.
a. The third vase of flowers is the largest (larger than the other two). **b.** The third vase of flowers is the most expensive (more expensive than the other two). **c.** The third vase of flowers is the most elegant (more elegant than the other two). **d.** The third vase of flowers is the prettiest (prettier than the other two). **e.** The first vase of flowers is the simplest (simpler than the other two).

Vocabulary Review

Have students read the instructions and complete the exercise.

Answers
1. luxury 2. performance 3. damage
4. advertising 5. feature 6. survivors
7. deserve 8. talent

THE PERFECT MATCH

OBJECTIVES

- To talk about job interviews
- To use the present perfect tense to relate the past to the present
- To use the present perfect tense to talk about repeated past actions
- To use the present perfect tense with **How long**
- To understand grammar clues
- To identify sentence stress
- To make generalizations
- To make inferences
- To write supporting details
- To use adjectives ending in **–ing** and **–ed**

GETTING STARTED

Warm Up

Preview

- Lead a discussion about jobs and job interviews. Ask, *What qualifications (type of experience, skill) does someone need to get a good job?* If necessary, introduce or review **salary, education, major, graduate, personality,** and **experience.** Say, *Joe makes $100 a week. His **salary** is very low.* Then say, *Bill went to a good high school and an excellent university. He got a good **education.*** Say, *In college, students **major** in a certain subject, such as English or science.* Then tell students that when people finish school, they **graduate.** Say, *I'm going to describe Diane's **personality.** She is friendly and outgoing.*

  Continue: *Eileen has worked here for fifteen years. She has a lot of **experience.***

- Check understanding of **employer, employee, apply, application,** and **improve.** Say, *An **employee** works for someone. The **employer** is the boss.* Say, *Jerry needs a job. He is going to **apply** for a job at the Smith Company.* For **application,** use realia. Say, ***Editors** are in charge of making books, newspapers, and magazines.*

Option: Vocabulary Notebooks See page TEviii.

Presentation

❶ Have students work in small groups to answer the questions.

Option: You may want to ask students: *What points are important to keep in mind when preparing for an interview?*

Option: Have students work in pairs to write (and perform) a quick sketch of a typical interview using the new vocabulary words.

❷ Play the recording or read the audioscript aloud one or more times.

Audioscript: The audioscript for Exercise 2 appears on page T155.

> **Answers**
> **Conversation 1:** experience **Conversation 2:** education **Conversation 3:** reason for leaving last job

Option: Ask additional questions:

Conversation 1: What does Ms. Christie like to do? (travel, do restaurant work)

Conversation 2: What job is Mr. Fox applying for? (editor)

Conversation 3: What does Ms. Roberts dislike about her current job? (Employees have to work 12 to 14 hours a day and on Saturdays and Sundays; the boss doesn't pay a person who arrives even a minute late.)

Option: Ask additional discussion questions:

- Which job applicant is best qualified for the job? Why do you think that?

 Workbook: Practice 1

Figure It Out

See page T66.

THE PERFECT MATCH

GETTING STARTED

Warm Up

1. What kinds of information do employers want to find out during job interviews? How can you best get ready for a job interview? Make a list of answers for each question.

2. Listen to the conversations. What information is the employer trying to find out from each job applicant? Write the number of the conversation in the correct box.

   ☐ education
   ☐ reason for leaving last job
   ☐ present salary
   ☐ number of years at last job
   ☐ experience

Figure It Out

Discoveries magazine is looking for a reporter to travel all over the world and write adventure articles. Ms. Tyler is interviewing Cristina Vela for the job.

A.

Ms. Tyler: So, Ms. Vela, you're interested in working for *Discoveries?*

Cristina: That's right. I've written lots of articles for newspapers.

Ms. Tyler: Oh? What newspapers have you worked for?

Cristina: Well, I've sold articles to the *New Kensington Star* and a few other newspapers.

Ms. Tyler: Have you ever written an adventure article?

Cristina: No, I haven't, but I've done some adventurous things to get information for my articles. I've even taken risks.

Ms. Tyler: Tell me about one of them.

Cristina: Well, once I wanted to report on prisons, so I stole something from a store. I spent five days in prison. It was horrible, but later I wrote an article about my experiences there. When the public read the article, they were upset and complained. Since then, the prisons have really improved.

Ms. Tyler: That certainly is interesting and adventuresome.

B.

Ms. Tyler: And how long have you been a reporter for the *Star?*

Cristina: Since last July … so, for about a year.

Ms. Tyler: And why are you applying for a job with us?

Cristina: Because I'd like to work abroad. I've never crossed the Atlantic.

Ms. Tyler: Have you ever been up the Amazon River?

Cristina: No, I haven't, but I'd love to go. I've always dreamed about doing a story on the rain forests.

Ms. Tyler: Well, Ms. Vela, I like your enthusiasm. I think you'd be perfect for the job. When can you start?

3 Answer the questions.

a. What kind of person is *Discoveries* magazine looking for?

b. What experience does Cristina Vela have?

c. How did Cristina get information for her article on the prison?

d. Do you think Cristina Vela is right for the job? Why or why not? Would you want this job?

e. People have different criteria for choosing a job, such as money or flexible work hours. What criteria are important to you?

4 Vocabulary Check Match the words with their meanings.

_____ **1.** employer   **a.** boss

_____ **2.** salary   **b.** to do things that can be dangerous

_____ **3.** to take risks   **c.** unhappy and angry

_____ **4.** to upset   **d.** to say bad things about

_____ **5.** to complain   **e.** interest, excitement

_____ **6.** enthusiasm   **f.** money paid for work

Figure It Out

Preview

Check understanding of **adventure, take risks, prison, upset,** and **enthusiasm.** Ask students what kinds of movies they like and list the names of some **adventure** movies. Explain that a person who does something dangerous is **taking a risk.** The person may succeed, but there is a chance of failure. Tell students that people who are convicted of crimes such as stealing are sent to **prison.** Ask students what makes them happy, sad, and **upset.** Explain that **upset** is not as strong as **angry.** Ask students what their hobbies are. Ask what they are **enthusiastic** about doing in their free time. Tell students that **improve** means "become better."

Presentation

❸ Have students read the interview and answer the questions.

> **Answers**
> **a.** Someone with enthusiasm who has experience writing adventurous, interesting newspaper articles. **b.** She's sold articles to the *New Kensington Star* and a few other newspapers. She's also done adventurous things to get information for her articles. **c.** She stole something from a store and spent five days in prison. **d.** and **e.** Answers will vary.

🜨 **Option:** Write the following exercise on the board. Ask students to name their most important criteria in choosing a job. Would they add any criteria to the list? Have students rank the criteria from most important to least important. Then have them compare their ratings in pairs, in small groups, or as a class. Do they agree? Which criteria do most students feel are important? Unimportant?

_____ money

_____ power

_____ adventure

_____ being famous

_____ personal interests

_____ family's opinion

🜨 **Option:** Ask additional comprehension questions:

- How did the public react to Cristina's article on prisons? (They were upset and complained.) What happened because of that reaction? (The prisons improved.)

- How long has Cristina been a reporter for the *Star*? (for about a year)

- Why is Cristina applying for the job? (She'd like to work abroad. She's never crossed the Atlantic.)

- Why would she like to visit the Amazon? (She's always dreamed about doing a story on the rain forests.)

🜨 **Option:** Ask if students can think of any additional questions Ms. Tyler could ask. Have pairs of students make up short dialogues in which Ms. Tyler is more interested in Cristina's education, last job, career goals, and so on. Students should perform their skits for the class.

🜨 **Option:** Point out the word **adventurous** in the dialogue. Can students think of other adjectives that end in **–ous?** (famous, dangerous) Ask, *What are the noun forms of these adjectives?* (adventure, fame, danger)

☑ ❹ **Vocabulary Check** Have students work alone and then check answers with a partner. Assign this exercise as homework if there isn't time to finish it in class.

> **Answers**
> **1.** a **2.** f **3.** b **4.** c **5.** d **6.** e

 Workbook: Practice 2

🜨 **Option: Vocabulary Notebooks** See page TEviii.

Talk About It

 Option: If students need extra practice with the present perfect tense, postpone this activity and Workbook Practice 3 until after you've completed the grammar exercises for this unit or Workbook Practice 4.

Presentation

❺ Ask selected students to model the dialogue for the class. Then have students work in pairs taking turns being the employer and the job applicant as they work through all the items. Circulate and offer assistance. Make notes of student errors, but don't interrupt to correct them; you want to encourage fluency. Have selected pairs perform their dialogues for the class. Refer to your notes and write errors on the board without identifying who made them. Then correct the errors as a class.

 Option: Have students brainstorm other jobs and the experience necessary to do them. Pairs of students should write interviews and perform them for the class. After each presentation, ask the class if they think the applicant would get the job or not.

Workbook: Practice 3

GRAMMAR

The Present Perfect: Relating the Past to the Present

Preview

• With students' books closed, ask questions using **Have you ever ...** and the present perfect tense; for example, *Have you ever been abroad? Where have you traveled in your own country?* Pay attention to how students use the present perfect tense in their answers, but don't correct errors yet.

• Explain that we use the present perfect when we're thinking about how something in the past has had an impact on the present. We use this tense with time expressions that mean "for the time up to the present," such **as ever**, **so far**, and **up to now**. The present perfect tense is often used in news reporting to describe recent news events that have happened in the past: A tornado *has flattened* the downtown area. Two burglars *have stolen* a Picasso painting from the city museum. The present perfect is not used if a specific time in the past is mentioned. Instead, the simple past is used; for example, Yesterday afternoon, a tornado *flattened* the downtown area. Last night around midnight, two burglars *stole* a Picasso painting from the city museum.

• Introduce **journalism** (the activity of writing for newspapers, TV, etc.) Say, *A **journalist** is someone who writes for the newspapers, magazines, radio, TV, etc.*

Talk About It

 5 With a partner, take turns being an employer and a job applicant. Ask and answer questions using the cues.

Example:

job: reporter
experience: writes articles for the *Herald*/a year

State job and ask about past experience.

A: I see you want a job as a reporter. What kind of experience have you had?

Tell experience.

B: Well, I've written several articles for the *Herald*.

Ask about length of time.

A: And how long have you worked at the *Herald*?

Tell length of time.

B: For about a year.

a. **job:** history teacher   **experience:** teaches at Valley High School/September 1989

b. **job:** computer technician   **experience:** fixes computers for Unex/last March

c. **job:** store clerk   **experience:** sells records at Cactus Records/five years

d. **job:** tennis teacher   **experience:** works for Atlas Health Club/five months

e. **job:** waiter   **experience:** works at Maxim's Restaurant/August 1996

GRAMMAR

The Present Perfect: Relating the Past to the Present

We use the present perfect tense (*have*/*has* + past participle) to talk about an action that happened sometime in the past, but is still relevant in the present. This use is often signaled by time words such as *before, ever, so far, up to now, always,* and *never.*

> **A:** **Have** you ever **worked** as a journalist?
>
> **B:** I've never **worked** for a daily, but last year the local newspaper published one of my stories.
>
> **A:** Really? What other kinds of stories **have** you **written**?
>
> **B:** So far, I've only **written** this one.

1 Many common verbs have irregular past participles. Complete the chart with the past participles.

is	was	_____	do	did	_____	begin	began	_____
have	had	_____	take	took	_____	get	got	_____
go	went	_____	make	made	_____	see	saw	_____
write	wrote	_____	come	came	_____	meet	met	_____

2 Melanie Gibson is interviewing Indira Jones for a job as a guide. Write the correct form of the verb on the line.

MELANIE: So, Indira, you want to be an adventure guide in the Andes.

INDIRA: Yes, Ms. Gibson, I **(1. always, love)** _____ the Andes.

MELANIE: And **(2. you, ever, work)** _____ as an adventure guide before?

INDIRA: Yes, so far I **(3. take)** _____ a group of grandmothers on a white-water raft trip in Colorado. And two years ago, I **(4. cross)** _____ a 16,000-foot mountain pass in Nepal with a group of teens … in the winter.

MELANIE: Impressive, but the Andes are different. **(5. you, study)** _____ to be a guide?

INDIRA: Well, last summer I **(6. take)** _____ a course in outdoor survival. They **(7. teach)** _____ us about outdoor medical emergencies. But generally, in my life, I **(8. learn)** _____ most from hands-on experience.

MELANIE: Well, Indira, you sound like the perfect guide for an adventure trip to Machu Pichu.

The Present Perfect: Repeated Past Actions

The present perfect tense also expresses an action that has repeated at unspecified times in the past. To ask questions, we use *How many* or *How often*.

> **A:** How many adventure stories **have** you **written** so far?
>
> **B:** Well, up to now, I**'ve finished** four, but I'm working on another now.
>
> **A:** How often **have** you **had** a close call on these trips?
>
> **B:** Only four times. I**'ve had** good luck.

Presentation

❶ Have students work alone to fill in the past participles and then compare answers with a partner.

> **Answers**
> **Column 1:** been, had, gone, written
> **Column 2:** done, taken, made, come
> **Column 3:** begun, gotten, seen, met

Language Note: The irregular past participle of **get** in British English is **got**. In American English, it is **gotten**, except when used with **have**: **have got**.

Ⓢ Option: Have students compete in a spelling bee. Say the base form of a verb and have students say and then spell the past participle. Each correct answer earns 1 point. You can play this game with students competing against each other individually or as teams. Mix up regular and irregular past participles. The student/team with the most points at the end of the game wins.

Ⓢ Option: Read several sentences in the present perfect tense without contracting the subject and verb. Have students say the subject-verb back in its contracted form. You can use sentences like these: *I have* never studied French. *She has* applied for a job there. *We have* always tried our best.

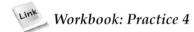 *Workbook: Practice 4*

❷ Have students work alone and then compare answers with a partner.

> **Answers**
> 1. have/'ve always loved 2. have you ever worked 3. have/'ve taken 4. crossed
> 5. Have you studied/Did you study 6. took
> 7. taught 8. have/'ve learned

Ⓢ Option: Have pairs of students develop their own quiz of five or six sentences using the simple past or present perfect tense (with blanks for the answers). Check the sentences and then have students exchange papers with neighboring partners and take the quiz for further practice in contrasting the simple past and the present perfect.

The Present Perfect: Repeated Past Actions

Preview

- Ask selected students questions with **How many** and **How often**. Don't correct errors yet, but do take note of whether students use the present perfect tense or not.

- Go over the dialogue in the box. Explain that the present perfect can be used to talk about how often something was repeated in the past.

Presentation

❸ Have students work with a partner to ask and answer questions. Then ask students to report to the class some of their partners' answers. While students are discussing their life experiences, encourage partners to ask follow-up questions to get more information.

Answers

a. How many times/How often have you traveled abroad? **b.** How many times/How often have you attended a concert? **c.** How many times/How often have you had a close call? **d.** How many times/How often have you used the Internet? **e.** How many times/How often have you fallen in love? **f.** How many times/How often have you fallen asleep in class? **g.** How many times/How often have you lost something important? **h.** *Answers will vary.*

The Present Perfect Tense with *How long*

Preview

Explain the different uses of **for** and **since** with the present perfect tense. We use **for** when discussing a length of time in the past: for a week, for a long time. **Since** is used when referring to a starting time in the past: since 1989, since last Wednesday. Ask selected students to make up sentences about their own life experiences using **for** and **since** and the present perfect.

Presentation

❹ Have students work alone and then review answers as a class. Make sure students understand the difference in meaning between the sentences in each pair.

Answers
1. b 2. a 3. a 4. b

🜨 **Option:** Have students draw their own personal time lines. Encourage them to show major events in their lives. They should then take turns showing and explaining them to a

partner. Encourage students to use the present perfect tense with both **for** and **since.** Students who are listening should practice asking questions with **How long** and the present perfect.

Example:

A: I began to study English in 1999.

B: How long have you studied English?

A: I've studied English for one year. I've studied English since 1999.

🜨 **Option:** Have students bring in information on a favorite artist, writer, movie star, or sports figure. They should make a time line showing the major events in that person's life. Other students should then ask questions about that person using the present perfect.

🜨 **Option:** Have students bring in pictures of friends or family members and talk about their work history and other activities. Students should use the simple past tense when describing jobs/activities these people did in the past but no longer do, for example, "My uncle worked for a telephone company for two years." Students should use the present perfect tense to describe jobs/activities these people started in the past and are still doing at the present time, for example, "My father has worked for the telephone company for two years." Students who are listening should take notes and be prepared to answer questions about the information they've heard, for example, "Does Fran's uncle work for the telephone company now?"

Link *Workbook: Practices 5, 6, 7*

☑ ❺ **Check Your Understanding** In this exercise, students determine in which situations the present perfect tense would be used. They should work alone and then compare answers with a partner.

Answers
Giving your boss or teacher an update on a project, Interviewing a person about his travel experiences abroad, Asking a person about the length of time at your school

3 With a partner, take turns asking about your life experiences. Ask questions with *How many times* or *How often.*

Example: fly an airplane

A: How many times have you flown in an airplane?

B: Up to now, I've flown four times. *or* I've never flown before.

a.	travel abroad	**e.**	fall in love
b.	attend a concert	**f.**	fall asleep in class
c.	have a close call	**g.**	lose something important
d.	use the Internet	**h.**	idea of your own

The Present Perfect Tense with *How long*

We use the present perfect tense to talk about an action that began in the past and continues up to the present moment. To ask about the length of time, we use *How long,* and we generally answer with *for* or *since.*

> **A:** So, how long **have** you **taken** pictures of famous people?
>
> **B:** I've **photographed** famous people ever **since** I graduated from school.
>
> **A:** And how long **have** you **worked** as a freelance journalist?
>
> **B:** I've **been** a reporter **for** about three years now.

4 Match each sentence with its meaning. Write the letter on the line.

_____ **1.** He has worked as a nurse for two years.

_____ **2.** He worked as a nurse for two years.

      a. He worked as a nurse for two years, but isn't doing this job now.

      b. He began working as a nurse two years ago, and is still a nurse.

_____ **3.** How long did you live in Mexico City?

_____ **4.** How long have you lived in Mexico City?

      a. You don't live in Mexico City now.

      b. You live in Mexico City now.

5 **Check Your Understanding** In which situations are you likely to use the present perfect tense? Check your answers with a partner's.

☐ Giving your boss or teacher an update on a project

☐ Inviting a friend to your house for lunch

☐ Interviewing a person about his travel experiences abroad

☐ Asking a friend for her opinion about a movie

☐ Asking a person about the length of time at your school

With your partner, choose one of the situations you checked. Imagine yourselves in the situation and write a dialogue.

6 **Express Yourself** Walk around the room and find someone who has done each of the activities listed below. When you find someone, continue the conversation by asking a follow-up question.

Example: travel abroad

A: Have you ever traveled abroad?	**A:** Have you ever traveled abroad?
B: Yes, I have. I went abroad last year.	**B:** Unfortunately, I haven't.
A: Where did you go?	
B: I went to Cairo.	

a. take music lessons **d.** surf the Internet **g.** see a famous person

b. go to a live concert **e.** apply for a job **h.** be in the hospital

c. be in a car accident **f.** go scuba diving **i.** idea of your own

LISTENING and SPEAKING

Listen: A Job Interview

 Before You Listen

a. What are some of the jobs people do to make a movie?

b. What does a stuntman do? List some examples.

Understanding Grammar Clues You understand more if you listen for grammar clues, like word endings and auxiliary verbs. These clues signal such aspects as singular and plural, or present, past, and future time frames.

 2 A stuntman is interviewing for a job. Listen and complete the chart.

Name:	*Hal Hunk*
Length of time as a stuntperson:	
First stunt:	
Age:	
Stunt experience:	*has driven cars and motorcycles*
Most recent stunt:	
Stunts never tried:	

6 Express Yourself Have selected students report to the class about someone who has done an activity, for example, "Berta has taken music lessons since she was seven, in other words, for ten years."

Option: Do Exercise 6 as a competition. Students have to find a different person who has done each of the activities listed in the exercise. Once they've found someone who has done an activity (and asked a follow-up question to get additional information), they should write down the person's name and continue. (They cannot use a person's name more than once.) The winner is the first student to find people who have done all the activities and can report who they are and one detail about each one.

LISTENING and SPEAKING

Listen: A Job Interview

Presentation

1 Before You Listen Have students work in small groups to read the questions. If necessary, bring in pictures of some of the people who work on movies. You might have to assist students with additional vocabulary to do this exercise: **actor, cameraman, director, editor, executive producer, makeup person, producer, production assistant, screenwriter, script supervisor, wardrobe director.**

Check understanding of **stuntman/stuntperson** (the person who does dangerous action scenes in a movie in place of the actor). Ask students to name any stuntpeople they know. Ask, *What kinds of stunts have you seen? Which movies have you seen them in?*

Understanding Grammar Clues
Explain to students that they can catch the finer nuances of what's being said if they listen for grammar clues to assist in getting the meaning.

2 Play the recording or read the audioscript aloud one or more times. Have students complete the chart.

Audioscript: The audioscript for Exercise 2 appears on page T155.

> **Answers**
> **Length of time as a stuntperson:** six years.
> **First stunt:** He jumped off a train in a cowboy movie. **Age:** fifteen. **Stunt experience:** He has fallen off buildings. **Most recent stunt:** He had to fight with two live tigers. **Stunts never tried:** He's never jumped out of a plane; he's never fought a monster.

Option: Play the recording or read the audioscript aloud again. Have students write down the verbs they hear in the simple past and the present perfect tenses. Ask, *What things did Hal Hunk do in the past? What things that he started in the past does he still do in the present?*

Option: Ask additional discussion questions:
- Which stunt sounds the most dangerous? Why?
- Which stunt would you like to try? Why?
- Would you ever like to work as a stuntperson? Why or why not?
- What other job connected with making a movie would you like to try? Why do you think it would be interesting?

 Workbook: Practices 8, 9

Pronunciation

Presentation

🎧 **❸** Review the information in the box. Then play the recording or read the sentences aloud. Students should listen the first time, practice saying the words along with the recording the second time, and then try reading the dialogue with a partner, paying attention to the sentence stress.

🎧 **❹** Students should work alone to identify the sentence stress in the dialogue. Then play the recording or read the sentences aloud for students to check their answers. Review the answers as a class. Then assign partners for students to practice the dialogue. Observe pairs of students practicing the dialogue. Listen for the correct sentence stress. Make notes of student errors, but don't interrupt to correct them; you want to encourage fluency. Write errors on the board without identifying who made them. Then correct the errors as a class.

> **Answers**
> A: so, crime
> B: lot, mayor, half
> A: amazing, else
> B: city, traffic
> A: year, next

Option: Have partners practice the dialogue together and then ask selected students to perform in front of the class.

Option: Read other sentences from this unit (or other units) and have students say where the sentence stress falls.

 Workbook: Practice 10

Speak Out

➡️ **Making Generalizations** Introduce the different expressions used to make general statements. Have selected students practice making their own sentences using these expressions. If necessary, give them an example to start out: *Generally speaking, it's cheaper to live in the country than the city.*

Presentation

❺ Have students discuss the questions in small groups and use the expressions for making generalizations. Circulate to make sure they are using the expressions correctly.

Option: Have students debate one of these issues using expressions for making generalizations:

- More women should be allowed in male-dominated fields.

- Women should be required/allowed to serve in the military.

- More men should stay at home and take care of the children while women work.

Option: Have students write paragraphs describing specific jobs and who has done them traditionally.

Pronunciation

> **Sentence Stress**
>
> In every thought group, a group of words that expresses a thought, the last content word is usually stressed more than the others. The stressed syllable of this word is called sentence stress. Other content words are less stressed.

3 Listen to the dialogue. The syllable in bold carries the sentence stress.

A: /For a **year** now,/Ms. Holmes has been **may**or./What's she accomplished so **far**?/

B: /She's hired fifty new po**lice** officers./

4 Read the dialogue. For each thought group, predict which words carry the sentence stress and underline them.

A: /And so,/what has Ms. Holmes done about crime?/

B: /She's done a lot./ While she's been mayor,/crime has decreased by half./

A: /That's amazing!/ What else has she done?/

B: /She's made bicycle lanes all over the city/and closed several streets to traffic./

A: /All in one year!/ I can't wait to see what's next./

Now listen to the dialogue and check your answers with the class. Then practice the dialogue with a partner, focusing on the correct sentence stress.

Speak Out

 STRATEGY **Making Generalizations** When you want to make general statements that are true most of the time, use these expressions.

In most cases, ...	Most people have ...	Generally speaking, ...
People usually ...	In general, ...	Most people now believe ...

5 With two other students, discuss these questions.

a. What jobs do men usually have in your country today? What jobs do women usually have in your country today?

b. In your country, have traditional jobs for men and women changed in the last fifty years? Why or why not? How do you feel about this?

Read About It

1 **Before You Read** What skills do you think a newspaper reporter should have? Check your top three choices. Compare your answers with a partner's.

- ☐ solving problems
- ☐ getting along with people
- ☐ thinking quickly
- ☐ giving opinions
- ☐ organizing meetings

- ☐ listening carefully
- ☐ writing clearly
- ☐ interviewing
- ☐ taking notes
- ☐ meeting deadlines

Nellie Bly, Newspaperwoman

Elizabeth Cochrane, known as Nellie Bly, was an exceptional woman who worked to make life better for everybody. When she was about eighteen years old, she read an article in the *Pittsburgh*
5 *Dispatch* that spoke out against women. She was very upset, so she wrote a letter called "What Girls Are Good For" to the editor. This letter impressed the editors and they gave her a job.

Bly's career with the *Dispatch* began with a
10 series of articles about divorce. The public reacted very strongly for or against her articles. The editors, however, were surprised because they never believed that a young woman could write such controversial stories.

15 Bly's next articles were about the lives of the women who lived in boarding houses in Pittsburgh. Then she wrote about poor sections of the city, about employees in shops who worked long hours for low salaries, and about conditions in the prisons.

20 After Bly moved to New York City, Joseph Pulitzer, a famous newspaperman, asked her to write about conditions in mental hospitals for his paper, the *New York World*. She pretended to be crazy and within twenty-four hours, she was in a mental hospital. After ten days, she returned with stories about violent nurses, terrible food, and unsanitary conditions. These
25 stories were again controversial, but helped to improve hospital conditions.

This success encouraged Bly to write other stories. She jumped off a boat into the Hudson River so she could write a story about the rescue crew. She got herself arrested and spent time in prison. Her stories about prison conditions forced the authorities to separate men and women prisoners.

READING and WRITING

Read About It

Presentation

❶ Before You Read Have students work alone and then compare answers with a partner. You can also have students rank their top three choices in order of importance. Take a class survey and see what the top three skills are. (*Answers will vary.*)

Option: Have students rank all the qualities in the list according to importance. Have them write 1 for most important and 10 for least important. Which qualities do most students believe are important? Unimportant?

❷ Have students read the article beginning on page 72 and then work with a partner to determine the meaning of the words from context. Circulate to help as necessary. After you've gone over the definitions as a class, ask students what clues they used to figure out the meanings of the words. Were some words harder to define than others? Why?

Answers
Other answers are possible.
a. impressed: made people notice **b.** controversial: causing disagreement or argument **c.** pretended: acted as if something was true when it wasn't **d.** crazy: insane **e.** success: good results **f.** authorities: officials, people in charge **g.** instead: in place of **h.** response: answer **i.** gave in: agreed, was persuaded **j.** followed: paid attention to **k.** achieved: reached **l.** popularity: how much you are liked by others

🔨 **Option:** You may want to give each pair of students two or three words to define. Then put pairs together to exchange information. Alternatively, you can call on selected pairs to read their definitions aloud to the class. In this way, the whole class can work together on the definitions.

➡ **Making Inferences** Explain to students that inferences are opinions or ideas that are not clearly stated in the text but that we can figure out from our reading.

❸ Have students work alone and then compare answers with a partner. Then discuss the answers as a class.

Answers:
a. no **b.** yes **c.** yes **d.** no **e.** yes

🔨 **Option:** Ask additional comprehension questions:

- Why did Nellie Bly write a letter called "What Girls Are Good For"? (She was very upset about a newspaper article that spoke out against women.)

- What were her first articles about? (divorce) How did the public react? (They reacted very strongly either for or against her articles.)

- What did Bly do to get her story on mental hospitals? (She pretended to be crazy and spent ten days in a mental hospital.) On prison conditions? (She got herself arrested and spent time in prison.)

- How long did it take Bly to travel around the world? (72 days, 6 hours, and 10 minutes)

🔨 **Option:** Have students skim the article quickly, close their books, and then retell Nellie Bly's story to a partner.

Think About It

Presentation

❹ Have students discuss whether they think Nellie's methods were appropriate or not. Could she do the same thing today? What are some problems with her methods?

🔨 **Option:** Have students think of some current controversial issues (pollution, the homeless, and so on). Then have them work in groups to think of original ways of gathering information to draw attention to the problem. Groups should present their ideas to the class.

🔨 **Option:** Ask students what they think the most controversial issues are today and what Nellie Bly would say about them.

❺ Have students discuss the question with a partner. They can look back at the article if necessary.

❻ Have students work in pairs to list what they can infer from the article about Nellie Bly's personality. What qualities do they like about her? Which ones do they find less attractive? How popular would Nellie Bly be if she lived in today's society?

30   Because of a popular novel at the time, *Around the World in Eighty Days*, by Jules Verne, Bly decided she would travel around the world in fewer than eighty days. When Pulitzer wanted to send a man instead, her response was quick. "If you do," she said, "I'll leave at the same time and race against him!"

35   Pulitzer finally gave in, and she left New York on November 14, 1889. She crossed the Atlantic, interviewed Jules Verne in Paris, and traveled through the Suez, Somalia, Calcutta, Singapore, Yokohama, and San Francisco. Her readers followed her trip closely. When she arrived in New York, the whole city was amazed. She had made the trip in seventy-two days, six hours and

40 ten minutes.

     Bly continued to write stories after her journey, but she never again achieved the popularity she once had. She died in 1922 of pneumonia, at the age of fifty-five.

2   Find these words in the article and use the context to determine their meanings. Write short definitions on a sheet of paper. Work without a dictionary. Discuss your answers with the class.

a. impressed (line 7)	**e.** success (line 26)	**i.** gave in (line 35)
b. controversial (line 14)	**f.** authorities (line 28)	**j.** followed (line 38)
c. pretended (line 22)	**g.** instead (line 33)	**k.** achieved (line 41)
d. crazy (line 23)	**h.** response (line 33)	**l.** popularity (line 41)

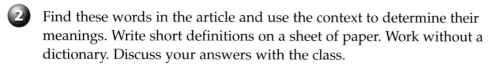 **STRATEGY**   **Making Inferences** You can often figure out the writer's opinions or ideas even if they are not directly stated. You do this with other information in the text. In other words, you make inferences based on what you read.

3   Read each sentence and decide if the inference is one the text supports or one the text does not support. Write *yes* or *no*.

_____ **a.** Bly never got married.

_____ **b.** Conditions in mental hospitals were very bad.

_____ **c.** Pulitzer thought Bly was a good reporter.

_____ **d.** Pulitzer thought Bly was too young to go on a trip around the world.

_____ **e.** Bly was sure she could beat a man in a race around the world.

Think About It

4   Do you think the methods Nellie used to get information for her articles were fair? Why or why not?

5   Do you think Nellie faced unnecessary difficulties because she was a woman? Give examples.

6   What inferences can you draw about Nellie's personality?

Write: Supporting Details

In a well-developed paragraph, the supporting sentences are explained with supporting details. These details (facts, examples, experience, description) give specific information about each supporting point.

 7   Read the paragraph and complete the outline.

    I believe Sarah Lewis is the best candidate for the position of English Instructor at Miles College. Ms. Lewis comes to the department with excellent credentials. First, she has a strong educational background. She holds two master's degrees, one in communication studies and one in linguistics. She also has a wide range of experience. She has taught in a refugee program in Indonesia, in a business program in Turkey, and in a university program in California. Finally, Ms. Lewis is truly professional and well respected. She has written several articles and presented at conferences. Her colleagues and students comment on how hard she works for her classes and the program. I am certain that Ms. Lewis will make a lasting contribution to our teaching staff.

Outline

Topic Sentence (Main Idea): *I believe Sarah Lewis is the best candidate for the position of English Instructor at Miles College.*

Supporting Point 1:	*Has a strong educational background*
Detail 1:	*MA in communication studies*
Detail 2:	*MA in linguistics*
Supporting Point 2:	_____
Detail 1:	_____
Detail 2:	_____
Detail 3:	_____
Supporting Point 3:	_____
Detail 1:	_____
Detail 2:	_____
Detail 3:	_____

Write About It

8   Your boss asked you to find a new employee. You interviewed several people and chose one of them. Write a one-paragraph report to your boss explaining your choice. First, choose a specific job. Then give the person you selected a name. Write a paragraph explaining why the person is a match. Talk about the person's education, experience, and personality.

  Check Your Writing Reread your paragraph. Use the questions below and revise your paper as necessary.

- Are the supporting sentences ordered logically?
- Are the supporting points explained with details?
- Are verb tenses used correctly?

Write: Supporting Details

Students read the presentation in class or for homework.

✺ Option: You might want to introduce the following vocabulary before having students read the paragraph in Exercise 7: **credentials:** qualifications; **master's degree:** an advanced degree that is higher than a bachelor's degree; **linguistics:** the study of language; **refugee:** a person who has had to leave his or her country, especially because of war; **lasting:** continuing for a long time; **contribution:** something you give to help make something else successful.

Presentation

❼ Have students work alone to read the paragraph and complete the outline. Then they should compare answers with a partner.

> **Answers**
> **Supporting Point 2:** Has a wide range of experience **Detail 1:** Taught in a refugee program in Indonesia **Detail 2:** Taught in a business program in Turkey **Detail 3:** Taught in a university program in California **Supporting Point 3:** Professional and well respected **Detail 1:** Written several articles **Detail 2:** Presented at conferences **Detail 3:** Colleagues and students say she works hard for her classes and the program

Write About It

Presentation

❽ Have students write a paragraph to their boss explaining who they would like to hire. Remind them to include the job title and/or a brief description. They can write the paragraph in class or as homework. If students will do their writing at home, have them first brainstorm in class so that you can check that step.

 Workbook: Practice 11

☑ ❾ Check Your Writing Students should revise their assignments based on the suggestions given. They can do a final grammar check before handing the paragraph in.

Vocabulary Expansion: Adjectives ending in –ing and –ed See page T146.

> **Answers**
> 1. interesting, interested 2. boring, bored
> 3. confusing, confused 4. frightening, frightened 5. surprising, surprised 6. embarrassing, embarrassed 7. exciting, excited
> 8. entertaining, entertained

EVALUATION

See page TExi.

Unit 7 Achievement Test

Self-Check See **Check Your Knowledge** on page 56 of the Workbook.

Dictation Have students review the sentences in Exercise 2 on page 68. Then present the sentences as dictation. (See instructions on page TExv.)

Communication Skills

1. Have students tell you what kinds of questions are asked in interviews. Then have them play the parts of an interviewer and job applicant. Notice their use of vocabulary to talk about job experience, education, and qualifications. Students should take turns playing the parts of both interviewer and job applicant.

2. Have students tell you about some of the highlights of their life (most memorable/interesting experiences). They should tell you about those experiences using the present perfect tense and **for/since.**

ASK THE EXPERTS

OBJECTIVES

- To talk about personal problems
- To use **should, ought to,** and **had better**
- To listen for the main idea
- To identify intonation patterns
- To ask for and give advice
- To practice skimming
- To write an informal letter
- To use expressions with **break**

GETTING STARTED

Warm Up

Preview

Check understanding of **expert.** Can students name an expert who gives advice on radio or TV or who writes for a newspaper or magazine? What do they think of him/her? Ask, *Are any of you experts in a particular field?*

Presentation

❶ Have students work with a partner to make a list of problems people can have. Then have pairs of students form larger groups and compare answers. Finally, have selected students read a problem from their list. Compile a list on the board. Ask, *How many of these problems do you face in your life?*

☻ **Option: Vocabulary Notebooks** See page TEviii.

🎧 ❷ Make sure that everyone understands the exercise. Play the recording or read the audioscript aloud one or more times. Tell students they do not have to understand every word to do the activity.

Audioscript: The audioscript for Exercise 2 appears on page T156.

Answers
Conversation A: school problem
Conversation B: health problem
Conversation C: family problem

☻ **Option:** Before doing Exercise 2, have students anticipate what key words they might hear in the listening. (For example, under "health problem," students might anticipate they would hear the word "doctor.") Students should make a list and then check off the words they actually hear.

☻ **Option:** Have students give advice to the people whose problems they just heard.

☻ **Option:** Ask additional comprehension questions:
Conversation 1: How many questions did Annie miss on her test? (almost half)
Conversation 2: What's wrong with Betty? (One of her back teeth really hurts.)
Conversation 3: What have Harry and Jenny been arguing about? (the kids) What does Jenny think about the parents' roles? (They have to make rules for their children.)

❸ Have students discuss in pairs who they go to for advice. Ask them to give details. Ask, *Who do you ask for advice and why? What kind of advice do you seek?* (Answers will vary.)

☻ **Option:** Have students write a brief dialogue about asking someone for advice. If students are uncomfortable writing something so personal, have them write an imaginary dialogue.

 Workbook: Practice 1

Figure It Out

Preview

- Check understanding of **newspaper columnist.** Ask, *Can you name a famous newspaper columnist who gives advice? What do you think of him/her? What kinds of problems does he/she address?*

(Additional Preview activities and Exercise 4 teaching notes appear on page T76.)

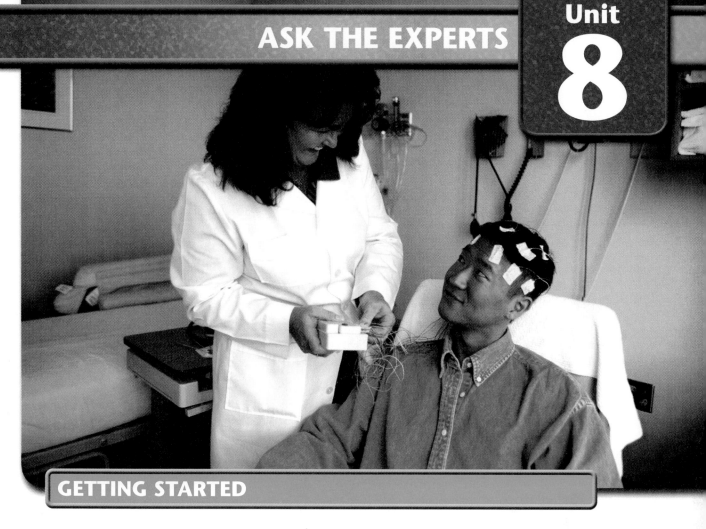

GETTING STARTED

Warm Up

1 We all have problems during our lives such as problems with our health or problems with our family. What other problems can people have? Make a list.

2 You are going to hear three conversations. What kind of problem is each person having? Write the letter of the conversation.

- ☐ health problem
- ☐ work problem
- ☐ school problem
- ☐ family problem

3 When you have a problem, who do you ask for advice?

Figure It Out

4 "Ask Andy Summers" is an advice column in the newspaper. People with problems write to Andy Summers and he responds with advice. On the next page, match the problem with the advice by writing the letter on the line.

Problem

_____ **1.** My teacher is taking my class on a trip to England. All of my friends are going, but my parents say that I'm too young to travel abroad. I'm seventeen years old, but my parents think that I'm still a baby! What should I do?

_____ **2.** My best friend always borrows money from me and never pays me back. Last month, he asked me for $500. Now he says that if I give him another $500, he'll be able to pay me back everything he owes me next July. Do you think I should believe him?

_____ **3.** My husband and I both make good salaries, but he spends money as if we were millionaires! He shops all of the time and he always pays by credit card. Now we have no money at all and we owe thousands of dollars. What advice can you give me?

_____ **4.** My son loves loud rock music. I can't stand rock, so one day I threw all his CDs away. Now he won't speak to me. What do you think I ought to do?

_____ **5.** Last summer thieves broke into our house while we were on vacation and took everything. This year my husband refuses to go on vacation because he's afraid it'll happen again. I don't want to stay home all summer. What should I do?

_____ **6.** I asked my boss for more money, but she refused. She said that I'm always late and take too many coffee breaks. I want a new job with a better boss. My friends say that I'd better not leave my job right away. What do you think?

_____ **7.** On my last vacation, I gained a lot of weight. Now my clothes are too tight and I can't stop eating. Can you give me some advice?

_____ **8.** My son and his wife have three beautiful children. The trouble is that they want me to watch their children while they're at work. I love my grandchildren, but I don't like watching them every day. What should I do?

Advice

a. I think your friend may not be able to return your money. Maybe you should find a new friend.

b. I agree with your friends. It sounds like you're not a very good worker. You'd better not quit the job you have now. In fact, you'd better work harder if you want to keep your job.

c. I advise you to go on vacation alone. Leave your husband at home to watch your house.

d. I think people like your husband shouldn't have credit cards. You should cut his credit cards in half and throw them away.

e. You should go on a diet. Don't eat candy or desserts. You ought to start exercising more, too. Join a health club and go there every day.

f. I think you ought to tell them that you're too busy to babysit.

g. You ought to apologize to your son. You should probably offer to buy him some new CDs, too.

h. You should ask them to consult with your teacher. Then they'll find out that you'll be with your teacher and your friends.

5 Look at the problems and the advice again. Do you agree or disagree with the advice? Why? If you disagree, can you think of better advice?

- Check understanding of **(travel) abroad** (Problem 1), **borrow (money)**, **pay back**, **owe** (Problem 2), **credit card** (Problem 3), **throw away** (Problem 4), **refuses** (Problem 5), and **gain weight** (Problem 7). Ask, *Have you ever gone to another country? Have you ever **traveled abroad?*** Have a student come to the front of the class and pantomime **borrowing (money)**, **owing** it, and **paying** it **back**. You can also use pantomime to demonstrate **throw away** and **gain weight**. Ask students for the opposite of **refuse** (accept/take) and **gain weight**. Show students a **credit card** if they don't already know what it is.

⊛ **Option: Vocabulary Notebooks** See page TEviii.

Language Note: In the first problem, **baby** is used metaphorically. Here it means "someone who is not old enough to take care of himself/herself." The parents think their child is too young to go on a trip unsupervised.

Presentation

❹ Have students read the instructions, and make sure they understand the exercise.

Answers
1. h 2. a 3. d 4. g 5. c 6. b 7. e 8. f

⊛ **Option:** You may want to tell the students that the abbreviation of **had better** is **'d better** (Problem 6). In very fast speech, speakers of American English often drop the **'d** entirely, so that *I'd better* sounds more like *I better*: "I better not leave my job right away."

❺ Have students work in pairs or small groups and decide whether they agree or disagree with the advice that was given. If they disagree, they should rewrite the advice.

⊛ **Option:** Have selected students read their advice aloud. After several students have given advice on the same problem, have the class vote on the best piece of advice.

⊛ **Option:** Have students close their books and paraphrase the letters and the advice.

⊛ **Option:** Ask additional comprehension questions:

1. Where is the class going? (to England)

2. How much has the friend already borrowed? ($500) How much more does the friend want to borrow? ($500)

3. What does the woman's husband do? (He shops all the time and always pays by credit card.)

4. Why is the husband afraid to go on vacation? (He's afraid thieves will break into the house and take everything again.)

5. Why did the boss refuse the employee's request for more money? (The employee is always late and takes too many coffee breaks.)

⊛ **Option:** Ask additional discussion questions:

- Do people ever come to you for advice? If so, what do they ask? If not, why not?

- How does it make you feel when people ask you for advice? When they don't?

- Do you think you are/would be a good advice giver?

⊛ **Option:** Bring in a real advice column and have students read it. (They can add unfamiliar vocabulary words to their notebooks.) Do the students agree with the advice given by the columnist? If they disagree, have them give better advice.

☑ ❻ **Vocabulary Check** Have students work alone and then check answers with a partner.

Answers
a. borrowed b. advised c. consult d. can't stand e. thief f. salary

 Workbook: Practice 2

 Option: Vocabulary Notebooks See page TEviii.

Talk About It

 Option: If students need extra practice with giving advice and warnings, postpone this activity until after you've completed the grammar exercises for this unit or Workbook Practices 4 and 5.

Preview

Check understanding of **hot line.** Ask, *Have you ever called a hot line? What kinds of problems do people call about?*

Cultural Note: "Talk radio" has become very popular in the United States. Listeners call in to a radio station to discuss a particular topic (anything from politics to car repair) or to get advice on their personal problems.

Presentation

❼ Have students read the instructions and ask selected students to model the dialogue for the class. Then have students work in pairs taking turns being the caller and adviser. Circulate and offer assistance. Make notes of student errors, but don't interrupt to correct them; you want to encourage fluency. Have selected pairs perform their dialogues for the class. Refer to your notes and write errors on the board without identifying who made them. Then correct the errors as a class.

 Option: Have students discuss whether they would call in to a hot line to get advice on problems in any of these areas:

- money
- school
- parents
- work

- health
- car
- love life

If they wouldn't call in to a hot line, who would they consult about these problems?

 Option: Ask, *Are you familiar with any hot lines in your city or country?* Lead a class discussion.

 Workbook: Practice 3

Vocabulary Check Fill in the blanks with the correct words from the box.

owe	advised
can't stand	consult
borrowed	thief
salary	refuse

a. Clyde _____ my favorite CD yesterday. He says that he'll return it on Friday.

b. Tom says his neighbors are too noisy. He asked me what he should do. I _____ him to move.

c. I want to buy a computer, but I don't know much about them. I want to _____ with a computer expert first.

d. I _____ my roommate's bad habits.

e. A _____ grabbed my purse and ran away. He got all of my money and credit cards.

f. I don't make enough money. My boss ought to raise my _____.

Talk About It

7 *Help Line* is an advice hot line. People with problems call in and ask for advice. With a partner, take turns being the adviser and the caller. Use the cues.

Example: Your phone bill is too high.

> Explain problem; ask for advice.

A: The phone company says that I made thirty calls to Australia last month, but I don't even know anyone in Australia! They're going to turn off my phone if I don't pay. What should I do?

> Give advice.

B: You should call the phone company and complain.

> Reject advice.

A: I don't think that'll work.

> Give advice.

B: Well, maybe you should write a letter to the phone company and explain the situation.

> Accept advice.

A: That's probably a better idea.

a. Your neighbors are noisy at night.
b. Someone in your family is a couch potato.
c. You don't know how to use your new computer.
d. Someone owes you a lot of money.
e. Your new bike doesn't work right.
f. You don't like your boss.
g. You can't stop smoking.
h. Idea of your own.

```
International Long Distance
TCT Calling Plan from 212-555-5555

No.  Date     Time      Place        Area-Number     *    Min.   Amount
1    Jan 08   05:48PM   AUSTRALIA    0613784293      S    45     21.60
2    Jan 13   08:23PM   AUSTRALIA    0614942217      X    32     15.36
3    Jan 13   08:24PM   AUSTRALIA    0618934392      X    24     11.52
4    Jan 14   06:06PM   AUSTRALIA    0616843470      S    54     25.92
Total TCT Calling Plan calls from 212-555-5555:             74.40

Total International Long Distance                            74.40
```

Giving Advice: *Should, Ought to*

To ask for and give advice, we can use the modals *should* or *ought to*.

> **A:** How **should** I **tell** my boss I'm looking for another job?
>
> **B:** You **shouldn't say** anything. You **should wait** till you have another job.
>
> **A:** I don't know. I think I really **ought to say** something now.

 1 **Check Your Understanding** Read the letter to Andy Summers. Then complete Andy's answer with *should, shouldn't,* or *ought.*

July 15

Dear Andy Summers,

My wife and I have been married for only a few weeks but we are having a lot of problems. We love each other but we have very different lifestyles. I like to get up late and she likes to get up early. She likes to go to the theater but I like to watch TV. She likes to go to fancy restaurants but I like pizza and hamburgers. I like to listen to rock music but she only likes classical music. We love each other a lot but we are driving each other crazy. I'm afraid that if we don't solve our problems, we are going to break up. What should we do?

Sincerely,

In Love But Not Happy

July 25

Dear In Love,

It's good to hear that with all of your problems, you are still in love. To solve your problems, you and your wife **(1.)**_____ to have a talk. You **(2.)**_____ agree to get up a little earlier and your wife **(3.)**_____ to agree to get up a little later. You **(4.)**_____ go to the movies with your wife once in a while and she **(5.)**_____ to stay home with you and watch TV once in a while, too. You **(6.)**_____ eat pizzas and hamburgers all of the time. This food is bad for your health. Also, you and your wife **(7.)**_____ find some restaurants that you both like. You **(8.)**_____ listen to rock music all of the time. No one can relax when rock music is playing. Maybe you **(9.)**_____ to throw away your rock albums and start listening to classical music.

Sincerely,

Andy Summers

GRAMMAR

Giving Advice:
Should, Ought to

Preview

- Before looking at the grammar presentation, see if students can create sentences using **should** and **ought to** to give advice. Ask students to make a sentence with **ought to** in the negative. Explain that **ought to** is rarely used in questions or negative statements. Then go over the information in the box.

- Check understanding of **lifestyle**. Ask, *What kind of lifestyle do you lead? Is your lifestyle the same as your parents'?* Lead a class discussion.

Presentation

☑ **❶ Check Your Understanding** In this exercise, students complete Andy's letter with **should(n't)** or **ought to**.

> **Answers**
> 1. ought 2. should 3. ought 4. should
> 5. ought 6. shouldn't 7. should 8. shouldn't
> 9. ought

 Option: Bring in a first aid book and have students give advice for treating various ailments, such as snake bites or burns, using **should(n't)** or **ought to**.

 Workbook: Practices 4, 5

Giving a Warning: *Had better*

Preview

- Explain that **had better** is used to give a warning. It can sometimes sound threatening and is not used in polite requests. The tone of **had better** is more pressing or urgent than **should** or **ought to**.

- Have the class practice making sentences with **had better** and **had better not**.

Presentation

❷ Have students read the sentences and discuss the situations in which they might say them. *(Answers will vary.)*

Softening Advice

Preview

Ask students if they know how to give advice in a "softer" way than **should** and **ought to.** Write their ideas on the board.

Presentation

❸ Students work alone to rewrite the dialogue using the expressions **I (don't) think, Do you think** to soften advice. Have students check answers with a partner. Ask selected students to perform the dialogue for the class.

> **Answers**
> **1.** Do you think I should visit … **2.** I think you ought to go … **3.** I think you had better take … **4.** Do you think I should stay at … **5.** I don't think you should stay there.

 Workbook: Practice 6

❹ Students read the situations and give advice using the expression **should**, or give a warning with **had better/had better not**. *(Answers will vary.)*

Option: Give students additional practice in making advice sentences negative.

- I think we should go to the movies.
- She should stay at home.
- We'd better borrow some money.
- I think she should ask for a raise.

Language Note: Students may have trouble using **should**, **ought to**, and **had better** after **think**. Remind students that there is never inversion of the subject and **should, ought to,** or **had better** after **think**.

- Do you think (that) we should go?
- I don't think (that) we should go.
- I think (that) you should help me.

You may also want to tell the class that **that** is optional after **think**.

Option: Have students consider these additional situations and give advice.

- A friend is on a trip abroad and has lost his passport.
- A friend is going to New York, where you've been many times. Suggest some interesting places to visit.
- A friend is coming to visit your city and wants to stay in a hotel. Give him some advice.
- A friend wants to know what he should pack before he leaves on a big trip. Make some recommendations.

 Workbook: Practices 7, 8

Giving a Warning: *Had better*

When we want to give strong advice or a warning, we use *had better/had better not* + verb.

> **A:** I still think I should tell my boss I'm looking for another job.
>
> **B:** You'**d better take** my advice. You'**d better not tell** him, or you might not have a job at all!

2 In which situation might you say each of the following statements? Discuss your answers with a partner.

    a. You'd better leave it alone.

    b. You'd better not tell anyone.

    c. I'd better go study.

    d. You'd better not drink that.

    e. He'd better apologize

    f. We'd better not take the car.

Softening Advice

We often use *think* when we ask for or give advice with *should, ought to,* or *had better.* This makes the advice "softer."

> **SON:** **Do** you **think** I **should take** my credit card on my trip?
>
> **DAD:** Yes, and I **think** you **ought to hide** your money in your shoe!
>
> **SON:** Dad, **don't** you **think** you **should relax** a little?

3 Rewrite the dialogue. Use *I think, I don't think,* or *Do you think* in the numbered sentences.

    A: I'm taking a trip to California. **(1.)** Should I visit San Francisco?

    B: Yes, it's really beautiful! **(2.)** You ought to go to Los Angeles, too.

    A: I hear that it's really warm in California. I can leave all my winter clothes at home!

    B: Not really! It can get cold in San Francisco in the summer. **(3.)** You had better take some warm clothes with you.

    A: OK. What about hotels? **(4.)** Should I stay at the West Hollywood Hotel in Los Angeles?

    B: **(5.)** You shouldn't stay there. It's too expensive.

4 Consider the situations. For each, give advice with *should* or a warning with *had better/had better not.*

    a. Anna loves to play volleyball. There is a new gym near her home.

    b. The doctor says you're too thin. If you lose more weight, you will probably get sick.

    c. That part of the city is dangerous! If you go there at night, be careful.

    d. I read a wonderful book recently. I think you'd like it, too.

    e. Put that medicine where the kids can't reach it.

    f. Paolo is writing a paragraph and he doesn't know how to spell some words.

5 Work with a partner. Look at the pictures. Take turns asking for and giving advice, using a form of *think*.

 a.

 b.

 c.

 d.

 e.

 f.

Example:

A: What do you think he should do?

B: I think he ought to do the dishes.

6 **Check Your Understanding** In which situations are you likely to use *should*, *ought to*, or *had better*? Check your answers with a partner's.

- ☐ Recommending a vacation spot to a friend
- ☐ Telling a friend how to get a driver's license
- ☐ Making an appointment to see a dentist
- ☐ Discussing a problem you have with a friend
- ☐ Comparing your health club with a friend's

7 **Express Yourself** With a partner, choose one of the situations you checked above. Imagine yourselves in the situation and write a dialogue using different expressions of advice.

LISTENING and SPEAKING

Listen: *Ask Olga!*

1 **Before You Listen** Many radio and TV programs offer advice. People call on the phone and describe their problems, and listeners call in to give them advice. Why do you think that people ask for advice on these programs? Why do you think people call in to give advice?

STRATEGY **Listening for the Main Idea** You can understand more easily when you focus on getting the main idea of a conversation. Listen for key words or phrases that are repeated or stressed.

❺ Students ask and answer questions using a form of *think.* Tell students that there may be more than one possible answer for each illustration.

Answers
Question: What do you think he/she should do?
Possible answers: a. I think he ought to do the dishes. **b.** I don't think he should watch so much TV. **c.** I think she should turn down her radio. **d.** I don't think he should read the paper while crossing the street. **e.** I think he'd better not smoke at a gas station. **f.** I think he should slow down.

☑ **❻ Check Your Understanding** This exercise asks students to identify specific situations for giving advice.

Answers
Recommending a vacation spot to a friend, Telling a friend how to get a driver's license

✖ **❼ Express Yourself** This activity is communicative and interactive. It connects the grammar point—in this case, giving advice—to the students' personal lives.

Listen: *Ask Olga!*

Presentation

❶ Before You Listen Check understanding of **personal problem.** Say, *We call a problem with a husband, wife, or child a personal problem.* Personal problems can also occur between friends. Have students tell you what kinds of personal problems people might have. Clarify **Better Business Bureau.** Ask students what they could do if they bought something and it didn't work properly. Then tell students that in many countries, each city has a Better Business Bureau to help people with consumer problems. Ask students to name consumer problems they have had. What did they do in each situation?

Option: Have students work in small groups to come up with a list of personal problems. Have them report to the class and put their ideas on the board.

Option: To personalize the discussion, ask students if they would ever call a radio program to get advice. If so, in what situation would they do it and why? If not, why not?

➡ **Listening for the Main Idea** Have students read the strategy. Explain that in this listening activity they will be listening for the main idea. Tell students that they shouldn't worry about understanding every word. Rather, they should focus attention on key words and phrases that will help them understand the main idea.

🎧 ❷ Before listening, make sure students understand the vocabulary for the two problems they will be listening to on the radio call-in program *Ask Olga!* Then play the recording or read the audioscript aloud one or more times. Have students check the correct box for each problem.

Audioscript: The audioscript for Exercises 2 and 3 appear on page T156.

> **Answers**
> **Problem 1:** a personal problem
> **Problem 2:** a problem with something he bought

 Workbook: Practice 9

🎧 ❸ Play the recording or read the audioscript aloud one or more times so that students can write their answers.

> **Answers**
> **Problem 1:** She wants to leave school and get married. **Advice 2:** She should take her parents' advice **or** She shouldn't get married.
> **Problem 2:** His used car keeps breaking down. **Advice 1:** Never buy a used car **or** He should sell it and buy a new car.
> Answers may vary.

🌐 **Option:** Ask additional comprehension questions:

Problem 1: How old are the people involved? (The young woman is twenty-one and her boyfriend is twenty-seven.) What do her parents think? (They think her boyfriend is too old for her.) What happened to Listener B when she was young? (She got married when she was still in college. After a year, they broke up, and she never finished college.)

Problem 2: What is wrong with the car now? (The engine has broken down.) According to Listener C, what does everybody know? (Used cars always break down.)

🌐 **Option:** Have students vote on which advice they agree with. Then lead a class discussion. Students on each side of the issue should explain why they voted as they did.

Pronunciation

Students read the explanation in the box in class or as homework.

Presentation

🎧 ❹ Play the recording or read the audioscript aloud two or more times. Pause between sentences to allow students time to circle the correct answer. Have students work with a partner and go over their answers. Then go over the answers as a class.

Audioscript: The audioscript for Exercise 4 appears on page T156.

> **Answers**
> **a.** rising **b.** rising/falling **c.** rising **d.** rising/falling **e.** rising/falling **f.** rising **g.** rising/falling **h.** rising **i.** rising/falling **j.** rising/falling

 Workbook: Practice 10

Speak Out

➡ **Asking for and Giving Advice** Go around the class and ask students to give their advice on various topics. Don't worry about correcting errors at this point. Then have students review the expressions for asking for and giving opinions.

🌐 **Option:** You may wish to have student volunteers state current personal problems in small groups or as a class. Have other students offer advice. Encourage responses to be "soft" (see page 79).

Review the expressions *From my point of view … , As I see it … , It seems to me that …* when giving an opinion.

2 Listen to the radio program *Ask Olga!* What kind of problem is each person asking about? Check your answer.

Problem 1
☐ a problem with money
☐ a personal problem
☐ a problem at school

Problem 2
☐ a problem with someone at work
☐ a problem with something he borrowed
☐ a problem with something he bought

 3 Listen to the program again. Complete the chart.

Problem 1	Advice 1	Advice 2
	She should get married.	

Problem 2	Advice 1	Advice 2
		He should go to the Better Business Bureau.

Pronunciation

Intonation Patterns

Yes/no questions have a rising intonation pattern.

Should we go alone?

Statements and information questions have a rising-falling intonation pattern.

No, you should ask Jonathan.

Why should I do that?

---

4 Circle the intonation you hear.

a.	rising	rising/falling	**f.**	rising	rising/falling
b.	rising	rising/falling	**g.**	rising	rising/falling
c.	rising	rising/falling	**h.**	rising	rising/falling
d.	rising	rising/falling	**i.**	rising	rising/falling
e.	rising	rising/falling	**j.**	rising	rising/falling

Speak Out

STRATEGY **Asking for and Giving Advice** When solving problems, you ask for and give advice. Sometimes you agree with people's advice and sometimes you don't.

Asking for Advice	Giving Advice
What do you think …	I think they should …
Do you think they should …	They ought to …
Should they …	In my opinion, they'd better …

5 Your city has received a large amount of money to solve one of its problems. Work in groups of three. Each student should read a different problem and then explain the problem to the group. As a group, decide which problem the city should spend the money on. Ask for advice and give advice.

a. In some neighborhoods, there are many thieves, and people are afraid to go out at night. Sometimes the thieves hurt or kill people to get their money. The city needs more police officers.

b. People are worried about the traffic problem. More and more people have cars. There are terrible traffic jams. Sometimes traffic stops completely. The city needs to build wider streets and new roads.

c. People are upset about the amount of air pollution in the city. Factories put huge quantities of smoke in the air. Cars, trucks, and buses add more pollution. If the city tells the companies to put in pollution controls, many factories will close. The city needs to help the factories pay for pollution controls.

READING and WRITING

Read About It

1 **Before You Read** In the past, people usually got advice from their families and friends. What are some different ways of getting advice today?

STRATEGY **Skimming** Before reading a text, it is a good idea to get a general idea of what the text is about. Skim, or read quickly, to find the main ideas.

2 Quickly skim the text. What is the main idea of paragraph one? Of paragraph two? Compare your answers with a partner's.

Help Is Out There

In the past, when people had problems, they went to relatives or friends to get advice. Today, thanks to technology, it is possible to get advice from radio shows, TV programs, telephone hot
5   lines, and the Internet.

Advice is everywhere. Listeners across the United States can call up radio programs to talk about their problems and get or give advice on the air. For example, the popular radio show *Car Talk*
10   gives advice on problems listeners are having with their cars. TV viewers can watch as people tell their life stories and describe their difficulties on many well-known talk shows such as *Sally Jesse Raphael* or *The Oprah Winfrey Show*.

Presentation

❺ Have students read the instructions. Then have students work in groups of three, discussing which problem they think the city should tackle. Circulate and offer help. Make notes of student errors, but don't interrupt to correct them; you want to encourage fluency. Have selected pairs perform their dialogues for the class. Refer to your notes and write errors on the board without identifying who made them. Then correct the errors as a class.

Option: Have students work individually, in pairs, or in small groups to write dialogues in which a parent gives advice to a child, a teacher gives advice to a student, or a friend gives advice to another friend. Ask pairs or groups to share their dialogues with the class.

READING and WRITING

Read About It

Presentation

❶ Before You Read Have students work in pairs or small groups to come up with a list of ways people get advice today.

Option: Put students' lists on the board and have the class rank the items according to their effectiveness.

➡ Skimming Explain to students what skimming is [reading quickly to get a general sense of the main ideas(s)]. Ask, *Do you ever skim materials in your native language? If so, what materials are they? Why would you skim something rather than read slowly? What are the advantages/disadvantages to skimming something?*

❷ Have students work alone to skim the text for the main ideas. Then they can compare answers with a partner.

Answers

Paragraph One: People used to go to friends or relatives to get advice.

Paragraph Two: Now people can get advice from a variety of sources.

Option: If there is time, have students read the remaining paragraphs and find the main idea for each one. Have selected students put their answers on the board and check them as a class. Ask students to explain their answers. Allow students to offer other choices and explain why.

❸ Have students define the terms in the box in their own words. Then have them skim the reading to check their answers.

Answers
Internet (l. 26): a system of connected computers around the world that provides rapid access to many kinds of information
newsgroup (l. 33): a group on the Internet that discusses a particular interest
chatting (l. 37): communicating instantly in real time by typing messages back and forth between computers
Web site (l. 41): a collection of documents that may have text, images, sound, and video that is found on the Internet

❹ Have students work alone to guess the meaning of the words from context. Circulate to help as necessary.

Answers
a. problems **b.** people who give advice
c. the place where you get something (in this case, advice) **d.** fast, quick **e.** a chronic disease **f.** an abbreviation for Internet

❺ Have students compare answers with a partner. What clue words helped them get their answers?

Option: Compare answers as a whole-class activity. List the words from Exercise 4 (a–f) on the board. Have individual students write the clue words that helped them figure out the meanings of the words. Did most students agree on the clue words?

Option: Ask, *Have you had any experience with a newsgroup? Have you ever visited a Web site? If so, what were your favorites?* Lead a class discussion.

Frequently, audience members on these shows make comments and give their own advice to the talk-show guests. Other people with problems can dial telephone hot lines, specialized services that offer immediate access to advice counselors. Callers may get advice on what to do about a snakebite, how to cook low-fat meals, or even how to solve a homework problem. But by far the fastest growing source of advice and help is the Internet, a system of connected computers around the world that provides rapid access to many kinds of information.

There are several ways to give and get advice on the Internet. Computer users may join a newsgroup, a kind of electronic discussion group that focuses on one subject. For example, people with diabetes may join a group to read articles on how to deal with this chronic disease, while people interested in improving their golf game can join a newsgroup specializing in golf. Another way to get advice on the Internet is through chatting, one of the Net's most popular features. In text-based chatting, people communicate instantly in real time by typing messages back and forth. In multimedia chat, people can have voice conversations and live video communication. Yet another way to get advice or solve a problem is through visiting Web sites.

Web sites are collections of documents that may have text, images, sound, and video. Each Web site has its own electronic address. For example, if students want to check English grammar, they can visit the following address: http://www.hiway.co.uk/~ei/intro.html.

To sum up, it is clear that technological advances today have given people many more ways to give advice, get advice, and solve their problems.

3 In your own words, define the computer terms in the box. Share your definitions with the class.

> Internet
> chatting
> newsgroup
> Web site

4 Use the context to guess the meaning of the following words. Write your answers on a sheet of paper.

   a. difficulties (line 11)   **d.** rapid (line 28)
   b. counselors (line 20)   **e.** diabetes (line 34)
   c. source (line 25)   **f.** Net (line 37)

5 What clue words in the context helped you figure out the meaning of each word? Compare your words with a partner's.

Think About It

6 Is it easier to get advice from a friend or from a stranger? Why?

7 Can you trust advice you find on the Internet? How do you know?

8 What experience have you had using the Internet? Have you ever asked for advice or solved a problem using the Internet? Explain.

Write: An Informal Letter

We send informal letters to family members, friends, and people we do not have important business relationships with. An informal letter has several standard parts: the date, the greeting, the body, the closing, and the signature.

9 Look at the letter to Andy Summers on page 78. Use it to answer the questions.

a. Where do we put the date on a letter? The greeting? The closing? Where do we write the first line of a letter?

b. How did the writer order the information in the letter? Write 1 to 3.

____ request for advice

____ identification of the problem

____ explanation of the problem

Write About it

10 You need some advice. Write a letter to Andy Summers. First, choose a problem. (For example, maybe you got a bad grade, you need money, or you don't like your job.) Brainstorm and focus your ideas. Then write a letter. Make sure that your letter identifies the problem, explains the problem, and requests advice. Don't forget to include the date, a greeting, and a closing. Use the letter on page 78 as an example.

 11 **Check Your Writing** Exchange papers with a partner. Read your partner's letter, and using the questions below, suggest ways to improve the letter.

- Are the parts of the letter easy to identify?
- Is the problem identified in the first sentence?
- Is the problem explained well?
- Does the writer ask for advice?

Think About It

Presentation

6 Have students think about the question and then discuss it in pairs.

7 Ask students to discuss this question in pairs and then join another pair to compare answers.

8 Students should talk about their experiences with the Internet. If they have solved a problem, they should go through the steps they took.

Option: If students were planning their own Web site, what would it feature? Who would be the intended audience? What would its purpose be?

Write: An Informal Letter

Students read the presentation in class or for homework.

Option: Bring in a sample letter with the different parts clearly identified. Ask students if there are any differences in how informal letters are written in their language.

Presentation

9 Students should refer to the letter to Andy Summers on page 78 to answer these questions.

Option: Review the meaning of **signature** (your name written the way you usually write it, for example, at the end of a letter or on a check). Ask students which letter on page 78 has a **signature**. (Dear In Love,)

> **Answers**
> **a. date:** top left-hand side; **greeting:** below date, left-hand side; **closing:** bottom of letter, left-hand side; **first line of letter:** below greeting, indented from left-hand side
> **b.** 3, 1, 2

Language Note: There are many different ways to write an informal letter. The **date** and the **closing** may appear on the right-hand side, the date may be written without the year or left off entirely, and **Dear** may be substituted with **Hi,**—or **Hello.**

You may want to remind students that when we include the year in the date, the year is set off by a comma, for example, Nellie Bly left New York on November 14, 1889, to travel around the work.

 Workbook: Practice 12

Write About It

Presentation

10 Have students write their own letter seeking advice.

 Workbook: Practice 11

☑ **11 Check Your Writing** Have students exchange papers and use the questions to give suggestions on how to improve the letter. Students should revise their letters based on the suggestions.

Vocabulary Expansion: Expressions with *break* See page T147.

> **Answers**
> **A. 1.** up **2.** even **3.** the law **4.** down **5.** the ice **6.** in
> **B. 1.** e **2.** a **3.** d **4.** c **5.** f **6.** b

> **EVALUATION**
> See page TExi.
>
> **Unit 8 Achievement Test**
>
> **Self-Check** See **Check Your Knowledge** on page 64 of the Workbook.
>
> **Dictation** Have students review the sentences in Exercise 6 on page 77. Then present them as a dictation. (See instructions on page TExv.)
>
> **Communication Skills**
>
> **1.** Play the part of the caller on a radio call-in program while a student plays the adviser. As students speak, listen for their use of language for giving advice.
>
> **2.** Have students work in pairs to discuss the problems on page 76. Observe pairs of students discussing the problems. Listen as students take turns in explaining the problems, and asking for, giving, and accepting advice.

STRESSED OUT

OBJECTIVES

- To talk about stress
- To use relative pronouns in adjective clauses to describe people and things
- To identify opinions
- To identify contrastive stress
- To express preferences
- To understand reference
- To write a paragraph using examples
- To use expressions with **take**

GETTING STARTED

Warm Up

Preview

Check understanding of different words used to describe emotions: **happy, sad, angry, tired, jealous, nervous, confident, shocked, worried, calm, frightened, depressed, anxious,** and **disappointed.** Bring pictures or photos of people to class and ask students to identify the emotions the people are feeling. Check understanding of **stress.** Ask, *How do you feel when you're stressed out?*

Presentation

❶ Have students work with a partner to make a list of what makes people feel stressed out. Then compile the different lists on the board. As a class, rank the most stressful situations.

✪ **Option:** Have students talk about stress in their own lives. What stresses them out? What do they do in the situation? Ask, *How stressed out are you?* Have students show hands as you read off each category: *not stressed at all, sometimes stressed, frequently stressed, always stressed.* Record the answers on the board.

✪ **Option:** Make a list of the most stressful jobs and have students vote on which one is the most stressful. Ask, *Why is this job the most stressful?* Lead a class discussion.

Language Note: In the first conversation, **pop** refers to **soda pop.** In some areas of the United States, a soft drink is referred to simply as **soda. Pepsi Cola** and **Coca-Cola** are two examples of soda pop.

🎧 ❷ Make sure that everyone understands the exercise. Play the recording or read the audioscript aloud one or more times. Tell students they do not have to understand every word to do the activity.

Audioscript: The audioscript for Exercise 2 appears on page T157.

> **Answers**
> **a.** Bob **b.** Judy **c.** Mark

 Workbook: Practice 1

✪ **Option:** Have students give advice to the stressed-out people in Exercise 2.

✪ **Option:** Ask additional questions:

Conversation A: How does Sue feel about her new job? (She loves it.)

Conversation B: What will happen if Judy loses her job? [She won't be able to (give money) help out her brother in college.]

Conversation C: When does Mark always worry? (when he has to catch a plane)

✪ **Option:** Have students write a brief dialogue about a time when they were stressed out. If students are uncomfortable writing something so personal, have them write an imaginary dialogue.

Figure It Out

See page T86.

GETTING STARTED

Warm Up

1 Many people complain about stress in their lives. These people feel nervous and upset. When someone is under too much stress, we say that this person is "stressed out." What makes people stressed out?

2 Listen to the conversations. Who is stressed out? Circle the name.

  a. Sue/Bob
  b. Judy/Chris
  c. Sandy/Mark

Figure It Out

3 How well do you handle stress? Fill out the questionnaire on page 86 to find out. Circle one or more letters for each question.

Questionnaire

1. *You always carry an expensive, brown briefcase. You are on the bus, and the man who is sitting next to you keeps looking at your briefcase. Finally, he says that your briefcase is the one that he lost on the bus last week. You:*
   a. get nervous.
   b. get angry and tell him the briefcase is yours.
   c. don't listen to him and continue reading.
   d. tell him that maybe his briefcase is in the lost and found.

2. *You are alone in an elevator that has stopped between floors. You:*
   a. begin to shout for help.
   b. feel very nervous and frightened.
   c. ring the alarm and calmly wait for help.
   d. read the newspaper you have in your briefcase.

3. *You are going on vacation with your family on Saturday. On Friday morning, an executive who is very important asks you to start work on a new project right away. She says that you can go on vacation next month. You:*
   a. laugh nervously.
   b. feel anxious, but finally agree.
   c. politely refuse and tell why.
   d. suggest that you can start the project after your trip.

4. *You have a friend who wants to borrow some money. He always pays it back, but it takes a long time. Today he needs thirty dollars, but you want to use this money to buy a birthday present for another friend. You:*
   a. get really upset and tell him to find the money some place else.
   b. lend him the money and disappoint your other friend.
   c. explain why you can't lend him the money.
   d. offer to help him learn to use his money more carefully.

5. *You are returning from a trip abroad. You have brought eight Swiss watches with you. The customs officer who is checking your baggage has just told you that the limit is two watches. You:*
   a. begin to get upset.
   b. say that you are very, very sorry.
   c. calmly admit that you have brought in too many watches.
   d. smile and tell him that you didn't know that the limit was two watches.

4 Count 1 point for every **a** or **b** answer you did *not* circle and 1 point for every **c** or **d** answer you *did* circle. Then find your score in the chart.

16–20	You handle stress better than most people. You stay calm in situations that make other people very nervous.
11–15	You are a person who sometimes feels stress, but not very often.
6–10	Situations that cause stress are frequent in your life. You should try to relax a little!
0–5	You feel stressed out too often! You should learn how to calm down from people who know how to handle stress.

Figure It Out

Preview

- If they haven't done so already, have students make a list of situations that have stressed them out in the past. To help students focus their thoughts, ask them to think of situations that happen at work, at school, at home, or when traveling. How did they handle each situation? Have them share answers with a partner.

- Check understanding of **lost and found** (item 1), **borrow, lend** (item 4), and **customs officer** (item 5). Ask, *What does the bus driver do when he/she finds personal belongings left behind on the bus?* Explain that the place to claim lost articles is called the **lost and found** (office). Review **borrow** and **lend**. Ask, *If I don't have money and want to get some from a friend, what can I do? What can my friend do?* (I can **borrow** it. My friend can **lend** it.) Explain that a **customs officer** is the person who checks travelers' luggage when they enter one country from another country.

- 🌐 **Option: Vocabulary Notebooks** See page TEviii.

Presentation

❸ Have students read the instructions and complete the questionnaire on page 86 alone.

❹ Have students calculate their scores. Circulate and provide help as necessary. Find out how many students are in each category. You may want to graph the results. Do the students agree with their scores? Were they surprised by the outcome? Lead a class discussion.

🌐 **Option:** Ask, *If you could choose your own answer, how would you react to the situations in the questionnaire?* Have students work in groups to come up with alternative solutions to the situations. Ask selected students to give their answers and write them on the board. Are the solutions more or less stressful than the ones given in the questionnaire?

🌐 **Option:** For homework, have students give the questionnaire to friends or family members and graph the results.

☑ ❺ **Vocabulary Check** Have students work alone and then check answers with a partner.

Answers
1. b 2. a 3. d 4. f 5. c 6. e 7. g

 Workbook: Practice 2

🌀 **Option: Vocabulary Notebooks** See page TEviii.

Talk About It

🌀 **Option:** If students need extra practice with adjective clauses (including relative pronouns as subjects and objects), postpone this activity until after you've completed the grammar exercises for this unit or Workbook Practices 3, 4, and 5.

Preview

With students' books closed, ask if they ever read health magazines. Ask, *What kinds of topics are in those magazines? What do they say about stress?*

Presentation

❻ Have students read the instructions and ask selected students to model the dialogue for the class. Then have students work in pairs taking turns being the reporter and the expert as they work through all the items. Circulate and offer assistance. Make notes of student errors, but don't interrupt to correct them; you want to encourage fluency. Have selected pairs perform their dialogues for the class. Refer to your notes and write errors on the board without identifying who made them. Then correct the errors as a class.

🌀 **Option:** You may want to give students time before they do Exercise 6 to come up with reasons for why they find one situation more stressful than another.

🌀 **Option:** Suggest additional situations to discuss, such as getting married/getting divorced or starting a new job/retiring.

🌀 **Option:** Lead a class debate, with each team explaining why their topic (for example, having money problems) is more stressful than the other (for example, having problems with their children). Have students who are observing serve as judges and vote on the winners in the debate. Ideally, each student should get to serve on at least one debate team.

🌀 **Option:** For a homework assignment, have students give advice to people who face the situations in the exercise. They should review the structures they learned in Unit 8 on giving advice, giving a warning, and softening advice.

GRAMMAR

Adjective Clauses

Preview

Before looking at the grammar presentation, check students' knowledge of the grammar structure. Ask a student to stand up. Prompt that student to look at another student and say a sentence about that person, "I talked to the student who …" then continue to ask selected students to stand and make sentences about other students. "I talked to the girl who is wearing glasses." See if they can come up with other sentences using **which** and **that**. (Don't worry about errors. This is an exercise to check their knowledge.) Then go over the information in the box.

5 **Vocabulary Check** Match the words and their meanings.

_____ **1.** to handle   **a.** afraid

_____ **2.** frightened   **b.** to control

_____ **3.** anxious   **c.** to make someone feel sad

_____ **4.** to suggest   **d.** nervous

_____ **5.** to disappoint   **e.** the most you can have

_____ **6.** limit   **f.** to say an idea

_____ **7.** to calm down   **g.** to stop being nervous

Talk About It

6 A reporter for a health magazine is talking to an expert on stress. With a partner, take turns asking and answering questions.

Example: change jobs a lot/never change jobs

Ask for a comparison.

A: Who has more stress—people who change jobs a lot or people who never change jobs?

Give a comparison.

B: People who change jobs have more stress than people who don't.

Ask for an explanation.

A: Why do you think that?

Give an explanation.

B: Because people who change jobs a lot have to make many adjustments in their lives, and that's stressful.

a. have money problems/have problems with their children

b. lose their jobs/change work hours every week

c. travel a lot on business/work weekends

d. work for a male boss/work for a female boss

e. give up smoking/go on a diet

GRAMMAR

Adjective Clauses

Adjective clauses define, or give more information about, a noun. They are generally introduced by a relative pronoun (*that, who, whom, which*) and come after the noun they describe.

I have a friend.	*adjective clause* I have a friend **who is stressed out**.
He's listening to a tape.	*adjective clause* He's listening to a tape **which will relax him**.
Many people are stressed out.	*adjective clause* Many people **that I know** are stressed out.

1 Look at the example in the box on page 87:

   a. What does *who* refer to? _____

   b. What does *which* refer to? _____

   c. What does *that* refer to? _____

2 Imagine a stressed-out friend of yours.
Finish the sentences.

   a. I have a friend who _____,
      and who _____.

   b. She works at a place which _____.

   c. She has a car that _____.

We often use adjective clauses to define general words such as *the one, someone, anyone, people, something, anything, everyone.*

> In this job, we need **someone** who never gets angry.
>
> **Everything** that happens at work stresses Leslie out.

3 Finish the sentences about your other stressed-out friend, Tom.

   a. Tom doesn't know anyone who _____.

   b. Everything that _____ costs too much.

   c. He doesn't like anything that _____.

   d. He should talk to someone who _____.

Relative Pronouns as Subjects

Relative pronouns can be the subject of the adjective clause. *That* and *which* refer to things. *That* and *who* refer to people.

	Subject	Verb phrase
I read an article	**that**	explains the physical effects of stress.
	which	
I met the doctor	**that**	wrote the article.
	who	

4 Combine each pair of sentences. Use *who* for people and *that* for things.

Example:

I read a book. The book describes how to reduce stress.

I read a book that describes how to reduce stress.

   a. The book is about techniques. The techniques can help you control stress.

   b. The doctor is an expert on stress. The doctor wrote the book.

   c. The book says that running is a technique. This technique can lower stress.

   d. People feel much better. People run three times a week.

   e. Older people often feel depressed. These people live alone.

Presentation

❶ Have students work alone and then compare answers with a partner.

> **Answers**
> **a.** a friend **b.** a tape **c.** Many people

❷ Have students work alone and then compare sentences with a partner. Then ask selected students to put their sentences on the board and correct them as a class. (*Answers will vary.*)

 Option: Give students additional practice with adjective clauses. Write these examples on the board and have students read their completed sentences to the class.

- I'm reading a book that _____.

- My city/school/country is famous for [a zoo] that [many schoolchildren visit].

- _____ is a famous singer/sports hero/actor who _____.

- Sonia got a new (camera) for her birth-day which _____.

❸ Have students read the grammar explanation and then work alone, comparing answers with a partner. (*Answers will vary.*)

Relative Pronouns as Subjects

❹ Have students read the grammar explanation and then combine the sentences. Go over answers as a class.

> **Answers**
> **a.** The book is about techniques that can help you control stress. **b.** The doctor who wrote the book is an expert on stress.
> **c.** The book says that running is a technique that can lower stress. **d.** People who run three times a week feel much better.
> **e.** Older people who live alone often feel depressed.

Link ***Workbook: Practice 3***

Relative Pronouns as Objects

Preview

Explain that relative pronouns can also be used as objects. Practice making sentences with relative pronouns as both subjects and objects.

Presentation

☑ **❺ Check Your Understanding** In this exercise, students determine which relative pronouns are used as subjects and which as objects. Have students read the grammar presentation and do the exercise. They should work alone and then compare answers with a partner.

Answers

a. **Who** is a subject pronoun. It cannot be left out. b. **That** is an object pronoun and can be left out. c. **That** is an object pronoun and can be left out. d. **Which** is a subject pronoun. It cannot be left out. e. **Who** is a subject pronoun. It cannot be left out.

❻ Have students work in pairs to complete the paragraph, and then review answers as a class.

Answers

1. (which) 2. who 3. (which) 4. which
5. (which) 6. who 7. which 8. who

 Option: Bring in sentences from easy newspaper or magazine articles. Have students locate adjective clauses with relative pronouns (some may have been deleted) and identify them as either subjects or objects.

Link *Workbook: Practices 4, 5, 7, 8*

Relative Pronouns as Objects

A relative pronoun can be the object of the adjective clause. In this case, the pronoun can be left out.

	Object	Subject	Verb		
I read the book	**which**	Dr. Stone	wrote.		Formal
I read the book	**that**	Dr. Stone	wrote.		
I read the book	—	Dr. Stone	wrote.		Informal
The man	**whom**	I	met	is an expert on stress.	Formal
The man	**who**	I	met	is an expert on stress.	
The man	**that**	I	met	is an expert on stress.	
The man	—	I	met	is an expert on stress.	Informal

 5 **Check Your Understanding** Underline the relative pronouns used as subjects. Circle the relative pronouns used as objects. If the pronoun can be left out, put parentheses ( ) around it.

   a. The workers who performed repetitive tasks suffered from stress.
   b. Here are the books on stress that I told you to read.
   c. The child that we saw on the elevator was frightened.
   d. Environmental problems which cause stress include noise and air pollution.
   e. Students who need to get good grades often feel stressed out.

6 Read the paragraph. Write *who* or *which* on the line. If the relative pronoun is not necessary, put it in parentheses ( ).

One thing **(1.)** _____ doctors recommend for people **(2.)** _____ are under a lot of stress is running. Running is a sport **(3.)** _____ anyone can do. It is also a sport **(4.)** _____ doesn't require a lot of special equipment. The only things **(5.)** _____ runners need are running shoes and a place to run. Most people **(6.)** _____ run regularly say that the best place to run is a street or a park. People run outdoors all year round, even in places **(7.)** _____ are cold in the winter. According to experts, people **(8.)** _____ are interested in lowering stress must run for at least twenty to thirty minutes three times a week.

7 **Express Yourself** Look at how adjective clauses are used in definitions. Then, with a partner, complete the chart. Share your sentences with the class.

Example:

A: How would you define a "modem"?

B: It's a device that's used to connect your computer to the Internet.

Item	Verb	Class	Defining Information
A thermometer	is	an instrument	that measures temperature.
A cell phone		a device	
Chocolate	is		
Politicians		people	
A fax machine		a machine	
A stuntman	is		
Idea of your own			

LISTENING and SPEAKING

Listen: Stressful Jobs

1 **Before You Listen** How stressful do you think these jobs are? In column 1, rank them from 1 (highest stress) to 6 (lowest stress).

	1	**2**		**1**	**2**
librarian	_____	_____	banker	_____	_____
police officer	_____	_____	firefighter	_____	_____
sports star	_____	_____	actor/actress	_____	_____

 Identifying Opinions Listen for expressions such as *personally*, *I think*, *in my opinion*, and *as I see it*. These tell you that the speaker is giving his or her own opinion.

 2 Listen to the interview with an expert on stress. In column 2, write his ranking for stress (1 is the highest, 6 is the lowest).

 3 Listen to the interview again. What expressions did the speaker use to indicate he was giving his opinion?

 4 Compare your rankings with the expert's. Did you rank the jobs differently? Why? Share your ideas with the class.

❼ Express Yourself This activity is communicative and interactive. It connects the grammar point—in this case, adjective clauses—to the students' personal lives. *(Answers will vary.)*

 Link *Workbook: Practice 6*

Option: Give students a list of items to define and compile a class dictionary.

LISTENING and SPEAKING

Listen: Stressful Jobs

Preview

- Review the kinds of jobs that are the most stressful.

- Check understanding of **profession** (job), **enormous** (very large), **danger, popularity**, and **performance**. For **danger, popularity**, and **performance**, see if students can come up with other forms of the words (dangerous, popular, perform). Explain that you can **gain popularity** as well as **lose popularity**. (The latter is found in the audioscript.) Ask students if they know of another noun that goes with **gain** and **lose** (gain/lose weight).

Presentation

❶ Before You Listen Have students read the jobs and rank them according to how stressful they think they are. They should write their answers in the first column.

➡ **Identifying Opinions** Have students read the strategy. Explain that for these listening activities they will first listen and rank the jobs from most to least stressful. Then they will listen for language used to indicate that someone is giving an opinion. Ask students if they know any expressions used to give an opinion. (Don't correct errors at this stage.)

 ❷ Play the recording or read the audioscript aloud one or more times. In column 2, have students rank the stress

level of the jobs according to the expert and compare answers with a partner.

Audioscript: The audioscript for Exercises 2 and 3 appears on page T157.

> **Answers**
> librarian, 6; police officer, 2; sports star, 3; banker, 5; firefighter, 1; actor/actress, 4

Language Note: In American English, there has been a move toward making language more gender neutral, especially when referring to professions. Therefore, **policeman** has become **police officer** and **fireman** has become **firefighter**. Many jobs now use the word "person" in their names, for example, **TV anchorperson**, or have dropped "person" entirely: **chair, anchor**.

Option: Ask additional comprehension questions about jobs and stress.

What is some advice for people in stressful jobs? (Get plenty of rest and exercise and eat lots of fresh fruit and vegetables.)

 ❸ Play the recording or read the audioscript aloud again. Have students make notes of the language used to give an opinion.

> **Answers**
> here's my opinion, I think, I'd say, In my opinion

Option: You may want to remind students of other expressions used to give opinions, such as **As I see it, In my view, It seems to me, From my point of view, As far as I'm concerned**.

Link *Workbook: Practice 9*

❹ Have students discuss the questions in small groups, then as a class. *(Answers will vary.)*

Option: Give students other professions to rank. Some examples: **babysitter, construction worker, dancer, farmer, stuntperson, teacher, zookeeper**.

Pronunciation

Preview

- Ask selected students to ask general questions. Answer each one by emphasizing some information in the sentence. See if students can identify the pattern and come up with a rule before you go over the information in the pronunciation box.

- Students read the explanation in the box in class or as homework.

Presentation

❺ Have students practice saying the sentences with a partner. Circulate and provide assistance. Then have students switch partners so that they can practice with other students.

❻ Play the recording or read the audioscript aloud two or more times. Pause between sentences to allow students time to write. Have students work with a partner and go over their answers. Then go over the answers as a class.

Audioscript: The audioscript for Exercise 6 appears on page T157.

> **Answers**
> 1. a 2. b 3. a 4. a 5. a

 Workbook: Practice 10

⊛ **Option:** For further practice, read several sentences with one piece of information clearly stressed in each one. Then ask students to compose a question that would elicit each sentence. They should read their question back to you. Say, *I went downtown yesterday to buy a new **bicycle**.* Students then write and say, "**What** did you buy?"

Speak Out

➡ **Expressing Preferences** Go around the class and ask students to give their opinions on various topics. Don't worry about correcting errors at this point. Then review language for asking for and giving opinions.

Pronunciation

Contrastive Stress

In English we use stress and intonation to emphasize or contrast certain information.

What did Zoltan buy? He bought a **car**. (not a **bike**)

Did Zoltan **sell** a car? No, he **bought** a car. (not **sold**)

Who bought a car? **Zoltan** bought a car. (not **Karl**)

 5 Work with a partner. Take turns saying the sentences aloud. Is your partner emphasizing the right information?

a. I never drove my father's new **car**, but I drove his new **motorcycle**.

b. I never drove my father's **new** car, but I drove his **old** car.

c. I never drove my **father's** new car, but I drove my **mother's** new car.

d. I never drove **my** father's new car, but I drove **your** father's new car.

e. I never **drove** my father's new car, but I **rode** in my father's new car.

f. I never drove my father's new car, but **you** drove my father's new car.

 6 Listen to the answer and circle the letter of the correct question.

1. a. Who bought the best computer?
   b. Which computer is best?

2. a. Which computer did he buy at the mall?
   b. Where did he buy his new computer?

3. a. Who bought the cheapest computer?
   b. Which computer did Dan buy?

4. a. How often does Dan use the computer lab?
   b. What time does Dan use the computer lab?

5. a. Whose computer was the most powerful?
   b. What was Dan's computer like?

Speak Out

STRATEGY **Expressing Preferences** To indicate that you like one person or thing more than another, you use certain expressions. These expressions signal preferences.

I prefer ...	I much prefer ...	Would you rather ... ?
I like ... more than ...	I'd rather ...	I'd rather not ...

7 Work in groups of three. For each word in the box, tell what kinds of things you prefer.

movies	music
books	TV programs
restaurants	clubs
friends	bosses

Example:

A: I like movies that have happy endings.

B: Not me! I prefer movies that are frightening.

C: Really? I think scary movies are stressful. I'd rather see movies that teach me something.

READING and WRITING

Read About It

 1 Before You Read

a. What do you know about chocolate? Where does it come from? What is it made of?

b. The following article about chocolate appears in this unit on stress. What do you think chocolate and stress have to do with each other?

STRATEGY **Understanding Reference** Pronouns are used as substitutes for other words. They can refer to words or phrases that appear earlier or later in the text. By paying attention to pronoun reference, it is easier to understand connections between ideas.

Chocolate: A World Favorite

Chocolate, one of the most popular foods in the world, has a history as rich as its flavor. Chocolate comes from the beans of the cacao tree, a plant that has grown in the Americas for
5   at least 4,000 years. As long ago as the twelfth century, Indian families drank chocolate at marriages and other ceremonies. However, chocolate was not known in Europe until 1528, when the Spanish explorer Hernán Cortés
10   brought it to Spain.

    Drinking chocolate soon became popular in Spain and quickly spread to the rest of Europe. Three hundred years later, a scientist in Holland learned how to make chocolate into
15   candy. As the years passed, people in countries such as Belgium, Switzerland, and England began to make many kinds of chocolate candy. Today the making of chocolate is a multibillion dollar industry.

Cacao beans

Presentation

❼ Have students work in groups of three discussing what kinds of things they prefer. Circulate and offer help. Make notes of student errors, but don't interrupt to correct them; you want to encourage fluency. Have selected pairs perform their dialogues for the class. Refer to your notes and write errors on the board without identifying who made them. Then correct the errors as a class.

✿ Option: Have students memorize or write out a dialogue about their likes and dislikes. Encourage them to use props (real or imaginary) and to place their dialogue in an interesting setting (for example, a restaurant). Students should perform their skits, and the class can vote on the most entertaining, silliest, and so on.

✿ Option: Teach and practice additional language for expressing preferences:

- Expressing likes: **I (really) like … ; I'm crazy/nuts/wild about …**

- Saying what you prefer: **I tend to prefer/like … ; On the whole, I … ; If it was up to me, I …**

READING and WRITING

Read About It

Preview

With students' books closed, say that they're going to read an article about something that is eaten worldwide and is very popular. Ask, *What do you think it is?* Make a list of possibilities on the board. Then have students open their books to check the answer.

Presentation

❶ Before You Read Have students work in pairs or small groups to discuss the questions.

✿ Option: Have students work in small groups. Assign question **a** to half of the groups and question **b** to the other half. After students have had time for discussion, exchange ideas as a class.

➡ Understanding Reference Explain to students that pronoun reference is helpful because it makes it easier to understand the connection between ideas. Also explain that using pronoun reference in their own writing will make their work easier to read, less redundant, and more sophisticated. Alternatively, you can first ask students to tell you why pronoun reference is important.

❷ Have students read the article beginning on page 92 and answer the comprehension questions.

Answers
a. Chocolate came from the Americas.
b. The Spanish explorer Hernán Cortés brought it to Spain. c. It gives people quick energy and lowers stress.

Language Note: You might want to point out the difference in meaning depending on the tense used. For example, "Where <u>did</u> chocolate come from?" asks for the place of origin. "Where <u>does</u> chocolate come from?" asks for the name of the plant that produces chocolate.

⊕ **Option:** To give students an opportunity to practice their skimming skills, have them read the entire article in one or two minutes and then close their books and tell you what it's about. Alternatively, assign a different paragraph to each student in a group. Give students a few seconds to skim the paragraph and then summarize it for their group.

⊕ **Option:** Ask additional comprehension questions:

• Where does chocolate come from? (the beans of the cacao tree)

• How was it used in the twelfth century? (as a drink at marriages and other ceremonies) When did it arrive in Spain? (1528)

• Who first made chocolate into candy? (a scientist in Holland)

• Why do mountain climbers carry chocolate? (It gives them quick energy.)

• What do some people think of when they eat chocolate? (the food and comfort they received from their mothers)

❸ Have students work alone underlining the words each pronoun refers to. Then ask them to compare answers with a partner.

Answers
a. chocolate b. the cacao tree/a plant
c. chocolate d. chocolate e. statues
f. mountain climbers g. people h. people
i. people

❹ Have students work alone or with a partner writing short definitions. Assign this exercise for homework if there isn't time to complete it in class.

Answers
Other answers are possible.
a. traditional actions used at important social or religious events b. business
c. taste d. mixed e. things that are used to make something f. having to do with the body g. power h. having to do with the mind i. want, desire j. make someone remember something

⊕ **Option:** Assign two of the words to different pairs. Then have students exchange definitions with other students. This is a quick way to exchange a lot of information in little time. Circulate and offer help.

Think About It

Presentation
❺ Have students discuss the questions in pairs.

❻ Have students discuss this question in pairs and then join another pair to compare answers. What does the class in general think?

⊕ **Option:** Divide students into two teams to debate the positive and negative qualities of chocolate. Teams should be encouraged to add reasons to their list that aren't found in the reading.

⊕ **Option:** Have students write a brief story about a time when they enjoyed chocolate (or some other treat) as a child. They should focus on where they were and how they felt at the time. Have them include what the treat looked like and how it tasted.

20   There are many reasons why chocolate is so popular. People like its rich, delicious flavor. Some people think that chocolate is even better when combined with other ingredients, such as fruit and nuts. Also, candy makers can make chocolate into decorative shapes, from flowers and hearts to animals, and even to huge statues that weigh as much as 220 pounds (100 kilos).

25   In addition, eating chocolate has helpful physical effects. The sugar and fat in chocolate give people quick energy. This is why mountain climbers often carry chocolate with them. For this same reason, people like to have a candy bar when they're feeling tired.

        Eating chocolate has mental effects, too. Many people crave chocolate in times
30 of stress or emotional upset. Some psychologists explain that people associate chocolate with the happy times of their childhoods. The taste of chocolate reminds them of the food and comfort they received from their mothers. However, physical scientists have developed another explanation. They say that one
35 ingredient of chocolate, phenylethylamine, seems to lower stress.

        There is no doubt that chocolate, with its unique physical and psychological effects and its unmatched flavor, is one of the world's favorite foods.

2 Answer the questions.

   a. Where did chocolate come from?

   b. Who brought chocolate to Europe?

   c. What effect does chocolate have on the human body?

3 Find the following pronouns in the article and underline the word(s) each one refers to. Check your answers with the class.

   a. its (line 2)   **d.** its (line 20)   **g.** they (line 28)

   b. that (line 4)   **e.** that (line 23)   **h.** their (line 31)

   c. it (line 10)   **f.** them (line 27)   **i.** they (line 32)

4 Use the context to determine the meanings of the words. Write short definitions on a sheet of paper. Work without a dictionary.

   a. ceremony (line 7)   **f.** physical (line 25)

   b. industry (line 19)   **g.** energy (line 26)

   c. flavor (line 21)   **h.** mental (line 29)

   d. combined (line 21)   **i.** crave (line 29)

   e. ingredients (line 22)   **j.** remind (line 32)

Think About It

5 Do you ever eat when you feel stressed out? What do you eat? Does eating that food make you feel better? Why?

6 The article talks about the good effects of eating chocolate. What are some bad effects of chocolate?

Write: Using Examples

One kind of supporting detail is examples. Examples illustrate your ideas and make your writing easier to understand. Examples can be signaled by expressions like *for example*, *for instance*, *like*, and *such as*.

 Read the paragraph and answer the questions.

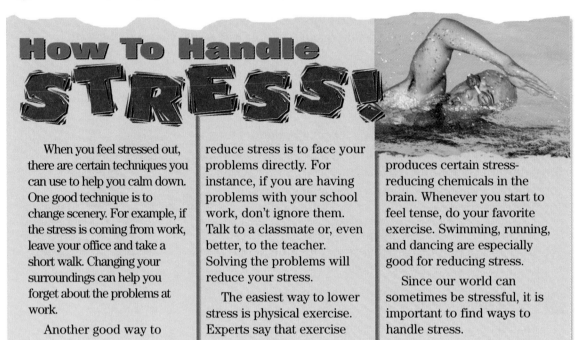

How To Handle STRESS!

When you feel stressed out, there are certain techniques you can use to help you calm down. One good technique is to change scenery. For example, if the stress is coming from work, leave your office and take a short walk. Changing your surroundings can help you forget about the problems at work.

Another good way to reduce stress is to face your problems directly. For instance, if you are having problems with your school work, don't ignore them. Talk to a classmate or, even better, to the teacher. Solving the problems will reduce your stress.

The easiest way to lower stress is physical exercise. Experts say that exercise produces certain stress-reducing chemicals in the brain. Whenever you start to feel tense, do your favorite exercise. Swimming, running, and dancing are especially good for reducing stress.

Since our world can sometimes be stressful, it is important to find ways to handle stress.

a. There are three examples in the paragraph. What are they?

b. How are they signaled?

c. What general statements do they support?

Write About It

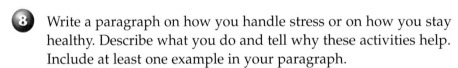 Write a paragraph on how you handle stress or on how you stay healthy. Describe what you do and tell why these activities help. Include at least one example in your paragraph.

 Check Your Writing Reread your paragraph. Does it say what you want it to say? Use the checklist and make revisions as needed.

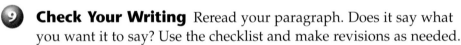

- Does the topic sentence state the main idea clearly?
- Are the supporting sentences ordered logically?
- Are there enough details and at least one specific example?

Write: Using Examples

Preview

- Students read the presentation in class or for homework.

- Explain how examples are used in writing to illustrate ideas. Ask students to go back to the article on chocolate on page 92 and see if they can find examples used by the writer to support ideas.

Presentation

❼ Have students read the paragraph and answer the questions.

> ### Answers
> **a.** leave your office and take a short walk; talk to a classmate or the teacher; swimming, running, and dancing **b.** For example, For instance **c.** One good technique is to change scenery; Another good way to reduce stress is to face your problems directly; The easiest way to lower stress is physical exercise.

Write About It

Presentation

❽ Have students write their own paragraph about handling stress or staying healthy. They can write the paragraph in class or as homework. If students will do their writing at home, have them first brainstorm in class so that you can check that step.

☑ **❾ Check Your Writing** In this exercise, students exchange papers and use the questions to give suggestions on how to improve the paragraph. Students should revise their assignments based on the suggestions given.

 Workbook: Practices 11, 12

Vocabulary Expansion: Expressions with *take*
See page T148.

> ### Answers
> **1.** i **2.** a **3.** c **4.** h **5.** g **6.** j **7.** b **8.** e
> **9.** d **10.** f

EVALUATION

See page TExi.

Unit 9 Achievement Test

Self-Check See **Check Your Knowledge** on page 72 of the Workbook.

Dictation Have students review the sentences in Exercise 4 on page 88. Then present sentences as a dictation. (See instructions on page TExv.)

Communication Skills

1. Ask students how they feel in different situations. Pay attention to how they use vocabulary describing emotions. Some possible situations: eating a favorite food, on summer vacation, before a big exam.

2. Show pictures of different objects (or bring them into class) and have students describe the objects using adjective clauses. Show pictures of people and have students use adjective clauses to describe them.

3. Ask students to describe their preferences in movies, books, and TV programs. Pay attention to their use of adjective clauses.

Review Units 7–9

Review unit exercises can be assigned as homework or done in class. You can use them in different ways.

- Give the review exercises as a quiz. Students work alone and turn in their answers to you.

- Use review exercises as you would other exercises in the book. Students work alone and then compare answers with a partner.

- Have students work alone and then review answers as a class. Have selected students write their answers on the board, and correct any errors as a class.

❶ Have students read the instructions and complete the exercise. For a comparison of the simple past and present perfect tenses, have students refer to Unit 7, pages 67–69.

Answers
1. have 2. Have (you) ever used 3. have always sent 4. haven't been 5. did (you) find out 6. saw 7. do (you) need
8. Have (you) translated 9. have never heard 10. is

❷ Have students read the instructions and complete the exercise. For a comparison of the simple past and present perfect tenses, have students refer to Unit 7, pages 67–69.

Answers
1. Have (you ever) wished 2. describes
3. found 4. receive 5. has helped

❸ Have students read the instructions and complete the exercise. For a review of time expressions, have students refer to Unit 7, pages 67–69.

Answers
a. ever b. last month c. yet d. since e. still
f. so far

1 Complete the conversation with the correct form of the verbs. Use the simple present, simple past, or present perfect tense.

BILL: Hello, Acme Translation Services? I **(1. have)** _____ a letter that I need translated right away.

ACME: **(2. use, ever)** _____ you _____ our company before?

BILL: No. I **(3. send, always)** _____ my work to Speedy Translations up to now, but I **(4. be, neg.)** _____ satisfied, so now I'm trying you.

ACME: How **(5. find out)** _____ you _____ about our company?

BILL: I **(6. see)** _____ your ad in the paper.

ACME: What language **(7. need)** _____ you _____?

BILL: Urdu. **(8. translate)** _____ you _____ Urdu before?

ACME: Sir, we **(9. hear, neg.)** _____ of that language. I'm sorry.

BILL: What? I can't believe it. What kind of company **(10. be)** _____ this?

2 Complete the passage with the correct form of one of the verbs in the box. Use the simple present, the simple past, or the present perfect tense.

decide	help
describe	receive
find	wish

Are you happy in your present job? **(1.)** _____ you ever _____ that you had a different, more exciting job? If so, subscribe to our monthly newsletter, the *Job Bulletin*. The *Job Bulletin* **(2.)** _____ all the positions available in our area. Last year, over 1,275 happy people **(3.)** _____ the job of their dreams through our newsletter. We **(4.)** _____ letters from satisfied customers every month, thanking us for our help. The *Job Bulletin* **(5.)** _____ people find work for over fifteen years! Let us help you, too.

3 Complete the sentences with an appropriate word or expression from the box.

ever	last month
so far	yet
still	since

a. Have you _____ sat at a cafe and watched the people go by?

b. The company hired six new employees _____.

c. Larry can't go because he hasn't finished his homework _____.

d. My husband has been a couch potato _____ he was a teenager!

e. What? You _____ haven't paid the bills?

f. Do we need film? How many photos have you taken _____?

4 Read each situation and write one sentence giving advice. Use *should*, *shouldn't*, *ought to*, or *had better*.

a. My daughter is always late to work, and I'm afraid she's going to lose her job.

_____

b. Pavel saw Eva cheat on the last math test.

_____

c. Antonio has studied English for six years, but he still cannot speak it well.

_____

d. I don't know why Zack does so badly on tests. He stays up all night to study.

_____

e. The president of the company wants to make his employees happy.

_____

5 Complete each sentence with a relative pronoun. Use *who, whom,* or *which*. If the relative pronoun is not necessary, put it in parentheses ( ).

a. That student over there is the one _____ won the Special Achievement Award.

b. Can you lend me your copy of the novel _____ I lost?

c. My computer is the one invention _____ I couldn't live without!

d. The librarian _____ handles reference books is busy.

e. The child _____ performed that piece plays four other instruments.

Vocabulary Review

Complete the sentences with words from the box.

can't stand	industry
controversial	enthusiasm
had better	lend
stress	salary
handle	

1. Most doctors agree that constant _____ has serious health effects.

2. I really _____ people who don't wait their turn.

3. She is the youngest candidate, but the boss likes her energy and _____.

4. You _____ turn in that report today or you'll get into deep trouble!

5. The boss promised Sarah an increase in _____.

6. I don't think you should _____ Frank that money. He always takes forever to pay back what he owes.

7. Nellie Bly wrote about _____ social topics of her day.

8. The making of chocolate is a multi-billion dollar _____.

❹ Have students read the instructions and complete the exercise. For a review of **should, shouldn't, ought to,** and **had better,** have students refer to Unit 8, pages 78–79.

Answers
Other answers are possible. **a.** She'd better get to work on time. **b.** Eva shouldn't cheat on tests. **c.** Antonio ought to study more. **d.** Zack should do better on tests. **e.** He should increase their salaries.

❺ Have students read the instructions and complete the exercise. For a review of adjective clauses, have students refer to Unit 9, pages 87–89.

Answers
a. who **b.** (which) **c.** (which)
d. who **e.** who

Vocabulary Review

Have students read the instructions and complete the exercise.

Answers
1. stress **2.** can't stand **3.** enthusiasm
4. had better **5.** salary **6.** lend
7. controversial **8.** industry

YOU'VE GOT TO BE KIDDING!

OBJECTIVES

- To talk about records
- To use the present perfect and present perfect progressive tenses to talk about what has been happening
- To listen to confirm predictions
- To identify unstressed *h* words
- To express surprise or disbelief
- To distinguish fact and opinion
- To write a paragraph using transitions
- To make opposites with the prefixes **–un** and **–in**

GETTING STARTED

Warm Up

Preview

Check understanding of **gold medal**, **race**, **break a record** (conversation a), **encyclopedia**, **luxury** (conversation b), **contest**, **finish line**, and **better luck next time** (conversation c). Ask, *What medals do the top three finishers in the Olympics receive?* (**gold**, silver, and bronze). For **break a record**, talk about someone who won a medal in the Olympics or some other contest. Say, *Florence Griffith Joyner won a* **gold medal**. *She ran faster than any other woman in history. She* **broke the record** *for running 100 meters.*

- Explain that any game someone can win is a **contest**. A **race** is a contest to see who can go the fastest. Say, *In a running* **race**, *the first person who crosses the* **finish line** *is the winner.* Ask, *What can you say to a friend who has just lost an important race?* Introduce **Better luck next time.**

- Show your students an **encyclopedia** and ask them to explain what it's used for. Explain that **luxury** goods are very expensive.

Language Note: *Luxury* is used to describe expensive clothing, possessions, and surroundings that are desirable but not necessary. It is a word often used by advertisers to give the impression that something is fancy and hard to obtain.

🌐 **Option: Vocabulary Notebooks** See page TEviii.

Presentation

❶ Have students list different sports and any famous athletes who have set records in these sports. Compile a list on the board. Then have students think of other kinds of records people have set.

🌐 **Option:** Before doing Exercise 2, have students anticipate what key words they might hear in the listening. Students should make a list of these words and check off the ones that they actually hear.

🎧 ❷ Make sure that everyone understands the exercise. Explain that the first conversation deals with a swimming record, the second is about a work situation, and the third is about a contest. Play the recording or read the audioscript aloud one or more times. Tell students they do not have to understand every word.

Audioscript: The audioscript for Exercises 2 and 3 appears on page T158.

> **Answers**
> **a.** yes **b.** yes **c.** no

🌐 **Option:** Ask students to tell you what they could say to the two people who broke the records. Elicit expressions such as **Congratulations! Well done! Good job! You did it! I'm really proud of you!**

🎧 ❸ Play the recording or read the audioscript aloud again. Tell students to listen for the records that are mentioned.

> **Answers**
> **a.** 100-meter (swimming) race **b.** selling the most encyclopedias **c.** running while carrying glasses

(Option exercises for Exercise 3 appear on page T98.)

YOU'VE GOT TO BE KIDDING!

GETTING STARTED

Warm Up

1 Many people want to be the best in what they do. In sports, for example, runners and swimmers try to break records. Think of some athletes who have broken sports records. What records did they break? What other kinds of records do people try to break?

2 You are going to hear conversations with three people who tried to break records. Circle **yes** if the person broke the record and **no** if the person did not.

    a. yes/no   **b.** yes/no   **c.** yes/no

3 Listen to the conversations again. What record was the person trying to break?

    a. _____

    b. _____

    c. _____

Figure It Out

A.

MOM: Ruby, put that book down! You've been reading it for hours now. I need your help in the kitchen.

5 **RUBY:** But this book is great! Just let me finish this part and then I'll help you. I'm reading about a man who has set world records for eating glass and metal.

MOM: Why do you waste your time on
10 science fiction?

RUBY: It's not science fiction. It's true! Michel Lotito is a real person from France, and he has been eating glass and metal since 1959.

15 **MOM:** You're kidding me!

B.

MOM: How much glass has he eaten?

RUBY: Well, so far, he's eaten six chandeliers. And remember, he's been eating metal objects all that time, too.

20 **MOM:** What kind of metal objects?

RUBY: It says here that he has eaten ten bicycles, seven TV sets, a shopping cart, and ...

MOM: That's incredible! How long did it take him to eat the shopping cart?

25 **RUBY:** He finished it in four and a half days.

MOM: That's amazing! And he's been doing this for over thirty years? If he's not careful, he's going to end up in a coffin. Let me see that book.

RUBY: Here. Look at this part.

30 **MOM:** Gee, he even ate a small airplane! This is unbelievable!

RUBY: Come on, I'll give you a hand in the kitchen now. Maybe we should make a glass and metal salad for dinner tonight. And maybe we can have the Eiffel Tower for dessert.

4 Answer the questions.

a. How long has Michel Lotito been eating glass and metal?

b. What unusual objects has he eaten?

c. What are Ruby and her mother going to do?

d. Why do some people do unusual things such as eating glass and metal and climbing skyscrapers?

e. What unusual thing would you try?

Michel Lotito

(Exercise 3 Options continued from page T97.)

Option: Have students talk about their own experiences. Have they ever entered a contest or a race? What happened? Were they satisfied with the outcome? Have selected students tell their stories to the class.

Option: Ask additional comprehension questions about the daughter, Bill, and Lou.

Figure It Out

Preview

Check understanding of (A) **metal**, **science fiction**, (B) **chandelier**, **shopping cart**, and **unbelievable**. Show students pictures of objects made of glass and **metal**. Give the names of some famous science fiction books or movies in the students' native language. Ask, *Do you like **science fiction?*** and ask for a show of hands. Show the picture in the Student Book of the **chandelier**. Can students tell you the origin of the word? (It comes from French.) Draw a picture of a **shopping cart** on the board or pantomime going shopping. Explain that **unbelievable** (like **incredible** and **amazing**) is a word you say when you're really surprised by something you've just seen or heard.

Language Note: Note the initial "sh" sound of **chandelier**. To **end up in a coffin** means "to die." Students don't need to memorize this expression.

Option: Vocabulary Notebooks See page TEviii.

Option: Before students read the dialogue and answer the questions, have them practice their scanning skills. Write these numbers on the board and have students find what they refer to: **a.** 1, **b.** $4\frac{1}{2}$, **c.** 6, **d.** 7, **e.** 10, **f.** 1959.

> **Answers**
> **a.** the number of shopping carts or airplanes Michel Lotito has eaten **b.** the number of days it took him to eat the shopping cart **c.** the number of chandeliers he has eaten **d.** the number of TV sets he has eaten **e.** the number of bicycles he has eaten **f.** the year he started eating glass and metal

Presentation

❹ Have students read the dialogue and answer the comprehension questions, working alone. Then have them compare answers with a partner. Alternately, have students skim the dialogue and then close their books. They should then summarize the dialogue for a partner.

> **Answers**
> **a.** since 1959 **b.** He's eaten chandeliers, bicycles, TV sets, a shopping cart, and a small airplane. **c.** They're going to make dinner. **d.–e.** *Answers will vary.*

Option: Ask additional comprehension questions:

- Why does Ruby's mother want her to stop reading? (She needs Ruby's help in the kitchen.)
- Where is Michel Lotito from? (France)
- What kind of salad does Ruby joke about making? (glass and metal salad)

Option: Ask, *What kind of strange record would you like to try to break?* Have students discuss in small groups. Ask selected students to report back to the class.

Option: Ask students if they agree with Ruby's mother that science fiction is a waste of time. Alternatively, have students comment on Ruby's behavior. Would a teenager in their culture respond to a parent as Ruby does in her first speech (line 5)? Lead a class discussion.

 Workbook: Practices 1, 2

☑ **❺ Vocabulary Check** Have students work alone and then check answers with a partner.

Answers
1. e 2. a 3. d 4. b 5. c

🌐 **Option: Vocabulary Notebooks** See page TEviii.

Talk About It

🌐 **Option:** If your students need extra practice with the present perfect tense or present perfect progressive tense, do this activity until after you've completed the grammar exercises for this unit or Workbook Practice 3.

Preview

With students' books closed, ask students to tell you about a TV show they saw or a magazine article they read about someone who set a record. Who was the show/article about? What did the person do? Was the show/article interesting? Why or why not?

Presentation

❻ Have students read the instructions and ask selected students to model the dialogue for the class. Then have students work in pairs taking turns being the host and the guest as they work through all the items. Circulate and offer assistance. Make notes of student errors, but don't correct them; you want to encourage fluency. Have selected pairs perform their dialogues for the class. Refer to your notes and write errors on the board without identifying who made them. Then correct the errors as a class.

 Workbook: Practice 4

🌐 **Option:** Have students make up dialogues, substituting their own names. Encourage them to make the records comical and surprising. Alternately, use a book such as the *Guinness Book of World Records* for factual information that students can incorporate into their dialogues.

GRAMMAR

The Present Perfect Progressive Tense: Unfinished Past Actions

Preview

* Go over the grammar presentation and explain that this structure is used for past actions that have continued up to the present and will probably continue into the future. Ask selected students to say a sentence each using the present perfect progressive tense. They should mention an action that they started in the past and are still doing now, for example, "I have been studying English for three years."

* Review the contracted forms, for example, "I've been studying … "

* Brainstorm expressions used with the present perfect progressive tense: **so far, up to now, since then, how long, for (a year)**, and so on.

* Check understanding of **collect** and **collection.**

5 **Vocabulary Check** Match the words with their definitions.

_____ **1.** set records (lines 7–8)　　**a.** not use well

_____ **2.** waste (line 9)　　**b.** hard to believe

_____ **3.** objects (line 18)　　**c.** help

_____ **4.** incredible (line 23)　　**d.** things

_____ **5.** give a hand (line 32)　　**e.** be the best

Talk About It

6 Each of the guests on today's *That's Amazing!* show has set a world record. Work with a partner. Take turns being the TV show host and the guest. Ask and answer questions using the cues.

Example: Jose Montero's record:
　　　　　　hit songs written in one year

> *Ask about number of actions until present.*
> **A:** Jose, you've just set the world record for songwriting. How many hits have you written so far this year?
>
> *Tell number of actions until present.*
> **B:** I've written seven so far this year.
>
> *Ask about length of time.*
> **A:** How long have you been writing songs?
>
> *Tell length of time.*
> **B:** I've been composing songs for ten years now … basically since I moved to Hollywood.

a. Gary DiAngelo's record:　　countries visited in one year

b. Judy Grant's record:　　film awards won in lifetime

c. Keiko Mayahara's record:　　sports medals received in lifetime

GRAMMAR

The Present Perfect Progressive Tense: Unfinished Past Actions

The present perfect progressive (*have/has* + *been* + verb–*ing*) is used to talk about unfinished past actions or actions that began in the past, are happening now, and will probably continue into the future.

> **A:** How long **have** you **been singing** opera now?
>
> **B:** Well, I**'ve been working** at the Opera Cafe for a year now.
>
> **A:** **Have** you **liked** your job as a singing waitress?
>
> **B:** Oh yes, I**'ve broken** 100 glasses! I'm the high note of the evening.

1 Write an appropriate verb in the present perfect progressive tense.

1. A: Did Michel Lotito really eat six chandeliers?

    B: Why, yes. He _____ glass since 1959.

2. A: I understand Natalia has won several swimming medals.

    B: That's right. She _____ medals ever since she was a child.

3. A: I hear Lola and Manuel won the prize for the best dancers.

    B: Yes, they _____ in contests since they met each other in 1998.

4. A: Is it true that Charles got the award for the person who has traveled the most?

    B: Yes, it is. He _____ for more than forty years now.

5. A: I hear you have a huge rock collection.

    B: Yes, I _____ rocks for five years now.

The Present Perfect vs. the Present Perfect Progressive

We use the present perfect tense to talk about actions completed at an indefinite time in the past, but which still have importance in the present.

> He**'s read** the book, so he knows the ending. *(the action is complete)*
>
> He**'s been reading** the book, but he hasn't finished yet. *(the action is incomplete)*

The present perfect tense is often used to tell how many times someone has done an action. The present perfect progressive tense often stresses how long someone has been doing an action.

> He's read the book **five times**.
>
> He's been reading the book **for over a month**.

2 **Check Your Understanding** Match the sentences with their meanings. Write the letter on the line.

_____ **1.** I've collected stamps for years. I'm starting to get bored with them.

_____ **2.** I've been collecting stamps for years. I'm going to look for more when I go on vacation.

_____ **3.** I collected stamps when I was young.

a. I collected stamps, but I stopped several years ago.

b. I collected stamps in the past, but I may stop soon.

c. I began collecting stamps a while ago, and I am still an active stamp collector.

Presentation

❶ Have students work alone and then compare answers with a partner.

> **Answers**
> **1.** has/'s been eating **2.** has/'s been winning **3.** have/'ve been dancing **4.** has/'s been traveling **5.** have/'ve been collecting

 Workbook: Practice 3

Language Note: You might want to mention that stative verbs (those that refer to conditions that do not change, such as sense verbs and verbs of knowing) are not usually used in the present perfect progressive tense. How many stative verbs can students name? Have them check their list against the verbs given in Unit 2 on page 16. Additional stative verbs are listed on page T16.

The Present Perfect vs. the Present Perfect Progressive

Preview

Have students go over the grammar presentations. Explain that one major difference in usage is that the present perfect is often used to emphasize *completion* of an action; the present perfect progressive is often used to focus on *duration* of an action. Write sentences like these on the board to illustrate:

1. I've done my homework and now I'm finished. (present perfect: emphasis on completion)

2. I've been doing my homework for an hour. (present perfect progressive: emphasis on duration)

Presentation

☑ **❷ Check Your Understanding** In this exercise, students match the sentences with their meanings. They should work alone and then compare answers with a partner.

> **Answers**
> **1.** b **2.** c **3.** a

🌐 **Option:** Ask students if they **have a collection**, **have collected**, or **have been collecting** anything as a hobby: stamps, coins, baseball cards, comic books, and so on. Make a list of the hobbies on the board. You may wish to survey the class to see which hobby is most popular. To check students' understanding of present perfect vs. the present perfect progressive, you may wish to ask students, *Who has collected (stamps)?* and then ask, *Who has been collecting (stamps)?* Check to see that students answer only one question.

Answers
4. c 5. a 6. b

 Workbook: Practice 9

❸ Have students complete the sentences with the proper form of the present perfect or present perfect progressive and compare answers with a partner.

Answers
a. has been growing, has reached **b.** has seen, have been showing **c.** hasn't cut **d.** has played **e.** has been serving, has sold

 Workbook: Practices 5, 6

Option: Write the names of the two tenses on the board. Divide the class into teams. One member from each team should come to the front of the class. Give the base form of a verb and point to one of the tenses, for example, *run; present perfect.* The first student who writes the correct form of the verb, for example, "has/have run," on the board wins a point for his or her team. Students get an additional point for spelling the form correctly.

 ❹ **Express Yourself** These activities are communicative and interactive. They connect the grammar point—in this case, the use of the present perfect and present perfect progressive tenses—to the students' personal lives. Students should ask each other about their different activities, using the items provided.

 Workbook: Practices 7, 8

❺ Students work in groups of three to ask and answer questions about their activities. *(Answers will vary.)*

Ⓧ **Option:** Have students practice forming questions using **how long** and the present perfect progressive tense, for example, (teach English) "How long have you been teaching English?" Other possibilities: watch TV, work at the same job, collect stamps, jog.

Ⓧ **Option:** Have students work in pairs to interview each other about their hobbies and other activities. Then they should present a brief biographical sketch to the class, using the present perfect and present perfect progressive tenses as appropriate. Alternately, have students write a sketch of a family member for homework.

_____ **4.** She's driven race cars since she was a teenager, but now she wants to learn to fly a plane.

_____ **5.** She's been driving race cars for two years.

_____ **6.** She drove a race car three years ago.

a. She drives a race car now, and she will probably drive it in the future.

b. She doesn't drive a race car now, but she did in the past.

c. She began driving race cars years ago, but she may stop soon.

3 Complete the sentences with a form of the present perfect or the present perfect progressive. Some verbs may be negative.

a. Paul Miller of California **(grow)** _____ his mustache for eleven years now. So far, it **(reach)** _____ a length of more than 6 feet (1.8 meters).

b. Sal Piro of New York City **(see)** _____ the film _The Rocky Horror Picture Show_ more than 870 times. Movie theaters **(show)** _____ that film for over eleven years now.

c. Georgia Sebrantke of West Germany **(cut)** _____ her hair since she was born. It's now 10 feet long and still growing.

d. Jan Leighton of the United States **(play)** _____ more than 3,350 different roles so far in his career as an actor.

e. McDonald's, the world's largest chain of hamburger restaurants, **(serve)** _____ hamburgers since 1955. McDonald's **(sell)** _____ more than 90 billion hamburgers.

4 **Express Yourself** Ask a partner about his or her activities.

Example: have any hobbies

A: Do you have any hobbies?

B: Yes, I collect stamps.

A: How long have you been collecting stamps?

B: Since I was ten years old.

a. play a musical instrument
b. exercise regularly
c. own a bike or car
d. look up information on the Internet
e. belong to any clubs or teams
f. idea of your own

5 Work in groups of three. Report your partner's current activities to the group.

Listen: The Talk Show Guest

 Before You Listen
Do UFOs (**u**nidentified **f**lying **o**bjects) exist?
Some people say they have actually seen them.
Do you believe in UFOs? Why or why not?

 Listening to Confirm Predictions You can
often predict in a general way what a talk will be
about. As you listen, focus on information that tells
you if your guesses are correct. Listen to confirm
your predictions.

 You're watching TV and the announcer says, "Next on *That's Amazing!*,
an interview with a man who says he's seen a UFO and met beings
from another planet." With a partner, predict what probably happened
to the man.

 Listen and compare your ideas with the real story.

Now listen to the interview again and answer the questions.

  a. How long has Mr. Quintero been a farmer?
  b. Where did the space people take Mr. Quintero?
  c. What problems has he been having recently?

Pronunciation

> **Unstressed *h* Words**
>
> Unstressed function words beginning with *h* (*him, her, his, have*, etc.) usually drop the
> initial **/h/** sound. The word is then linked to the previous word.
>
> This is **his** medal, not **her** medal. (stressed, no reductions)
>
> Ruby read ̶his book, and so did ̶her Mom. (unstressed, *h* is dropped)
>   (read'is)   (did'er)
>
> How long ̶have you been reading this?
>   (long've)

 Work with a partner. Predict how to say the words. Draw a line
through the letter *h* when you think it's not pronounced. Then draw
a line linking the function word to the previous word.

  A: So Hilary, how long have you and Henry been living in Prague?

  B: I just got here, but Henry's been here for half a year.

  A: How does he like it here? Has Prague been good to him?

  B: He says he's the happiest he's ever been.

LISTENING and SPEAKING

Listen: The Talk Show Guest

Preview

- Ask students, *Do you believe in astrology? Ghosts? Mind reading? Palmistry? UFOs?*

- Check understanding of **to persuade**, **unidentified flying object**, **outer space**, **fantastic**, **spaceship**, and **to grab**. Explain that **fantastic** (like **amazing** and **incredible**) is said when you hear or see something that's unbelievable or very surprising. Point at the sky to teach **space** and indicate that **outer space** is very far away. Unidentified flying object is what UFO stands for, and space people travel in them or in **spaceships** (or so some people believe!). Pantomime **to grab** by picking up a nearby object very quickly.

Language Note: UFO is an acronym. Students don't need to know the word, but they should learn how to ask about them, for example, "What does UFO stand for?" You should also tell students that sometimes each letter in an acronym is pronounced separately (like UFO), but that generally acronyms are pronounced as words (like **NATO**—North Atlantic Treaty Organization). Can students come up with other acronyms?

Presentation

❶ **Before You Listen** Put students in small groups to read and discuss the questions. They should give reasons to support their opinions. Have students with opposite views work together, or ask students to take the opposite position of what they really believe for the sake of the discussion. Put students' ideas on the board.

➡ **Listening to Confirm Predictions**
Have students read the strategy. Explain that we can often predict some of the expressions and ideas we will hear when we know the general topic. Give students some situations and ask them to come up with ideas and words they might expect to hear: a bank robbery, a terrible storm, and so on. Ask selected students to state some of their ideas.

❷ Have students work in pairs to make predictions about what they think they will hear. Circulate and provide help. Make a list of the students' predictions on the board and have students copy it.

❸ Play the recording or read the audioscript aloud one or more times. Have students compare their predictions with what they actually heard. (*Answers will vary.*)

Audioscript: The audioscript for Exercises 3 and 4 appears on page T158.

❹ Play the recording or read the audioscript aloud again while students answer the questions. They should compare answers with a partner.

> **Answers**
> **a.** for thirty years **b.** They took him into the spaceship. **c.** He's been having bad dreams about the space people.

 Option: Ask additional comprehension questions about the show that Amy watched on TV. Ask specific questions about Mr. Quintero and what happened to him.

Link *Workbook: Practice 10*

 Option: Have students write dialogues between someone who has just seen a UFO and a police officer or a TV reporter. Have students perform their dialogues for the class.

Pronunciation

Presentation

❺ Have students read the explanation in the box in class or as homework and then make predictions with a partner. Circulate and provide assistance.

> **Answers**
> A: long_have
> B: got_here, been_here
> A: to_him
> B: says_he's, happiest_he's

Answers
A: like his
B: and his, and his, and his
A: sure he, adores his
B: for him

 Workbook: Practice 11

 6 Play the recording or read the sentences in Exercise 5 in the Student Book one or more times and have students check their answers.

7 Have students reread the dialogue with a partner. Go over any problem areas with the class.

Speak Out

➡ **Expressing Surprise or Disbelief** Go around the class and ask students to practice the expressions in the box. Don't worry about correcting errors at this point.

8 First check understanding of **chemist** (scientist), **countryside** (area outside cities and towns), and **unique** (very unusual). Then have students take turns reading one of the texts. They should then close their books and retell the story to the rest of the group. Students who are listening should react with surprise, using the expressions in the box. After all students have had a chance to read, they should discuss which text they think is false. Encourage students to use language for disagreeing from Unit 1 (page 7) and persuasive language from Unit 6 (page 59). Ask each group to report back to the class. How did they reach their decision?

Answer
Text C is false.

Option: With students' books closed, ask additional comprehension questions. Students should give answers in their own words.

Text A: What does Carolyn James paint? (bright, happy pictures of the English countryside) Why are her paintings unusual? (She is totally blind.)

Text B: What are Bill Harding's clothes made of? (real grass that is still alive and growing) What is he looking for? (a company to sell his clothes)

Text C: How long has Frank Faruggio been working on his project? (eleven years) What is it? (a soft-drink bottle you can eat)

 Workbook: Practice 12

Option: Have students look for a newspaper or magazine article about a strange or unusual event or person. They should bring the article to class and explain the story in their own words.

A: Wow! That's amazing! He must really like his job.

B: He does, and his boss, and his office, and his house.

A: And I'm sure he adores his wife, Hilary.

B: I hope so. Anyway, I'm really happy for him.

  Now listen to the dialogue and check your predictions.

7 Practice reading the dialogue, focusing on linking the words.

Speak Out

 Expressing Surprise or Disbelief When you hear information that is surprising or hard to believe, you can use these expressions.

Wow!	That's hard to believe.	Oh, come on!
That's amazing!	You can't be serious.	I can't believe it.
You're kidding me!	Are you really sure that ...	No way!

8 Work in groups of three. Each student reads one of the texts below. Then close your books and take turns telling the stories to each other. As a group, decide which of the stories is false. (Only one is false.) Use the language for showing surprise to react to your partners' stories.

A. Carolyn James has been painting bright, happy pictures of the English countryside since 1980. She has sold many of her paintings for thousands of dollars. She begins by sitting in a pretty place and drawing it. Later, she finishes her paintings at home. James's paintings are unusual not only because they are beautiful—they are also unusual because she is totally blind.

B. Bill Harding is a performer from Chicago, Illinois, who has some very unique clothes. They are made of real grass that is still alive and growing. Harding has developed a special technique to grow grass between pieces of cloth. He has been looking for a company to sell his grass pants, shirts, dresses, and shoes, but so far no one has been interested.

C. Frank Faruggio is a chemist from Atlanta, Georgia, the home of Coca-Cola. He has spent eleven years on an unusual project. He has been working on the world's first soft-drink bottle you can eat. After people drink the soft drink, they can eat the bottle. He says that his bottles will be ready for supermarkets by 2005.

Read About It

1 **Before You Read**

    a. Reference books, such as a telephone book or thesaurus, are useful tools for finding information. List as many reference books as you can.

    b. One kind of reference book is a book of records. What information can you find in this sort of book?

STRATEGY **Distinguishing Fact and Opinion** When you read, it is important to tell the difference between facts and opinions. Facts are statements that are known to be true. Opinions are expressions of a writer's ideas, beliefs, or emotions.

A Record-Breaking Book

    People have always been interested in learning about world records. They want to know the biggest, smallest, fastest, slowest, longest, shortest, oldest,

5 and youngest. However, until 1955 there was no single reference book that contained comparative information on world records. The first book of this kind was the *Guinness Book*

10 *of World Records*.

    The idea for this book came from Hugh Beaver, who was an executive of Arthur Guinness Son and Co., Ltd. One day, after seeing some birds flying, he

15 told his friends that he thought that those birds were probably the fastest birds in Britain. Several of his friends disagreed with him. However, when they tried to settle the argument by looking in

20 various reference books, they found out that none contained the information that they were looking for. As a result, Beaver decided that his company ought to put out a book that would present all sorts of superlatives and world records.

READING and WRITING

Read About It

Presentation

❶ Before You Read Have students work in pairs or small groups to list as many **reference books** as they can. Then discuss what information can be found in each of these books. Ask students, *What information can you find in a **book of records**?* Compare this information with the information that can be found in reference books. Same? Different? Have students give as many examples of reference books as possible.

Option: Have students work in pairs. Have some of the pairs list as many reference books as they can and what information they think they will find in each sort (type) of book. Have the rest of the pairs make a list of what can be found in a book of records. Match pairs with different assignments. Have them exchange ideas, and discuss what information in each book can be considered **fact** and what is considered **opinion.** Selected pairs can share their ideas with the class.

➡ Distinguishing Fact and Opinion
Explain to students that it is important to be able to identify facts and opinions. Ask students to give examples of facts and opinions. Alternatively, give several practice sentences:

- Reference books are an important part of any library. (opinion)
- This reference book has 422 pages. (fact)
- The reference book I bought yesterday is fantastic. (opinion)

❷ Have students read the article beginning on page 104 and determine whether the statements are true or false.

Answers
a. F b. T c. F

🌐 **Option:** Read additional true/false comprehension statements:

- There was a more popular reference book than the *Guinness Book of Superlatives* published in 1950. (false)

- The disagreement over which birds were the fastest in Britain was settled easily. (false)

- Norris and Ross McWhirter had a small fact and figure agency in London. (true)

- The first edition of the reference book was called *The Guinness World Record Book*. (false)

- *The Guinness Book* sells millions of copies each year. (true)

🌐 **Option:** To give students an opportunity to practice their skimming and summarizing skills, have them read the entire article in one or two minutes, close their books, and then summarize the main points for a partner. Alternatively, one partner could summarize information about the book and the other could concentrate on Hugh Beaver and the creation of the *Guinness Book of World Records*.

❸ Have students work alone identifying facts and opinions. Then ask students to compare answers with a partner.

Answers
a. F b. F c. F d. F e. O

❹ Have students work alone or with a partner writing short definitions. Assign this exercise for homework if there isn't time to complete it in class.

Answers
Other answers are possible.
a. (only) one b. had, held c. agree about who is right d. publish e. books, people, etc. that provide information f. what is known g. a book that sells a lot of copies h. usually a newer copy of a book in which some of the details have been changed but that remains basically the same

🌐 **Option:** Have different pairs of students write definitions for two of the words. When students are finished, have them exchange definitions with other pairs. This is a quick way to exchange a lot of information in little time. Circulate and offer help.

Beaver began to look for authors. Soon he heard of Norris
25 and Ross McWhirter, who ran a small fact and figure agency in
London. They found and checked facts for people and so had
gathered a large collection of information from newspapers,
magazines, reference books, and other sources. Beaver
interviewed the two brothers in order to test their knowledge
30 of records and unusual facts. He found their knowledge
amazing and hired them. On August 27, 1955, the *Guinness
Book of Superlatives* went on sale in bookstores. In four
months it became a best seller. Later, the name of the book
was changed to the *Guinness Book of World Records*.

35 The *Guinness Book of World Records* has fascinated
people ever since it came out. The public continues to buy new versions of the book
every year. In fact, since 1988, the book has had average sales of 60 million copies a
year in 25 languages. This number equals 168 stacks of books each as tall as Mount
Everest. Even today, this book continues to break its own record as the fastest selling
40 book in the world!

2 Read the statements. Write **T** (true) or **F** (false).

a. _____ Beaver and his friend found that the birds were in fact the
fastest birds in Britain.

b. _____ Beaver hired Norris and Ross McWhirter to write a book.

c. _____ At first, the *Guinness Book of Superlatives* was not popular.

3 Decide if each statement is a fact **(F)** or opinion **(O)**. Write **F** or **O**.

_____ a. People have always been interested in world records.

_____ b. Hugh Beaver was an executive of Arthur Guinness,
Son and Co., Ltd.

_____ c. Beaver thought Norris and Ross McWhirter's knowledge
was amazing.

_____ d. On August 27, 1955, the *Guinness Book of Superlatives*
went on sale.

_____ e. The *Guinness Book of World Records* is a fascinating book.

4 Use the context to guess the meanings of the
words. Write synonyms or definitions on a
sheet of paper. Work without a dictionary.

a. single (line 6)
b. contained (lines 7 and 21)
c. settle (line 19)
d. put out (line 22)
e. sources (line 28)
f. knowledge (line 29)
g. best seller (line 33)
h. version (line 36)

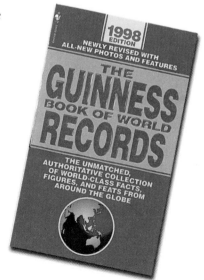

Think About It

5 Which is more useful—studying hard and memorizing many facts, or knowing where to look to get facts when you need them? Why?

6 In addition to reference books, today many people use the Internet to get information. Do you think you can trust information found on the Internet? How can you tell if it is accurate?

Write: Using Transitions

To connect our ideas in writing, we use linking words, called transitions. These words tell readers what to expect next in a paragraph. Some transitions show relationships such as time and rank. Others signal additional information (*and, also, in addition*) or effect/result (*so, therefore, for this reason*).

7 Combine the sentences to form a paragraph. Use the linking words in the box. Write the paragraph on a sheet of paper.

after that	in addition
as a result	soon
finally	therefore
for example	

  a. I have been breaking records for walking on my hands for a long time.
  b. I set a record in 1988 when I walked one mile.
  c. I tried to walk farther, but my arms were not strong enough.
  d. I began a very difficult training program.
  e. I began lifting weights.
  f. I tried to walk a little farther on my hands every day.
  g. I began to increase my distances.
  h. I broke a record by walking on my hands from New York to Montreal.

Write About It

8 Imagine that you have just set a world record. Pick a record and tell how you set it. Make sure that your paragraph has a clear topic sentence, several supporting sentences, and a concluding sentence. Use transition words in your paragraph.

9 Exchange papers with another student. Make suggestions to your partner. If there are places where you need more information, write a question to the writer in the margin.

10 **Check Your Writing** When you get your paper back, use the questions below and make revisions as needed.

- Is the main idea developed with enough supporting ideas and details?
- Are transition words used to show relationships between ideas?
- Are verb tenses used correctly?

Think About It

Presentation

❺ Have students discuss the questions in pairs. Then ask selected students to report back to the class.

❻ Have students divide into two opposing teams to debate the accuracy of the Internet.

Write: Using Transitions

Preview

Students first read the presentation in class or for homework. Explain that transitions in writing can make the information flow, join points together to add more information, show a cause and result, or compare/contrast information. Ask students to go back to the article on the *Guinness Book of World Records* on page 104 and find examples of transitions.

Presentation

❼ First explain that this exercise uses only linking words that signal additional information or effect/result. Tell students that there is more than one way to link the sentences. Circulate and help as necessary.

Answers

Other paragraphs are possible.
I have been breaking records for walking on my hands for a long time. <u>For example</u>, I set a record in 1988 when I walked one mile. <u>After that</u>, I tried to walk farther, but my arms were not strong enough. <u>Therefore</u>, I began a very difficult training program. <u>Soon</u> I began lifting weights. <u>In addition</u>, I tried to walk a little farther on my hands every day. <u>As a result</u>, I began to increase my distances. <u>Finally</u>, I broke a record by walking on my hands from New York to Montreal.

Write About It

Presentation

❽ Have students write a paragraph about setting a world record. They can write it in class or as homework. If students will do their writing at home, have them first brainstorm in class so you can checked that step.

 Link *Workbook: Practice 13*

❾ Have students exchange papers and do a peer-editing exercise. Use these questions as a guide to provide positive feedback and give students ideas for how to revise their paragraphs.

- What was most interesting about the paragraph? (and/or surprising)

- What is one thing you read about that you wanted to learn more about?

- What is one thing that you didn't read about that you wanted to?

☑ **❿ Check Your Writing** Students should use the questions and suggestions to revise their paragraphs.

Vocabulary Expansion: Making opposites with prefixes *un-* and *–in* See page T149.

Answers

A. **1.** unusual **2.** unidentified **3.** infrequently **4.** inexpensive **5.** unfriendly **6.** unmarried **7.** unbelievable **8.** incredible

B. **1.** unusual **2.** unidentified **3.** infrequently **4.** inexpensive **5.** unfriendly **6.** married **7.** believable **8.** incredible

---

EVALUATION

See page TExi.

Unit 10 Achievement Test

Self-Check See **Check Your Knowledge** on page 80 of the Workbook.

Dictation Have students review the sentences in Exercise 3 on page 101. Then present them as a dictation. (See instructions on page TExv.)

Communication Skills

1. Ask students questions and have them answer with sentences that emphasize both completion and duration. Pay careful attention to students' use of the present perfect and present perfect progressive.

2. Read some surprising statements (for example, from the *Guinness Book of World Records*) and observe the language students use to express surprise.

FROM RAGS TO RICHES

OBJECTIVES

- To talk about changes
- To use **used to** + verb to talk about past habits
- To use **get used to/be used to** to talk about adjusting to changes
- To listen for tone of voice
- To identify when **to** is reduced
- To introduce a new topic and return to a topic
- To summarize what you've read
- To write a summary
- To identify **get** vs. **be**

GETTING STARTED

Warm Up

Preview

- Check understanding of **lottery** and **sales are up**. If possible, show students a lottery ticket. Lead a class discussion about lotteries. Ask, *How do lotteries work? Are they good or bad? Do you think it's a good idea to play the lottery?* Explain that in the United States some individual states have lotteries. The profits are used to help pay for public education, including building schools, buying computers, and so on. Is there a lottery in the students' city or country? If so, what are the profits used for?

- Ask students for another way to say **sales are up** (sales are increasing) and to give the opposite (sales are down).

- ⊛ **Option: Vocabulary Notebooks** See page TEviii.

Presentation

❶ Have students work in pairs or small groups to discuss the questions. If they don't personally know anyone who has gone from rags to riches, ask them to discuss someone famous whom they've read about or seen on TV. Alternatively, have students imagine how a person's life would change after winning the lottery. Compile a list of possible changes on the board. Are most of the changes positive or negative? Lead a class discussion.

⊛ **Option:** First, have students anticipate what key words they might hear in the listening. Students should make a list and then check off the words they hear.

🎧 ❷ Make sure that everyone understands the exercise. Play the recording or read the audioscript aloud one or more times. Tell students they do not have to understand every word to do the activity.

Audioscript: The audioscript for Exercise 2 appears on page T158.

Answers
Conversation 1: bottom right-hand picture
Conversation 2: bottom left-hand picture
Conversation 3: top right-hand picture

⊛ **Option:** Ask additional comprehension questions:

Conversation 1: What was the winning lottery number? (82709)

Conversation 2: What two things does Mr. Lee ask the man to do? (call the factory and tell them they need more workers; tell the workers he is going to give everyone a big raise)

Conversation 3: How much does the speaker think the coin is worth? (a fortune)

❸ Have students work in pairs to brainstorm. Then have them join another pair and compile their lists. Call on selected students and make a list on the board. Lead a class discussion.

⊛ **Option:** Have students debate the question "Can money buy happiness?" Ask some students to serve as judges and pick the winning team.

Figure It Out

See page T108.

GETTING STARTED

Warm Up

1 When someone gets rich quickly, we say that the person has gone "from rags to riches." Do you know of anyone who has gone from rags to riches? (A businessperson? A movie star? A musician?) How has the person's life changed?

2 Listen to the conversations. How did the people get rich? Write the number of the conversation in the box. There is one extra picture.

3 "Money can't buy happiness" is an old saying. Do you agree? What are the advantages and disadvantages of being rich? Brainstorm a list.

Figure It Out

A few numbers on a lottery ticket have completely changed the lives of George and Mary Buck and their three children. Susan Johnson of WXYZ-TV is interviewing them.

A. **SUSAN:** Well, Mr. and Mrs. Buck, it's been six months since that lucky day! How are you getting used to your new life of luxury?

GEORGE: It's been great! But we've had to make a lot of adjustments.

	SUSAN:	Really? What kinds of adjustments?
5	**GEORGE:**	Well, I used to get up early and work long hours. I never used to spend much time with the children because I went to bed right after dinner. I was always exhausted by the end of the day.
10	**MARY:**	And I was always worrying about money. There never seemed to be enough to pay all the bills. We never went to fancy restaurants or took nice vacations.
15	**GEORGE:**	Now our lives are completely different. We sleep late, have our meals by the pool, and take long trips. I can even afford to buy Mary gold jewelry!

| **B.** | **SUSAN:** | What kinds of things have you bought? |
| 20 | **GEORGE:** | Well, our house, of course. Plus, we bought each of our children a new car. They used to take the bus to school. Now they drive! |

	SUSAN:	Have you gotten used to your new house?
25	**MARY:**	Well, it's much larger than our old one. It's got a huge pool, a bowling alley, a private movie theater, and all the latest appliances.
	GEORGE:	And of course, we don't have to cook or clean anymore because we have a chef and a maid.

C.	**SUSAN:**	Has your social life changed much?
30	**GEORGE:**	It sure has! I used to go bowling with my friends after work. Now I can invite them to bowl here.
	MARY:	And I never used to go to the movies. It was too expensive. But now I can invite all of my friends to watch the latest movies right here at home.
35	**SUSAN:**	So, is it true that money can buy happiness?
	MARY:	Not really. We still have a few worries, but being rich has made some things a lot easier!

Figure It Out

Preview

- Check understanding of (A) **adjustments**, **exhausted**, **fancy**, and **jewelry**; (B) **bowling alley** and **appliances**; (C) **social life**. Explain that adjustments are changes. In this case they refer to changes in behavior. Ask students what kinds of adjustments in behavior or schedule they had to make to take your English class. Tell students that **exhausted** means "very tired." Show students pictures of **fancy** houses, cars, and clothes. Pantomime the words (wearing) **jewelry** and bowling. Explain that a **bowling alley** is a place where people bowl, or go bowling. Give a list of different household **appliances**: dishwasher, dryer, microwave oven, and so on. As you mention each appliance, have students raise their hands if they have one in their home. Explain that **social life** relates to things and activities that you do with other people, especially for enjoyment.

- Write these two questions on the board and have students skim the dialogue for the answers. Set a time limit. When the time is up, have students close their books and tell their answers to a partner.

  1. How did Mr. and Mrs. Buck use to live?

  2. How have their lives changed?

🌀 **Option: Vocabulary Notebooks** See page TEviii.

Presentation

❹ Have students read the dialogue and answer the questions alone. Then have students compare answers.

> ### Answers
> **a.** They won the lottery. **b.** George used to get up early and work long hours. He never spent time with the children. He was always exhausted and used to go to bed right after dinner. Mary was always worrying about money and bills. They never went to fancy restaurants or took nice vacations. **c.** It was too expensive. **d.–e.** *Answers will vary.*

⊛ **Option:** Ask additional comprehension questions about the Bucks.

- What kinds of things have the Bucks bought? (the house, new cars)

- What is different about their new house? (It's much larger than the old one. It has a huge pool, a bowling alley, a private movie theater, and all the latest appliances.)

- How has their social life changed? (They invite their friends to bowl and watch the latest movies at their house.)

⊛ **Option:** Have students imagine that they've won the lottery. What did they use to do before they won? What do they do now? Students can share ideas in small groups.

⊛ **Option:** On the board, list possible things students could do if they won the lottery, for example, travel around the world, buy a big new house, put all the money in the bank, and so on. Or you may wish to have students use their ideas from the previous option.

Ask students to rank the items according t o their personal preferences. Then have all the students who ranked the same items one and two sit together and discuss their choices. Alternatively, have students with very different lists discuss why they ordered the items as they did.

 Workbook: Practice 1

☑ **❺ Vocabulary Check** Have students work alone and then check answers with a partner. Assign this exercise as home

work if there isn't time to finish it in class. Alternatively, have students work in pairs and write definitions for only two or three items. Then have them trade definitions with another pair. For speaking practice, have students explain their definitions to each other.

> ### Answers
> **a.** great comfort **b.** changes **c.** very tired **d.** statements that tell you how much you owe **e.** to be able to pay for (something) **f.** machines that do jobs in your home **g.** cook **h.** cleaning person **i.** current

⊛ **Option: Vocabulary Notebooks:** See page TEviii.

Talk About It

⊛ **Option:** If students need extra practice with the structure **used to** + verb, postpone this activity until after you've completed the grammar exercises or Workbook Practice 2.

Preview

With students' books closed, ask them what kinds of things did they use to do five years ago that they no longer do. Have selected students share their answers. Don't worry about correcting grammatical errors yet; just listen to see how familiar students are with the target structure.

Presentation

❻ Have students read the instructions and ask selected students to model the dialogue for the class. Then have students work in pairs taking turns being the interviewer and one of the children. Circulate and offer assistance. Make notes of student errors, but don't interrupt to correct them; you want to encourage fluency. Have selected pairs perform their dialogues for the class. Refer to your notes and write errors on the board without identifying who made them. Then correct the errors as a class.

GRAMMAR

See page T110.

4 Answer the questions.

a. How did the Buck family get rich?

b. What did they use to do before they got rich?

c. Why didn't Mary Buck use to go to the movies?

d. Imagine you win the lottery. How will your life be different? What will you do? Name five things.

e. There is a saying, "Love of money is the root of all evil." Do you agree? Why or why not?

 5 **Vocabulary Check** Write a synonym or short definition for each of the following words. Work without a dictionary.

a. luxury (line 2)	d. bills (line 12)	g. chef (line 28)
b. adjustments (line 3)	e. afford (line 18)	h. maid (line 28)
c. exhausted (line 7)	f. appliances (line 26)	i. the latest (line 33)

Talk About It

6 You are interviewing the Buck children about what they used to do before they got rich and what they do now. With a partner, take turns asking and answering questions about the cues below. The first is done for you.

Ask about past routine.

A: Did you use to eat out in expensive restaurants?

Describe past routine.

B: Oh no, we never used to eat out in fancy restaurants. We always used to eat at home.

Current Activities	**Past Activities**
a. eat out in expensive restaurants	always eat at home
b. play computer games	not have a computer
c. watch movies in a private theater	not go to the movies
d. go to live concerts	listen to old tapes
e. drive a car to school	take the bus to school
f. ask the chef to cook something	prepare our own meals
g. wear new designer clothes	wear the same clothes for a long time

GRAMMAR

Habitual Actions in the Past: *Used to* + Verb

When we talk about actions that happened regularly in the past, we can use the simple past tense with an adverb of frequency or an expression of frequency.

> George and Mary **frequently had** hot dogs in their backyard when they lived in their old house. They **never ate** gourmet foods.

We can also use the expression *used to* + verb to talk about past habits or past routines. *Used to* is pronounced /yuwstə/.

> **A:** In those days, Mary and George **used to serve** their guests hamburgers and hot dogs. They **didn't use to have** a fancy chef.
>
> **B:** **Did** they **use to eat** off of paper plates then?
>
> **A:** Of course. They didn't have a dishwasher in those days.

1 Look at the sentences in the box above. Circle the answer.

    a. In affirmative sentences we use   **use to**   **used to**.

    b. In negative sentences we use   **use to**   **used to**.

    c. In questions we use   **use to**   **used to**.

2 Fill in the blanks with the correct form of *used to*.

MARY: George, I'm bored. I think I **(1. be)** _____ happier before we won the lottery.

GEORGE: You're kidding me! Now we have everything that money can buy.

MARY: I know, but I miss my old friends. Jane and I always **(2. do)** _____ our laundry at the Laundromat every week. And Cathy and I **(3. go)** _____ grocery shopping together. We **(4. try)** _____ to plan inexpensive meals. Now the chef and the maid do everything.

GEORGE: You **(5. think, *neg.*)** _____ our life was so good.

MARY: I know, but I do now. We **(6. be)** _____ happy just being together. Remember?

GEORGE: Of course I remember. But why **(7. you, worry)** _____ about money all the time? And why **(8. you, complain)** _____ that you had to work too hard? Now we never have to worry about money again.

MARY: True. But money isn't everything.

3 David started his first year at college two months ago and is living in an apartment with two roommates. His life has really changed. Complete the chart with what you imagine used to happen at home.

Home	College
David's mother used to make all the meals.	David cooks for himself.
	He gets up at 10:30 a.m.
	He does his laundry every other week.
	He pays bills.
	He comes home when he wants.
	He studies in the library.

GRAMMAR

Habitual Actions in the Past: *Used to* + Verb

Preview

- Go over the grammar explanations on pages 109–110. Explain that **used to** is used to talk about actions that happened regularly in the past. The simple past + adverb or expression of frequency also indicates actions that happened regularly in the past. The difference is that **used to** always indicates that a change has taken place. The routine, habit, or situation in the past has to have changed. To state that something happened in the past, use the simple past tense, for example, "I passed my exam last month."

- You might want to add that **used to** has no present, progressive, or perfect tense and no infinitive or **–ing** form. Ask, *What verb form do we use to talk about present habits or states?* (the simple present tense)

Presentation

❶ Have students work alone and then compare answers with a partner.

> **Answers**
> a. used to b. use to c. use to

Language Note: Make sure students understand the difference between **used to** and the verb **to use**. These expressions look similar and can be confusing for some students.

❷ Have students work alone and then compare answers with a partner.

> **Answers**
> 1. used to be 2. used to do 3. used to go
> 4. used to try 5. didn't use to think 6. used to be 7. did you use to worry 8. did you use to complain

 Workbook: Practice 3

Option: Have students review the ideas they had and the lists they made earlier about the different things they do now vs. what they used to do if they won the lottery. They should rewrite the sentences in the affirmative and the negative, paying careful attention to using the structure **used to** + verb correctly. Ask selected students to share their sentences with the class.

❸ Have students work alone to complete the exercise. *(Answers will vary.)*

> **Sample Answers**
> David <u>used to get</u> up at noon. <u>Now</u> he gets up at 10:30 a.m.
>
> David <u>used to ask</u> his mother to do his laundry. <u>Now</u> he does his laundry every other week.

 Workbook: Practice 4

⊕ **Option:** Instead of doing Exercise 4, have selected students write their answers to Exercise 3 on the board. Discuss and correct the sentences as a class.

❹ Have students share their answers with a partner. Circulate and help as needed.

⊕ **Option:** For further practice, give students several situations and have them make up sentences using **used to.**

- Last year you lived in a cold climate. This year you moved to a hot climate. (*Example:* "I used to wear a heavy coat, hat, and gloves every day. Now I wear shorts.")

- Last year you didn't work and you had a lot of free time. This year you are working full time.

- Last year you didn't have confidence in your English. This year you are more confident.

Get used to and Be used to

Preview

With students' books closed, ask selected students to make up sentences using **get used to** and **be used to** to see how familiar they are with these structures. Then go over the grammar explanations.

Explain that **get used to** refers to the process of adjusting to changes.

Be used to is the structure that may give your students more trouble. It indicates that you have experienced something long enough so that you are now accustomed to it. It indicates that you are now familiar with the situation.

Used to is followed by the base form of the verb, for example, "*I used to play the piano when I was a child.*" **Get used to** and **be used to** are followed by the –**ing** form of the verb, for example, "I am used to <u>playing</u> the piano for my family every evening." **Get used to** and **be used to** can also be followed by a pronoun or a noun phrase.

 Workbook: Practice 2

Presentation

☑ ❺ **Check Your Understanding** In this exercise, students determine which structure is used in each situation. They should work alone and then compare answers with a partner.

Answers
b, a

❻ Have students work in pairs to discuss their answers. Then go over the answers as a class.

Answers
a. is getting used to living in **b.** is used to/has gotten used to **c.** is use to/has gotten use to

 Workbook: Practice 5

4 With a partner, ask and answer questions about what David used to do.

Example:

A: Did David use to cook for himself?

B: No, he never used to cook. His mother used to make all the meals. Now, he cooks for himself, but he only knows how to microwave food.

Get used to and Be used to

When we are in the process of adjusting to changes, we use the expression *get used to* + verb–*ing*. When we have finished adjusting, we use the expression *be used to* + verb–*ing*.

> **A:** How have you adjusted to living in Barcelona?
>
> **B:** At first, it was difficult, but now I love it. And I**'m** even **getting used to eating** lunch at 2 p.m. and dinner at 9 p.m.
>
> **A:** **Are** you **used to speaking** Catalan yet?
>
> **B:** Oh, yes. I have no problems with Catalan.

Get used to and *be used to* can also be followed by a noun phrase or pronoun.

> **A:** When you moved to Barcelona, was it hard to **get used to Catalan**?
>
> **B:** No, actually, I **got used to it** pretty fast—thanks to Catalan TV.

 5 **Check Your Understanding**

Which form means "you have finally adjusted to changes"?

a. *get used to* + verb–*ing*   **b.** *be used to* + verb–*ing*

Which form means "you are still adjusting to changes"?

a. *get used to* + verb–*ing*   **b.** *be used to* to + verb–*ing*

6 Read about Kyung-mi. Write a correct form of *be used to* or *get used to* on the line. Discuss your answers with a partner.

a. Kyung-mi has just moved from a village in Korea to New York City. After a year, it all seems a little less strange to her. Kyung-mi _____ to New York, slowly but surely.

b. Kyung-mi studied English in Korea for many years. After a year of living and studying in New York City, she is no longer afraid to speak English. Finally, Kyung-mi _____ speaking English.

c. At first, Kyung-mi was surprised at all the different people in New York City. On the subway, she used to stare at young people who wore colorful clothes and had crazy hairdos. Now she hardly notices them. Kyung-mi _____ seeing a lot of different kinds of people.

7 Use the correct form of *used to*, *get used to*, or *be used to* with the verbs in parentheses. You may need to use the negative.

GLORIA VANDERBILT

Gloria Vanderbilt is from one of the richest families in New York. She's always been rich, but she hasn't always been happy. In fact, Vanderbilt **(1. be)** _____ very unhappy. As a child, she lived with an aunt, but her aunt **(2. spend)** _____ much time with her. Vanderbilt never had any real friends because she didn't go to school. Private teachers **(3. come)** _____ to her house to teach her.

At age seventeen, Vanderbilt went to Hollywood and her life changed. She quickly **(4. dance)** _____ at famous clubs. She even **(5. date)** _____ movie stars. But she was still not happy. She thought people liked her only for her money.

Now Vanderbilt is a very successful clothing designer. Millions of people wear her jeans. Her success changed her social life, too. Finally, she made friends who like her for herself. She **(6. be)** _____ famous and popular. Gloria Vanderbilt is happy at last.

 8 **Check Your Understanding** In which situations are you likely to use *used to* + verb?

- ☐ Talking about when you were a child
- ☐ Describing what your life was like before you bought a car
- ☐ Explaining to a friend how to use a cellular phone
- ☐ Deciding whether to buy a laptop or a desktop computer
- ☐ Interviewing someone who has just moved to a new country about their past

Compare your answers with a partner's.

9 **Express Yourself** With a partner, pick one of the situations you checked above. Imagine yourselves in the situation and write a dialogue.

❼ Have students work alone and then compare answers with a partner. Go over the answers as a class and have students explain their choices.

Answers
1. used to be 2. didn't use to spend/never used to spend 3. used to come 4. got used to dancing 5. used to date 6. is used to being

✪ **Option:** Have students think back to when they first started learning English. Ask, *What are you still getting used to? What are you already used to?* Have them respond with sentences about their own experience, for example, "I'm still getting used to speaking English in front of other people," "I'm used to looking up words in an English-English dictionary."

☑ ❽ **Check Your Understanding** In this exercise, students determine in which situations they would use **used to** + verb. They should work alone and then compare answers with a partner.

Answers
Talking about when you were a child, Describing what your life was like before you bought a car, Interviewing someone who has just moved to a new country about their past

▦ ❾ **Express Yourself** This activity is communicative and interactive. It connects the grammar point—in this case, **used to** + verb—to the students' personal lives. After students have completed their dialogues, ask selected students to perform them for the class.

✪ **Option:** Have students write a dialogue dealing with one of the situations in Exercise 8 for homework.

LISTENING and SPEAKING

Listen: What Went Wrong?

Preview

- With students' books closed, ask what they prefer to do on vacation: go to a big city for sightseeing and nightlife or visit a small village next to a beautiful beach for relaxing? Divide the class into two groups and have each group talk about their vacation setting.

- Check understanding of **impatient, neutral, humorous, sad, irritated, hesitant, enthusiastic, sarcastic,** and **angry**.

Presentation

❶ **Before You Listen** Have students open their books and read the question. Put students in small groups for discussion. At the end of the activity, put students' ideas on the board. Do they know of a place where this actually happened? Where is it? What happened? Lead a class discussion.

➡ **Listening for Tone of Voice** Have students read the strategy. Explain that it is important to focus not only on the speaker's words but also on the tone the speaker is using. The tone can tell you what the speaker really means or feels.

🎧 ❷ Play the recording or read the audioscript aloud one or more times. Have students circle the words that indicate the tone of each speaker's voice.

Audioscript: The audioscript for Exercises 2 and 3 appears on page T158.

Answers
a. neutral b. irritated c. enthusiastic

🎧 ❸ Have students read the items and predict which statements will be true and which will be false. Play the recording or read the audioscript aloud one or more times. Have students compare their predictions with what they actually heard. Then have them compare answers with a partner.

Answers
a. T b. T c. F; Now the young people are always looking for people from other places to marry. d. F; There are more than 13,000 hotel beds for tourists. e. F; A lot of the people aren't used to all the changes.

 Option: Ask additional comprehension questions about what the children used to do and what the tourists do. What changes in St. Napa have the villagers noticed?

Option: Have students talk about their hometown and how it has changed. Alternatively, have students research and present information on a tourist destination that has changed. They should use the target grammar structures in their presentation.

Link *Workbook: Practice 6*

❹ Have students work in pairs to discuss how the villagers solved their problems. You may wish to write the students' ideas on the board. Then have them compare their solutions to the one on page 116. Did any pair figure out what the villagers really did? Do the students think their solution was any better then the villagers' solution?

Pronunciation

Presentation

🎧 ❺ First have students read the explanation about unstressed **to** in class or as homework. Then play the recording or read the conversation aloud. Students should draw a line through **to** when it's reduced. Have students compare answers.

Answers
To is reduced in the following phrases.
A: going t̸o do
B: going t̸o go, want t̸o come
A: got t̸o study
B: used t̸o studying

 Link *Workbook: Practice 7*

Listen: What Went Wrong?

1 **Before You Listen** Many travelers look for small villages and clean beaches that are relatively unknown and free of tourists. Eventually, other tourists find these places. What happens when these places become popular?

STRATEGY **Listening for Tone of Voice** When you listen, pay attention to the speaker's tone of voice. The tone tells you how he or she is feeling or what he or she really means.

2 Listen to an interview with people from a small village that suddenly became very popular. Circle the correct answer.

    a. The interviewer's tone is   impatient   neutral   humorous.
    b. The villager's tone is   sad   irritated   hesitant.
    c. The young villager's tone is   enthusiastic   sarcastic   angry.

3 Listen again. Write **T** (true) or **F** (false) on the line. Correct any false statement.

    ——— **a.** Most of the people used to be farmers or fishermen.
    ——— **b.** The young people never used to go out dancing in clubs.
    ——— **c.** Many local couples have gotten married in the last five years.
    ——— **d.** There are 1,300 hotel beds for tourists.
    ——— **e.** The people are used to the tourists' customs.

4 With a partner, discuss how the villagers solved their problems. Then look on page 116 to check your answer.

Pronunciation

Unstressed *to*

Like other function words, *to* is usually unstressed. The vowel sound **/uw/** is reduced to /ə/, and sometimes the /t/ is dropped. *To* is also linked to the word before it.

I **used to** get up early.	/yustə/	She's **going to** get up early.	/gənə/
You **ought to** get up earlier.	/ɔtə/	I've **got to** get up early.	/gɔtə/
I **want to** get up early.	/wanə/	I **have to** get up early.	/hæftə/

---

5 Read the conversation. Predict how to pronounce *to*. Then listen to the conversation. Draw a line through *to* if it is reduced.

    A: What are you going to do tonight?
    B: I'm going to go to the movies. Do you want to come along?
    A: I can't. I've got to study. Don't you have to study, too?
    B: Yes, but I'm going to the movies first. Don't worry. I'm used to studying late.

Check your answers with a partner. Then practice reading the dialogue, focusing on the correct pronunciation of *to*.

Speak Out

STRATEGY **Introducing a New Topic and Returning to a Topic** When you want to change the subject of a conversation or return to the previous topic, you can use certain words and expressions.

Introducing a New Topic	Returning to a Topic
That reminds me …	But to get back to …
Speaking of …	As I was saying …

 Work in groups of three. Imagine a profession that you used to have. Discuss your past experiences with the group.

Example:

A: I used to be a clown. I really liked my job. I was a clown for ten years! I used to work in all the most famous circuses.

B: That reminds me of when I went to the circus to paint pictures of the performers. You see, I used to be a painter.

C: Really? I love art. I used to live right by the Modern Art Museum.

A: Well, as I was saying, I used to work in really big circuses …

READING and WRITING

Read About It

 Before You Read Describe the home of your dreams. Is it a huge house? A luxury apartment? Is it in the country or the city? What special features does it have?

STRATEGY **Summarizing** One way to help you understand and remember a reading is to summarize the most important ideas in a few simple words. When you summarize, include the main idea of each paragraph and use your own words.

 Read the following article and decide which ideas you would include in a summary of the reading.

San Simeon—One Man's Dream

San Simeon, a fantastic estate on the central California coast, was the brainchild of William Randolph Hearst. Hearst, a newspaper and magazine publisher, was one of the richest men of the early twentieth century. His dream was to use his wealth to build a huge castle filled with the world's most beautiful art and architecture.

❻ Have students practice reading the dialogue with a partner. Then ask selected students to perform their dialogue for the class.

Speak Out

➡ **Introducing a New Topic and Returning to a Topic** Explain to students that certain expressions signal when you want to introduce a new topic or return to a previously discussed topic.

Presentation

❼ Go over the expressions in the box and have students read the conversation. Give students a few minutes to think of a profession and a list of what they used to do in that job. Have groups of three students practice their conversations, and then ask selected students to perform for the class.

Option: You may want to teach some additional expressions used to introduce a new topic: **By the way; Oh, before I forget; Just to change the subject for a moment; Incidentally;** and an additional expression to return to a topic: **As I said before.**

 *Workbook: Practice 8*

READING and WRITING

Read About It

Presentation

❶ Before You Read Have students work in pairs or small groups to describe the house of their dreams. Then have selected students report to the class.

Option: If students are having trouble getting started, give them some questions to focus their discussion:

- Where is your dream house located? Is it near a park? The ocean? The mountains?
- How many rooms does it have?
- What kind of view does it have?

➡ **Summarizing** Explain to students that summarizing is an important skill to learn. To demonstrate, return to the article about Gloria Vanderbilt on page 112. Can students summarize it in one or two sentences? Remind them that they don't have to include details. A summary should include the main points to give someone who hasn't read the article a general idea about what it is about.

❷ Have students read the article for homework and come to class prepared to write a summary. Alternatively, give students a time limit to skim the article for the main ideas. Then have them work in small groups to summarize the article together.

Option: Have students underline important information in each paragraph of the article about Sam Simeon. Then have them use the information to construct their summary. If there's time, have students compare summaries with a partner. Which summary do they think is more complete? Why?

 Workbook: Practices 9, 10

❸ Have students work alone and then compare answers with a partner.

> **Answers**
> **a.** to use his wealth to build a huge castle filled with the world's most beautiful art and architecture **b.** Hearst designed many of the rooms and Julia Morgan designed the house. **c.** from every part of the world

Option: Have students scan the article for the following expressions containing numbers. What do they refer to? **a.** 1920 (the year Hearst began building his castle) **b.** 200,000 (the number of acres the estate covered) **c.** 50 (the number of miles the private beach covered) **d.** 1937 (the year Hearst died) **e.** 1958 (the year Sam Simeon became a public museum)

Option: Alternatively, have students write sentences about what happened in each of these years: 1920 (Hearst began building San Simeon), 1937 (Hearst died), and 1958 (San Simeon became a public museum).

Option: Ask additional comprehension questions:

- What was Hearst's profession? (He was a newspaper and magazine publisher.)

- What did he do when a guest said that the swimming pool was too small? (He began building the largest heated outdoor pool in the world.)

- What happened to San Simeon in 1958? (It became a public museum.)

Option: Ask additional discussion questions:

- What do you think of Hearst's achievement?

- Would you like to visit the Hearst castle? If so, what would you like to see? If not, why not?

❹ Have students work alone writing synonyms or short definitions. Alternatively, students can work with a partner. Assign this exercise for homework if there isn't time to finish it in class.

> **Answers**
> **a.** idea **b.** riches; money and property **c.** making a circle around **d.** finally **e.** destroyed **f.** had a new opinion about (something) **g.** happy with (something) **h.** valuable things

Option: Have different pairs of students write definitions for only two of the words. Then have students exchange definitions with another pair. This is a quick way to exchange a lot of information in a little time. Circulate and offer help.

5   Hearst began building his castle in 1920.
He named it San Simeon, but he used to refer
to it and the surrounding hillside as "the
ranch," a simple place for his family and
friends to gather. Eventually, in addition to
10   the castle, he built three villas for guests and
a zoo. The estate covered more than 200,000
acres, with a private beach over 50 miles long.

Hearst designed many of San Simeon's

San Simeon

rooms himself, but he chose the architect Julia Morgan to design the house. Hearst and
15   Morgan worked on the house for many years. They often changed their plans in order
to make the house better. At times, they even tore down what they had built because
Hearst had changed his mind. When Morgan told him that the view from his bedroom
windows would not be very good, he added a second floor so his bedroom would be
higher and have a better view. After a guest mentioned that the swimming pool was
20   too small, Hearst began building the largest heated outdoor pool in the world.

Hearst used the finest wood and stone to build his castle. In addition, he sent
people all over the world to find beautiful objects to fill its rooms. They brought back
Greek statues, Spanish wood ceilings and furniture, entire rooms from European
castles, and even complete buildings to use as building materials. Hearst's art
25   collection, the largest ever owned by one man, contained treasures from every part of
the world and was worth millions of dollars. However, Hearst never felt satisfied with
his castle. He continued working on it, planning more rooms and buildings, until his
death in 1937.

Many people wonder if San Simeon made Hearst happy.
30   Perhaps not. When people entered the house after he died,
they found that many of the treasures were still in their
boxes. Hearst had never looked at or enjoyed some of his
most beautiful possessions. Also, the constant changes that
he made may show that, for him, the house was never
35   perfect or complete.

San Simeon has been a public museum since 1958.
Since then, hundreds of thousands of people have seen for
themselves one of the world's largest and most beautiful
examples of the power of money.

William Randolph Hearst

 Answer the questions.
   a. What was Hearst's dream?
   b. Who designed San Simeon?
   c. Where did Hearst buy the objects he put in his castle?

 Using the context, write a synonym or definition of each word.
   a. brainchild (line 1)   **e.** tore down (line 16)
   b. wealth (line 3)   **f.** changed his mind (line 17)
   c. surrounding (line 7)   **g.** satisfied with (line 26)
   d. eventually (line 9)   **h.** treasures (line 31)

⑤ Summarize each paragraph of the article on San Simeon.

Example: Paragraph 1

San Simeon was built by William Hearst, one of the wealthiest men of the twentieth century. It is a large house full of beautiful art and architecture.

Think About It

⑥ What are some examples of interesting architecture in your country? Who built these buildings? What are they used for?

⑦ Ancient treasures of great beauty, such as the Aztec carvings in Mexico or the fragments of temples and statues in Greece, form part of the world's cultural heritage. Should people have the right to buy these treasures for themselves or should they belong exclusively to their country of origin?

Write: Summarizing

A summary presents the most important ideas of a reading in a shortened form. It should include the main ideas and main supporting points, but not the details. The first sentence of a summary usually mentions the title and the main idea of the text.

Write About It

⑧ Write a summary of the reading in Unit 9, "Chocolate: A World Favorite." You can start like this:

> *The article "Chocolate: A World Favorite" explains the popularity of chocolate throughout the world.*

 ⑨ **Check Your Writing** Exchange papers with a partner. Use the questions below to give your partner feedback. Then, revise your paper as necessary.

- Does the first sentence name the article and give the main idea?
- Does the summary include only the main ideas and the main supporting points, not details?
- Is the summary written in the writer's words?

Answer to Exercise 4 on p. 113: The people built another village on a hillside, not far from the old village. The people work in the old village, but go home to their new village.

❺ Have students complete a written summary of each paragraph in the article "San Simeon—One Man's Dream," on pages 114–115. Review as a class.

Think About It

Presentation

❻ Have students work in pairs or small groups to discuss these questions. Then have each pair or group of students report to the class.

☸ Option: Have students use realia to present information in class on one or two buildings in their city that they think should be preserved as **landmarks** (building designated as having historical or aesthetic significance).

❼ Have students work in small groups to discuss this question. Alternatively, have two teams of students debate it.

Write: Summarizing

Presentation

Review paragraph structure (Unit 1, page 10), topic sentence (Unit 3, page 29), supporting sentences (Unit 4, page 41), and ordering supporting sentences (Unit 6, page 62).

Write About It

Presentation

❽ With students' books closed, ask them what they remember about the article in Unit 9, "Chocolate: A World Favorite"; or have students go back and skim the article. Then list the details and ideas on the board. Tell students to choose the details they think are important to include in their summaries. They can write the summary in class or as homework. If students will do their writing at home, have them first brainstorm in class so that you can check that step. Students should work alone at this stage.

☑ ❾ Check Your Writing In this exercise, students exchange papers and do peer-editing. In addition, you can have students answer these three questions when

reading their partner's summary:

- Was anything important left out of the summary?
- Were any details included that should have been left out?
- What is one thing your partner did in his/her summary that you liked?

These questions should provide positive feedback and give the students ideas for how to rewrite their summaries.

Vocabulary Expansion: *Get* vs. *be* See page T150.

> **Answers**
> A. 1. are 2. are/'re getting 3. is/'s
>   4. is/'s getting 5. is/'s 6. is/'s getting
>   7. is/'s 8. is/'s getting
> B. **Miss:** a friend, a baseball game, a TV program, an appointment, a plane
>   **Lose:** a friend, a baseball game, the car keys, ten dollars, five pounds

EVALUATION

See page TExi.

Unit 11 Achievement Test

Self-Check See **Check Your Knowledge** on page 88 of the Workbook.

Dictation Have students review the sentences in Exercise 2 on page 110. Then present them as a dictation. (See instructions on page TExv.)

Communication Skills

1. Ask students how their lives have changed in the past five years. What did they use to do that they no longer do? Pay careful attention to their use of **used to** + verb to describe habitual past actions.

2. Ask students how their lives have changed recently. Which changes are they still getting used to? Already used to? Pay careful attention to their use of **get used to** and **be used to**.

3. Have students talk about their vacations. Interrupt them so that they have to use expressions to return to the same topic and introduce a topic.

HIT THE JACKPOT

OBJECTIVES

- To talk about games and game shows
- To use the first conditional to talk about possible results
- To use conditionals with **unless**
- To listen for numbers
- To identify unstressed **you**
- To describe consequences
- To understand text organization
- To write instructions
- To use expressions with **miss** and **lose**

GETTING STARTED

Warm Up

Preview

Check understanding of **jackpot** (the most valuable prize in a game or lottery) and **hit the jackpot** (win the prize). Explain that a **jackpot** can also refer to an amount of money that increases each time someone tries to win it and fails.

Presentation

❶ Have students work in pairs or small groups to discuss the questions. Ask, *Do you like game shows? Why or why not? What is your favorite game show? Why do you like it? What game show is currently most popular? Why do people like it?* Lead a class discussion.

🌀 **Option:** Before doing Exercise 2, have students anticipate what key words they might hear in the listening exercise. Students should make a list and then check off the words that they actually hear.

🎧 ❷ Make sure that everyone understands the exercise. Play the recording or read the audioscript aloud one or more times. Tell students they do not have to understand every word to do the activity.

Audioscript: The audioscript for Exercise 2 appears on page T159.

Answers
Conversation 1: *The $44,000 Question*
Conversation 2: *What's My Occupation?*

🌀 **Option:** Ask additional comprehension questions:

Conversation 1: How does Ms. Phillips feel? (a little nervous) What is the last question? (Who invented the sport of basketball?)

Conversation 2: What does the mystery person do? (She's the first woman to be a pilot of the Concorde jet.)

🌀 **Option:** Play one of these game shows:

- *Twenty Questions:* A student thinks of a word or expression and the other students have to guess it by asking only yes/no questions. Students who ask a question and get a *yes* answer can ask another question. If they get a *no* answer, the next student asks a question.

- *True/False Elimination Game:* Read a true/false statement. Students who believe it's true should stand on one side of the room, students who believe it's false on the other. Students who choose the wrong answer are eliminated. After each statement, more students will drop out until one person is left as the winner.

- *What Do You Know?* All students start with a fictitious amount of money, for example, $500. Ask a question, first telling students the topic: movies, sports, history, and so on. Students then decide how much money (up to a limit of $100) they want to bet. Students who get the right answer win the money they bet. If they're wrong, the amount is subtracted from their total. Ask five to eight questions. The student with the most money left at the end of the game is the winner.

Figure It Out

See page T118.

GETTING STARTED

Warm Up

1 Some TV game shows give people a chance to win big prizes. When someone wins a big prize, such as a new house or a car, we say that he or she has "hit the jackpot." What kind of game shows have you seen on TV? Do you like game shows? Why or why not?

2 You are going to listen to parts of two game shows. What do you think the name of each show is? Write the number on the line.

_____ *Name the Song!*   _____ *What's My Occupation?*
_____ *The $44,000 Question*   _____ *Guess the Price!*

Figure It Out

Jackpot Shop is a popular TV game show that takes place in a shopping mall. Contestants try to win fabulous prizes, such as computers, TVs, cars, appliances, and jewelry.

A.   **BETTY:**   Hello, and welcome to the show! I'm your hostess, Betty DiGato. This week our contestants are Maria Duran and Peter Flanigan. [*applause*] Maria and Peter, I hope you aren't too nervous.

PETER: Not at all, Betty, this is my third week on the show, so I'm getting used to it.

MARIA: I'm thrilled to be here, but yes, I'm a bit nervous. I've never been on TV before!

BETTY: Before we begin, I want to make sure you understand the rules. First, you pick out one of our fabulous prizes from any of the shops in the mall. Then you have to answer a question. If the prize is inexpensive, the question will be easy. However, if you choose a more expensive prize, such as a digital TV, the question will be harder. If you answer correctly, you win the prize. Do you have any questions?

MARIA: If I make a mistake, do I get the prize?

BETTY: No, if you make a mistake, you won't win anything. And you'll have to give back the most expensive prize you've won.

B. **BETTY:** Remember, the player who has the most prizes at the end of the game gets to answer the jackpot question! And if the player answers correctly, he or she hits the jackpot. The jackpot is ten minutes of free shopping in the mall. If the player answers the jackpot question incorrectly, he or she still gets to come back and play again next week.

MARIA: What if I don't answer any questions correctly?

BETTY: You'll still get a copy of my autobiography, *Famous in Fifteen Minutes*. Everybody's a winner on *Jackpot Shop*!

3 Answer the questions.

  a. How do players win prizes on *Jackpot Shop?*

  b. What happens if a player answers a question incorrectly?

  c. What is the jackpot?

  d. Would you like to participate in a game show? Why or why not?

  e. What is more important for a game-show contestant, intelligence or luck? Why?

  f. Do you consider yourself a lucky person? Why or why not?

4 **Vocabulary Check** Write definitions for the following words.

  a. hostess (line 1)

  b. contestants (line 2)

  c. thrilled (line 6)

  d. rules (line 9)

  e. pick out (line 9)

  f. fabulous (line 9)

  g. hit the jackpot (line 20)

  h. copy (line 25)

  i. autobiography (line 25)

  j. winner (line 26)

Figure It Out

Preview

Check understanding of **mall** and **autobiography**. Ask students if they ever go shopping in a **mall**. Explain that an **autobiography** is a book a person writes about his or her own life. Have students read anyone's autobiography recently? If so, whose? What can they say about it? Whose autobiography would they most like to read?

⊗ **Option: Vocabulary Notebooks** See page TEviii.

Presentation

❸ Have students work alone, reading the dialogue and answering the questions. Students should compare answers with a partner.

> **Answers**
> **a.** by answering correctly **b.** If they make a mistake, they don't win anything and they have to give back the most expensive prize they've won. **c.** ten minutes of free shopping in the mall **d.–f.** *Answers will vary.*

⊗ **Option:** Alternatively, have students skim the dialogue quickly and then close their books. Ask them to retell the rules of the game in their own words to a partner.

⊗ **Option:** Ask additional comprehension questions:

- How does Peter feel about being on the show? (He's not at all nervous.) Maria?

(She's thrilled to be on the show and a bit nervous.)

- What happens if the contestant chooses an inexpensive prize? (The question will be easy.) An expensive one? (The question will be harder.)

- What happens if the contestant answers the jackpot question incorrectly? (He or she can come back and play again next week.)

☑ ❹ **Vocabulary Check** Have students work alone and then check answers with a partner. Assign this exercise as homework if there isn't time to finish it in class. Alternatively, have students work in pairs and write definitions for only two or three items and then trade definitions with another pair. For speaking practice, students shouldn't just copy the definitions but explain them to each other.

> **Answers**
> **a.** in this case, the woman who runs the game show **b.** people who are competing and trying to win the money or another prize **c.** very excited **d.** instructions for what you can and cannot do **e.** choose **f.** wonderful, fantastic **g.** win the prize **h.** (one) book, magazine, record, or other item **i.** a book written by a person about his or her own life **j.** the person who wins something, such as a contest or race

⊗ **Option: Vocabulary Notebooks** See page TEviii.

Talk About It

 Option: If students need extra practice with the first conditional structure, postpone this activity until after you've completed the grammar exercises for this unit or Workbook Practices 2 and 3.

Presentation

❺ Have students read the instructions. Then ask selected students to model the dialogue for the class. Have students work in pairs taking turns being the host/hostess and one of the contestants as they work through all the items. Circulate and offer assistance. Make notes of student errors, but don't interrupt to correct them; you want to encourage fluency. Have selected pairs perform their dialogues for the class. Refer to your notes and write errors on the board without identifying who made them. Then correct the errors as a class.

GRAMMAR

The First Conditional: Possible Results

Preview

- With students' books closed, explain that it is helpful to divide conditional sentences into two groups: those that talk about situations that are real or possible and those that refer to situations that are unreal or imaginary. The first conditional structure talks about situations that are real or possible. Ask students various questions to give them practice in using the structure: *If you don't come to class tomorrow, what will happen? If you pass/fail your most important exam, what will happen? If you learn to speak English fluently, what will you do?*

- Go over the grammar explanation. Explain that there are two parts to a conditional sentence: the **if** clause or conditional clause ("If the player answers right,") and the main clause or result clause ("he gets the prize"). When verbs in both clauses are in the simple present tense, the sentence shows a cause-and-effect relationship. When the verb in the main clause uses **will**, the sentence shows a result in the future: "If we win today, we **will** fly to Rio." Explain that the **if** clause can be placed at the beginning or the end of the sentence. Point out the difference in punctuation depending on the placement of the **if** clause.

Presentation

❶ Have students work alone and then compare answers with a partner.

> **Answers**
> **1.** win **2.** will we go **3.** will/'ll go **4.** win
> **5.** go **6.** will/'ll take **7.** travel **8.** won't/will not go **9.** will/'ll visit **10.** will/'ll relax
> **11.** will/'ll visit **12.** won't/will not go
> **13.** won't/will not go **14.** will we do
> **15.** don't/do not win

Talk About It

5 You are checking with Betty DiGato about the rules of *Jackpot Shop*. Work with a partner. Use the cues and take turns asking questions.

Example: answer question correctly

Ask a question about a condition.

A: What happens if I answer the question correctly?

State the possible result of the condition.

B: If you answer the question correctly, you'll win the prize.

a. pick out cheap prize
b. answer question incorrectly
c. my opponent gets answer correct
d. choose expensive prize

e. not get any questions right
f. answer jackpot question correctly
g. not give back prizes
h. make mistake with jackpot question

GRAMMAR

The First Conditional: Possible Results

In conditional sentences, the *if* clause is the condition, and the main clause is the result of that condition. First conditional sentences show results that are possible in the present or future.

Condition	Result
If + present simple	*present simple*
If the player **answers** right,	he **gets** the prize.
If + present simple	*will + verb*
If we **win** today,	we **will fly** to Rio.
If we **don't win**,	we**'ll stay** home.

The *if* clause can come before or after the main clause.

A: **If we go to Brazil,** we'll stay in Rio.

B: No, I won't go to Brazil **if we don't go up the Amazon.**

1 Complete the conversation with the simple present or future tense of the verbs.

THELMA: If we **(1. win)** _____ a trip, where **(2. we, go)** _____?

EARL: We **(3. go)** _____ to Brazil if we **(4. win)** _____, right?

THELMA: Right, and if we **(5. go)** _____ to Brazil, we **(6. take)** _____ a trip up the Amazon.

EARL: No, Thelma. If we **(7. travel)** _____ to Brazil, we **(8. go, neg.)** _____ up the Amazon. We **(9. visit)** _____ Rio and **(10. relax)** _____ on the beach. And we **(11. visit)** _____ Salvador de Bahia. I've always wanted to go there.

THELMA: Well, I've always wanted to take a boat up the Amazon. If you **(12. go, neg.)** _____ up the Amazon with me, I **(13. go, neg.)** _____ to Salvador de Bahia with you.

EARL: OK. But what **(14. we, do)** _____ if we **(15. win, neg.)** _____?

2 You are going to study abroad next year. What will you do if these things happen to you? Write your responses on a sheet of paper.

Example: What if you can't understand the language?

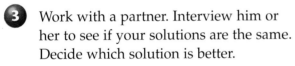

If I can't understand the language, I'll ask people
to repeat.

   a. What if you lose your traveler's checks?
   b. What if you don't get along with your host family?
   c. What if you don't like the food?
   d. What if your parents come to visit?
   e. What if you run out of money?
   f. What if you lose your passport?
   g. What if you get sick?
   h. What if you fall in love?
   i. Idea of your own.

3 Work with a partner. Interview him or her to see if your solutions are the same. Decide which solution is better.

Example:

   A: What'll you do if you can't understand the language?
   B: No problem. I'll hire a translator.
   A: What'll you do if you can't find a translator?
   B: In that case, I'll use gestures.

Conditionals with *Unless*

Unless means *if not*. We use *unless* with negative conditions to express requirements or give a strong warning.

Required Condition	Result
If Earl **does not win**,	he **won't go** to Bahia.
Unless Earl **wins**,	he **won't go** to Bahia.
Unless you **go** up the Amazon,	I **won't go** to Bahia.

Option: Have students play a memory game using the first conditional. The first student should complete the following sentence: "If I hit the jackpot, I'll _____." The second student says the first student's sentence, for example, "If he hits the jackpot, he'll buy a car," and adds his/her own sentence: "If I hit the jackpot, I'll travel around the world." Each student in turn repeats what has been said before (changing the pronoun reference as necessary) and adds his/her own sentence. A student who can't repeat the entire chain is out.

 Workbook: Practice 1

❷ Have students brainstorm in small groups before they write their own answers. (*Answers will vary.*)

❸ Have students compare their answers for Exercise 2. Each pair should share their best answer for each question with the class. Which pair has the best answer of all? (*Answers will vary.*)

Option: Lead a class discussion about the situations in Exercise 2. Which situations have students experienced? Which would they least like to experience? Not mind experiencing? Why?

Conditionals with *Unless*

Preview

With students' books closed, ask selected students to make sentences using **unless**. Explain that **unless** means "except if." In other words, situation Y won't happen ("I won't go to Bahia") except if condition X exists ("unless you go up the Amazon").

Presentation

❹ Have students work alone and then compare answers with a partner. Go over the answers and make sure students understand when to use **unless**.

Answers

1. if 2. unless 3. unless 4. unless 5. if

 Option: Have students practice the dialogue. Ask selected students to perform it for the class.

❺ Have students practice the dialogues. Then ask selected students to perform them for the class. *(Answers will vary.)*

Link *Workbook: Practices 2, 3*

 Option: Bring in or have students bring in newspaper articles. Have students practice making up sentences based on what they've read using the first conditional and **unless**. For example, based on an article about increasing prices for electronic goods, students might say: "If prices don't go down, I won't buy a new television" or "I won't buy a new television unless prices go down."

More on First Conditionals

Preview

Go over the grammar explanation and have selected students read the example sentences in the box. For further practice, elicit other sentences using **should, ought to, can,** and the imperative in first conditionals.

Presentation

❻ As a class, brainstorm different ideas Mrs. Lee might suggest. Then have students work with a partner to make and practice dialogues, taking turns playing the parts of Mr. and Mrs. Lee. Ask selected students to perform for the class. *(Answers will vary.)*

Link *Workbook: Practice 4*

 Option: To practice the imperative in the first conditional, have students compose advice to give to Mary Lee directly, for example, "If you get stressed out, **call** us immediately."

4 Complete the dialogue with *if* or *unless*.

EARL: I won't go to Brazil **(1.)** _____ we don't stay for at least two weeks. There's no point in going **(2.)** _____ we can enjoy it.

THELMA: Well, I won't go **(3.)** _____ we stay a month. Brazil's the fifth largest country in the world and there's so much to see.

EARL: We won't be able to see the Iguaca Falls **(4.)** _____ we have more time.

THELMA: And **(5.)** _____ we don't see those falls, I'm not going!

5 You are confirming plans with a friend. With a partner, make dialogues using the cues.

Example:

A: You'll go camping with us this weekend, won't you?
B: Of course I will, unless it rains.

a. go camping this weekend
b. get tickets for the new Spielberg movie tomorrow
c. go sightseeing with me after your job interview
d. begin dance lessons next fall
e. sail up the Amazon next summer
f. join the gym in January
g. idea of your own

More on First Conditionals

We can use *should, ought to, can,* and imperatives in first conditionals.

> If you go to Mexico, you **ought to go** to the Yucatan.
>
> If you go to the Yucatan, you **shouldn't miss** the Mayan ruins at Chichen Itza.
>
> If you get tired of the ruins, **drive** to the beach.

6 Mary Lee is going to start college soon. Her father is afraid that everything will go wrong, but Mrs. Lee is sure everything will be OK. Work with a partner. Make dialogues using the cues.

Example: not like her roommate

MR. LEE: What will happen if she doesn't like her roommate?

MRS. LEE: If she doesn't like her roommate, she can move to another apartment.

a. need money
b. get sick
c. forget to call us
d. not get good grades
e. miss home
f. not learn to cook
g. get stressed out
h. need a car
i. want to drop out
j. idea of your own

☑ 7 Check Your Understanding In which situations are you likely to use the first conditional? Check your answers with a partner's.

- ☐ Talking about your experiences with dating
- ☐ Warning someone about playing the lottery
- ☐ Describing how the sun affects planets
- ☐ Telling about a frightening experience that you had
- ☐ Explaining the rules of a sport to someone

8 Express Yourself With your partner, choose one of the situations you checked above. Imagine yourselves in the situation and write a dialogue using the first conditional.

LISTENING and SPEAKING

Listen: *Jackpot Shop!*

1 Before You Listen On *Jackpot Shop*, contestants answer questions to win prizes. In the game shows you know about, what do contestants have to do to win prizes?

STRATEGY **Understanding Numbers** Facts and statistics often include numbers. When you listen to take notes or to answer questions, it is important to focus carefully on the numbers you hear.

2 Maria Duran and Peter Flanigan are ready to start playing *Jackpot Shop*. Listen to the program and answer the questions.
- **a.** What prizes did Maria try to win?
- **b.** What prizes did Peter try to win?
- **c.** Who won *Jackpot Shop*?

3 Listen to the program again and circle the correct answers.
- **a.** Today's Jackpot Shop is show number _____.
  - 301   341   431
- **b.** Today is Maria's _____ time on the show.
  - 1st   3rd   4th
- **c.** Hernán Cortéz brought chocolate to Europe in _____.
  - 1258   1308   1528
- **d.** Peter and Maria want the combination VCR and color TV with the _____-inch screen.
  - 19   25   29
- **e.** Ray Kroc sold _____ of McDonald's hamburgers before he died.
  - thousands   millions   billions
- **f.** The American Dream car prize is worth _____.
  - $200,000 $2,000,000 $2,000,000,000

☑ ❼ **Check Your Understanding** In this exercise, students determine in which situations the first conditional is used. They should work alone and then compare answers with a partner.

> **Answers**
> Warning someone about playing the lottery, Explaining the rules of a sport to someone

❽ **Express Yourself** This activity is communicative and interactive. It connects the grammar point—in this case, the first conditional—to the students' personal lives. When students write their dialogues, make sure they use at least one sentence containing **unless**. Have students present their dialogues to the class.

LISTENING and SPEAKING

Listen: *Jackpot Shop!*

Presentation

❶ **Before You Listen** With students' books closed, ask students if they remember the rules for the show *Jackpot Shop*. If necessary, have students reread the conversation beginning on page 117. Then ask them to retell the rules of the game in their own words. Have students open their books and read the question. Put them in small groups to discuss game shows.

⊕ **Option:** Have students discuss these questions about game shows:

- What is the most expensive prize you've ever seen someone win? The most disappointing?

- Would you walk across a bed of burning coals to win a big prize? What is something you absolutely would *not* do no matter how big the prize was?

➡ **Understanding Numbers** Have students read the strategy. Explain that it is important to listen for numbers because they can provide details of a listening passage.

❷ Play the recording or read the audioscript aloud one or more times. Have students answer the questions.

Audioscript: The audioscript for Exercises 2 and 3 appears on page T159.

> **Answers**
> **a.** a (good) dictionary, a compact disc player, and a combination VCR and color TV (with a 29-inch screen) **b.** a (Marie de Nouvelle 24-karat) gold watch, a combination VCR and color TV (with a 29-inch screen), the American Dream Car **c.** Maria

❸ Have the students read the items and predict the answers. Play the recording or read the audioscript aloud one or more times. Have students compare their predictions with what they actually heard. Then they should compare answers with a partner.

> **Answers**
> **a.** 341 **b.** 1st **c.** 1528 **d.** 29 **e.** billions **f.** $2,000,000

⊕ **Option:** Ask additional comprehension questions:

- Where was the famous singer John Lennon born? (Liverpool, England)

- When did Ray Kroc die? (1984)

- How large was William Randolph Hearst's estate? (200,000 acres)

- How long did it take Nellie Bly to travel around the world? (less than eighty days)

 Workbook: Practice 5

⊕ **Option:** Have students play their own version of *Jackpot Shop*. For prizes, you can bring in pictures from magazines or draw them on the board. Have students make up questions for each other in various categories: TV shows, books, famous people, history, movies, sports, fashion, and so on.

Pronunciation

Presentation

❹ Students read the explanation in the box in class or as homework. Practice saying different sentences with unstressed **you** and have students repeat after you. Have students work alone to make predictions.

❺ Play the recording or read the dialogue in Exercise 4 aloud so that students can check their answers. Have selected students perform the dialogue for the class.

> **Answers**
> A: if y~~ou~~ hit, what'll y~~ou~~ do
> B: Do <u>you</u> know what y~~ou~~'ll do, if <u>you</u> win
> A: Do y~~ou~~ want
> B: I'll tell y~~ou~~ what, I'll invite <u>you</u>, if <u>you</u> win, <u>you</u> can invite

 Workbook: Practice 6

Speak Out

➡ **Describing Consequences** Explain that conditional sentences can describe the result if a certain condition is or isn't present. Have selected students give additional conditional sentences.

Presentation

❻ Have students work in groups of three. You might want to put all the students representing a particular group together first to brainstorm ideas. Students should read the applicable paragraph on page 124 and prepare arguments before presenting their ideas in their own words. After a few minutes, have selected students report to the class about their discussion. Who was most successful at persuading? Why?

 Workbook: Practice 7

Option: Have students continue the activity discussing real charitable organizations, for example, Red Cross (emergency relief), SPCA (Society for the Prevention of Cruelty to Animals), Head Start (teaches disadvantaged children to read and write). As an extension, have students choose a charity and raise money for that organization. As a class, students should discuss why they're choosing the organization and what benefits their donation will bring.

Pronunciation

> **Unstressed *you***
>
> The word *you* is usually unstressed and pronounced **ya** or /yə/. Sometimes the **y** sound links with the word before, creating a new sound—**d + y = /dj/** and **t + y = /ch/**.
>
> If you win, what'll you do?　　　　　　Don't you want to play?
> /yə/　　　　　　/yə/ *(reduced)*　　　　　/donchjə/ *(reduced and linked)*
>
> Did you buy the TICKet?
> /dɪdjə/ *(reduced and linked)*

4 Predict the pronunciation of *you*. Underline *you* if it is stressed. Put a line through it if it is unstressed.

A: If you hit the jackpot, what'll you do?

B: I don't know. Do you know what you'll do if you win?

A: Of course! I'll go on a cruise to Greece. Do you want to come?

B: I'll tell you what. Let's make a deal. If I win, I'll invite you along, and if you win, you can invite me.

A: It's a deal!

5 Listen to the dialogue and check your answers. With a partner, practice reading the dialogue, focusing on the pronunciation of *you*.

Speak Out

STRATEGY **Describing Consequences** When you want to talk about the possible results or consequences of an action, you can use conditional forms.

> If **X** happens, **Y** will happen.　　　　Unless **X** happens, **Y** will/won't happen.
> If **X** doesn't happen, **Y** won't happen.

6 Every year the City Club donates money to the group that can best help the city. This year the finalists are the City Opera, the Clean World Club, and the Hospital Helpers.

Work with two other students. Each of you represents a different group. Persuade the other students that your group should get the money.

Example:

A: Well, I think the City Opera deserves the money. If it doesn't get the money, the opera will close for the rest of the year.

B: That's a good cause, but people are more important, and unless the hospital gets that new X-ray machine, patients will not get the quality care they need.

City Opera

The City Opera has been performing in the city for over thirty-five years. Each year they perform fifteen operas. Many important opera stars come to the city to sing. A lot of visitors come to the city to see the operas, too. The tickets are expensive, but the opera also performs for free in high schools and colleges in the city. Every summer they give free performances in the park. If the City Opera does not get the money, it will have to close.

Clean World Club

The Clean World Club is a group of about 200 people who work hard to keep the city clean. The Clean World Club watches the factories to make sure that they do not pollute. It recycles old bottles, cans, and newspapers. It also has a Clean City Day once every month. On these days, the people in the club clean the streets, parks, and rivers. Last year the club also planted over 500 trees. If the club doesn't get the money, it will not be able to do its work.

Hospital Helpers

The Hospital Helpers is a group of about 400 people who buy new machines and furniture for the City Hospital. Last year they built a new emergency room for the hospital. They also bought the hospital over 100 new beds. This year, the hospital needs a new X-ray machine. If the club does not get the money, the hospital will not get the new machine.

READING and WRITING

Read About It

1. Before You Read What games did you use to play as a child? What games do you play now? How are they different from the games you used to play?

STRATEGY **Understanding Text Organization** As you read, you will understand more if you look at how writers organize their ideas. One writer may compare two solutions to a problem. Another writer may begin with historical information and then describe recent events. Another writer may classify items. Most writers use a combination of these patterns. Pay attention to how the text is organized.

READING and WRITING

Read About It

Presentation

❶ Before You Read Have students work in small groups discussing the questions. Then lead a class discussion. Have selected students come to the front of the class to explain the games they used to play, either acting them out with a partner (for athletic games) or drawing them on the board (for board games). List on the board all the games students mention and take a class survey. Who else used to play these games? Which one(s) did students like the most? Students should then talk about the games they play now and how they're different.

You may want to teach some helpful expressions for discussing games: **The object of the game is to** _____; **First you roll the dice/draw a card, then you** _____; **It's important (not) to** _____; **If you** _____, **then you're out of the game; The first one to** _____ **wins the game.**

➡ **Understanding Text Organization**
Explain to students that they can quickly pick out information they need from a text once they understand how it is organized. There are three common ways of organizing text:

- Pro and con: comparing the two sides of a question or a problem

- Chronological: presenting information in the order it happened, beginning with the past and moving to the present or future

- Classification: putting information in different categories

❷ Have students read the article for homework and come to class prepared to describe how the text is organized.

❸ Have students work alone and then compare answers with a partner.

Answers
a. Games were related to telling the future, to war, and to funeral ceremonies. **b.** strategy games and chance games **c.** They let people practice cooperation and competition and test people's ability to think. They are also sources of entertainment.

Option: Ask additional comprehension questions:

- Why did people throw animal bones in ancient times? (to tell the future)

- Where was the oldest known board game discovered? (in a cemetery in Ur, Iraq)

- What do strategy games depend on? (players' skills and abilities)

Option: Ask additional discussion questions:

- Which of the games in the article have you played? Which would you like to play? Why?

- Can you think of any other reasons why games are still important today?

❹ Have students work alone or with a partner writing synonyms or short definitions. Assign this exercise for homework if there isn't time to finish it in class.

Answers
Other answers are possible.
a. very old **b.** changed, grew into **c.** beginnings **d.** head of a group, person in charge **e.** comes from, was made in **f.** plan **g.** luck **h.** is the result of

Option: Have different pairs of students write definitions for only two of the words. Then have students exchange definitions with another pair. This is a quick way to exchange a lot of information in a little time. Circulate and offer help.

2 As you read "Board Games Past and Present," notice how the writer organizes her ideas.

Board Games Past and Present

Board games are a favorite pastime in countries around the world. In fact, board games of different sorts have played an important role in the lives of people since the beginning of time and continue to be important today.

In the past, games were related to telling the future, to war, and to funeral
5 ceremonies. For example, in ancient times, people threw animal bones to tell the future. Later, the art of throwing animal bones developed into games with dice. Archaeologists have found board games with dice from as early as 3000 B.C. Other games, such as chess, had their origins in war. In chess, a game that originally came from Iran, the markers represent two armies. The players are the leaders of their
10 armies. In some societies, board games were so important that people left them with the dead. The oldest example of a board game was discovered in a cemetery in Ur, Iraq. Experts think that it dates from 3500 B.C.

Most board games fall into one of two types, strategy games and chance games. In strategy games, the result of the game depends on the players' skills and abilities.
15 Players must move their markers within rules and think about what the other players are going to do. The player who thinks of the best moves will win. Three strategy games are the Chinese war game Weigi, its Japanese cousin Go, and chess.

In other games, chance is important. Most of these games are race games. Players move their markers around the board from start to finish. The first player to arrive at
20 the finish is the winner. The results of the game depend on chance—usually the throw of dice. Parcheesi, originally from India, is a chance game that is popular in many countries today.

Why have games been important in many times
25 and places? Experts say that games let people practice cooperation and competition, two valuable skills. Games also test people's abilities to think. In addition, games are sources of entertainment. For all these reasons, games continue to be a part
30 of our culture.

3 Answer the questions.

   a. What were the earliest uses of games?
   b. What are the main kinds of board games?
   c. Why are games still popular today?

4 Use the context to guess the meanings of the following words. Write a synonym or short definition. Do not use a dictionary.

a. ancient (line 5)	**e.** dates from (line 12)
b. developed (line 6)	**f.** strategy (line 14)
c. origins (line 8)	**g.** chance (line 18)
d. leader (line 9)	**h.** depend on (lines 20–21)

Consider the organization of the reading. Circle the letter of the correct answer. In paragraph two, the writer:

  a. ranks games from the most difficult to the easiest
  b. describes the general history of games
  c. lists favorite games

In paragraphs three and four, the writer:

  a. criticizes games
  b. explains why games are important
  c. classifies types of games

Think About It

 What are your favorite games? Are they strategy games or chance games?

Write: Instructions

When you tell someone how to do something, you must write very clear instructions. First, analyze your audience so that you know how much information to present. Then think of all the equipment needed to play and all the steps involved. You also need to define any unfamiliar terms. Finally, organize the steps as they happen, and use transitions to signal the order.

Write About It

 Think of a simple game you know how to play well. In a paragraph, explain how to play the game. Be sure to give the name of the game, the main objective, and all the materials needed. Then present the rules. Use the example below as a model.

> In the game Tic-Tac-Toe, the winner is the person who first gets three Os or three Xs in a straight line. The line can be vertical, horizontal, or diagonal. This game is usually played with pencil and paper. First, a grid of nine squares is drawn. One of two players uses the symbol X and the other player uses the symbol O. The player who goes first decides where he or she wants to mark his or her X or O, and draws it in one of the squares. Next the other player does the same. Then the first player draws an X or O again, then the other player, and so on. Tic-Tac-Toe is a strategy game, so it is important for each player to block the line his or her opponent wants to form while trying to make his or her own line of three symbols in a row.

  Check Your Writing Exchange papers with a partner. Using the questions below, make suggestions to your partner on ways to make the instructions clearer.

  - Are the steps (rules) presented in a logical order?
  - Are transitions used to help the reader follow the rules?
  - Are unfamiliar terms defined?

❺ Have students work in pairs to answer the questions.

Answers
b, c

Think About It

Presentation

❻ Have students discuss which games they prefer, strategy games or chance games.

Option: Have each student in a group present his or her favorite strategy or chance game. Then the group can choose the game they'd most like to play. Alternatively, have each group prepare handouts and props and give a class presentation about their favorite game. The class then votes on which game sounds most interesting.

Option: Bring in or have students bring in some games to play in class. Tell students that they must explain the rules in English.

Write: Instructions

Presentation

Students read the presentation in class or for homework.

Write About It

Presentation

❼ With students' books closed, have students tell you about a situation when they had unclear instructions for doing something. What were they doing? What finally happened? What about the instructions made them difficult to follow? Lead a class discussion. Then have students read the model paragraph and discuss it with a partner. How is it organized? Review expressions for discussing game playing (Before You Read, page T124).

Link *Workbook: Practice 8*

❽ **Check Your Writing** In this exercise, students exchange papers and do peer-editing. In addition, you can have students answer these three questions when reading their partner's paragraph:

- Is it clear how to win the game?
- What do you do during the game?
- What, if anything, should you avoid doing in the game?

These questions should provide positive feedback and give students ideas for how to rewrite their instructions.

Vocabulary Expansion: The different meanings of *miss* and *lose* See page T151.

Answers
a. 6 **b.** 2 **c.** 4 **d.** 1 **e.** 3 **f.** 5

EVALUATION

See page TExi.

Unit 12 Achievement Test

Self-Check See **Check Your Knowledge** on page 94 of the Workbook.

Dictation Have students review the paragraph on the City Opera on page 124. Then present it as a dictation. (See instructions on page TExv.)

Communication Skills

1. Ask students how their lives will change in these situations: if they win the lottery, get a new job, move to another city/country, or get a pet. Pay attention to their use of the first conditional.

2. Have students use their sentences from item 1 to generate conditional sentences with **unless**. For example, "If I win the lottery, I'll go to Paris" becomes "I won't go to Paris **unless** I win the lottery."

Review Units 10–12

Unit review exercises can be assigned as homework or done in class. You can use them in different ways.

- Give the review exercises as a quiz. Students work alone and turn in their answers to you.

- Use the review exercises as you would other exercises in the book. Students work alone and then compare answers with a partner.

- Have students work alone and then review answers as a class. Have selected students write their answers on the board, and correct any errors together.

❶ Have students read the instructions and complete the exercise. For a comparison of the present perfect and present perfect progressive tenses, have students refer to Unit 10, pages 99–100.

Answers
1. have/'ve been having 2. has/'s been acting 3. has/'s been locking 4. has/'s been playing 5. has/'s been 6. has/'s been hiding 7. has/'s been making 8. have/'ve built

❷ Have students read the instructions and complete the exercise. For a comparison of **used to, get used to,** and **be used to,** have students refer to Unit 11, pages 109–111.

Answers
1. used to 2. is/'s getting used to/is used to 3. used to 4. is/'s getting used to 5. is used to/has gotten used to

❸ Have students read the instructions and complete the exercise. For a review of the first conditional, have students refer to Unit 12, pages 119–121.

Answers
a. will/'ll have b. won't/will not eat c. visit d. don't/do not get out of e. doesn't/does not turn off f. will/'ll win

1 Complete the conversation with the correct form of the verbs in parentheses. Use the present perfect or present perfect progressive tense.

JANE: Rose, what's wrong? You look worried.

ROSE: I am. I **(1. have)** _____ problems with my son Joey.

JANE: Really? About what?

ROSE: Well, Joey **(2. act)** _____ really different lately. He **(3. lock)** _____ the door to his room and he **(4. play)** _____ his music really loud at night.

JANE: Don't most boys go through that stage?

ROSE: Maybe, but Joey wasn't like that before. And he **(5. be)** _____ so secretive. He **(6. hide)** _____ strange things in his backpack, and **(7. make)** _____ weird noises in his room.

JANE: Well, here he comes now with a package.

ROSE: Hi Joey. What's that?

JOEY: It's a surprise for you, Mom! I **(8. build)** _____ you a birdhouse for your flower garden. I hope you like it!

2 Complete the passage with the correct form of *used to*, *get used to*, or *be used to*.

Jennifer's life is very different from the way it was last year. She **(1.)** _____ live with Hannah, a classmate from school. This year she's living alone. It is hard to adjust, but she **(2.)** _____ being alone in the apartment. She and Hannah **(3.)** _____ spend Sunday mornings eating a long breakfast and reading the paper. Now Jennifer **(4.)** _____ spending Sunday morning eating alone at the neighborhood cafe. One adjustment was easy to make, though. Jennifer **(5.)** _____ the extra closet space right away!

3 Complete the sentences with the correct form of the verbs in parentheses. Some verbs may be negative.

a. If I get in the ticket line early, I **(have)** _____ a better chance of getting concert tickets, don't you think?

b. She **(eat)** _____ her food unless it has a lot of salt on it.

c. If you **(visit)** _____ Barcelona, be sure to see the architecture of Gaudì.

d. You are going to catch a cold if you **(get out of)** _____ those wet clothes.

e. If she **(turn off)** _____ the TV, she'll become a couch potato.

f. If the contestant answers this last question, he **(win)** _____ a trip to Hawaii.

4 Complete each sentence with a verb that makes sense. Use the correct form.

   a. If I don't get paid today, I _____ money from my father.
   b. We _____ the picnic if it rains.
   c. I know Alex _____ you if you ask him politely.
   d. Unless the alarm clock _____, I never wake up on time.
   e. Jason _____ to the meeting unless we invite him.
   f. If Elena _____ the race, she will be very disappointed.

5 Match the sentences with the closest meaning.

   1. ____ Max has been looking for a job for six months.
   2. ____ Max looked for a job last month.
   3. ____ Max hasn't looked for a job yet.

   a. Max is not looking for a job anymore.
   b. Max is still looking for a job.
   c. Max is still studying and will work in the future.

   4. ____ Katya used to play the violin.
   5. ____ Katya is used to playing the violin.
   6. ____ Katya can't get used to playing the violin.

   a. Katya practices the violin regularly.
   b. Katya has stopped playing the violin.
   c. Katya is having trouble playing the violin.

Vocabulary Review

Use the words and expressions in the box to complete the sentences.

afford	origin
thrilled	treasures
wealth	rules
break the record	give me a hand
best seller	fabulous

   1. I'm really busy here; I need some help. Could you _____?
   2. Now that the Buck family has won the lottery, they can _____ to buy anything they want.
   3. When Lucy met Rock N. Roller in person, she was so _____ that she fainted!
   4. The game of chess had its _____ in war.
   5. My son's goal is to _____ for chewing the most pieces of gum at one time!
   6. The _____ of this game are confusing; what do I do next?
   7. Examples of some of the world's architectural _____ can be found at the Cloisters museum in New York City.
   8. _____ doesn't guarantee happiness, as everybody knows.
   9. The *Guinness Book of World Records* is an annual _____.
   10. That diamond necklace is worth millions. Isn't it _____?

❹ Have students read the instructions and complete the exercise. For a review of the first conditional, have students refer to Unit 12, pages 119–121. *(Answers will vary.)*

> **Sample Answers**
> **a.** 'll have to borrow **b.** 'll cancel **c.** will go with **d.** rings **e.** doesn't come **f.** loses

❺ Have students read the instructions and complete the exercise. For a comparison of the present perfect and present perfect progressive tenses, have students refer to Unit 10, pages 99–100. For a comparison of **used to, get used to,** and **be used to,** have students refer to Unit 11, pages 109–111.

> **Answers**
> 1. b 2. a 3. c 4. b 5. a 6. c

Vocabulary Review

Have students read the instructions and complete the exercise.

> **Answers**
> 1. give me a hand 2. afford 3. thrilled
> 4. origin 5. break the record 6. rules
> 7. treasures 8. Wealth 9. best seller
> 10. fabulous

Base Form	Simple Past	Past Participle
be: am, is, are	was, were	been
become	became	become
begin	began	begun
bend	bent	bent
bite	bit	bitten
blow	blew	blown
break	broke	broken
bring	brought	brought
build	built	built
buy	bought	bought
catch	caught	caught
choose	chose	chosen
come	came	come
cost	cost	cost
cut	cut	cut
do	did	done
draw	drew	drawn
drink	drank	drunk
drive	drove	driven
eat	ate	eaten
fall	fell	fallen
feel	felt	felt
find	found	found
fight	fought	fought
fit	fit	fit
fly	flew	flown
forget	forgot	forgotten
freeze	froze	frozen
get	got	gotten
give	gave	given
go	went	gone
grow	grew	grown
have, has	had	had
hear	heard	heard
hide	hid	hidden
hit	hit	hit
hold	held	held
hurt	hurt	hurt
keep	kept	kept
know	knew	known
leave	left	left

IRREGULAR VERBS

Base Form	Simple Past	Past Participle
lend	lent	lent
lie	lay	lain
lie	lied	lied
light	lit	lit
lose	lost	lost
make	made	made
mean	meant	meant
meet	met	met
pay	paid	paid
put	put	put
quit	quit	quit
read	read	read
ride	rode	ridden
ring	rang	rung
rise	rose	risen
run	ran	run
say	said	said
see	saw	seen
sell	sold	sold
send	sent	sent
set	set	set
sing	sang	sung
sit	sat	sat
sleep	slept	slept
speak	spoke	spoken
speed	sped	sped
spend	spent	spent
stand	stood	stood
steal	stole	stolen
strike	struck	struck
swim	swam	swum
take	took	taken
tell	told	told
think	thought	thought
throw	threw	thrown
understand	understood	understood
wake	woke	woken
wear	wore	worn
win	won	won
write	wrote	written

THE INTERNATIONAL PHONETIC ALPHABET

IPA SYMBOLS

Consonants

/b/	**b**a**b**y, clu**b**	/s/	**s**alt, medi**c**ine, bu**s**
/d/	**d**own, to**d**ay, sa**d**	/š/	**s**ugar, spe**ci**al, fi**sh**
/f/	**f**un, pre**f**er, lau**gh**	/t/	**t**ea, ma**t**erial, da**t**e
/g/	**g**ood, be**g**in, do**g**	/θ/	**th**ing, heal**th**y, ba**th**
/h/	**h**ome, be**h**ind	/ð/	**th**is, mo**th**er, ba**th**e
/k/	**k**ey, cho**c**olate, bla**ck**	/v/	**v**ery, tra**v**el, o**f**
/l/	**l**ate, po**l**ice, mai**l**	/w/	**w**ay, any**o**ne
/m/	**m**ay, wo**m**an, swi**m**	/y/	**y**es, on**i**on
/n/	**n**o, opi**n**ion	/z/	**z**oo, cou**s**in, alway**s**
/ŋ/	a**ng**ry, lo**ng**	/ž/	mea**s**ure, gara**g**e
/p/	**p**aper, ma**p**	/č/	**ch**eck, pi**c**ture, wat**ch**
/r/	**r**ain, pa**r**ent, doo**r**	/ǰ/	**j**ob, refri**g**erator, oran**g**e

Vowels

/ɑ/	**o**n, h**o**t, f**a**ther	/o/	**o**pen, cl**o**se, sh**ow**
/æ/	**a**nd, c**a**sh	/u/	b**oo**t, d**o**, thr**ough**
/ɛ/	**e**gg, s**ay**s, l**ea**ther	/ʌ/	**o**f, y**ou**ng, s**u**n
/ɪ/	**i**n, b**i**g	/ʊ/	p**u**t, c**oo**k, w**ou**ld
/ɔ/	**o**ff, d**augh**ter, dr**aw**	/ə/	**a**bout, penc**i**l, lem**o**n
/e/	**A**pril, tr**ai**n, s**ay**	/ɚ/	moth**er**, Sat**ur**day, doct**or**
/i/	**e**ven, sp**ea**k, tr**ee**	/ɝ/	**ear**th, b**ur**n, h**er**

Diphthongs

/ɑɪ/	**i**ce, st**y**le, l**ie**	/ɔɪ/	**oi**l, n**oi**se, b**oy**
/ɑʊ/	**ou**t, d**ow**n, h**ow**		

THE ENGLISH ALPHABET

Here is the pronunciation of the letters of the English alphabet, written in International Phonetic Alphabet symbols.

a	/e/	n	/ɛn/
b	/bi/	o	/o/
c	/si/	p	/pi/
d	/di/	q	/kyu/
e	/i/	r	/ɑr/
f	/ɛf/	s	/ɛs/
g	/ǰi/	t	/ti/
h	/eč/	u	/yu/
i	/ɑɪ/	v	/vi/
j	/ǰe/	w	/'dʌbəlˌyu/
k	/ke/	x	/ɛks/
l	/ɛl/	y	/wɑɪ/
m	/ɛm/	z	/zi/

UNIT VOCABULARY

STARTING OUT

Nouns
chart
communication
culture
education
experience
hobby
opinion

Verbs
to communicate (with)
to get acquainted (with)
to get down to business
to get to know

UNIT 1

Nouns
cartoon
channel
comedy
commercial
couch potato
detective
documentary
fact
frequency
habit
program
science fiction
soap opera
television guide

Verbs
to participate in
to scan
to turn on
to turn off

Adjectives
bored
favorite
main

Adverbs
almost
ever
generally
how often
normally
once
once in a while
rarely
seldom
twice

UNIT 2

Nouns
band
executive
exercise
film
fortune
gift shop
guard
gym
lobby
nut
privacy
ring
security
snack bar
towel
voice
wig

Verbs
to believe
to come off
to exercise
to film
to follow
to get out of
to hold
to investigate
to lie on
to miss
to practice
to relax
to wait

Adjectives
bald
embarrassing
fantastic
private
public

Adverbs
anymore
still

Expressions
left alone

UNIT 3

Nouns
age
appearance
condition
couple
height
length
location
neighborhood
possession
price
quality
size
speed
truck
weight
yard

Verbs
to compare
to contribute
to purchase
to wonder

Adjectives
attractive
cheap
crowded
enormous
far
gorgeous
huge
jealous
light
low
modern
narrow
perfect
poor
rich
traditional

Expressions
keep up with the Joneses

UNIT 4

Nouns
album
award
compact disc (CD)
entertainment
fan
hit
jazz
opera
prize
record
rock (and roll)
soul
talent
tape
technology

Verbs
to accompany
to appear
to become
to discover
to grow up
to invent
to participate in
to perform
to spread

Adjectives
popular
well-known

Adverbs
finally

UNIT 5

Nouns
accident
alarm
argument
baggage
close call
counter
damage
direction
disaster
earthquake
fire
flood
gate
hurricane
passenger
reaction
storm
tornado

Verbs
to cause
to check in
to damage
to destroy
to get ahead of
to hide
to interrupt
to land (a plane)
to notice
to recover
to rescue
to save (someone)
to scream
to shatter
to shout
to strike
to take off (a plane)

Adjectives
awful
major
minor

Adverbs
as
when
while

Expressions
first of all
in fact

UNIT 6

Nouns
ad
advertisement
advertising
appointment
candy bar
chance
engine
feature
luxury
microwave oven
power
product
soap
wheel

Verbs
to deserve
to own
to persuade
to recommend
to spend

Adjectives
advanced
amazing
comfortable
modern
powerful
up-to-date

Adverbs
right away

Expressions
for example
for instance
namely

UNIT VOCABULARY

UNIT 7

Nouns
application
adventure
candidate
employee
employer
employment
experience
major
prison
popularity
qualification
salary
stunt
success

Verbs
to achieve
to apply

to complain
to fight
to improve
to steal
to take risks

Adjectives
controversial
perfect

qualified
upset

Adverbs
since

Expressions
so far
up to now
in general

UNIT 8

Nouns
advice
credit card
diet
health
hot line
millionaire
pollution
salary
thief
traffic jam

Verbs
to advise
to borrow
to break into
to consult
to gain (weight)
to lose (weight)
to owe

to pay back
to quit
to refuse
to solve
to throw away

Modals
had better
ought to
should

Adjectives
fancy
personal
rapid

Expressions
can't stand

UNIT 9

Nouns
elevator
ingredients
limit
lost and found
pay check
project
stress
technique

Verbs
to calm down
to disappoint
to handle
to keep
to lower
to rank
to remind

Adjectives
anxious
calm
depressed
mental
physical
stressed-out

Expressions
according to
personally
in my opinion
I'd rather

UNIT 10

Nouns
athlete
chemist
collection
contest
encyclopedia
glass
medal
metal
object

record (the best done)
reference book
result
spaceship
waste (of time)

Verbs
to break (a record)
to collect

to develop
to give a hand
to exist
to kid
to reach
to set (a record)
to waste

Adjectives
blind
incredible

unbelievable
unusual

Expressions
as a result
for this reason
in addition

UNIT 11

Nouns
adjustment
advantage
appliance
bill
chef
dishwasher
driver's license

Laundromat
laundry
lottery
maid
meal
social life
treasure

Verbs
to adjust
to afford
to be used to
to get used to
to bowl

Adjectives
exhausted
latest

Adverbs
eventually

UNIT 12

Nouns
autobiography
condition
copy
effect
host (of a show)
hostess (of a show)

jackpot
loser
mistake
pastime
player
rule
winner

Verbs
to depend on
to give back
to get along with
to go camping
to hit the jackpot
to make sure

to play
to recycle

Adjectives
fabulous
thrilled

Adverbs
unless

INDEX

Numbers indicate units.

CONTENTS

SCOPE AND SEQUENCE

Unit	Theme	Topics	Functions	Grammar	Listening and Speaking	Reading and Writing	Pronunciation	Vocabulary Expansion
1	What's on TV?	TV habits, couch potatoes	• Talking about habits, opinions, and general truths • Talking about frequency • Stating opinions • Expressing agreement and disagreement	Simple present tense; Future events; Frequency adverbs and expressions	**Listening:** Coming Soon! ➡ Listening for specific details **Speaking:** What's Your Opinion? ➡ Expressing opinions	**Reading:** TV Programs ➡ Scanning **Writing:** The paragraph	–s/–es ending	Two-word verbs: *find out, look up, turn on, turn up, turn down, turn off*
2	People Watching	Privacy, people watching, paparazzi	• Talking about what is happening • Making appointments	Present progressive tense; Present time; Future time; Stative verbs	**Listening:** Where Are They? ➡ Making inferences **Speaking:** The Meeting ➡ Making appointments	**Reading:** The Right to Privacy ➡ Guessing meaning from context **Writing:** Narrowing a topic	syllables	Expressions with *have*
3	Keeping Up with the Joneses	Upward mobility, jealousy, comparing possessions	• Comparing and contrasting two items • Expressing preferences • Asking for agreement	Comparative adjectives; *Not as ... as*; Talking about similarities	**Listening:** Choosing a Restaurant ➡ Listening for criteria **Speaking:** Alternatives ➡ Agreeing and disagreeing	**Reading:** Mall Crawlers: A Teenage Stereotype ➡ Identifying main ideas **Writing:** The topic sentence	stressed syllables	Nouns, adjectives, and their opposites
4	And the Beat Goes On!	Music around the world	• Talking about what happened • Signaling chronological order • Keeping a conversation going	Simple past tense; Adverbs of sequence	**Listening:** Music Around the World ➡ Listening to complete a chart **Speaking:** First-time experiences ➡ Keeping a Conversation Going	**Reading:** The Story of Jazz ➡ Noticing chronological order **Writing:** Supporting sentences	–ed ending	Nouns ending in –ance and –ment
5	Close Calls	Accidents, disasters	• Talking about what was happening • Telling a story	Simple past and past progressive tenses; Time clauses with *when, while, as*	**Listening:** A News Story ➡ Listening for sequence **Speaking:** A Close Call ➡ Telling a story	**Reading:** The San Francisco Earthquake of 1906 ➡ Making predictions **Writing:** The concluding sentence	content vs. function words	Expressions with *get*
6	The Best in Life	Ads, advertising	• Comparing and contrasting three or more items • Arguing, counterarguing, and conceding	Superlative; Making comparisions with adverbs and nouns	**Listening:** Advertisements ➡ Listening to draw conclusions **Speaking:** Five Thousand Dollars ➡ Arguing, counterarguing, conceding	**Reading:** The World of Advertising ➡ Noticing examples **Writing:** Ordering supporting sentences	numbers	Adjectives ending in –able, –ible, and –ful

Unit	Theme	Topics	Functions	Grammar	Listening and Speaking	Reading and Writing	Pronunciation	Vocabulary Expansion
7	The Perfect Match	Jobs, job interviews, past experience	• Talking about what has happened • Stating generalizations	Present perfect tense; *How many, how often, how long; For, since*	**Listening:** A Job Interview ➡ Understanding grammar clues **Speaking:** Men's/Women's jobs ➡ Making generalizations	**Reading:** Nellie Bly, Newspaper-woman ➡ Making inferences **Writing:** Supporting details	Sentence stress	Adjectives ending in *–ing* and *–ed*
8	Ask the Experts	Advice, hotlines	• Offering, accepting, and rejecting advice • Talking about what one should, ought to, and had better do	*Should, ought to; Had better*	**Listening:** Ask Olga! ➡ Listening for the main idea **Speaking:** City Problems ➡ Asking for and giving advice	**Reading:** Help is Out There ➡ Skimming **Writing:** An informal letter	Intonation patterns	Expressions with *break*
9	Stressed Out	Stress, handling stress	• Describing specific people and objects • Expressing preferences	Adjective clauses; Relative pronouns as subjects; Relative pronouns as objects	**Listening:** Stressful Jobs ➡ Identifying opinions **Speaking:** Personal preferences ➡ Expressing preferences	**Reading:** Chocolate: A World Favorite ➡ Understanding references **Writing:** Using examples	Stress and intonation	Expressions with *take*
10	You've Got to Be Kidding!	Records, record breakers, incredible feats	• Talking about what has been happening • Expressing surprise and disbelief	Present perfect progressive tense; Present perfect vs. present perfect progressive tense	**Listening:** The Talk Show Guest ➡ Listening to confirm predictions **Speaking:** True Stories ➡ Expressing surprise and disbelief	**Reading:** A Record-Breaking Book ➡ Distinguishing fact and opinion **Writing:** Using transitions	Reducing "h" sounds	Making opposites with prefixes *un–* and *in–*
11	From Rags to Riches	Sudden wealth, changes in habit and lifestyle	• Talking about past habits • Talking about changes and adjusting to changes • Changing the subject of conversation	Habitual actions in the past: *Used to + verb; Get/Be used to*	**Listening:** What Went Wrong? ➡ Listening for tone of voice **Speaking:** Past experiences ➡ Introducing a new topic and returning to a topic	**Reading:** San Simeon—One Man's Dream ➡ Summarizing **Writing:** Summarizing	Reducing "to"	*Get* vs. *be*
12	Hit the Jackpot	Game shows, games, consequences of actions	• Talking about cause and effect • Speculating about the future • Describing consequences	First conditional possible results; *If, unless*	**Listening:** Jackpot Shop! ➡ Understanding numbers **Speaking:** The City Club ➡ Describing consequences	**Reading:** Board Games Past and Present ➡ Understanding text organization **Writing:** Instructions	Unstressed "you"	The different meanings of *miss* and *lose*

Unit 1

What's on TV?

Two-word Verbs

English has many two-word verbs. They are made of a verb and another word, such as **off**, **on**, or **up**. The two-word verb has a different meaning from the verb alone.

Example:

Please **turn** the page.

Joaquin, please do your homework before you **turn on** the TV.

a. Which verb means "change"?

b. Which verb means "start a machine"?

Read the story. Match the underlined words with the meanings given below. Write the letters on the lines.

I'm a couch potato. I love to watch TV! I buy a television guide every week because I want to **(a.)** <u>find out</u> what programs are on TV. Movies are my favorite, so I **(b.)** <u>look up</u> the ones I can see that week. As soon as I get home from work, I get something to eat and drink, and I **(c.)** <u>turn on</u> the TV. I like to watch rock music videos on TV, so I always **(d.)** <u>turn up</u> the TV as high as possible when a good video is on. When my wife comes home from work, she usually likes to **(e.)** <u>turn down</u> the TV. She says that it's too noisy. Sometimes she tells me to **(f.)** <u>turn off</u> the TV. She says that she hates TV. My wife doesn't understand me. No one understands a couch potato.

_____ **1.** start a machine

_____ **2.** learn

_____ **3.** make the sound loud

_____ **4.** make the sound quiet

_____ **5.** find in a book

_____ **6.** stop a machine

Unit 2

People Watching

Expressions with *have*

In English, the verb **have** appears in many different expressions. When **have** is part of an expression, there can be many different meanings.

A. *Match the underlined words with their meanings. Write the letters on the lines.*

_____ **1.** We <u>had some friends over</u> to our house.

_____ **2.** What did you <u>have on</u> yesterday?

_____ **3.** I <u>had a great time</u> at your party.

_____ **4.** Friday is a holiday. We <u>have the day off</u>.

_____ **5.** Did you hear? Mona <u>had a baby</u>!

_____ **6.** Please <u>have a seat</u>.

_____ **7.** We <u>had lunch</u> in this great Italian restaurant.

_____ **8.** That's your second dessert. I didn't know you <u>had a sweet tooth</u>.

a. have a vacation day

b. liked to eat sweet things

c. sit down

d. wear

e. enjoyed myself

f. invited people to come

g. gave birth

h. ate

B. *Now match these sentences with the sentences in Part **A**. Write the numbers on the lines.*

_____ **A.** The doctor will see you in a minute.

_____ **B.** No, I didn't know that. That's great news!

_____ **C.** I haven't danced so much in years!

_____ **D.** We had dinner. Then we listened to music.

_____ **E.** I wore a red dress and black shoes.

_____ **F.** Where is it? I'd like to go there.

_____ **G.** I'm going to visit some friends in Boston.

_____ **H.** Yes, I do. I really like pie and ice cream.

Unit 3

Keeping Up with the Joneses

Nouns, adjectives, and their opposites

Many nouns and adjectives have related forms. The noun **length**, for
example, is related to the adjective **long**. Many adjectives have opposites,
too. The opposite of **high** is **low**. Some words have similar meanings such
as **high** and **tall**.

A. *Complete the chart, using a dictionary if necessary. Then compare answers
with a partner.*

Noun	Adjective	Opposite	Can Describe
1. length	long		line, hair
2.	wide	narrow	street, river
3. height		low	hill, price
tall		person, tree	
4. size	big		room, ball
5. weight		thin	person, leg
	heavy		person, box

B. *Complete the sentences with the correct words from the chart in Part A. More
than one answer is possible for some sentences.*

1. My sister cut her hair yesterday. It was getting very _____.

2. His bedroom is 12 feet long and 10 feet _____.

3. My father and I are the same _____. We're both 6 feet tall.

4. I'm eating too much. The doctor told me to lose _____.

5. Tom's laptop computer is east to carry. It's very _____.

6. This shirt is too small. Do you have a bigger _____.

7. We wanted to buy the CD player, but the price was too _____.

8. No trucks or buses could be on Main Street. It was too _____.

And the Beat Goes On!

Nouns ending in –*ance* and –*ment*

Many verbs change to nouns when we add the ending –**ance** or –**ment**.

A. *Complete the chart, using a dictionary if necessary. Can you think of any other nouns that end in –ance or –ment? (Add them to the chart.)*

Verb	Noun
1. perform	performance
2. disappear	
3. appear	
4. attend	
5. accompany	accompaniment
6. entertain	
7. agree	
8. disagree	
9. excite	
10. retire	
11.	
12.	

B. *Complete the sentences with the correct verbs or nouns in the chart in Part A.*

1. The Rolling Stones are going to _____ on April 24.

2. Can you _____ my party on Saturday night?

3. My father will _____ me to the driving test next week.

4. TV and movies are two popular kinds of _____.

5. My parents and I _____ that there is too much violence on TV.

6. Marie and Joanne had a _____, so they aren't friends now.

7. The children can't sleep now because they had too much _____ today.

8. Sandra's father is going to _____ this year. He's been teaching for thirty years.

Unit 5

Close Calls

Expressions with *get*

A. *Complete the paragraph with words in the box. If no word is necessary, write an X.*

in	out of
off	to
on	up

It was my first day at my new job, so I got

(1.) _____ early. I got **(2.)** _____

dressed quickly and ate breakfast as fast as I could. I kissed my

husband good-bye and went outside to get **(3.)** _____

my car. The car wouldn't start! I got **(4.)** _____ my car

and walked to the bus stop. I got **(5.)** _____ the bus

at Rush Street and got **(6.)** _____ near my office.

When I finally got **(7.)** _____ work, I was almost an

hour late. My boss got **(8.)** _____ angry and I got

(9.) _____ fired!

B. *Match the expressions with* **get** *in Column A with the correct definitions in Column B. Write the letters on the lines.*

A	**B**
_____ **1.** get in	**a.** wake up
_____ **2.** get dressed	**b.** lose your job
_____ **3.** get off	**c.** enter a car
_____ **4.** get up	**d.** arrive at
_____ **5.** get fired	**e.** exit a bus
_____ **6.** get on	**f.** exit a car
_____ **7.** get to	**g.** enter a bus
_____ **8.** get out	**h.** put on clothes

Unit 6

The Best in Life

Adjectives ending in *–able*, *–ible*, and *–ful*

Many nouns and verbs change to adjectives when we add the ending **–able, –ible,** or **–ful**.

A. *Complete the chart, using a dictionary if necessary to help with spelling. Can you think of any other nouns or verbs that fit in this category? (Add them to the chart.)*

Noun or Verb	Adjective
1. help	helpful
2. beauty	
3. care	
4. comfort	comfortable
5. collect	
6. believe	
7.	
8.	

B. *These six sentences are missing nouns, verbs, or adjectives from the chart in Part A. Complete the sentences with the correct words.*

1. Thank you for the book. It was very _____ .

2. A thing of _____ is a joy forever.

3. Be _____ with that watch! It's very expensive.

4. I like riding in your new car. It's very _____ .

5. Can I have the stamp on your letter? I _____ stamps.

6. I don't _____ in UFOs. Do you?

Unit 7

The Perfect Match

Adjectives ending in *–ing* and *–ed*

In English, we can make adjectives by adding **–ing** or **–ed** to the base form of a verb, for example, **amaze: amazing, amazed**. Nellie Bly was **amazing**. The public was **amazed**.

Complete the chart. Then write sentences using the adjectives ending in **–ing** *and* **–ed**.

Verb	Adjective ending in *–ing*	Adjective ending in *–ed*
1. interest		
2. bore		
3. confuse		
4. frighten		
5. surprise		
6. embarrass		
7. excite		
8. entertain		

1. _____
_____
2. _____
_____
3. _____
_____
4. _____
_____
5. _____
_____
6. _____
_____
7. _____
_____
8. _____
_____

Unit 8

Ask the Experts

Expressions with *break*

A. *Complete these expressions using* **break** *with words from the box.*

down	even
the ice	in
the law	up

1. We had been dating for three years but decided to stop seeing each other because we were always fighting. We decided to **break** _____.

2. My company didn't make any money last year, but we didn't lose any money either. My company **broke** _____.

3. You shouldn't **break** _____ because the police will catch you.

4. My car is always **breaking** _____. I'm going to have to get it repaired or buy a new one.

5. I'm shy, so when I go to a big party, I have trouble **breaking** _____. It's difficult to know what to say.

6. I locked my keys inside my car, so we had to **break** _____ to get them.

B. *Match the expressions with* **break** *in Column A with the correct definitions in Column B.*

A	B
_____ **1.** to break into	**a.** have no money
_____ **2.** to be broke	**b.** hurt someone
_____ **3.** to break a record	(because you don't love them)
_____ **4.** to break out	**c.** escape from
_____ **5.** to take a break	**d.** do something better than
_____ **6.** to break	anyone has before
(someone's) heart	**e.** enter a place (house, car) illegally
	f. stop working

C. *Can you think of any other expressions with* **break***?*

Unit 9

Stressed Out

Expressions with *take*

*The verb **take** is used in many different expressions. Read the letter and figure out the meaning of the underlined expressions. Then match each expression with its meaning.*

Dear Ken,

I'm really enjoying my first year of college. I'm **(a.)** taking a class in photography. We are learning how to **(b.)** take pictures with many kinds of cameras and film. Last week, our teacher let us **(c.)** take a look at a very old camera. She also let us **(d.)** take turns using it. Everyone got to use it. Next week we are going to **(e.)** take a trip to a park so that we can practice some more with our cameras.

Our teacher always helps us a lot. I find that when I **(f.)** take her advice, my pictures come out better. However, it **(g.)** takes a long time to do it right. Sometimes I spend hours with my camera. The class is fun, but it **(h.)** takes a lot of work, too. In fact, it is my hardest class—but I enjoy it the most. I'll be sorry when we **(i.)** take the final exam and the course is over.

I hope that you are **(j.)** taking it easy and enjoying yourself.

Your friend,

Gerardo

_____ **1.** answer a test   _____ **6.** relaxing

_____ **2.** in a class   _____ **7.** make photographs

_____ **3.** look at   _____ **8.** travel

_____ **4.** needs a lot of work   _____ **9.** one person after another

_____ **5.** needs many hours   _____ **10.** use someone's idea

Unit 10

You've Got to Be Kidding!

Making opposites with prefixes *un–* and *in–*

A. *Complete the chart with the form of each word that means the opposite. Use a dictionary if necessary. Then make a sentence with each of the opposites.*

Word	Opposite
1. usual	
2. identified	
3. frequently	
4. expensive	
5. friendly	
6. married	
7. believable	
8. credible	

B. *Complete the sentences with the correct form of the words from the chart in Part A.*

1. This is very _____ weather! It usually doesn't snow this time of year.

2. Some people believe in UFOs or _____ flying objects.

3. I don't go to the movies very often. They are very expensive now, so I go _____.

4. There's a big sale on cassettes and CDs at the mall. They're very _____ now.

5. Our new neighbors are very _____. We seldom see them, and they never talk to us.

6. My brother didn't get _____ until he was thirty-eight years old.

7. What a wonderful movie! The story was _____, and the actors were great.

8. He ran the marathon in 2 hours and 10 minutes. That's _____.

Unit 11

From Rags to Riches

Get vs. be

*The verb **get** refers to a process. The verb **be** refers to a state.*

| I'm single now, but I**'m getting married** next month. | (process) |
| My sister **is married**. She**'s been married** for two years. | (state) |

*Complete the following sentences with the correct form of **get** or **be**.*

My boyfriend and I **(1.)** _____
engaged, but not for much longer. We **(2.)**
_____ married in just two days! I
know that he **(3.)** _____ a little
overweight, but I don't care. He looks as
handsome to me as he did when he was thin. I
also know that he **(4.)** _____ bald,
but if he loses all his hair, he can wear a wig.
I'll still love him!

My mother **(5.)** _____ very
happy for me, but she **(6.)** _____
more and more impatient with my father
because he won't help with the wedding plans.
She says he **(7.)** _____ upset because he
(8.) _____ older and his daughter is leaving home. I
told him that he isn't losing a daughter, he's gaining a son (-in-law).

Unit 12

Hit the Jackpot

The Different Meanings of *miss* and *lose*

A. *The verbs* **miss** *and* **lose** *can have different meanings. Match each underlined word with its meaning below.*

        Yesterday started out to be a really terrible day. First I got up late. I
(1.) <u>missed</u> my bus and had to wait an hour for the next one. I arrived at
work late, so I **(2.)** <u>missed</u> a meeting with my boss. She got angry. She
said, "If you arrive late again, you'll **(3.)** <u>lose</u> your job." I had lunch in a
restaurant, but when I went to pay, I discovered that I had **(4.)** <u>lost</u> my
wallet. After work, I played tennis with my friend Rosa, but I **(5.)** <u>lost</u>
every game. When I got home, I tried to call my old roommate, but she
wasn't at home. I've really **(6.)** <u>missed</u> her since she moved out. Later in
the evening a man called. He said that he had found my wallet. That's
how I met my future husband. To tell the truth, it wasn't such a bad day
after all!

_____ **a.** felt sad because someone is absent

_____ **b.** didn't attend

_____ **c.** wasn't able to find

_____ **d.** didn't get on

_____ **e.** not keep

_____ **f.** didn't win

B. *Read the list of items below. Put each item in the correct box in the chart.
Two of the items can go in both boxes.*

| a friend | a baseball game | the car keys | a TV program |
| ten dollars | a plane | five pounds | an appointment |

Miss	Lose

Student Book Audioscript

UNIT 1: What's on TV?

Page 1, Exercise 2

Announcer: Channel 1.

Woman: OK, Sam. We know you're in there! Come out with your hands up!

Man: I'll never give up! You'll have to come in and get me!

Woman: Let's go! Let's get him now!

Announcer: Channel 2.

Woman: The African elephant is the largest animal living in Africa. It is also in great danger. Every year, hundreds of elephants are killed. If governments do not stop the killing, soon there will be no more elephants.

Announcer: Channel 3.

Man: OK, Ms. Case. Here's your question. Who invented the electric light bulb?

Woman: Thomas Edison.

Man: That's right! You win $10,000!

Announcer: Channel 4.

Woman: My guest today is Margo Kay. Margo is the president of the Bank of Chicago. The Bank of Chicago is the largest United States bank to be headed by a woman. Margo also races cars. She has won races in several countries. Please join me in welcoming Margo Kay.

Announcer: Channel 5.

Man: Look! A huge green monster!

Woman: Where?

Man: Over there in the water!

Woman: It's Godzilla!

Man: Oh, no! Run!

Page 7, Exercise 2

Man: And now a look at some of the TV programs coming up next week on Channel 1, everyone's favorite channel. On Monday at 7:30, you can see *The Big Question*. On this exciting game show, people can win wonderful prizes … or they can lose everything!

Woman: Later Monday evening you can see everyone's favorite detective on *Nikki Danger—Police Officer*. In this week's show, Nikki gets a big surprise when she catches the killer of a rock star. Find out Nikki's surprise Monday at 8:00.

Man: After school, your children can watch *Amazing Animals*. This week, the show visits the lions at the famous San Diego Zoo in California. *Amazing Animals* starts at 4:00 on Tuesday.

Woman: On Wednesday evening, all you science fiction fans can see one of the great science fiction movies of all time on *Spaceship Theater*. The movie is *2001: A Space Odyssey*, and it's on at 8:30.

Man: This week, *Music City* features Rock N. Roller, who sings all his hit songs. See Rock sing on Thursday, starting at 7:00.

Woman: These and many other exciting programs are on Channel 1 next week. Watch them all!

Page 8, Exercise 6

1. sleeps	7. comes	13. wants
2. teaches	8. believes	14. uses
3. goes	9. asks	15. fixes
4. learns	10. changes	16. washes
5. makes	11. laughs	17. hikes
6. calls	12. describes	18. misses

UNIT 2: People Watching

Page 11, Exercise 1

Narrator: Conversation A

A: That woman looks like your boss. But doesn't your boss have blonde hair?

B: I can't believe it! It is my boss! She's wearing a red wig! And look at those glasses!

A: Well, I think she looks great!

B: No one at work will believe she goes out in public like that!

Narrator: Conversation B

B: Look at that bald man with all the cameras. What's he taking a picture of?

A: I don't know, but I hope his pictures turn out. None of the pictures I took on my vacation turned out OK.

B: Why not?

A: I forgot to put film in the camera!

Narrator: Conversation C

A: That band is good.

B: Yeah. I know they're students from the university, but they sound like professional musicians.

A: Oh, my gosh! Look who's watching them! It's Jack Michaelson! And he's got his guitar!

B: He's my favorite singer! He has a fantastic voice!

A: Do you think he'll play a song with the band?

B: Don't be silly! He's in town for a concert. He won't play for free!

Narrator: Conversation D

B: Look at those people over there. They look like they're really in love.

A: Ohhhh. He has a ring. I think he's going to ask her to get married.

B: This is so romantic. It's just like a movie.

Page 17, Exercises 2 and 3

Narrator: Conversation A

A: Bob has a new racket, but he's not playing well today.

B: No, he's not. He's missing a lot of balls.

A: I think he's tired. He normally plays very well.

B: Well, after running for two hours, I'd be tired, too!

Narrator: Conversation B

A: Aren't you enjoying this show, Bill?

B: Not really, Mary.

A: You're kidding! I think it's a great comedy!

B: Well, I don't think it's funny. I'm tired. I'm going to take a nap. Call me when the detective show comes on.

Narrator: Conversation C

A: Look, Judy! Liz Tyler, the movie star, is sitting at that table!

B: I see her, Mary! She's drinking pineapple juice! And eating a hot dog!

A: She's really beautiful, but she sure has strange tastes!

B: I think it looks great. I'm going to order a hot dog and some pineapple juice, too.

Narrator: Conversation D

A: It's really hot today.

B: Yeah. Do you want to go in the water and cool off?

A: OK. But I don't know how to swim.

B: You can't swim? But it's easy! Come on. I'll teach you.

Narrator: Conversation E

A: What's happening in the lobby?

B: Nothing much. But there's a lot of excitement at the pool.

A: Oh? What's going on?

B: Rock N. Roller is trying to swim, but there are hundreds of people watching and screaming at him.

A: Let's send some guards down there to help him.

UNIT 3: Keeping Up with the Joneses

Page 21, Exercises 1 and 2

Narrator: Conversation A

A: Our neighbors have a new car!

B: Oh? What's it like?

A: Well, it's bigger and faster than ours. It's a lot more expensive, too.

B: Hmmmm. You know, dear, our car is getting old! And it's very small.

A: I know. Let's go look for a new car tomorrow.

Narrator: Are these people trying to keep up with the Joneses?

Narrator: Conversation B

A: Well, honey, are you happy with our new swimming pool?

B: Yes, I am. You know I love to swim, and our pool is longer, wider, and deeper than our neighbor's pool.

A: You're right. No one in the neighborhood has a better pool than ours.

Narrator: Are these people keeping up with their neighbors?

Narrator: Conversation C

A: Hey, Paula! Look! We got a new color TV. It's bigger, better, and more expensive than our old one.

B: Gee, Maria, you're lucky! We still have our old black-and-white TV.

A: That's OK, Paula. You can watch your favorite programs at my house.

Narrator: Is Paula's family keeping up with Maria's family?

Page 26, Exercises 2 and 3

Woman: Excuse me, sir. Is there a good restaurant in this neighborhood?

Man: Well, there are two nearby—Andy's Restaurant and the Starlight Diner.

Woman: Which one is better?

Man: It all depends. Each one has its good points and its bad points.

Woman: Well, what about price? I don't have a lot of money. Which one is cheaper?

Man: Oh, they're both pretty cheap. But I suppose Andy's Restaurant is a little cheaper than the Starlight.

Woman: And which one do you think is cleaner? I hate dirty restaurants!

Man: Well, let's see. I'd say that Andy's Restaurant is cleaner. It's definitely a lot newer than the Starlight. In fact, there's only one problem with Andy's Restaurant.

Woman: What's that?

Man: Well, sometimes it gets very noisy. It's small and it gets pretty crowded.

Woman: Is the Starlight as noisy as Andy's Restaurant? I really like peace and quiet!

Man: I'm sorry to say it's a lot worse! The Starlight is even smaller and more popular than Andy's Restaurant, so it's noisier and more crowded all the time.

Woman: Well, how's the food in both places? I'm really more interested in good food than anything else.

Man: I think the Starlight is OK, but it's not great. The food is much better at Andy's.

Woman: Which of these restaurants do you usually eat in?

Man: Eat in restaurants? Why, I never eat in restaurants. My son lives with me, and he's the best cook in town!

UNIT 4: And the Beat Goes On!

Page 39, Exercise 2

Professor: We are now going to listen to some examples of folk music. We'll hear selections from Africa, Asia, the Middle East, and the Caribbean. Many of these kinds of folk music were used for more than just entertainment. We will talk about some of the special uses each one has.

One of the examples that first comes to mind is drum music. The wooden drum music of Western Africa played an important role in communicating over long distances. Drummers used tone and rhythm to send messages from village to village. In this way, people could get in contact with each other very easily.

There are other kinds of drum music. In Barbados, West Indies, for example, drums are made from metal oil containers. They produce a unique sound and can be used to play a melody. The steel drums of Barbados are used to accompany singing and dancing at village festivals.

In Japan, a special type of music called koto music had a different use. Musicians played the koto to accompany plays in the classical theater.

Another kind of folk music is Vedic song, which comes from India. Vedic song had rules for composition set down in very old writings. This type of music was used for telling stories and poetry.

As a last example, we can mention music from the Arabian countries. One kind of song was the Huda song. Huda song has a special rhythm which imitated the rhythm of a camel's walk. Experts believe that people thought this music would keep them safe from spirits in the desert.

As you can see, music had many more purposes than just entertainment.

UNIT 5: Close Calls

Page 43, Exercise 1

Narrator: Conversation A
A: Where's your car?
B: In the garage. A truck almost hit me while I was driving to school. I had to turn so quickly that I hit a tree.
A: Were you hurt?
B: No. My car was damaged, but I'm all right.
A: That was really a close call!

Narrator: Conversation B
(BUZZZZZZZZZZZZZZ)
A: What's that?
B: The smoke alarm! Come on! We have to get out of the house!

A: Don't go that way! The curtains are burning!
B: We can go out the back door. Hurry up! It's getting hot in here!

Narrator: Conversation C
A: Where were you when the thunderstorm started?
B: My husband and I were playing golf.
A: Didn't the lightening strike near you?
B: Too close! We were so afraid we ran under the nearest tree!
A: You're kidding!

Narrator: Conversation D
A: Hurry up, honey. That cloud is coming closer and closer.
B: At least in the basement we'll be safe from the winds.
A: Yes, I just hope it won't cause as much damage as last time. Remember all the trees that were blown down?

Narrator: Conversation E
A: We had a close call last weekend when we went skiing. We got caught in a blizzard.
B: That's awful! What happened?
A: Well, we couldn't drive—there were huge snowdrifts and we couldn't see at all. It was freezing cold and the winds were really strong.
B: I'm glad you got home safely!

Page 48, Exercise 2

Announcer: A woman caught a thief at Park City Mall today. Here is Ali el Khatabi reporting.
Reporter: "Why me?" was Mrs. Mildred Martin's first reaction to her close call at the supermarket. Mrs. Martin, please tell us what happened.
Mrs. Martin: Well, I came here this morning with my children to do some shopping. Normally, we come on Saturday, but we didn't have a thing in the house to eat. Anyway, after shopping, my kids and I were in the parking lot. They were getting into the back seat, and I was putting the groceries in the trunk. I noticed a man walking toward me, but, you know, I didn't think anything of it. Then suddenly, he was right next to me, and he grabbed my purse! He was trying to run away, but I pushed him and he fell over a bag of groceries. All of my money was in that purse!
Reporter: Well, Mrs. Martin, we know you hit the thief on the head, too. How did you do that?
Mrs. Martin: I just gave him a taste of the supermarket's weekly special—a bottle of milk right on the head!
Reporter: So there you have it, folks. When the thief woke up, the police were waiting to take him away.

UNIT 6: The Best in Life

Page 53, Exercise 2

Narrator: Ad A

Woman: I was working at my desk when suddenly I realized that I felt terrible. I was so tired that I couldn't work. So I bought some Fun Time candies. I bit into them and tasted their rich chocolate flavor and fresh, delicious nuts. I felt better right away. Whenever you feel hungry, try some Fun Time candies!

Narrator: Ad B

Woman: My old soap was drying my skin. My skin felt dry and hard. Then I decided to try Reid's Beauty Soap. Reid's Beauty Soap is made from special plants that keep your skin looking fresh, soft, and young! Try Reid's Beauty Soap today. You'll see and feel the difference!

Narrator: Ad C

Man: The new Tiger is a winner! This is the fastest, most powerful vehicle on the road. It can go from 0 to 70 in ten seconds. It uses very little gas and its engine hardly ever needs repairs. Test drive a Tiger today! You'll see that the Tiger is for you!

Pages 58–59, Exercises 2 and 3

Narrator: Ad A

Man: I say, hey-now, hey-now, ready to go, 'Cause with my new Click pen, I don't write slow.
I say hey-now, hey-now, what do you say? Buy yourself a Click pen right away! Buy a Click, Click, Click, Click, Click, Click! Get a kick with Click, Click, Click, Click, Click!

Narrator: Ad B

Woman: Hi! As president of Skyways Airlines and a mother of four children, I often don't have time to cook when I get home from work. That's why I buy Wheeler's Country Style Soups. They're the only soups that taste better than my homemade soup. Wheeler's Country Style Soups are made with fresh vegetables. They're delicious! My children love them. So when I'm too tired to cook, I know that I can open a can of Wheeler's Country Style Soup and my family will love it! Serve your family Wheeler's Country Style Soup tonight!

Narrator: Ad C

Woman: Simply the most beautiful, most elegant, most expensive, and most accurate watches ever made! Marie de Nouvelle Swiss watches! Marie de Nouvelle Swiss watches.

Narrator: Ad D

(little girl and little boy)

Dee Dee: Mommy's birthday is tomorrow, Jimmy. What can we get for the best mommy in the world?

Jimmy: I know, Dee Dee. Let's get her flowers. Flowers are the best way to show your love.

Dee Dee: That's a great idea. Let's buy them at Mary Jane's Flower Shop. Mary Jane's has the prettiest flowers in town.

Narrator: Mary Jane's Flower Shop has the freshest flowers for all occasions. Mary Jane's is open Monday through Saturday from 9 a.m. to 9 p.m. and Sunday from 9 to 5.

UNIT 7: The Perfect Match

Page 65, Exercise 2

Narrator: Conversation 1

Interviewer: So, Ms. Christie, you want to work in the restaurant car on the Paris to Istanbul train?

Woman: That's right. I really like traveling, and I love restaurant work.

Interviewer: Do you have any experience working in a restaurant on a train?

Woman: Well, I don't exactly have experience on trains, but I have experience working in a restaurant. You see, I work on a ship on the Nile River in Egypt. I'm the head cook.

Interviewer: And what other experience have you had?

Woman: Well, before that, I was a flight attendant with Skyways Airlines.

Narrator: Conversation 2

Interviewer: Well, Mr. Fox, you're applying for the job as editor, right?

Man: That's right. I saw your ad in the employment office.

Interviewer: I see from your application that you went to Long Island University. When did you graduate?

Man: Last year.

Interviewer: What did you major in?

Man: English and advertising.

Narrator: Conversation 3

Interviewer: So, Ms. Roberts, why are you interested in finding a new job?

Woman: Well, I have a really terrible boss.

Interviewer: Oh really?

Woman: Yes. For example, if someone arrives only a minute late, he doesn't pay the person for the day.

Interviewer: Is that all?

Woman: No. We also have to work twelve to fourteen hours every day. We have to work every Saturday and Sunday, too.

Interviewer: I can see why you want to change jobs.

Page 70, Exercise 2

Interviewer: Come on in, Mr. Hunk. Have a seat.

Mr. Hunk: Thank you.

Interviewer: Your full name is Hal Hunk?

Mr. Hunk: That's right.

Interviewer: Your application says that you're interested in the job as stuntman. Have you had any experience doing stunts?

Mr. Hunk: Yes, sir, I have. I've been a stuntman for six years.

Interviewer: Really? When did you begin as a stuntman?

Mr. Hunk: I performed my first stunt when I was only fifteen.

Interviewer: What was your first stunt?

Mr. Hunk: I jumped off a train in a cowboy movie.

Interviewer: What other stunts have you done?

Mr. Hunk: Well, I've driven cars and motorcycles in detective and adventure films. I've fallen off every kind of building you can name.

Interviewer: Hmmmmm. Have you ever jumped out of a plane?

Mr. Hunk: No, I haven't, but I'd like to try.

Interviewer: Have you ever fought a monster?

Mr. Hunk: Well, so far I haven't ever fought a monster.

Interviewer: What was your most recent stunt?

Mr. Hunk: Well, the last thing I did was pretty exciting, even if I do say so myself. Last month, in an adventure movie, I had to fight with two live tigers. It was really dangerous, but everything went just fine.

Interviewer: Very interesting. Well, you certainly fill the bill for the job we have in mind. We'll let you know by the end of the month.

Mr. Hunk: Thank you very much.

UNIT 8: Ask the Experts

Page 75, Exercise 2

Narrator: Conversation A

Annie: I have a really big problem. We just got our history test back and I got a terrible grade. I got almost half the questions wrong!

Bill: Oh, no! Annie, what are you going to do?

Annie: I don't know! And I told my parents that I was going to do really well! What should I do?

Narrator: Conversation B

Betty: I feel terrible, Larry.

Larry: What's the matter, Betty?

Betty: One of my back teeth really hurts.

Larry: That's too bad! What are you going to do?

Narrator: Conversation C

Jenny: I'm so upset, Mary Jane. Harry and I have been arguing so much lately!

Mary Jane: What about, Jenny?

Jenny: We always argue about the kids. I believe that parents have to make rules for their children.

Mary Jane: I agree, but what about Harry?

Jenny: He says they're just kids and gives them anything they want. When Harry is there, the kids refuse to listen to me and I get angry. I don't know what to do!

Page 81, Exercises 2 and 3

(sound of phone ringing)

Olga: Hello, this is *Ask Olga*. What are you calling about?

Caller A: I have a huge problem. You see, I'm twenty-one years old and a university student. My boyfriend is twenty-seven and has a good job. My parents think that he is too old for me. My mother won't talk to him and my father can't stand him. But we really love each other, and he wants to get married. My boyfriend earns a good salary, and he says I can continue with school. I want to marry him, but I know my parents will be very upset. My mother says that she will never speak to me again if I get married now. What do you think I should do?

Olga: Well, let's ask our listeners.

Listener A: Hi, Olga. I have some advice for the caller. I think that it's wonderful that they're in love. That's the most important thing, isn't it? If people are really in love, I think that they should get married.

Olga: Thank you. We have another listener on the line with more advice.

Listener B: Hello, Olga. I have some advice for the caller. The same thing happened to me when I was young. I got married when I was still in college. I was still very young. My husband and I were very happy for the first six months. Then the problems started. We broke up after a year, and I never finished college. I think that you should think very carefully about marriage, and maybe you should take your parents' advice this time.

Olga: Thank you for your advice. *(sound of ringing phone)* We have another caller, now.

Caller B: I'm calling because I have a problem.

Olga: Go ahead.

Caller B: Well, I bought a used car three months ago, and I've had problems with it ever since. First, I had problems with the wheels. I took the car back, and the dealer fixed it for free. That was fine, but it took two weeks. Then, three weeks later, there was a problem with the electrical system. The lights went out one night when I was driving home. I took it back, and the dealer fixed it, but it was another two weeks. Now the engine has broken down, and the dealer doesn't want to fix it. He says that the guarantee was only for three months. So here I am with a car that won't work. What should I do?

Olga: Listeners, can you give this caller some advice?

Listener C: Hello, Olga. I have some advice. People should never buy used cars. Everyone knows that used cars always break down. I think the caller should buy a new car.

Olga: Thank you. We have another person with more advice.

Listener D: Hi, Olga. I have some different advice. I had trouble with a used car, too, so I went to the Better Business Bureau. The Better Business Bureau helps consumers solve their problems. I talked to a counselor there, who helped me get my car fixed for free. Every city has a Better Business Bureau. The caller should get in touch with the Better Business Bureau in his town.

Olga: Thanks! That's great advice! And now let's take a break. We'll be back right after this commercial.

Page 81, Exercise 4

a. Should I buy this car? **b.** You shouldn't buy a new car. **c.** Do you think that I should find a new job? **d.** Do you like the job you have now? **e.** My job is wonderful. **f.** Do you think that he'd better study more? **g.** I think he'd better study five hours every night. **h.** Should I go to San Diego? **i.** San Diego is wonderful in March. **j.** How is the weather in San Diego in March?

UNIT 9: Stressed Out

Page 85, Exercise 2

Narrator: Conversation A

Bob: How was your day at the office, Sue?

Sue: I had a great day! I just love my new job! Say, I'm really thirsty! Bob, would you get me a can of pop?

Bob: What!! I don't believe it!! I work too, you know. I had a hard day at the factory and I'm tired, too. I did all of the shopping after work, and I cleaned the house before you got home. Get the pop yourself!

Narrator: Conversation B

Chris: Do you think that you'll like working here, Judy?

Judy: To tell you the truth, Chris, I don't know yet. This is only my second day, and I've never worked in advertising before. My whole future depends on doing this job well. And if I lose this job, I won't be able to help out my brother who is in college studying to be a doctor.

Chris: I'm sure you'll do fine, Judy!

Narrator: Conversation C

Mark: Sandy, I told you to leave earlier!

Sandy: There is a little traffic, but there's plenty of time! You won't miss your plane. Calm down!

Mark: You know I always worry when I have to catch a plane.

Sandy: Look, Mark. If you miss this plane, there's another one in an hour.

Page 90, Exercises 2 and 3

Interviewer: Uh-huh, uh-huh … That's very interesting. My next question has to do with the kinds of jobs or professions that cause stress. In your opinion, what are the jobs that cause stress in people?

Expert: Well, it's not an easy question to answer. In fact, there are different experts who measure stress in different ways, but here's my own opinion. I think that people who work in jobs that have an element of physical danger feel huge amounts of stress. I'd say that firefighters feel enormous stress, for example. Firefighters often have to enter burning buildings where walls or ceilings can fall in on them.

Interviewer: I think that police officers must also be under a lot of stress, too.

Expert: That's right. Police officers who fight crime in the street all day feel almost as much stress as firefighters. They are in almost constant danger while they are at work.

Interviewer: And what are some professions that have very little stress?

Expert: Well, one profession that causes very little stress is banking. People who work as bankers have very little stress.

Interviewer: And the profession lowest in stress?

Expert: In my opinion, a librarian who spends all day in a quiet library has almost no stress at all!

Interviewer: What about people who have a lot of contact with the public, such as actors or sports stars?

Expert: Well, people in these occupations also experience a lot of stress. Actors, for example, get anxious about losing their popularity or giving a bad performance. Many of them are afraid of growing old, losing their popularity, not making money … Sports stars probably feel a little more stress than actors. They have to be at their best in every single game, and they are always afraid that they will lose. Still, they don't feel nearly as much stress as those people who work in dangerous conditions.

Interviewer: Now, let's talk a little about how people with stressful jobs handle it.

Expert: Sure! Getting plenty of rest is important. So is plenty of exercise. They should also try to eat lots of fresh fruit and vegetables.

Page 91, Exercise 6

1. Dan bought the best computer.
2. Dan bought his new computer at the **mall**.
3. Dan's **friend** bought the cheapest computer.

4. Dan **sometimes** uses the computer lab.
5. **Dan's** computer was the most powerful one in the shop.

UNIT 10: You've Got to Be Kidding!

Page 97, Exercises 2 and 3

Narrator: Conversation A
Daughter: Hey, Dad! Guess what!
Father: I know! You won the gold medal for swimming the fastest in the 100-meter race. And you broke your own record!
Daughter: How did you know that?
Father: Well, you're my daughter, aren't you?

Narrator: Conversation B
Mr. Atkins: Congratulations, Bill! You've sold more encyclopedias than any other salesperson in the company.
Bill: Why, thank you, Mr. Atkins. I really tried hard.
Mr. Atkins: And for that, the company is going to give you and your family the luxury edition of our finest encyclopedia! Completely free!
Bill: Thank you, sir. That's very nice of you.

Narrator: Conversation C
Bud: Hey, Lou, I heard that you entered the waiter's contest last week.
Lou: Yeah, Bud, I did. I wanted to break the record for running while carrying glasses.
Bud: How did you do?
Lou: I ran for thirty-five minutes and didn't drop a single glass, but then I tripped and fell down right before I reached the finish line.
Bud: Sorry to hear that. Better luck next time.

Page 102, Exercises 3 and 4

Ruby: So what happened on the *That's Amazing!* show today, Mom?
Mom: I don't know how you persuaded me to watch that crazy show! You know that I don't like to watch TV!
Ruby: But did you watch it?
Mom: Yes, it was about a man from Colombia. His name is Quintero. Liberato Anibal Quintero. He's been a farmer for thirty years.
Ruby: But, Mom, what did he do that was amazing?
Mom: Well, he says that he saw an unidentified flying object and met some people from outer space.
Ruby: Wow, that's fantastic! How did he meet them?
Mom: Well, he was outside with his cows when he saw a light in the sky. It came nearer and nearer and finally landed. It was a spaceship.
Ruby: Wow! So then what happened?
Mom: Well, he says that space people came out of the spaceship and grabbed him.
Ruby: You've got to be kidding!

Mom: No! They took him into the spaceship and gave him something to drink. He says that the drink was a strange color.
Ruby: What happened then?
Mom: He doesn't remember. The drink made him fall asleep. When he woke up, he was outside the ship on the ground. He says that ever since then he's been having bad dreams about the space people. He's afraid that they'll come back some day!
Ruby: Why doesn't he move so they can't find him?
Mom: Because his family has been living in the same place for thirty years, and he doesn't want to live anywhere else.
Ruby: Wow! What an incredible story. I hope that I see an unidentified flying object some day!
Mom: Ruby! You don't really believe in spaceships and space travelers, do you?
Ruby: Of course! I believe everything on *That's Amazing!* It's my favorite show.

UNIT 11: From Rags to Riches

Page 107, Exercise 2

Narrator: Conversation 1
A: I still can't believe that we won the lottery!
B: Sometimes it seems like a dream! The lucky number was eight-two-seven-oh-nine!

Narrator: Conversation 2
A: Business is great! Our sales are up 20 percent. Call the factory and tell them we need more workers.
B: Yes, Mr. Lee.
A: And tell the workers that I am going to give everyone a big raise.
B: That's great, Mr. Lee! Everyone will be happy!

Narrator: Conversation 3
A: Look at what I found in Grandpa's coin collection.
B: It's a gold coin! It must be worth a fortune!

Page 113, Exercises 2 and 3

[**I** = interviewer; **V1** = Villager 1; **V2** = Villager 2]

I: So, in your opinion, is the story of your village, St. Napa, a rags-to-riches story?
V1: Yes, in some ways it is. We used to be a poor town. Most of us were farmers or fishermen. We certainly didn't use to be rich, but we had happy and peaceful lives. Our children grew up, got married, and went to work here in the village. Now all of that has changed forever!
I: What happened?
V2: When tourists discovered St. Napa, they brought money to spend with them! They wanted clean and quiet beaches, but they also wanted to shop, eat out in nice restaurants, go dancing, and have fun! It's been great!

V1: No it hasn't!

I: Well, sir, how have things changed?

V1: For one thing, people never used to walk around town barefoot and only in their swimsuits, but the tourists do it all the time! And at night they go to the new dance clubs and stay out very late.

V2: Well, I love the new clubs. I get to meet interesting people from all over the world, and they like to dance and have fun just like me. All the young people from around here feel the same, too.

I: Interesting. And …

V1: Fun! Is that all life is about these days? Why, the young people here don't even think about staying in the village and carrying on the local traditions. They used to live here close to their parents and relatives. They used to marry each other, but now they are always looking for people from other places to marry.

I: I see. And what other changes have you seen?

V1: Well, the town used to be quiet, but now there are hundreds of restaurants, souvenir shops, and dance clubs. And last I heard, there are more than thirteen thousand hotel beds!

V2: Isn't that great? All the new businesses mean more jobs and more money for everyone!

V1: Well, we may be a richer village, but a lot of us aren't used to all these changes. We used to be happier when the town and the beaches were ours alone.

I: I appreciate your opinions on the changes here in St. Napa. Thank you for your time.

UNIT 12: Hit the Jackpot

Page 117, Exercise 2

Narrator: Conversation 1

Host: And now for your last question, Ms. Phillips. If you answer this question correctly, you'll win the $44,000 jackpot. Are you nervous?

Guest: Well, yes, I'm a little nervous, but I think that I can answer the last question.

Host: Good luck, Ms. Phillips. Here is your question. For $44,000, tell us who invented the sport of basketball?

Guest: I think it was Mr. James Naismith.

Host: Correct, Ms. Phillips. You hit the $44,000 jackpot!

Narrator: Conversation 2

Hostess: Now it's player number two's turn to ask our mystery person three questions. Remember, you have only three chances to figure out her occupation. Are you ready?

Guest: Yes, I am. Question one. Do you work at night or during the day?

Mystery Person: I have to work at night and during the day.

Guest: I see. Question two. Do you have to wear special clothes while you're at work?

Mystery Person: Why, yes, I do. That was a good question.

Guest: Question three. Are you a nurse?

Mystery Person: No, I'm not.

Hostess: Too bad, player two. Better luck next time. Now let's find out what our mystery person does.

Mystery Person: My name is Amanda Windsor. I'm the first woman to be the pilot of the Concorde jet, the fastest passenger airplane in the world.

Page 122, Exercises 2 and 3

[**B** = Betty, the hostess; **M** = Maria, a contestant; **P** = Peter, a contestant]

B: Welcome, everyone, to show #341 of *Jackpot Shop!* If you're ready, let's begin the game! Maria, today is your first time on the show, so you get the first turn. Remember, if you choose an expensive prize, your question will be hard. What prize do you want?

M: I'm going to start with something easy, Betty. I want a good dictionary.

B: OK. That's not very expensive at all. Here's your question. Who traveled to the New World in 1492?

M: Christopher Columbus.

B: That's right! Congratulations! *(audience applauds)* Now it's your turn, Peter. Are you ready?

P: Yes, I am, and I want a Marie de Nouvelle 24-karat gold watch.

B: That's an expensive prize, Peter. Here's your question. Who first brought chocolate to Europe from America in the year 1528?

P: Christopher Columbus.

B: *(raucous buzzer sounds)* Sorry, Peter. *(audience groans)* The answer is Hernán Cortés, the famous Spanish explorer. Better luck next time. Are you ready, Maria?

M: Yes, Betty. I want a compact disc player.

B: That's a little harder, Maria. Here's your question. What famous singer, born in Liverpool, England, in 1940, joined a band named after an insect?

M: I know! John Lennon of the Beatles!

B: Yes! *(audience applauds and whistles)* Are you ready, Peter?

P: Ready to go! And I'm going for the combination VCR and color TV with a 29-inch screen!

B: OK, Peter, that's a great prize. Here's your question. What famous opera star had a close call with the San Francisco earthquake of 1906?

P: Gosh, uh … was it Placido Domingo?

B: *(raucous buzzer sounds; audience groans)* Well, you know what that sound means, Peter. Sorry. It was Enrico Caruso. Ready, Maria?

M: You bet. And I want the same combination VCR and color TV that Peter wanted.

B: OK. Here's your question. This man founded the McDonald's hamburger chain and sold billions of burgers before he died in 1984. What was his name?

M: I … think it was … Ray Kroc.

B: Right again! *(audience applauds wildly)* Now it's Peter's turn. This is your last chance. If you want to win, you have to choose a prize more expensive than Maria's three prizes together.

P: Yeah, I know. Well, this is the big one. I want the American Dream Car!

B: Wow! That prize is worth $2 million! Be careful, Peter. Remember, Maria will win unless you answer correctly. Here's your question. San Simeon, on William Randolph Hearst's 200,000-acre estate in California, is one of the most beautiful castles in the world. When did he start building it?

P: Uh … gosh … uh … in 1918?

B: Sorry, Peter! *(buzzer sounds; audience groans)* He started building San Simeon in 1920. So, Maria, congratulations! *(audience claps and shouts; a bell rings wildly)* You're our winner! Are you ready for the jackpot question?

M: Yes, Betty. I'm as ready as I'll ever be.

B: OK. Now listen carefully. *(background noise of clock ticking or some other noise to indicate time passing)* What female newspaper reporter traveled around the world in the year 1890 in less than eighty days?

M: Oh, I know this! It was Nellie Bly!

B: That's right! *(bells and whistles and gongs ringing)* Congratulations! You've hit the jackpot! *(audience goes wild; fade-out)*

Workbook Audioscript

UNIT 1: What's on TV?

Practice 9

Pat: Well, Ann, I really love weekends, too. I get to do just what I want! Every Sunday morning I play soccer. It's great!

Ann: I thought you were a tennis player, Pat.

Pat: I am. I play tennis every Saturday afternoon.

Bob: Do you go swimming?

Pat: Yes, of course, but only every other week. You see, I play basketball twice a month. Well, I have to go now. I have a game.

Ann: I have to go, too.

Bob: Are you playing in the game, too?

Ann: No, I have to do my homework. I usually do it on Saturday afternoon, but today I want to do it early so that I can go to the art museum this afternoon. I like to go there once a month when the exhibits change. And every Sunday morning I go to the concert at the City Theater.

Bob: Gee, Ann, you spend every Sunday afternoon reading in the library, too. That's too much for me.

Ann: What do you usually do on weekends, Bob?

Bob: My idea of a great weekend is to sit on the couch in front of the TV with food, drinks, and a television guide!

Practice 11

1. closes	6. pushes
2. likes	7. falls
3. reads	8. continues
4. mixes	9. works
5. stops	10. finds

UNIT 2: People Watching

Practice 8

Peter: Hey, Carol. What are you doing on Friday night?

Carol: I'm going to the movies with my best friend, Judy. What about you?

Peter: Well, Friday night I'm staying home. My sister, her husband, and my nephew are coming to visit for the weekend. They're arriving on Friday afternoon.

Carol: That sounds like fun. How old is your nephew?

Peter: Eight.

Carol: And I guess you're taking him to the movies on Saturday afternoon, right?

Peter: Right. He's a cartoon nut, and, you know, I have to admit that I like them, too.

Carol: I hate them! I never go to cartoons with my little sisters any more. But guess where I'm taking them on Saturday afternoon.?

Peter: Where?

Carol: To the zoo. I'm a real animal nut.

Peter: Really? I am, too.

Carol: Why don't you have lunch with us on Sunday. Your nephew can meet my little sisters.

Peter: Sorry, I can't. I'm playing basketball with some friends at 1:00. Plus, I have to study for the exam all Sunday night. I'm really nervous about it.

Carol: I know what you mean. I'm nervous about it, too.

Peter: When are you going to study?

Carol: All Sunday afternoon and night! I'm staying home just to study.

Practice 9B

1. couches
2. bands
3. stories
4. managers
5. glasses
6. radios
7. horses
8. towels
9. exercises
10. beaches

UNIT 3: Keeping Up with the Joneses

Practice 9A

Pronunciation note: The name of the French city Nice is pronounced /nis/.

Travel Agent: Hi folks. Did you make a decision? Which city do you want to visit?

Thelma: We still can't decide. I want to see Fez, but Earl still wants to go to Nice.

Earl: That's right. I want a relaxing vacation, but Thelma wants something more exciting. Can you tell us more about these cities?

Agent: Sure. You know, Fez is really newer than Nice, but the old part still looks like it did in the ninth century.

Thelma: How interesting! Nice is older than Fez! But Nice seems so modern.

Agent: Well, Nice is more modern now, but it's really very old. The Greeks first lived there in 350 B.C. It has a long and interesting history.

Thelma: Tell us more about Fez. Are there lots of interesting things to buy? I love to go shopping!

Agent: Oh, Fez is great for shopping. Morocco is famous for many things, like beautiful rugs. You can buy beautiful purses, wallets, and jackets there, too. You can go shopping in Nice, but it's really better for relaxing on the beach.

Earl: What about hotels? I like big, modern hotels with all the conveniences.

Agent: Well, of course, there are big, modern hotels in Fez, but many hotels in Nice are even bigger and more modern.

Earl: Nice sounds good to me. I just want to relax and do nothing.

Thelma: Oh, Earl. We can relax and do nothing at home! I want foreign food, strange music, new experiences …

Earl: I'm telling you, Thelma. I don't want any of that spicy food or strange noise! Nice is nicer, more relaxing, and more comfortable than Fez!

Thelma: I'm sorry, but I don't agree! Fez is as nice as Nice. Also, it's cheaper and a lot more interesting!

Agent: Excuse me. I have an idea. I think you both need a little vacation alone. Thelma can go to Fez for a week and look for excitement. Earl, you can go to Nice and relax. Then you can spend your last two weeks together in Venice. You'll love Venice. It's very romantic.

Earl: That sounds perfect. What do you think, Thelma?

Thelma: Fez and Venice! Oh, Earl! Wait until my friends hear about this!

Practice 10B

1. condition
2. gorgeous
3. explain
4. friendly
5. compare
6. appearance
7. narrow
8. interesting
9. helpful

Practice 11B

On January 28, 1985, 45 pop stars decided to sing a simple song in a Los Angeles studio. They <u>called</u> the song "We Are the World." Michael Jackson and Lionel Richie wrote the song. Quincy Jones <u>arranged</u> it. The artists who <u>recorded</u> the song <u>included</u> Ray Charles, Tina Turner, Paul Simon, and many others. Thousands of people <u>listened</u> to the song and <u>wanted</u> to buy it. The money from the sales <u>helped</u> hungry people in Africa. These artists really <u>tried</u> to make the world a better place and succeeded.

UNIT 4: And the Beat Goes On!

Practice 12

Narrator: Dialogue 1

Mr. Lowe: Jack, I don't understand why you didn't pass this exam. You're usually a good student. What happened?

Jack: Well, Mr. Lowe, the truth is that I didn't study much. I didn't have time.

Mr. Lowe: Oh, really! Why?

Jack: Well, last week, I got a job at the music store. I work after school and on weekends.

Narrator: Dialogue 2

Doctor: So, Mr. Hollins, did you follow my instructions?

Hollins: Yes, doctor, I did.

Doctor: That's wonderful.

Hollins: Every day I got up early, turned on some rock music, and exercised. And I didn't eat any potatoes, bread, candy, or dessert all week.

Doctor: That's great! Let's see how much weight you lost. Congratulations! You lost eight pounds! You see, as the beat goes on, the fat comes off.

UNIT 5: Close Calls

Practice 9

Narrator: Conversation 1

Reporter: What were you doing when the lights went out?

Customer: I was getting a haircut. I almost lost an ear!

Reporter: Wow! That was really a close call!

Customer: Yeah. And now look at my hair! One side is much shorter that the other!

Narrator: Conversation 2
Reporter: And you, Ma'am. What were you doing?
Customer: My husband and I were choosing a sofabed for our daughter's first apartment. When the lights went out, my husband lay down and went to sleep.

Narrator: Conversation 3
Reporter: What about you, sir? What happened to you?
Customer: Well, I was buying a bottle of apple juice. When the lights went out, I dropped it, and it shattered. There was broken glass and apple juice all over the floor.

Narrator: Conversation 4
Reporter: Excuse me, Miss. What were you doing when the lights went out?
Customer: Well, my sister was trying on some shoes, and I was waiting for her. When the lights went out, we ran out of the store. When we got outside, we saw that she was wearing two different shoes!

Narrator: Conversation 5
Reporter: And what about you? What were you doing?
Customer: My friends and I were playing video games. When the lights went out, we lost our money! We want our money back so we can play another game.

Practice 11B

A: What were you doing when the lights went out?
B: I was getting a haircut. I almost lost an ear!
A: Wow! That was really a close call!
B: Yeah. And now look at my hair! One side is much shorter than the other!

UNIT 6: The Best in Life

Practice 8

Salesperson: Hi, can I help you?
Customer: Yes, I'm looking for a touring bike for a long trip I'm taking this summer.
Salesperson: Well, we have three touring bikes. We have the Road Rider, the Traveler, and the Mountain King.
Customer: What's the difference?
Salesperson: Each bike has advantages and disadvantages. The Road Rider has the most speeds—eighteen. That's five more speeds than the Traveler and the Mountain King.
Customer: Well, I don't need eighteen speeds, do I?
Salesperson: No, not really. You need a light, strong bike. The Mountain King is the lightest and strongest of the three. It's made of special metal, and it's great for long trips.

Customer: Are the other two a lot heavier?
Salesperson: Well, the Road Rider is a little heavier and the Traveler is the heaviest.
Customer: What about price?
Salesperson: The Mountain King is usually the most expensive, but right now it's on sale. Besides being light, it has a lot of special features, like a water bottle, a light, and mirrors.
Customer: Which one is cheapest?
Salesperson: The Traveler. But it's very heavy. It's not really good for a long trip.
Customer: I need to think this over a little.
Salesperson: OK, but remember, the sale ends next Tuesday.

UNIT 7: The Perfect Match

Practice 8

Betty: Hi, Marie. Have you finished getting ready for your trip?
Marie: No, I'm afraid I haven't, Betty. It seems that all I've done for days is stand in long lines all over the city.
Betty: Oh? Have you had some problems?
Marie: Well, yes and no. The camera store was closed, so I couldn't get the film I need. And I spent all morning waiting in line at the passport office. Then just when it was my turn, they closed.
Betty: That's terrible. Didn't anything go right?
Marie: Well, I did manage to buy two pairs of strong hiking boots. They were on sale at Rocky Mountain Shoes.
Betty: That's good. And what about your vaccination shots?
Marie: Oh, I've gotten them all. I did that last week. I had to wait in line for hours! But the nurse was very nice, and the shots didn't hurt at all.
Betty: I suppose you've finished all your packing by now.
Marie: Are you kidding? I've packed my big trunk, but I haven't started packing my suitcases! There are clothes all over my bedroom.
Betty: Well, in case I don't see you again before you go, have a safe trip and a great time. I can't really stay any longer. I have to get to the bank before it closes.
Marie: Wait, I'll go with you. I haven't picked up my money or my traveler's checks!

Practice 10B

A: Well, I see you've applied for the job.
B: Yes, I've wanted to change jobs for a while now.
A: And how long have you worked at your current job?
B: For five years.
A: And why do you want to leave your job after so many years?

B: Because I'm the smartest employee there, I've had the most education and I've got the most experience, but I've never gotten a raise. My boss hates me.

A: Well, OK, I see. Thank you for your time. We'll call you!

UNIT 8: Ask the Experts

Practice 9A, B

Narrator: Conversation 1

Nancy: Well, I really don't know what to do. Bill gets a stomachache almost every evening.

Grandma: I have just the thing for him, Nancy. Your grandfather had terrible stomachaches, too, and I always gave him a cup of this special tea. I make it from plants that I grow in the garden.

Nancy: And the tea cured his stomachaches?

Grandma: Yes, indeed. You should give him a cup of tea every time he has a stomach-ache. I'll show you how to prepare it.

Narrator: Conversation 2

Mrs. Potter: You'd better stop making so much noise, Timmy. I'll have to ask you to leave if you don't stop talking.

Timmy: I'm sorry, Mrs. Potter. I was asking Wayne about the encyclopedias.

Mrs. Potter: You should ask me. Which encyclopedia do you need?

Timmy: The one with all the maps in front. And where can I find a book on the history of Turkey? I need it for a report.

Mrs. Potter: You should learn how to find things in the library. Come over here and I'll show you.

Narrator: Conversation 3

Sylvia: Judy, I came to see you about my problem because I just can't talk to my mother about it.

Judy: Well, I know how you feel, Sylvia, but you should go to her with any problem you have. After all, she loves you and wants you to be happy.

Sylvia: She doesn't understand how I feel.

Judy: Of course your mother knows how you feel! Listen, I'm your best friend, and I'm telling you that you ought to talk to your mother about it!

Practice 10B

A: Joe, can I ask you a question? I need some advice.

B: Sure. No problem. What's the matter?

A: I'd like do buy a computer. Do you think I should buy a laptop? Or do you think I should buy a desktop?

B: Do you really need to take it with you?

A: Not really, but my friend has a laptop, and he really likes it.

B: I think you should buy a desktop. They're a lot cheaper and a better buy for your money.

A: I guess you're right. Thanks a lot.

UNIT 9: Stressed Out

Practice 9A, B

Narrator: Conversation 1

Sue: Oh, Mary, I can't decide which blouse to wear.

Mary: Why don't you wear the blouse that your mother gave you for your birthday, Sue?

Sue: No, I think I'll wear the blouse that I bought last week.

Narrator: Question one. Which blouse will Sue wear?

Narrator: Conversation 2

Edna: Look, Joyce! That man is walking out of the store without paying for those CDs!

Joyce: Which man, Edna? The one who has long brown hair?

Edna: No, the one who is wearing a green sweater.

Joyce: We'd better call the security guard!

Narrator: Question two. Which man will the security guard stop?

Narrator: Conversation 3

Liz: Alan, I can't decide which computer to buy. I like the one that's more expensive, but I really don't want to spend that much money.

Alan: I know, Liz, but the cheaper one isn't very fast. You should spend a little more money and get one that's fast.

Liz: You're right. Speed is important.

Narrator: Question three. Which computer will Liz buy?

Narrator: Conversation 4

Bill: Hey, Mark. That girl wants to talk to you.

Mark: Who? The girl who's standing near the window?

Bill: No, the girl who's standing near the door.

Narrator: Question four. Which girl wants to talk to Mark?

Narrator: Conversation 5

Customer: Do you have the new book by Dr. Ira Stone?

Clerk: Which book? The book that gives advice about stress?

Customer: No, the one that gives advice for parents.

Narrator: Question five. Which book does the customer want?

Practice 10B

Example:

A: Did Roger tell you about his problems?

B: No, Michael told me about them.

1. **A:** Did you say your grandfather's still sick?
   B: No, I said my grandfather's feeling great.
2. **A:** Did your friend pay you back all of the money?
   B: No, she only paid back some of the money.
3. **A:** Did you find a brown briefcase?
   B: No, I lost a brown briefcase.
4. **A:** You have the aisle seat, don't you?
   B: No, I'm next to the window.

UNIT 10: You've Got to Be Kidding!

Practice 10A, B

Narrator: Conversation 1

Sally: Mary! Nice to see you! What are you doing here?

Mary: I come here every week now, Sally. I'm on a diet and exercise program.

Sally: You look much better! How long have you been dieting?

Mary: Since November. What about you? Have you been exercising here long?

Sally: Not really. About two weeks.

Narrator: Conversation 2

Cindy: I can't believe that we've been waiting for twenty minutes.

Betty: I know. There are so many people here today.

Cindy: Do you think that we should go somewhere else for lunch?

Betty: We don't have time to eat anywhere else now. The boss has been watching to make sure that people come back from lunch on time. We'd better be careful or she'll catch us.

Narrator: Conversation 3

Doctor: How long have you been gaining weight?

Bill: Ever since I got my new job … about two months ago. I've been under a lot of stress, so I've been eating a lot.

Doctor: Well, you have to stop eating desserts. And no more chocolate!

Bill: No more chocolate! Doctor, that's my favorite food.

Practice 11B

A: So how long has Harry been away now?

B: Half a month, and he says he has been having a great time.

A: Have you talked with him on the phone?

B: Last night. He says his sister has taken him to all her favorite places, and she's been taking good care of him.

A: I'm happy he has been able to spend so much time with her.

B: Yeah, she's his favorite sister. He really likes her.

A: And I'm sure he also likes her cars, and her pool, and her huge house in Hawaii.

B: How horrible of you … , but how true!

UNIT 11: From Rags to Riches

Practice 6

Joan Kroc, Philanthropist

Reporter: Good evening, ladies and gentlemen. The subject of our profile today is Joan Kroc, the California millionaire.

Joan Kroc was not always a millionaire. She was born in St. Paul, Minnesota, in 1928. As a young woman, she started her career as a music teacher and professional piano player. Later, she became the music director at a TV station.

In 1957, Joan met Ray Kroc, the founder of the McDonald's hamburger restaurants. The couple got married in 1969.

Ray and Joan Kroc were among the richest people in the United States. They owned homes in California, Florida, and Chicago. They had a ninety-foot yacht and a forty-five-thousand-dollar Rolls Royce. Ray was a baseball fan, so in 1974 he bought the San Diego Padres baseball team.

But Ray and Joan didn't spend money just on themselves. They also donated millions of dollars to charity. And after her husband died in 1984, Joan started to give away even more money. She has given millions of dollars to hospitals and zoos and millions more to help the homeless. She gave Notre Dame University twelve million dollars to study peace issues, and she donated a million dollars to feed poor people in Africa. She also helps pay for sixteen Ronald McDonald Houses, places where the families of sick children can stay while the children are in the hospital.

Today experts think Mrs. Kroc is worth about $950 million. She ran the baseball team until she sold it in 1990 and is active in politics in California, but she prefers to work quietly behind the scenes. She lives on a thirteen-acre hilltop estate outside San Diego. The $14 million house covers 35,000 square feet and includes a four-bedroom guest house. The estate is surrounded by tall trees, so no one can see in. She feels this is necessary because so many people ask her for money. In fact once she had to excuse herself and leave a party because so many people were asking her to donate money to their favorite charities.

Practice 7B

A: When are you going to finish that book about Martin Scorcese?

B: I have to talk to my class about it tomorrow. Do you want to hear something interesting?

A: I know … Before Scorcese became a famous film director, he used to live in New York City's Little Italy neighborhood, and when he was a child, he used to like to watch the musicals of the 1940s and 1950s, and French New Wave films, and he used to work in documentary film, and …

B: Yes! That's amazing! You ought to help me with my report!

A: I'd like to, but I'm going to see GoodFellas. I've got to get going.

UNIT 12: Hit the Jackpot

Practice 5A, B

Raul: Marcia, what do I have to do to get on a game show?

Marcia: Well, Raul, for some shows it's easy. All you have to do is send in a letter. If they pick your letter, they'll invite you to be on the show. But on most shows, it's more difficult.

Raul: Really? Why is it more difficult on some shows than others?

Marcia: Well, there are so many shows that they need more than 10,000 people every year. The less popular shows will take nearly anyone who wants to be a guest. The more popular shows interview people who want to be a guest.

Raul: What happens in the interviews?

Marcia: Well, they'll ask you to talk about yourself. If they think that you have an outgoing personality, they'll put you on the show.

Raul: So, if I have an open, friendly personality, I'll get on a show?

Marcia: Not always. For example, a friendly personality is just fine for a show like *What's*

My Occupation? On this show, guests try to figure out the occupation of someone by asking questions. People really don't need a lot of education to do this. However, for shows like *Jackpot Shop,* guests have to answer difficult questions on many different subjects. On other shows, such as *Name the Song!,* guests have to listen to music and say the name of the song. To win, guests have to know a lot about music. To be a guest on either of these shows, you have to take a test. The test for *Jackpot Shop* asks difficult questions about history and science.

Raul: Wow! That sounds hard! Do you think that I'll get on a show?

Marcia: Maybe. Do you know that in Los Angeles there is a special school for people who want to be on game shows? If you really want to be on a game show, you can take classes there.

Raul: Is the school very expensive?

Marcia: No. In fact, it's free. You only have to pay them if you get on a show and win a prize. Then you have to pay twenty percent of your prize.

Raul: That sounds great! Where did you say the school is?

Practice 6A

Dorothy: So, Thelma, <u>where'll you</u> go first?

Thelma: Well, we're <u>going to</u> go to Brazil first, of course. We've always wanted to go there.

Dorothy: <u>What'll you</u> do there? Will you sail up the Amazon?

Thelma: Of course, and <u>we'll</u> go to Bahia too.

Dorothy: Will Earl go up the Amazon with <u>you</u>?

Thelma: Yes. I told <u>him</u> I won't go with <u>him</u> to Bahia unless he goes up the Amazon with me.

Dorothy: <u>Where'll you</u> go on the other two trips?

Thelma: Well, I want to go to New York, but Earl says Mexico is more relaxing …

Workbook Answer Key

UNIT 1: What's on TV?

Practice 1

A. Channel 3: comedy
Channel 5: documentary
Channel 6: soap opera
Channel 11: talk show
Channel 16: game show

Practice 2

1. couch potato
2. news
3. rarely
4. frequently
5. cartoons
6. entertainment
7. educational
8. activities

Practice 3

A. Answers will vary.

Practice 4

1. You don't have a TV.
2. He watches TV. Does he watch TV?
3. She doesn't love TV. Does she love TV?
4. It works. Does it work?
5. We want a new TV. We don't want a new TV.
6. They don't enjoy TV. Do they enjoy TV?

Practice 5

1. think
2. watch
3. don't develop
4. shows
5. sell
6. don't need
7. serves
8. encourages
9. permits
10. informs

Practice 6

A, B. Answers will vary.

Practice 7

A, B. Answers will vary.

Practice 8

1. How often do Americans elect a president? Once every four years.
2. How often does the calendar change? Once every month.
3. How often is the moon full? Once every 29 days.
4. How often do they award the Nobel Peace Prize? Once every year.
5. How often do we pay taxes? Once every year on April 15.
6. How often do they give Academy Awards? Once a year in March.
7. How often does the earth go around the sun? Once every 365¼ days.
8. How often do they hold the World Cup Football match? Once every four years.

Practice 9

Pat: go swimming/every other week
play basketball/twice a month
play tennis/every Saturday afternoon
Ann: do homework/every Saturday afternoon
go to the art museum/once a month
go to a concert/every Sunday morning
read in the library/every Sunday afternoon
Bob: watch TV and eat every weekend

Practice 10

Student A	Student B
1. loves	7. spend
2. want	8. know
3. watches	9. does
4. changes	10. takes
5. watch	11. sits
6. change	12. watches
	13. teaches

Practice 11

A. 1. /ɪz/
2. /s/
3. /z/
4. /ɪz/
5. /s/
6. /ɪz/
7. /z/
8. /z/
9. /s/
10. /z/

Practice 12

Main idea: My friend John is a real couch potato.
Unrelated sentences: I play the guitar and tennis.
His favorite lunch is pizza.

Check Your Knowledge

Vocabulary Check

1. news
2. cartoon
3. detective show
4. soap opera
5. talk show
6. documentary

Check Your Understanding

1. do you get up
2. get up
3. do you go
4. usually get
5. finish
6. don't get
7. Do you work
8. don't work
9. have
10. sometimes begin

UNIT 2: People Watching

Practice 1

A. Answers will vary
B. 1. They're in a restaurant.
2. They're at the airport.
3. They're at the beach/at the swimming pool.
4. They're at the gym.
5. They're at the library (or bookstore).

Practice 2

Practice 3

A, B. Answers will vary.

Practice 4

1. You're staying. You're not staying.
2. He's laughing. Is he laughing?
3. She isn't relaxing. Is she relaxing?
4. It's opening. Is it opening?
5. We're flying there. We're not (We aren't) flying there.
6. They're not running. Are they running?

Practice 5

1. is crying
2. is going
3. is happening
4. am cooking
5. don't like
6. love
7. are you hitting

T166

8. Are they fighting
9. fight
10. is throwing
11. don't understand
12. happen
13. am coming
14. am leaving

Practice 6

1. is raining
2. is shining
3. am studying
4. are bringing
5. are swimming/are sitting/
   are relaxing/are lying

Practice 7

1. still
2. anymore
3. still
4. anymore
5. anymore
6. still

Practice 8

	Carol	Peter
Friday night	going to the movies	staying home
Saturday afternoon	going to the zoo	going to the movies
Sunday afternoon	studying	playing basketball
Sunday night	studying	studying

Practice 9

A,B.
1. 2
2. 1
3. 2
4. 3
5. 2
6. 3
7. 2
8. 2
9. 4
10. 2

Practice 10

Student A
1. plays
2. swims
3. do
4. practices
5. writes
6. am writing
7. am
8. answering

Student B
9. am standing
10. is staying
11. exercises
12. Do, exercise
13. does, practice
14. does, do
15. help
16. want

Practice 11

Answers will vary.

Check Your Knowledge

Vocabulary Check

1. executive
2. hold
3. get out of
4. left alone
5. bald
6. lobby
7. lying
8. followed
9. fantastic
10. came off

Check Your Understanding

1. drives/is driving
2. relaxes/is relaxing
3. is taking/takes
4. wait/am waiting
5. are practicing/practice

UNIT 3: Keeping Up with the Joneses

Practice 1

Answers will vary.

Practice 2

A, B. Answers will vary.

Practice 3

1. taller than
2. bigger than
3. larger than
4. heavier than
5. more/less private
6. more/less famous
7. more/less relaxing
8. more/less beautiful
9. more/less popular
10. funnier than

Practice 4

1. nicer
2. better
3. more expensive
4. noisier
5. worse
6. taller
7. thinner
8. more attractive
9. more popular
10. more beautiful
11. more intelligent
12. better
13. older
14. harder
15. more patient

Practice 5

1. The workers are friendlier and more helpful.
2. The guests are more famous and more interesting.
3. The rooms are bigger and more comfortable.
4. The tennis courts are nicer and more private.
5. The pool is longer and deeper.
6. The gardens are larger and more attractive.
7. The lobby is newer and cleaner.
8. The Hideaway is prettier and more relaxing.

Practice 6

1. He wasn't as old as you drew him. Make him younger.
2. His hair wasn't as long as you drew it. Make it shorter.
3. His nose wasn't as big as you drew it. Make it smaller.
4. His eyes weren't as big as you drew them. Make them smaller.
5. His ears weren't as small as you drew them. Make them bigger.

Practice 7

A. Answers will vary.
B. Correct answers: 1. Canada is larger than the United States. 2. Lisbon is older than Rio de Janeiro. 3. The Nile is longer than the Amazon. 4. The Himalayas are higher than the Andes. 5. The Pacific is deeper than the Atlantic.

Practice 8

Questions will vary.

Practice 9

A. 1. Fez
   2. Nice
   3. Nice
   4. Nice
   5. Fez
   6. Nice
   7. Nice
   8. Nice
   9. Fez
   10. Fez

Practice 10

A, B
1. condition
2. gorgeous
3. explain
4. friendly
5. compare
6. appearance
7. narrow
8. interesting
9. helpful

Practice 11

Student A
1. bigger
2. better
3. deeper
4. more
5. taller
6. bigger
7. more
8. better

Student B
9. nicer
10. longer
11. wider
12. more interesting
13. prettier
14. more colorful
15. more jealous

Practice 12

Answers will vary.

Check Your Knowledge

Vocabulary Check

1. perfect
2. deep
3. attractive
4. neighbor
5. prices
6. heavy
7. enormous
8. wide

Check Your Understanding

1. deeper than
2. as expensive as
3. friendlier
4. more comfortable
5. bigger than
6. as large as
7. better
8. worse than

UNIT 4: And the Beat Goes On!

Practice 1

A. 1. folk
   2. rock and roll
   3. jazz
   4. classical
   5. rock
   6. country

B. Answers will vary.

Practice 2

A. 2. born
   3. beat
   4. fans
   5. albums
   6. won
   7. talent
   8. opera
   9. entertainment
   10. conductor

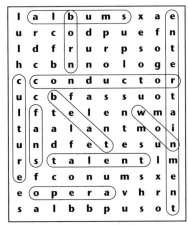

B. guitar, trumpet, clarinet, horn, drums, violin, piano, base fiddle

Practice 3

1. You arrived. Did you arrive?
2. He laughed. He didn't laugh.
3. She tried. Did she try?
4. It didn't escape. Did it escape?
5. We didn't talk. Did we talk?
6. They performed. They didn't perform.

Practice 4

1. blow
2. broke
3. begin
4. sell
5. found
6. write
7. took
8. cost
9. drive
10. fell
10. said

Practice 5

1. wrote
2. was
3. didn't sell
4. decided
5. became
6. sold
7. Did/sing

Practice 6

Answers will vary.

Practice 7

1. is
2. has
3. think
7. grew
8. lost
9. listen

4. invented
5. introduced
6. was
10. buy
11. perform
12. sing

Practice 8

Answers will vary.

Practice 9

Information Card for Student A
Name: Claude Debussy
Year of Birth: 1862
Place of Birth: Laye (near Paris), France
Major Works: *The Sea*, 1905; *Games,* 1912
Characteristics of Music: rhythm more important than melody
Year of Death: 1918

Information Card for Student B
Name: Wolfgang Amadeus Mozart
Year of Birth: 1756
Place of Birth: Salzburg, Austria
Major Works: *The Marriage of Figaro* (opera), 1786; *The Magic Flute* (opera), 1791
Characteristics of Music: always technically perfect
Year of Death: 1791

Practice 10

Paragraphs will vary.

Practice 11

1. /ɪd/
2. /d/
3. /d/
4. /ɪd/
5. /ɪd/
6. /d/
7. /ɪd/
8. /t/
9. /d/
10. /ɪd/

Practice 12

Dialogue 1
1. Jack (student) and Mr. Lowe (teacher)
2. at school
3. Jack's bad grade

Dialogue 2
1. Doctor, Mr. Hollins (patient)
2. at the doctor's office
3. Mr. Hollins' diet

Check Your Knowledge

Vocabulary Check
1. popular
2. performance
3. awards
4. talent
5. fans
6. opera
7. become
8. hit
9. entertainment
10. tape

Check Your Understanding
1. was
2. learned
3. had
4. decided
5. wrote
6. amazed
7. combined
8. sold
9. influenced
10. received

UNIT 5: Close Calls

Practice 1

Answers will vary.

Practice 2

1. tornado
2. passengers
3. counter
4. checking in
5. gate
6. baggage
7. Flight 62

Practice 3

Answers will vary

Practice 4

1. You weren't screaming. Were you screaming?
2. He was checking in. Was he checking in?
3. She wasn't sitting. Was she sitting?
4. It was raining. Was it raining?
5. We weren't shouting. Were we shouting?
6. They were hiding. They weren't hiding.

Practice 5

1. was
2. struck
3. moved
4. rained
5. started
6. died
7. lost
8. damaged
9. destroyed
10. caused
11. cost

Practice 6

1. were swimming
2. got
3. saw
4. was returning
5. were working
6. watched
7. were resting
8. played
9. were leaving
10. shouted

Practice 7

Answers will vary.

Practice 8

1. were living
2. didn't invent
3. was watching
4. shot, was planning
5. wasn't sailing, was sailing
6. were watching, landed
7. was working, discovered
8. made, called

Practice 9

Conversation 1: Hair Salon
Conversation 2: Discount Furniture
Conversation 3: Health Foods
Conversation 4: Women's Shoes
Conversation 5: Arcade

Practice 10

Answers will vary.

Practice 11

A: What, doing, when, lights, out
B: I, getting, haircut, I, almost, lost, ear
A: Wow, that, really, close, call
B: Yeah, how, look, hair, One, side, much, shorter, other

Practice 12

Set 1	Set 2
a. SS	**a.** SS
b. TS	**b.** SS
c. SS	**c.** SS
d. CS	**d.** CS
e. SS	**e.** TS
	f. SS

Check Your Knowledge

Vocabulary Check

1. damage
2. struck
3. save
4. escape
5. baggage claim
6. Tornadoes
7. gate
8. snack bar
9. accident
10. suddenly

Check Your Understanding

1. were checking in, destroyed
2. were arguing, told
3. were waiting, began
4. was recovering, were
5. was eating, struck
6. was moving, went

UNIT 6: The Best in Life

Practice 1

1. speed
2. power
3. taste
4. price

Answers may vary.

Practice 2

1. helicopter
2. features
3. powerful
4. deserve
5. luxury
6. advanced
7. appointment
8. ads

¹h	e	l	i	c	o	p	t	e	r
²f	e	a	t	u	r	e	s
			³p	o	w	e	r	f	u	l
			⁴d	e	s	e	r	v	e
			⁵l	u	x	u	r	y
⁶a	d	v	a	n	c	e	d
⁷a	p	p	o	i	n	t	m	e	n	t
			⁸b	u	s

Practice 3

Answers will vary.

Practice 4

1. more embarrassing, the most embarrassing
2. faster, the fastest
3. more exciting, the most exciting
4. safer, the safest
5. smarter, the smartest
6. heavier, the heaviest
7. more powerful, the most powerful
8. bigger, the biggest
9. more comfortable, the most comfortable
10. more interesting, the most interesting

Practice 5

1. the oldest
2. the longest
3. the most common
4. the largest
5. The shortest

Practice 6

Answers will vary.

Practice 7

A.
2. Myra does more homework than Butch.
3. Myra reads more novels than Bruce.
4. Myra plays tennis more often than Butch.
5. Butch watches the most TV of the three.
6. Myra watches less TV than Butch.
7. Bruce spends more time on homework than Butch.
8. Bruce visits more friends than Myra.

B. Answers will vary.

Practice 8

1. Road Rider
2. Traveler
3. Mountain King
4. Mountain King
5. Traveler
6. Mountain King

Practice 9

1. nice
2. $380
3. $318
4. cheaper
5. $315
6. $350
7. $315
8. $314
9. better
10. $314
11. nicest
12. most expensive
13. $380
14. $380
15. $350
16. $340
17. $340
18. $314
19. $26

Practice 10

Answers will vary.

Practice 11

Answers will vary.

Check Your Knowledge

Vocabulary Check

1. deserves
5. features
2. engine
3. appointment
4. means
6. amazing
7. luxury
8. own

Check Your Understanding

1. the most important
2. happier
3. stronger
4. weaker
5. the best
6. more important
7. fastest
8. (the) most reliable

UNIT 7: The Perfect Match

Practice 1

Answers will vary.

Practice 2

Professional Journalism: article, newspaper, reporter, story, magazine

Getting a Job: education, employer, résumé, experience, application, salary, cover letter

Practice 3

Answers will vary.

Practice 4

1. You've eaten. You haven't eaten.
2. He has gone. Has he gone?
3. She hasn't applied. Has she applied?
4. It has decreased. Has it decreased?
5. We've improved. We haven't improved.
6. They haven't complained. Have they complained?

Practice 5

Answers will vary.

1. Have you ever played an instrument?
2. Have you ever been in love?
3. Have you ever had a computer?
4. Have you ever been in a hospital?
5. Have you ever had a job?
6. Have you ever lived in another city?
7. Have you ever won a prize or an award?
8. Have you ever been on TV?

Practice 6

Answers will vary.

Practice 7

1. b
2. a
3. a

Practice 8

1. hasn't done
2. hasn't done
3. has done
4. hasn't done
5. has done
6. hasn't done

Practice 9

Answers will vary.

Practice 10

A: Well, job
B: yes, while
A: <u>current</u>
B: years
A: years
B: empl<u>oy</u>ee, edu<u>ca</u>tion, experi<u>en</u>ce, raise, hates
A: Well, see, time

Practice 11

Answers will vary.

Check Your Knowledge

Vocabulary Check

1. employer
2. graduated
3. technician
4. complain
5. salary

Check Your Understanding

1. has taken
2. has gone
3. has had
4. was
5. sent
6. stayed
7. was
8. became
9. have given
10. protects
11. has improved
12. have continued
13. has lead
14. remain

UNIT 8: Ask the Experts

Practice 1

1a. dentist
2a. gardener
3a. teacher
4a. exercise teacher or doctor
5a. travel agent
6a. sales manager
1b.–6b. Answers will vary.

Practice 2

1. borrows
2. pays back
3. owes
4. millionaire
5. advice
6. credit card

Practice 3

Answers will vary.

Practice 4

1. should or ought to
2. should or ought to
3. shouldn't
4. should or ought to
5. shouldn't
6. should or ought to

Practice 5

1. should
2. shouldn't
3. should
4. shouldn't
5. should

Practice 6

1. I think you'd better take your passport.
2. I don't think you should sleep in the park.
3. I think you should visit the art museum.
4. I think you ought to write your grandmother a postcard.
5. Do you think we should go by plane or by train?
6. I think you'd better take a lot of money with you.

Practice 7

Answers will vary.

Practice 8

Answers will vary.

Practice 9

A. 1. b 2. b 3. a
B. 1. She should give her husband some special tea.
   2. He should be quiet and ask the librarian for help.
   3. She should talk to her mother.

Practice 10

A: /Joe,/➚/can I ask you a question?/➚/I need some advice./➘/
B: /Sure./➘/No problem./➘/ What's the matter/➘/
A: /I'd like do buy a computer. /➘/Do you think I should buy a laptop?/➚/Or do you think I should buy a desktop?/➚/
B: Do you really need to take it with you?/➚/
A: Not really,/➘/but my friend has a laptop,/➘/and he really likes it./➘/
B: I think you should buy a desktop./➘/They're a lot cheaper/➘/and a better buy for your money./➘/
A: I guess you're right./➘/ Thanks a lot./➘/

Practice 11

Answers will vary.

Practice 12

B. Answers will vary.

Check Your Knowledge

Vocabulary Check

1. solve
2. advice
3. throw away
4. gain
5. millionaires

Check Your Understanding

A. 1. should/ought to
   2. shouldn't
3. should/ought to
4. should/ought to
B. 1. had better
2. had better not
3. had better
4. had better not
5. had better
6. had better not

UNIT 9: Stressed Out

Practice 1

Answers will vary.

Practice 2

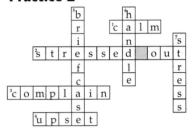

Practice 3

1. which
2. who
3. which
4. which
5. who, who
6. who, who

Practice 4

Answers will vary.

Practice 5

1. (that)
2. (who)
3. who
4. who
5. that

Practice 6

1. Enrico Caruso was an opera star who had a close call with an earthquake.
2. The American Dream is a car that is sixty feet long.
3. A paparazzo is a reporter who takes photos of famous people.
4. Nellie Bly was a reporter who helped make the world a better place.
5. A seismograph is a machine that measures earthquakes.

Practice 7

1. In picture A, the man who is in the helicopter is wearing a shirt with long sleeves. In picture B, he is wearing a shirt with short sleeves.
2. In picture A, the person who is coming out of the phone booth is old. In picture B, he is young.
3. In picture A, the person who is walking a dog is a man. In picture B, the person is a woman.

4. In picture A, the tall building has a clock. In picture B, it doesn't have a clock.
5. In picture A, both people who are in the black car are hurt. In picture B, only one of the people is hurt.

Practice 8

Answers will vary.

Practice 9

A. 1. She'll wear the blouse she bought last week.
2. The security guard will stop the man who is wearing a green sweater.
3. She'll buy the computer that is faster.
4. The girl who is standing near the door wants to talk to Mark.
5. The customer wants the book that gives advice for parents.

B. Answers will vary.

Practice 10

1. sick, great
2. all, some
3. find, lost
4. aisle, next to you

Practice 11

A, B. Answers will vary.

Practice 12

Answers will vary.

Check Your Knowledge

Vocabulary Check

1. upset   4. calm down
2. elevator   5. technique
3. stressed out   6. stress

Check Your Understanding

A. 1. that   5. (that)
2. who   6. that
3. that   7. who
4. (who)   8. (that)

B. Sentences will vary.

UNIT 10: You've Got to Be Kidding!

Practice 1

Answers will vary.

Practice 2

1. kidding   4. waste
2. metal   5. incredible
3. break

Practice 3

1. You've been talking. You haven't been talking.
2. He's been winning. Has he been winning?

3. She hasn't been laughing. Has she been laughing?
4. It has been raining. Has it been raining?
5. We've been reading. We haven't been reading.
6. They haven't been losing. Have they been losing?

Practice 4

Answers will vary.

Practice 5

1. have been playing
2. have been traveling/have traveled
3. has performed
4. have seen
5. has won
6. have played

Practice 6

1. How long have you been training for the Olympics?
2. How long have you known Ruby and her mom?
3. How long have you been married?
4. How long have you been hiking?
5. How long has your sister been writing poetry?
6. How long have you been playing the saxophone?
7. How long have you been (diving) in Madrid?

Practice 7

A: going to
B: want to
A: used to, used to, like to, used to
B: ought to
A: going to, got to

Practice 8

1. were   9. is
2. stole   10. have tried
3. rode   11. has been
4. hid   12. have been
5. died   wondering
6. looked   13. have been
7. found   looking
8. discovered   14. need

Practice 9

A. Meeting a friend.
Giving your boss an update.
Interviewing a marathon race winner.

Practice 10

A. 1. gym
2. restaurant
3. doctor's office

B. 1. a   3. b   5. c
2. a   4. c   6. a

Practice 11

A: So how long has Harry been away now?
B: Half a month, and he says he has been having a great time.
A: Have you talked with him on the phone?
B: Last night. He says his sister has taken him to all her favorite places and she's been taking good care of him.
A: I'm happy he has been able to spend so much time with her.
B: Yeah, she's his favorite sister. He really likes her.
A: And I'm sure he also likes her cars, and her pool, and her huge house in Hawaii.
B: How horrible of you … , but how true!

Practice 12

Answers will vary.

Practice 13

Answers will vary.

Check Your Knowledge

Vocabulary Check

1. set, record   4. collect
2. unusual   5. amazing
3. reference book 6. result

Check Your Understanding

1. have had
2. reported
3. has received
4. began
5. visited
6. has spoken/has been speaking to
7. has helped/has been helping
8. hopes
9. has given
10. ask

UNIT 11: From Rags to Riches

Practice 1

Answers will vary.

Practice 2

We didn't use to work all day. Did we use to work all day?

She's gotten used to working at night. Has she gotten used to working at night?

You are used to working with children. Aren't you used to working with children?

Practice 3

1. used to write
2. used to prepare
3. used to try
4. often used to put
5. used to serve
6. sometimes used to spend
7. had
8. killed

Practice 4

Answers will vary.

Practice 5

Answers will vary.

Practice 6

2. 1928
3. Ray Kroc
4. 1969
5. California, Florida, and Chicago
6. 1984
7. She gives it to charity.
8. San Diego

Practice 7

A: When are you going to finish that book about Martin Scorcese?

B: I have to talk to my class about it tomorrow. Do you want to hear something interesting?

A: I know…. Before Scorcese became a famous film director, he used to live in New York City's Little Italy neighborhood, and when he was a child, he used to like to watch the musicals of the 1940s and 1950s, and French New Wave films, and he used to work in documentary film, and …

B: Yes! That's amazing! You ought to help me with my report!

A: I'd like to, but I'm going to see *GoodFellas*. I've got to get going.

Practice 8

Answers will vary.

Practice 9

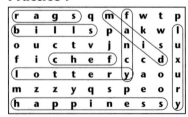

Practice 10

A. 1. c   3. a
   2. d   4. b

Check Your Knowledge

Vocabulary Check

1. castle   4. bills
2. lottery   5. adjustments
3. rags   6. wealth

Check Your Understanding

1. isn't used to eating
2. is used to driving
3. used to have
4. used to surprise
5. is used to being
6. is used to spending
7. used to do
8. got used to having
9. used to travel
10. is used to taking

UNIT 12: Hit the Jackpot

Practice 1

Answers will vary.

Practice 2

Answers may vary, but they should be similar to the following.

1. I'll be a couch potato when I'm older if I don't stop watching TV all the time.
2. I will do some serious people watching if I go to the Academy Awards in Hollywood.
3. If I want to keep up with the Joneses, I will have to buy a new car.
4. If I want to listen to the latest hit songs, I will have to buy some new CDs.
5. I'll hide under the counter if I see the mouse.
6. I won't have the best things in life unless I work very hard.
7. Unless I ask an expert, I won't get good advice.
8. I'm going to be stressed out unless I take a vacation soon.
9. I'll go from rags to riches if I win the lottery.
10. Unless I hit the jackpot, I won't be able to pay my bills.

Practice 3

A. 1. If
   2. unless
   3. If
   4. Unless
   5. unless

Practice 4

1. If you go to Peru, you can see Machu Picchu.
2. If you go to Russia, you can visit the Kremlin.
3. If you go to China, you can walk along the Great Wall.
4. If you go to Egypt, you can climb the pyramids.
5. If you go to France, you can have lunch at the Eiffel Tower.
6. If you go to Japan, you can see Mt. Fuji.
7. If you go to Brazil, you can sail up the Amazon.
8. Sentences will vary.

Practice 5

A. 1. 10,000
   2. intelligent
   3. Los Angeles
   4. twenty

B. 2. Go on an interview.
   3. Take a test.
   4. Go to school.

Practice 6

A. 1. where'll you   6. we'll
   2. going to   7. you
   3. wanted to   8. him (that)
   4. What'll you   9. him
   5. you   10. Where'll you

Practice 7

Answers will vary.

Practice 8

A. a. 2
   b. 4
   c. 3
   d. 5
   e. 1

Check Your Knowledge

Vocabulary Check

1. fabulous
2. hit the jackpot
3. rules
4. win
5. make sure

Check Your Understanding

A. 1. win, will travel
   2. have, ought to/should/had better talk
   3. don't stop talking, will ask
   4. will go, rains/won't go, stops raining
   5. go, will visit

B. 1. unless
   2. If
   3. Unless
   4. Unless
   5. if